Cambridge Entomological Club

Psyche

Cambridge Entomological Club

Psyche

ISBN/EAN: 9783741170720

Manufactured in Europe, USA, Canada, Australia, Japa

Cover: Foto ©Thomas Meinert / pixelio.de

Manufactured and distributed by brebook publishing software
(www.brebook.com)

Cambridge Entomological Club

Psyche

PSYCHE

A JOURNAL OF ENTOMOLOGY

Vol. 73   March, 1966   No. 1

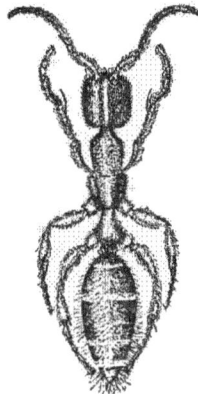

CONTENTS

PSYCHE is published quarterly by the Cambridge Entomological Club, the issues appearing in March, June, September and December. Subscription price, per year, payable in advance: $4.50 to Club members, $5.00 to all other subscribers. Single copies, $1.25.

Checks and remittances should be addressed to Treasurer, Cambridge Entomological Club, 16 Divinity Avenue, Cambridge, Mass.

Orders for back volumes, missing numbers, notices of change of address, etc., should be sent to the Editorial Office of Psyche, Biological Laboratories, Harvard University, Cambridge, Mass.

IMPORTANT NOTICE TO CONTRIBUTORS

Manuscripts intended for publication should be addressed to Professor F. M. Carpenter, Biological Laboratories, Harvard University, Cambridge, Mass.

Authors contributing articles over 4 printed pages in length may be required to bear a part of the extra expense, for additional pages. This expense will be that of typesetting only, which is about $10.00 per page. The actual cost of preparing cuts for all illustrations must be borne by contributors: the cost for full page plates from line drawings is ordinarily $12.00 each, and the full page half-tones, $18.00 each; smaller sizes in proportion.

AUTHOR'S SEPARATES

Reprints of articles may be secured by authors, if they are ordered at the time proofs are received for corrections. A statement of their cost will be furnished by the Editor on application.

The December, 1965 Psyche (Vol. 72, no. 4) was mailed March 10, 1966.

THE LEXINGTON PRESS. INC., LEXINGTON, MASSACHUSETTS

PSYCHE

| Vol. 73 | March, 1966 | No. 1 |

THE HABITS OF *PHEIDOLE RIDICULA* WHEELER WITH REMARKS ON HABIT PATTERNS IN THE GENUS *PHEIDOLE* (HYMENOPTERA: FORMICIDAE)

BY WILLIAM S. CREIGHTON[1]
Department of Biology, City College, New York

During 1965 the writer was able to study seven colonies of *Ph. ridicula* at La Feria, Texas. The observations in this paper were made on these colonies or on individuals transferred from them to observation nests. There are few North American ants as poorly known as *Ph. ridicula*. When W. M. Wheeler described this species in 1916 he had seen three specimens, all majors (1). One of these (the type) was taken by C. L. Scott at Brownsville, Texas. The other two, in the collection of the U. S. National Museum, came from San Diego, Texas, a town about 140 miles northwest of Brownsville. Except for these locality records no field data for *ridicula* were available and, as far as can be determined, no additional records have been published for this species.

The nests of *ridicula* are surprisingly difficult to find and this seems to be the reason why the species, which is a door-yard ant in the lower Rio Grande Valley, has escaped observation for the past fifty years. To judge from the La Feria colonies, *ridicula* prefers to nest in areas where there is a heavy cover of weeds, often nettles, common sunflower, Johnson grass and careless weed. These weeds not only conceal the nests but also the foragers which come from them. During December 1964 I made repeated visits to an area where there were two flourishing colonies of *ridicula*. It is now apparent that I often stood directly above these nests but neither was discovered until the covering weeds were removed. There are other features which make the nests of *ridicula* hard to find. A mature colony of this ant contains at least seventy-five majors and three

[1]Professor Emeritus, City College, New York
Manuscript received by the editor February 11, 1966
Published with a Grant-in-Aid of Research from the Society of the Sigma Xi.

hundred minors. These figures are based on totals secured by prolonged baiting of two of the colonies. Since neither nest was put out of action by the baiting it seems certain that the estimate is on the conservative side, yet there would be justification for the view that a much smaller population was present. There is rarely a conspicuous accumulation of excavated soil or of chaff around the nest entrance, for both are brought to the surface gradually and in small quantities. Even when a crater is built its diameter seldom exceeds three or four centimeters. Moreover, the crater is a transient structure for, since *ridicula* mixes the chaff with the excavated soil particles, the texture of the crater is loose and light and it is easily scattered by wind or rain. Hence much of the time the only indication of a *ridicula* nest is the nest entrance itself. This is never more than five millimeters in diameter and, more often, its diameter is about two millimeters. In addition, the nest entrance is frequently blocked up and drifted over with windblown dust and detritus. Early in this study the writer found it necessary to mark the nest entrances in order to be sure of their exact position.

There is a simple explanation for most of the above features. While *ridicula* will sometimes bring in other seeds, it is mainly interested in those of the careless weed, *Amaranthus palmeri*. These seeds are matured throughout the year, hence there is an ample supply of them at all times and large numbers are not garnered seasonally. Moreover, a great many of the *palmeri* seeds are free of any covering when they are brought to the nest. As a result there is no occasion for the production of a large chaff pile or an extensive crater since, in the genus Pheidole, both these features usually result from a seasonal excess of grass seeds which must be stripped and stored[2].

The soil in which *ridicula* nests is the Victoria loam, a fine-textured, compact soil which is virtually stone free. As the walls of excavations made in it are slow to crumble, there was every reason to expect that a *ridicula* nest could be fully exposed. Actually this proved to be impossible. It was easy to trace the main nest passage, which consists of an unbranched shaft of remarkably uniform diameter (about 2 mm.) that descends vertically through the soil to a depth of about thirty-two inches. It was not difficult to demonstrate the existence of lateral passages leading away from the main shaft, for the workers would open up the transected ends of these passages

[2]Similar considerations apply to *Ph. cerebrosior* Wh. which mainly garners the seeds of desert portulacas (*P. oleracea* Linné and *P. retusa* Engl.). This crop is seasonal but, since the seeds are bare when brought to the nest, no chaff pile results.

in the walls of the excavation. But to follow these passages to their ends was quite another matter. Although some of them were traced to a distance of two feet from the main shaft, no brood chamber or seed chamber was found. Nevertheless, it is possible to state that the nest of *ridicula* is diffuse with the seed and brood chambers widely separated.

The foraging responses of *ridicula* are flexible and this makes them difficult to describe. Much of the foraging occurs at night but it is misleading to characterize *ridicula* as a nocturnal forager. If the nest area is shaded, or if the day is overcast, foraging may occur over a twenty-four hour period. Even when the nest is not shaded foraging ordinarily continues until mid-morning. Foraging may be diffuse or the foragers may form columns. Most of the seeds brought in are picked up from surface litter and in this type of foraging columns rarely form. But when a concentrated food source is at hand, the foragers will converge on it and a column may result. The foragers seldom get far from the nest. In each of the seven colonies most of the foraging was done within ten feet of the nest entrance. The majors take no part in the foraging although they will leave the nest with the minors. When they do so they restrict their patrol to the area around the nest entrance and it is exceptional to find them more than a foot from it. During vigorous foraging there may be several majors outside the nest and their activities effectively clear the area of other ants.

There is little about the appearance of the major of *ridicula* to suggest its lethal behavior. From a structural standpoint Wheeler's choice of name is apt enough, for it would be hard to imagine a more top-heavy ant. But there is nothing ridiculous about the major in action. When it is on guard, either within the nest entrance or outside it, it attacks other ants with such efficiency that the victim usually has no chance to defend itself. The basic features of this attack are the same as those described for the major of *militicida* in 1959 (2). As the *ridicula* major approaches its victim the mandibles are opened to their widest extent. This is followed by a rapid lunge towards the victim during which the mandibles are snapped shut. Unlike the *militicida* major the major of *ridicula* does not hold the antennae close to the head during attack. They are usually held with the scapes at right angles to the long axis of the head and with the funiculi flanking the open mandibles (See Fig. 1). Because of the lateral expansion of the genae the mandibles can be opened to an astonishing extent, with the result that the major of *ridicula* seldom has difficulty getting the head or the thorax of its victim

Fig. 1. Major of *Pheidole ridicula* in the position it assumes when about to attack another ant.

between the mandibles. Perhaps this is why the *ridicula* major is much less deliberate in its attack and will strike the victim anywhere. Moreover, when the major of *ridicula* is aroused it will sometimes charge its own minors by mistake. It seldom kills them for the minor usually dodges under the closing mandibles to a safe position below the major's head. Nevertheless minors of *ridicula* are sometimes crushed by their own majors. In the encounters which occurred daily around each of the nests, the majors of *ridicula* rarely got the worst of it. They disposed of the majors of *Ph. floridana, metallescens* and *dentata* with ease and had little trouble with those of *Solenopsis geminata*. They would occasionally kill workers of *Pogonomyrmex barbatus* although this species was more often driven away than killed. There can, however, be no doubt about the high efficiency of the major of *ridicula* as a guard.

In addition to its activities as a guard the major of *ridicula* also functions as a seed crusher. Each of the flowers of *Amaranthus palmeri* produces a single, shiny, black seed about one millimeter in diameter, which resembles a tiny, blunt-edged discus. When these seeds are ripe they may fall out through a transverse slit which develops in the ovary wall or the ovary may be shed with the seed inside it. The minors strip the ovary wall away from such seeds after they are brought to the nest and the small amount of chaff which accumulates around the nest entrance is the result of this stripping. As far as could be determined the minors of *ridicula* cannot open the *palmeri* seeds; at least they never did so in the observation nests. When the major opens one of these seeds it picks it up by closing the mandibles on the lateral surfaces of the seed. Increasing pressure on these surfaces ultimately shatters the seed. In the observation nests the majors opened a number of seeds in quick succession. Their contents were then gradually eaten away by the minors. The majors take little interest in the seeds after they have opened them.

The behavior of *ridicula* runs counter to the "classic" view of the habits of *Pheidole* in several important respects. This view states that most species of *Pheidole* gather large quantities of grass seeds during a harvest period in late summer or early fall. These seeds are carried to the nest, stripped, and stored in seed chambers. The discarded hulls are built into a chaff pile. As a result of this the colony is provided with an abundant store of seeds which carries it over the time when no seeds are available. The account is usually rounded off with the statement that the stored seeds are opened by the major, whose large head and powerful jaws adapt it for seed crushing. There is nothing illogical in the above view. The only trouble is that, as the habits of the genus *Pheidole* become better known, it seems to fit fewer and fewer species.

Let us look for a moment at the matter of the use of stored seeds during periods when none are available. It is possible that a few species of *Pheidole* whose ranges extend into the northeastern United States *(Ph. bicarinata, davisi, morrisi* and *pilifera)* may behave in this fashion, for climatic conditions there often prohibit foraging over a period of five or six months. But this is assuredly not true of the bulk of our species, most of which forage all year long or at least for the greater part of the year. In addition, it can often be shown that there is no harvest period in the sense that the seeds are garnered when they have matured. Many species of *Pheidole* collect their seeds from surface litter and this litter furnishes a supply of seeds that may be worked for months after the seeds have ripened. The "harvest" may thus proceed throughout the entire winter and into the spring. *Ph. macclendoni, militicida* and *ridicula* all behave in this way. It seems plain enough that these species are not storing seeds against a period when seeds are not available, for there is either no such period or, if one exists, it is too brief to be of any significance.

There is the even more disturbing fact that many species of *Pheidole* do not confine themselves to a diet of seeds. No other North American species of *Pheidole* gathers greater quantities of seeds than does *Ph. (M.) rhea*. A large nest of this species may have several bushels of chaff around the nest entrances. But, when the foraging columns of *rhea* are observed it may be seen that the foragers often bring in seeds and insect remains in equal numbers. Allowing for the far smaller size of its colonies, the same behavior is true of *Ph. creightoni*. The matter becomes even more complex when it is necessary to deal with species which bring in insect remains during most of the year and gather seeds only at intervals. Such species are exceptionally difficult to handle for, unless they make a conspicuous chaff pile, which they often fail to do, the only way to prove that they have gathered seeds is to expose the seed chambers in the nest. This behavior is found in *Ph. bicarinata, cerebrosior, sitarches, rugulosa* and *xerophila*. It is only by stretching a point that these five species can be considered as harvesters, since their main reliance is on insect food. This leads directly to the problem of the strictly carnivorous species of *Pheidole*. In the writer's opinion there are considerably more of these than has been supposed. As early as 1908 W. M. Wheeler had recognized that *Ph. dentata* and *hyatti* are carnivorous and predacious (3). In 1955 Creighton and Gregg showed that *Ph. titanis* is termitophagus (4). In 1964 the writer pointed out that *Ph. (C.) clydei* is an entomophagus scavenger (5). But there are other species which can be added to this list. It should certainly include *Ph. grallipes* and *vallicola,* both of which are insectivorous and predatory. It also appears that *Ph. floridana* and *metallescens* belong here. In 1958 Van Pelt showed that both species are attracted to a variety of baits (6). But when they are not baited or allowed access to kitchen scraps, each brings insect remains to the nest. They have not been reported as seed collectors and the writer has been unable to find stored seeds in the nests.

The above discussion should show why it is misleading to characterize *Pheidole* as a genus of harvesters. There is obviously no possibility of applying such a designation to the growing number of carnivorous species, nor is the situation much better in the equally large number of species which utilize insect food at least as often as they do seeds. For the truth of the matter appears to be that species which subsist mainly on seeds are in the minority in the genus *Pheidole*. One further detail is pertinent in this connection. It now seems probable that the major of *Pheidole* functions more often as a guard than it does as a seed crusher. The writer has been able to observe the guarding function in the majors of *Ph. clydei, dentata, floridana, macclendoni, metallescens, militicida* and *ridicula*. Only in *ridicula* has the major also functioned as a seed crusher. It is obvious that the major of a carnivorous species can have no occasion to crush seeds and the fact that the guarding function cuts across food preferences would seem to indicate that it, rather than seed crushing, is the basic response of the major of *Pheidole*.

LITERATURE CITED

1. Wheeler, W. M., Proc. New Eng. Zool. Club, 6: 29-35 (1916).
2. Creighton, W. S. & Creighton, M. P., Psyche, 66: 1-12 (1959).
3. Wheeler, W. M., Bull. Amer. Mus. Nat. Hist. 24: 399-485 (1908).
4. Creighton, W. S. & Gregg, R. E. Univ. Colo. Studies, 3: 1-46 (1955).
5. Creighton, W. S., Psyche, 71: 169-173 (1964).
6. Van Pelt, A., Amer. Mid. Natural., 59: 1-57 (1958).

REVISIONARY NOTES ON THE GENERA
OF EUCHEILINI
(COLEOPTERA, CARABIDAE)

By Hans Reichardt[1]
Departamento de Zoologia, Secretaria da Agricultura,
São Paulo, Brazil

In the course of my studies on Neotropical Carabidae I have discovered several interesting taxonomic novelties about the endemic tribe Eucheilini which seem to be important enough to be reported on. Even though I have examined the types of the species of Eucheilini which are preserved in the Muséum National d'Histoire Naturelle, Paris, in July, 1964[2], it is as yet imposible to revise the tribe at the species level, since the species of *Inna*, one of the two genera of Eucheilini, are very poorly understood at present. Material in collections is very scarce. I hope that in the near future accumulation of enough specimens will allow a specific revision of this interesting tribe of Carabidae.

The material on which this revision is based has been borrowed (and partly also studied *in loco*) from the Departamento de Zoologia, São Paulo (CDZ), the Museu de la Universidad de La Plata, Argentina (MLP), the Museum of Comparative Zoology, Cambridge, Mass. (MCZ), the Muséum National d'Histoire Naturelle, Paris (MNHN) and the United States National Museum, Washington, D. C. (USNM). The loan of this interesting material is gratefully acknowledged.

The tribe and the genera included in this revision are not formally redescribed, since it seems to me that for the time being the characterization presented below is enough.

Tribe Eucheilini

Eucheilinae Bates, 1883, Biol. Centr. Amer., Col., 1 (1) :168.
Periglossinae Liebke, 1929 Ent. Anz., 9 :247. NEW SYNONYMY.
Euchilini; Csiki, 1932, Col. Cat., 124 :1585; Blackwelder, 1944, Bull. U.S.N. Mus., 185 :70.
Periglossini; Csiki, 1932, Col. Cat., 124 :1585; Blackwelder, 1944, Bull. U.S.N. Mus., 185 :70.
Eucheilini; Ball, 1960, Beetles of the U.S. :164.

---
[1]Currently at the Museum of Comparative Zoology, Harvard University
Manuscript received by the editor December 1, 1965.
[2]A trip supported by the Evolutionary Biology Committee at Harvard University; this support is gratefully acknowledged.

This small Neotropical tribe includes only two genera of small, Lebiini-like Carabidae. Their systematic position has been uncertain for a long time. Even though *Eucheila*, the type-genus, was described as early as 1829 (in Lebiini), the true relations to Helluonini were only recognized in 1883, when Bates erected the subfamily Eucheilinae to incorporate *Eucheila* and *Inna* (the latter also described in Lebiini, and at first considered as related to *Eucheila* by Bates), and placed it in the vicinity of the Helluonini.

In 1929 Liebke described the subfamily Periglossinae for a new Central-American genus, *Periglossium*. From his description and illustrations of this beetle, it is evident that *Periglossium* is a synonym of *Inna*, and consequently the name Periglossinae has to be suppressed.

The characters which link the Eucheilini to the Helluonini are the strangely modified mouthparts (Figs. 1-8). In spite of similarities, the Eucheilini are undoubtedly a distinct tribe, easily distinguished from the Lebiini by the completely different mouthparts and from the Helluonini by their general Lebiini-habitus, as well as by the antennae which are pubescent from the 4th segment on in Eucheilini (pubescent from base in Helluonini). The aedeagus of the Eucheilini was unknown up to now. I was able to dissect one male of *Eucheila strandi* (Liebke) and one of *Inna boyeri* (Solier) (see Figs. 11 and 12). The two aedeagi are very similar, and this fact strengthens the supposed relation between the two genera. The left paramere of the aedeagus is reduced, but still present, being somewhat lobate in the two species. The genitalia of Neotropical Helluonini are also unknown, so that no comparison can be made now.

Geographic distribution: The tribe is typically Neotropical, extending from Argentina to the southern United States (Texas). No species has yet been reported from the Antilles.

Key to genera

1. Labrum convex, covering apex of mandibles, with short setae only on lateral margins (Fig. 8) ; lateral margins of pronotum smooth, not crenulated ; pronotum with basal setae only ; tarsal claws pectinate .... *Eucheila* Dejean

    Labrum flat, not covering apex of mandibles, with 4 long setae on anterior margin, 2 longer ones and a series of short ones laterally (Fig. 3) ; lateral margins of pronotum crenulated ; pronotum with basal and latero-median setae ; tarsal claws simple .... *Inna* Putzeys

Eucheila Dejean

Eucheyla Dejean, in Dejean and Boisduval, 1829, Icon. Col. Eur., 1:60, 176-177 (type-species, by monotypy, *Eucheyla flavilabris* Dejean).
Eucheila; Dejean, 1831, Spec. gen. Col., 5:455-456; Chaudoir, 1848, Bull. Soc. Nat. Moscow, 21 (1):124; Lacordaire, 1854, Gen. Col., 1:148.
Euchila Dejean (nec *Euchila* Billberg); Agassiz, 1846, Nomencl. Zool. (emmendation); Gemminger and Harold, 1868, Cat. Col.. 1:155; Csiki, 1932, Col. Cat., 124:1585; Blackwelder, 1944, Bull. U.S.N. Mus., 185:70.

The genus was originally spelled *Eucheyla* by Dejean, who in the original description gave the Greek derivation of the name. It is obvious that this spelling was an incorrect transliteration. Dejean himself must have realized this, and in 1831 used the name *Eucheila* instead, without any mention of *Eucheyla*. According to article 32 of the International Code of Zoological Nomenclature, *Eucheyla* should be accepted as the "correct original spelling", since incorrect transliteration is not to be considered an inadvertent error (article 32, section a, ii). However, *Eucheyla* has remained unused as a senior synonym since 1829, and must, therefore, be considered a *nomen oblitum* (article 23, section b). *Eucheila* Dejean must, therefore, be considered the correct and valid name for the genus. *Eucheyla* Berlese, 1913, proposed as a subgenus of *Cheyletia* Haller, 1884 (Arachnida, Acari, Cheyletidae) is a junior homonym of *Eucheyla* Dejean, and has been replaced by *Neoeucheyla* Radford, 1950. Agassiz (1846) emmended the name to *Euchila,* which is, however, a junior homonym of *Euchila* Billberg, 1820 (Insecta, Lepidoptera).

Eucheila Dejean is easily distinguished from *Inna* Putzeys by the characters given in the generic key. The genus was described for a single species, *flavilabris* Dejean; however, material of *Inna strandi* Liebke from the type-locality, proves that Liebke's species is congenic with *flavilabris*.

Key to species of *Eucheila*

1. Metallic-brown species with dark brown appendages and lighter labrum; elytra 9-carinate .... *strandi* (Liebke)
    Metallic-green species (sometimes very dark), with yellow appendages and labrum; elytra with vestigial carinae ....
    .... *flavilabris* Dejean

Eucheila strandi (Liebke), new combination.
(Figs. 5-8, 11)

Inna strandi Liebke, 1939, Festschr. Emb. Strand, 5:121 (type from Jatai, Brazil, in Liebke's collection; probably destroyed).

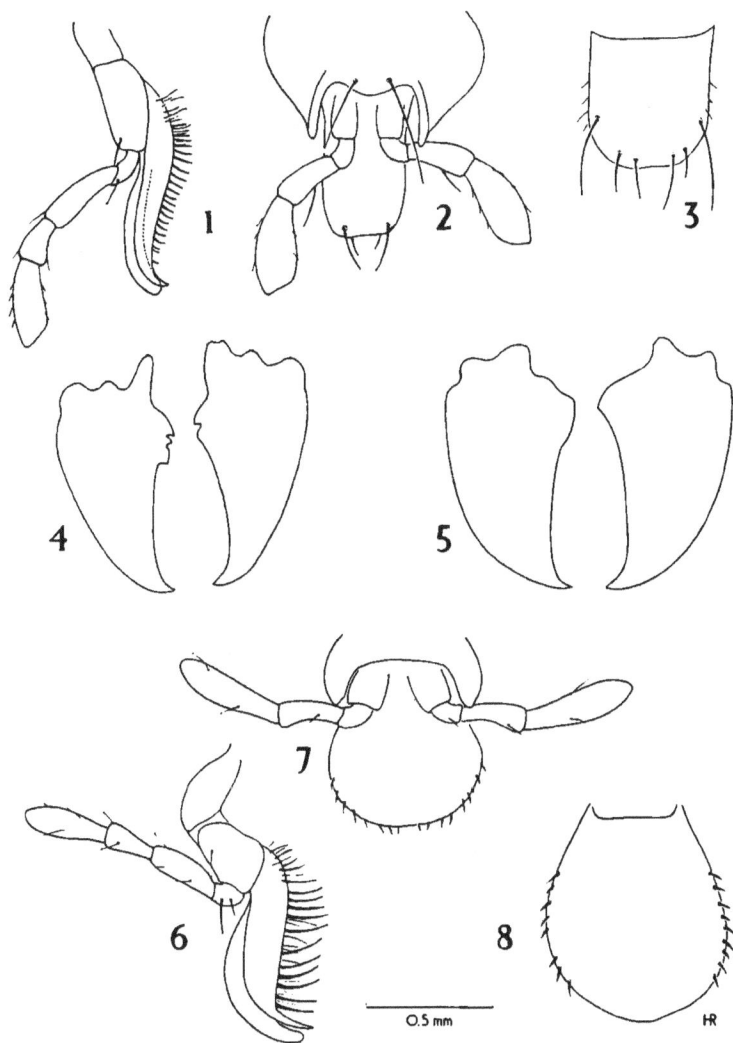

Figs. 1 — 4, *Inna boyeri* (Solier): Fig. 1, maxilla; Fig. 2, labium; Fig. 3, labrum; Fig. 4, mandibles; Figs. 5 — 8, *Eucheila strandi* (Liebke): Fig. 5, mandibles; Fig. 6, maxilla; Fig. 7, labium; Fig. 8, labrum.

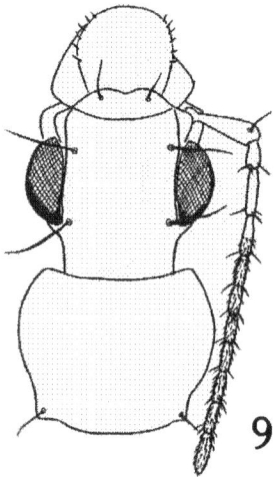

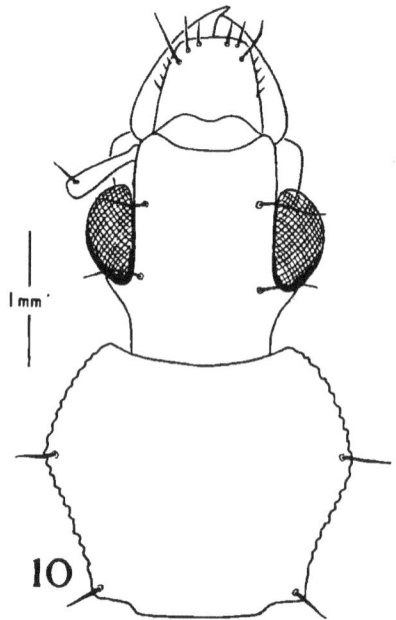

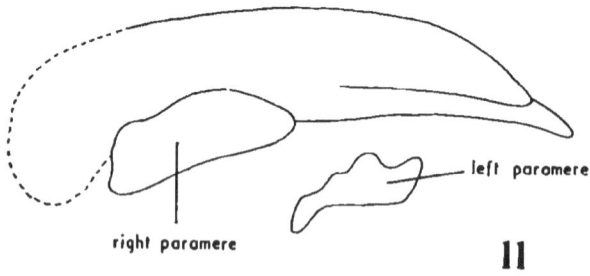

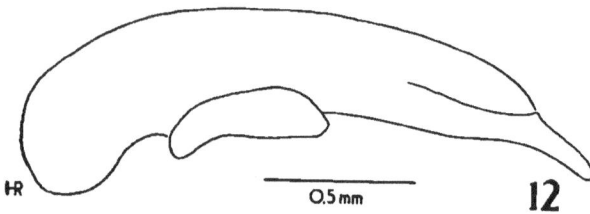

REICHARDT — EUCHEILINI

The pectinate claws, the very typical labrum and labium and the non-crenulated margin of the pronotum put this species without doubt in the same genus as *flavilabris*. It is easily distinguished by the different color and the well developed elytral carinae.

Examined specimens (6) : *Brazil: São Paulo,* Guatapará (1 ex., CDZ) ; *Goiás,* Jataí (3 exx., CDZ, MCZ) ; *Bahia,* no locality (1 ex., MNHN) ; *Ceará,* no locality (1 ex., USNM).

Euchila flavilabris Dejean
(Fig. 9)

Eucheyla flavilabris Dejean, in Dejean and Boisduval, 1829. Icon. Col. Eur., 1:178, pl. 8, fig. 3 (type from "environs de Rio-Janeiro", MNHN; examined).
Eucheila flavilabris; Dejean, 1831, Spec. gen. Col., 5:456-457; Lacordaire, 1854, Gen. Col., 1, pl. 4, fig. 4; Putzeys, 1863, Mem. Soc. Sci. Liège, 18:72. pl. 2, figs. 75-77.

Eucheila flavilabris is easily distinguished from *strandi* by the completely different color, especially that of the appendages. A few specimens are very dark, almost as brown as *strandi;* however, the elytral carinae are always vestigial and the appendages always yellow.

Examined specimens (14) : *Brazil: Bahia,* Salobro (1 ex., MNHN) ; *Minas Gerais,* Matusinhos (1 ex. MNHN) ; Serra do Caraça (1 ex., MNHN) ; *Rio de Janeiro,* Nova Friburgo (6 exx., MNHN) ; *Guanabara,* Rio de Janeiro (1 ex., MNHN) ; *São Paulo,* Estação Biológica de Boraceia, Salesópolis (2 exx., CDZ) ; *Santa Catarina,* no locality (1 ex., MNHN). *Argentina: Santiago del Estero,* near Icaño (1 ex., MNHN).

Inna Putzeys

Inna Putzeys, 1863, Mem. Soc. Sci. Liège, 18:71 (type-species, by monotypy, *Inna punctata* Putzeys) ; Chaudoir, 1872, Rev. Mag. Zool., (2) 23:219-221 (redescription).
Periglossium Liebke, 1929, Ent. Anz., 9:246-247 (type-species, by original designation, *Periglossium nevermanni* Liebke). NEW SYNONYMY.

Ten species of *Inna* are presently known, their distribution ranging from Argentina (*atrata* Dejean) to southern Texas (*texana* Schaeffer). My notes on the types suggest that some of the described species are synonyms, e.g., *Inna costulata* Chaudoir is differentiated from *granulata* Chaudoir only by color: *costulata* is coppery-metallic,

EXPLANATION OF PLATE 1
Fig. 9, *Eucheila flavilabris* Dejean, head and pronotum; Fig. 10, *Inna megala,* n. sp., head and pronotum; Fig. 11, aedeagus of *Eucheila strandi* (Liebke) ; Fig. 12, aedeagus of *Inna boyeri* (Solier).

while *granulata* is very dark brown, almost non-metallic. This color difference seems to be a very weak character, but since only the types are known, further decisions cannot be made now. It is also possible that *nevermanni*, from Costa Rica, is a synonym of *costulata*, which ranges from Colombia to Guatemala. The type of *Inna nevermanni* (Liebke) has probably been destroyed with part of Liebke's collection and no material is presently available from Costa Rica, so that nothing else can be said here.

The generic description of *Periglossium* Liebke does not differ in any respect from that of *Inna* Putzeys. There seems to be no reason to maintain *Periglossium,* which was probably described by Liebke when he did not know *Inna.*

Inna is easily distinguished from *Eucheila* by the characters given in the key.

Even though I have seen the types of most species, as mentioned above, I am presenting below new data only on two of the older species, of which material was available and could be identified. The recognition of the new species is based on comparison with the original descriptions of all the older species as well as on my notes on their types.

Ina boyeri (Solier)
(Figs. 1-4, 12)

Polystichus boyeri Solier, 1835, Ann. Soc. Ent. France, 4:111 (holotype male from "Colombia", MNHN; examined).
Inna boyeri; Chaudoir, 1872, Rev. Mag. Zool., (2) 23:241-242 (redescription).

I am referring to this species, originally described from Colombia, a series of 10 specimens from Barueri in the state of São Paulo, Brazil (CDZ, MCZ), which agree with the description and my notes on the type. *Inna boyeri* is very similar to *costulata;* however, it has more densely punctate pronotum and head, and is slightly larger in size.

Inna atrata (Dejean)

Cymindis atrata Dejean, 1831. Spec. gen. Col., 5:327 (holotype from "Buenos-Ayres", MNHN; examined).
Inna atrata; Chaudoir, 1872, Rev. Mag. Zool., (2) 23:243-244.

The type-specimen in the Paris Museum is very damaged: the left elytron and the left antenna are missing, as well as parts of several legs. The species is very characteristic, having a densely punctate head and being the smallest species of the genus.

Examined specimens (3): *Argentina: Buenos Aires,* Buenos Aires
(1 ex., MLP); Isla Martin Garcia (1 ex., MLP); *Misiones,* no
locality (1 ex., MLP).

Inna megala, n. sp.
(Fig. 10)

Description: Reddish-brown, with light, almost yellow appendages;
elytral margin very light brown. *Head* — densely punctate dorsally,
with longitudinal striation on antennal tubercules; whole surface
micro-reticulate. *Pronotum* — wider than long, slightly wider than
head; densely punctate on surface, with somewhat granulate aspect;
posterior angles more or less square; lateral margins turned upwards,
crenulated; median line in a slight depression which continues on
each side anteriorly (forming a Y). *Elytra* — with 8 irregularly
punctured sulci; 7 discal interstices more or less smooth, convex; 8th
and 9th interstices very slightly indicated only, mainly posteriorly;
almost twice as wide as pronotum, less than twice as long as wide;
elytral margin with setose punctures. *Measurements* — holotype, 3.7
× 10.3 mm; paratype, 4.1 × 10.9 mm.

Types: Paraguay: holotype female, Villarrica, F. Schade col.
(MCZ n. 31197); paratype female, Amambay, A. Schulze col.
(CDZ).

Inna megala is very similar to *planipennis* Bates, which is only
known from Mexico. The two species are of about the same size;
planipennis has a less densely punctured head, especially between the
eyes; the pronotum of *megala* is more transverse than that of *planipennis.*

Specific name: megala is derived from the Greek adjective *megas,*
meaning large.

REFERENCES

BALL, G. E.
    1960. Carabidae, in Arnett, The Beetles of the United States, pp. 55-
        182, 63 figs., Washington, D. C.
BATES, H. W.
    1881-1884. Carabidae in Biologia Centrali-Americana, Coleoptera, 1,
        299 pp., 13 color plates.
BLACKWELDER, R. E.
    1944. Checklist of the Coleopterous Insects of Mexico, Central Amer-
        ica, the West Indies and South America. Part 1. Bull. U.S.N.
        Mus., 185:1-88.
CHAUDOIR, M.
    1873. Mémoire sur la famille des carabiques. Bull. Soc. Nat. Moscow,
        21:3-134.

1872. Descriptions d'espèces nouvelles de carabiques de la tribu des troncatipennes, et remarques synonymiques. Rev. Mag. Zool., (2) 23 :219-221.

CSIKI, E.
1932. Carabidae, Harpalinae VII, in Coleopterorum Catalogus, pars 124 :1279-1598.

DEJEAN. P. F. M. A.
1829. In Dejean and Boisduval, Iconographie et histoire naturelle des Coléoptères d'Europe, 1, 400 pp., 60 pls., Paris.
1831. Spec. gen. Col., 5, 883 pp., Paris.

GEMMINGER, M. AND E. VON HAROLD
1868. Catalogus Coleopterorum . . . , 1, 424 pp., Monachii·

LACORDAIRE, J. T.
1854. Genera des Coléoptères . . . , 1. 486 pp., Paris.

LIEBKE, M·
1929. Laufkaeferstudien. VI. Ent. Anz., 9 :245-247, 261-265, figs.
1939. Neue Laufkaefer. Festschr. Embr. Strand, 5 :91-130, 21 figs.

PUTZEYS, J. A. A. H.
1863. Postscriptum ad clivinidarum monographiam atque de quibusdam alliis. Mem. Soc. Sci. Liège, 18 :1-78, figs.

SOLIER, A. J. J.
1835. Description de quelques espèces nouvelles de la famille des carabiques. Ann. Soc. Ent. France, 4 :111-121.

NOTES ON NEOTROPICAL TABANIDAE VIII. THE SPECIES DESCRIBED BY J. C. FABRICIUS[1]

By G. B. FAIRCHILD
Gorgas Memorial Laboratory, Panama, R. de. P.

During the summer of 1964 I had the opportunity of studying the types of Neotropical Tabanidae in Copenhagen with the financial aid of a travel grant from the Bache Fund of the National Academy of Sciences.

The existing type specimens of all insects described by Johann Christian Fabricius have recently been reviewed by Dr. Ella Zimsen (1964), of the Universitetets Zoologiske Museum in Copenhagen. The present notes concern only the neotropical Tabanidae. Studies of the Wiedemann types in Copenhagen will appear elsewhere. Fabricius type material was for a long time present in the Museums at Kiel and Copenhagen, but the Kiel collection has recently been deposited in Copenhagen. The Kiel material was much damaged by pests, while the Copenhagen material is generally quite well preserved.

I am greatly indebted to Dr. S. L. Tuxen for permission to study this material, and for comments on the results, and to Dr. Leif Lyneborg and Dr. Ella Zimsen, who helped greatly with advice and hospitality during my visit in Copenhagen.

Wiedemann (1828) discussed and redescribed most of Fabricius' species, and later authors have largely depended on his interpretations, as he studied the Fabrician specimens. More recently Philip (1954, 1960) has reported on a number of the Fabrician types, selected lectotypes, and corrected certain misidentifications. In the following list all the supposedly Neotropical Tabanidae described by Fabricius are cited, together with brief notes on their present condition, taxonomic status and whether deriving from the Kiel (K.) collection or the Copenhagen (C.) collection. Types of all but two species were seen. The species are listed alphabetically by modern genera, or subgenera, the genus in which they were placed by Fabricius added in parentheses where this differs.

As to the localities from which Fabricius' material came, I do not have information more definite than given in his descriptions. It is noteworthy, however, that all of his species from "America meridionali", except *Chrysops moerens* and possibly *Fidena analis,* have since been taken in Surinam or the Guianas. The localities of

[1]*Manuscript received by the editor February 12, 1966*

17

the remainder, Brasilia, Cajennae, and Americae insulis, have also
been confirmed by subsequent collecting.

LIST OF SPECIES

Acanthocera longicornis (Fab.) (Tabanus), 1775, Syst. Ent.,
p. 790, Brasilia. 1794, Ent. Syst., IV p. 371. Brasilia Mus. Dom.
Banks. The species should date from 1775, not 1794, as given by
Wiedemann and most subsequent authors. The descriptions are identical. I did not see the type, which should be in B.M., but is apparently lost. The species is the type of *Acanthocera* Macq. 1834.

Catachlorops rufescens (Fab.) (Tabanus), 1805, Syst. Antliat.,
p. 100, Amer, Merid. Dom. Smidt Mus. de Sehestedt. The single
type (C.) is intact though faded and dusty. It is labelled "T.
rufescens ex Am: Mer: Schmidt". Scutellum white-haired and white
transverse bands on at least second to fourth abdominal tergites. Legs
entirely dark. Beard, pleura and venter of abdomen entirely dark-
haired. Labella large and wholly sclerotized, palpi slender, brown,
black-haired. I give here figures of wing and head structures
(Fig. 1). Kröber's (1939) *C. rufescens* is entirely different, while
the type of his *C. scutellatus* in British Museum agreed closely with
notes and figures of type of *rufescens* Fab. *(New synonymy)*.

Chlorotabanus inanis (Fab.) (Tabanus), 1787, Mantissa Insect.
II, p. 356. Cajennae Dom. v. Rohr. The name should date as above
not 1794 as given by subsequent authors. Philip and Fairchild
(1956) have discussed the material in Copenhagen, which consists
of but the pin and labels of the original specimen (K.) and another
specimen (C.) in fair condition det. by Fabricius from Amer. Merid.

Chrysops costatus (Fab.) (Tabanus) 1794, Ent. Syst. IV, p. 373,
without locality; 1805, Syst. Antliat. p. 112, in America meridionali
Dom. Smidt. Mus. Dom Lund. There are three specimens (C.)
all in good condition, one of which is labelled type. This agrees with
current interpretations. One of the others is *C. ecuadoriensis* Lutz
or a related form. The name has been shown to be a synonym of *C.
variegatus* (De G.).

Chrysops laeta Fab. 1805, Syst. Antl., p. 112, in America meridionali Dom. Smidt. Mus. Dom. Lund. Philip (1955) has discussed the types and shown that *laeta* auct. is not Fabricius' species.
There are 3 specimens, two (C.) in good condition, the other (K.)
represented by wings only. The specimen described as *tuxeni* by
Philip is *formosa* Krob., *(New synonymy)* while the Kiel specimen
is probably *C. varians* var. *tardus* Wied. True *laeta* differs from
most allied species by the much shortened discal cell. Specimens in

Vienna labelled types are those studied by Wiedemann, and not, of course, true types. They are *varians* var. *tardus. C. tenuistria* Krob., whose type is lost, is very probably a synonym of *laeta* Fab. (NEW SYNONYMY).

Chrysops tristis (Fab.) (Tabanus) 1798, Ent. Syst. Suppl., p. 567, Cajennae Dom. v. Rohr. Of the type (K) only the name label remains. Two others specimens (C.) are in the collection, one of which bears a Lectotype label by Philip. Although not strictly types, these specimens were surely studied by Fabricius and Philip's action seems justified in the interests of stability, especially since subsequent workers have applied the name to at least 3 other species. I have an agreeing specimen from Surinam.

Chrysops moerens (Fab.) (Tabanus) 1787, Mantiss. Insect. II. p. 356 Cajennae Dom. v. Rohr. The type now consists of a single wing (K.). It is not a Neotropical species and is discussed elsewhere (Fairchild, 1966 in press).

Diachlorus bicinctus (Fab.) (Tabanus) 1805, Syst. Antliat. p. 102, America meridionali Dom. Smidt. Mus. Dom. Lund. The single type (C.) lacks one wing. It agrees with current interpretations, and is type of the genus.

Diachlorus curvipes (Fab.) (Haematopota) 1805, Syst. Antliat., p. 107. America meridionali Dom. Schmidt. Mus. Dom de Sehestedt. There are 2 females labelled type (C.) in good condition, and another (K.) not labelled type lacking head and abdomen. The two types agree with current interpretations, the other specimen is too damaged for certainty, but is probably the same.

Diachlorus podagricus (Fab.) (Haematopota) 1805, Syst. Antliat. p. 108. America meridionali. Dom. Smidt. Mus. Dom. de Sehestedt. Two females (C.) labelled type in good condition. The type of *D. nigrithorax* Kröb. 1930 in British Museum agrees with my notes on *podagricus,* and I believe is a synonym. (NEW SYNONYMY). Neither Kröber (1928) nor Lutz (1913) recognized the species.

Dichelacera cervicornis (Fab) (Tabanus) 1805, Syst. Antliat. p. 100. America meridionali. Dom. Smidt. Mus. Dom. Lund. Two females in good condition (C.) are labelled types, another (K.) lacks head and abdomen, but is probably the same. All agree with current concepts (Fairchild and Philip 1960).

Dichelacera damicornis (Fab.) (Tabanus) 1805, Syst, Antiliat. p. 101. America meridionali. Dom. Smidt. Mus. Dom. Lund. Two females in fair condition (C.) are labelled types. Another (K.) consists of but 2 legs and the wings. The types are as treated by Fairchild and Philip (1960) ; the Kiel specimen is probably the same.

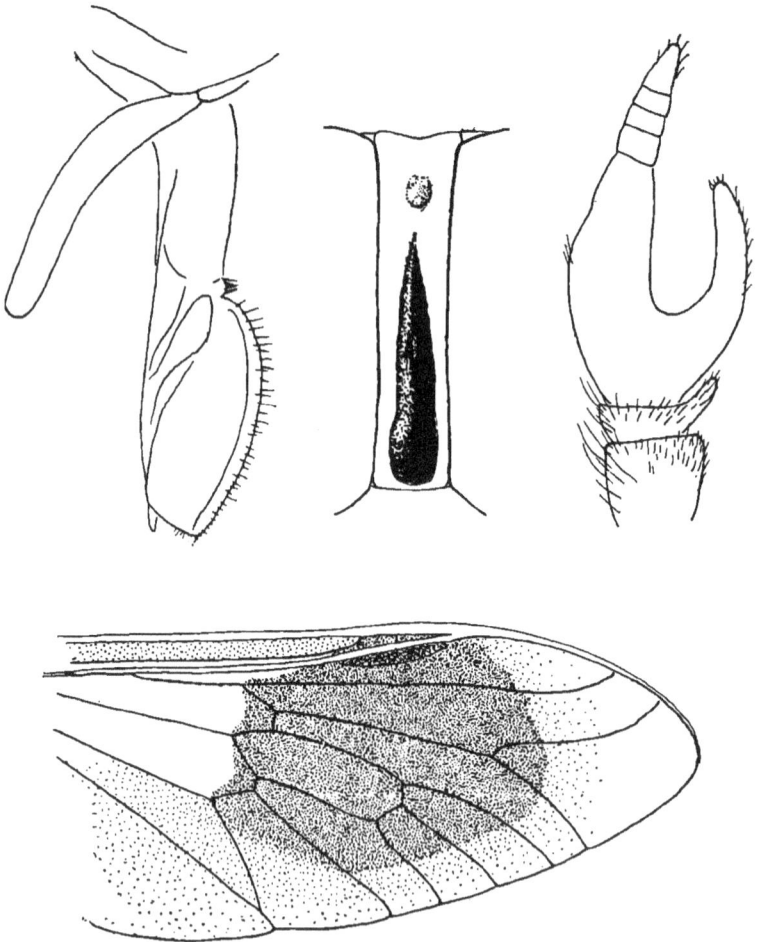

Fig. 1. *Catachlorops rufescens* (Fab.), palpi and proboscis, frons, antenna and wing. Proboscis and frons are to same scale, antenna at twice this magnification and wing about half magnification of frons. Holotype.

Dichelacera T. nigrum (Fab.) (Tabanus) 1805, Syst. Antliat. p. 101. America meridionali. Dom. Smidt. Mus. Dom. Lund. Two females in fair condition (C.) labelled type. Another (K) consists only of fragments of thorax and 1 wing. At least the types agree with current interpretations.

Fidena analis (Fab.) (Pangonia) 1805, Syst. Antliat. p. 91. America meridionali. Dom. Smidt. Mus. Dom. Lund. The type

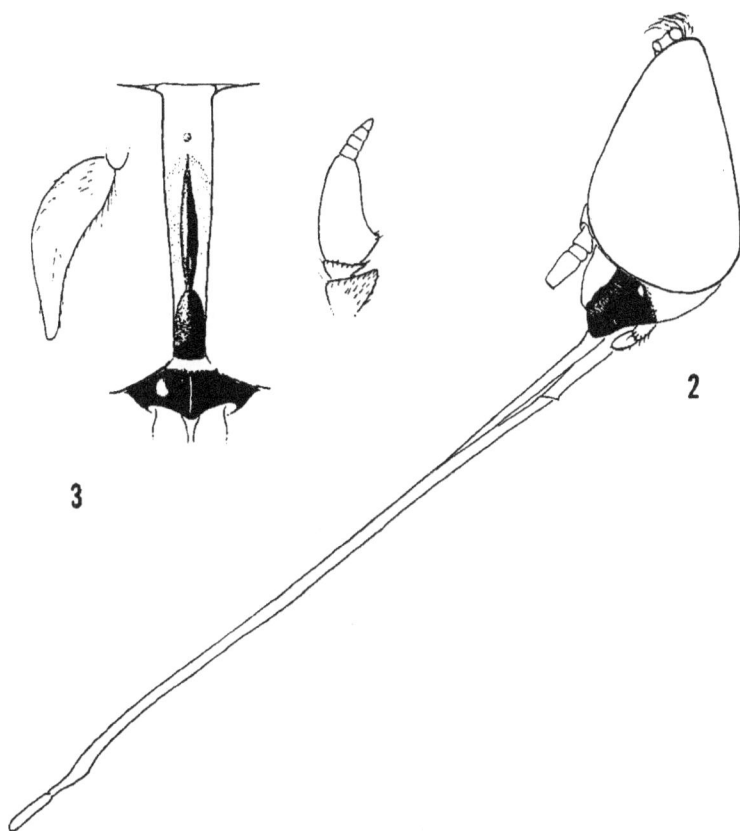

Figs. 2 and 3. Fig. 2. *Fidena analis* (Fab.), head in side view. Holotype.
Fig. 3. *Tabanus trivittatus* Fab., palpus. frons. antennae, all to same scale.
Lectotype.

is a male, labelled "P. analis ex Am: Mer: Schmidt." It lacks most
of third antennal segments, but is otherwise in good condition (C.).
This is not the species so identified by Lutz (1909) or Kröber
(1930). The legs are bicolored, femora black, tibiae & tarsi yellow,
beard and all thoracic hairs black. Clypeus pollinose dorsally, shiny
laterally. Wings entirely glass clear, veins yellowish, blackish only
at extreme base. Abdomen plump and inflated, the first two segments blackish, dark-haired, the remainder yellowish or yellowish
brown, wholly yellow-haired. Remains of antennae yellow. First
posterior cell narrowly open. It is structurally similar to *F. rhino-*

phora Bell. and *F. basilaris* Wied., differing in lacking darkened basal cells and coloring. It is possible that *Fidena oldroydi* Barr. from British Guiana is the female of *analis,* but direct comparison of specimens has not been made, and I had not seen specimens of the former when I studied the type of *analis. Oldroydi* seems to differ in having the wing veins brownish and patches of silvery hairs on sides of tergite 2. A figure of the head of the type of *analis* is included here (Fig. 2).

Lepiselaga crassipes (Fab.) (Haematopota) 1805, Syst. Antliat. p. 108. America meridionali Dom. Smidt. Mus. Dom. Lund. A single female (C.) labelled type is in good condition except for lack of antennae. It agrees with current interpretations.

Phaeotabanus cajennensis (Fab.) Tabanus) 1787, Mantissa Insect., II, p. 355. 1794, Ent. Syst., IV, p. 366-367, Cajennae Dom. v. Rohr. The type (K.) is fragmentary, with little remaining but shell of thorax and wings, and not determinable with certainty. Another specimen (C.) has an old determination label and a Metatype label by Philip. It is well preserved, the fore femora and basal halves of others black, agreeing with the darker specimens of the species, as currently understood, common in northern S. America.

Selasoma tibiale (Fab.) (Tabanus) 1805, Syst. Antliat. p. 102. America meridionali. Dom. Smidt. Mus. Dom. de Sehestedt. The type is intact, in good condition, and agrees with current concepts.

Stenotabanus stigma (Fab.) (Tabanus) 1805, Syst. Antliat. p. 104. Americae insulis. Dom. Smidt. Mus. Dom. Lund. Bequaert (1940) examined and reported on the types, which consist of a male and female (C.) in excellent condition. Another specimen (K.) is fragmentary, only body and one wing remaining. I can add nothing to Bequaert's comments.

Tabanus indicus Fab. 1805, Syst. Antliat., p. 103, America meridionali Dom. Smidt. Mus. Dom. Lund. Two specimens labelled type. One bears a label with "T. indicus ex Tranquebar", the other unlabelled, both are in fair condition and from the Copenhagen collection. The specimen from Tranquebar is an oriental species (Tranquebar is a town on the east coast of India). The unlabelled type is the common neotropical species currently being treated as *T. lineola* var. *carneus* Bell., but also represented by the types of *T. dorsiger* Wied. and *T. dorsovittatus* Macq. Philip (in press) has selected the Tranquebar specimen as lectotype, so the name will apply to an oriental species.

Tabanus lineola Fab. 1794, Ent. Syst. IV p. 369, America boreali Mus. Dom. Bosc. As previously noted by Philip (1942), a type specimen in the Kiel collection is fragmentary, consisting of wings, fore legs, part of thorax and first two abdominal segments almost completely denuded. Specimen bears an old label with "lineola" on one side and "49" on the other. The wings are glass clear, the costal cell not tinted and without appendix on third vein. Fore coxae pale grey pollinose, white haired; femora black, pale haired; tibiae with basal half white, apical half and tarsi black. Thorax blackish with notopleural lobes reddish, as are sides of mesonotum. Scutellum destroyed by pests. First abdominal tergite yellow with a pair of small round submedian dark integumental spots nearly touching in mid-line. Between them there are the remains of a whitish pollinose streak. Second tergite with a broad median dark stripe which is somewhat forked at its posterior end and fails to reach hind margin. This median dark integumental stripe is overlaid by vestiges of a narrow pale pollinose stripe. Nothing in the type contradicts present assignment of the name to the Nearctic form, though absence of scutellum prevents certainty that it is not *subsimilis* Bell. Wholly clear wings rule out Neotropical forms except *colombensis* Macq., which has darker and less contrastingly marked tergites. Use of this name by Kröber (1932) for southern Neotropical material is unwarranted. The Bosc specimen, not found in Paris, is probably lost.

Tabanus pellucidus Fab. 1805, Syst. Antliat., p. 97, America meridionali Dom. Smidt. Mus. Dom. de Sehestedt. The type (C) bears an old label with "T. pellucidus ex Am: Mer: Schmidt". It is on an old short pin, is extensively denuded, lacks antennae, mouth parts, palpi, and all legs; hole in subcallus and base of abdomen beneath. The beard and fore coxae white. Abdomen above reddish with traces of white sublateral patches, beneath with broad sublateral white-haired longitudinal bands. Wing veins brown-margined, first posterior cell closed and petiolate. It agreed closely with a homotype of *T. senior* Wlk. in shape of frons and all else remaining, except that wing cell closed further from margin. Another specimen (K.) not labelled type, lacks head, legs and one wing and is very dirty and denuded. In this the cell is open, but the specimen too fragmentary for certain placement. I believe the following names, whose types I have seen, to be synonymous as noted elsewhere (Fairchild 1966a in press). *T. crassicornis* Wied. 1821, *T. albibarbis* Wied. 1824, *T. angustifrons* Macq. 1847, *T. alboater* Wlk. 1850, *T. senior* Wlk. 1850, *T. atricornis* Big. 1892, and probably also *Chelommia amazonensis* Barr, 1949, of which I have not seen the type. The species is variable as to color, brown to black, and the first posterior

cell varies from open to long petiolate. The species was unrecognized
by Wiedemann, whose description (1828) differs in notable respects
from that of Fabricius, suggesting that he did not see the present
type. Subsequent students have done no better with the brief and
characterless description.

Tabanus quadripunctatus Fab. 1805, Syst. Antliat. p. 99. Amer-
ica meridionali Dom. Smidt. Mus. Dom. de Sehestedt. The type
(C.) bears an old handwritten label "T. 4 punctatus ex Am: Mer:
Schmidt" and is on an old short pin. Palpi, proboscis and outer half
of left wing missing, but otherwise the specimen in fair condition.
I have nothing to add to Philip's (1960) comments on it.

Tabanus trivittatus Fab. 1805, Syst. Antliat., p. 104, America
meridionali Dom. Smidt. Mus. Dom. de Sehestedt. The type (C.)
is labelled "T. 3 vittatus ex Am: Mer: Schmidt." and bears a red
lectotype label of Philip's, who discussed the types (1954). The other
specimen labelled type (C.) is det. Philip as *dorsiger* Wied. It lacks
the shiny subcallus, but through oversight I did not compare it with
the *dorsiger* type in Copenhagen. A final specimen (K) is fragmentary, lacking head and much of abdomen. What remains agrees with
the lectotype. The lectotype has orange antennae, the style slightly
darker. All femora black. Fore tibiae two-thirds, the others nearly
entirely, white. Palpi yellowish, almost wholly black-haired. Frontal
callus rugose. Wings very lightly tinted. The rather denuded
abdomen shows an even middorsal stripe. I give here a drawing of
the type (Fig. 3), which matches closely in proportions of frons and
antennae my homotype of *T. callosus* Macq., though slightly larger.
Specimens from Surinam are an even closer match to this figure,
though I did not have them available in Copenhagen, unfortunately.

REFERENCES

BEQUAERT, J.
    1940. The Tabanidae of the Antilles. Rev. Ent. 11(1-2): 253-369,
        figs. 1-32.
FAIRCHILD, G. B. AND C. B. PHILIP
    1960. A revision of the Neotropical genus *Dichelacera* subgenus *Diche-
        lacera* Macq. Studia Ent. 3 (1-4): 1-86, Pl. 1-7.
FAIRCHILD, G. B.
    1966. Some new synonymies in Tabanidae. Proc. Ent. Soc. Washington,
        in press.
FAIRCHILD, G. B.
    1966a Notes on Neotropical Tabanidae VII. The species described by
        C. R. W. Wiedemann. J. Med. Ent. In press.
KRÖBER, O.
    1925-1926. Die *Chrysops*-arten Sud-und Mittelamerikas nebst den arten
        den Inselwelt und Mexikos. Konowia 4:210-256, 319-375, Pl. 1-5.

1928. Die Amerikanischen Arten der Tabanidensubfamilie Diachlorinae End. Beih. z. Arch. f. Schiffs-u. Tropen-Hyg., etc., 32(2):73-123, figs. 1-26.
1930. Die Tabanidengattung Sackenimyia Big. Zool. Anz., 90(1-2):1-12, figs. 1-6.
1933. Das Subgenus Neotabanus der Tabanidengattung Tabanus s. lat. Rev. Ent. 3(3):337-367.
1939. Das Tabanidengenus *Catachlorops* Lutz. Verhoff. deutsche Kol. Mus. Bremen, 2(3):211-232, pl. 13-16.
LUTZ, A.
1909. Tabaniden Brasiliens und einiger Nachbarstaaten. Zool. Jahrb., Jena, Suppl., 10(4):619-692. Pl. 1-3.
1913. Tabanidas do Brasil e alguns estados visinhos. Mem. Inst. Osw. Cruz, 5(2):142-191, Pl. 12-13.
PHILIP, C. B.
1942. Notes on Nearctic Tabaninae. Part III. The *Tabanus lineola* complex. Psyche, 49(1-2):25-40.
1954. New North American Tabanidae, VII. Descriptions of Tabaninae from Mexico. Amer. Mus. Novitates, No. 1695, pp. 1-26, figs. 1-15.
1955. The types of *Chrysops laeta* Fabr. and a new species of Neotropical deerfly in the Copenhagen Zoological Museum. Ent. Medd., 27:70-75.
1960. Further records of Neotropical Tabanidae, mostly from Peru. Proc. Calif. Acad. Sci., Ser. 4, 31(3):69-102, fig. 1.
1966. New North American Tabanidae XVIII. New species and addenda to a Nearctic catalogue Ann. Ent. Soc. Amer., in press.
PHILIP, C. B. AND G. B. FAIRCHILD
1956. American biting flies of the genera *Chlorotabanus* Lutz and *Cryptotylus* Lutz. Ann. Ent. Soc. Amer., 49(4):313-324. fig. 1 and Pl. 1.
WIEDEMANN, C. R. W.
1828. Aussereuropaische zweiflugelige Insekten, 1:I-XXXII, 1-608, Pl. I-VIb.
ZIMSEN, ELLA
1964. The type material of J. C. Fabricius. Copenhagen, 1964, pp. 1-660.

TWO NEW AMERICAN ARADIDAE
(HEMIPTERA-HETEROPTERA)

By Nicholas A. Kormilev[1]

By the kind offices of Dr. John F. Lawrence, Museum of Comparative Zoology, Cambridge, Mass., I have had the opportunity to study several lots of Aradidae, collected by him on bracket fungi (Basidiomycetes: Polyporaceae) in various parts of North America. Two of the species were found to be new, and are described below, in order to facilitate a study of fungus-feeding insects now being undertaken by Dr. Lawrence. In the measurements, 25 units = 1 mm.

Aradus oviventris, new species
(Figs. 1 — 4)

TYPE DATA: Holotype, ♂, Rustler Park, 8 mi. W Portal, Cochise Co., Arizona, VIII.8.1961, J. F. Lawrence, coll. (Lot No. 918), ex Fomes *subroseus* [=*Fomes cajanderi* Karsten] on *Pinus* sp.; deposited in the American Museum of Natural History, New York. Paratypes, 6♂♂ and 6♀♀, same data; in the Museum of Comparative Zoology (MCZ No. 31201) and the author's collection.

DESCRIPTION: Male ovate, with rather broad abdomen; female more narrowed posteriorly. *Head* (Fig. 1) slightly longer than its width through eyes (♂ 32.5:28, ♀ 33:30); anterior process stout, rather short, slightly widened in middle, reaching to basal 1/5 of antennal segment II; antenniferous spines short and stout, acute, and slightly divergent; lateral tooth minute, but distinct; eyes subglobose. very prominent; preocular tubercles small, acute, the postocular blunt; vertex deeply and narrowly, semicircularly depressed, with two rows of rough granules in middle. *Antennae* (Fig. 2) less than twice as long as head (♂ 57:32.5, ♀ 57.5:33), and much narrower than fore femora; segment II subcylindrical, slightly widened in apical third, as long as head width including both eyes (♂), or one eye (♀); III subcylindrical, slightly widened toward apex; IV elongate-ovate; proportions of antennal segments; ♂ 6:28:13:10, ♀ 6.5:27:13:11; rostrum reaching to middle coxae, or, at most, to hind border of prosterum. *Pronotum* (Fig. 1) widest just behind middle, less than half as long as its maximum width (♂ 23:53, ♀

[1]365 Lincoln Pl., Apt. 2F, Brooklyn, New York
Manuscript received by the editor March 15, 1966.

21:55); anterior border subtruncate; anterolateral borders straight, with irregular teeth; the posterolateral slightly rounded; fore and hind lobes rather flat; interlobal depression shallow; carinae moderately prominent, granulate. *Scutellum* subtriangular, much longer than its width at base (♂ 30:23, ♀ 29:23); lateral borders barely convex, almost straight, feebly reflexed; disc flat, finely granulate in basal 2/5, more roughly so in apical 3/5; depressed at base, and moderately raised around depression; apex narrowly rounded. *Hemelytra* narrow, leaving entire connexivum and parts of tergum exposed, reaching genital lobes (♂), or tergum VII (♀); corium extending to suture between terga IV and V, its basolateral border expanded, rounded, and more or less reflexed. *Abdomen* longer than its maximum width across segment IV (♂ 90:75, ♀ 105:85); lateral borders strongly convex in both sexes, very finely serrate, and slightly notched at PE angles of connexiva; genital plates (Figs. 3 — 4) slightly convex posteriorly, and slightly notched at spiracles in male, more convex and less notched in female. *Color* testaceous; depression on vertex, apex of antennal segment II, basal 2/3 of III, entire IV, some spots on pronotum, and lateral borders of scutellum, darker, brown to piceous; posterolateral borders of pronotum, basolateral expansions on hemelytra, oval spots on terga III to VI, and round, callous spots on connexiva III to VI whitish; in some specimens posterior borders of connexiva II to VI, and R + M veins of corium, pinkish; ventral side testaceous, with some darker spots; hind borders of connexiva pink. *Total length:* ♂ 6.48 mm., ♀ 7.20 mm.; width of pronotum: ♂ 2.12 mm., ♀ 2.20 mm.; width of abdomen: ♂ 3.00 mm., ♀ 3.40 mm.

Aradus oviventris keys out to *Aradus basalis* in Parshley[2], but it may be separated from the latter species by the relatively shorter rostrum, reaching at most to hind border of prosternum, different shape of pronotum (with stronger teeth), relatively shorter antennae (only slightly longer than head and pronotum together), and color.

Aradus lawrencei, new species
(Figs. 5 — 8)

TYPE DATA: Holotype, ♂, 7 mi. NW Wilton, Hillsboro Co., New Hampshire, VII.30.1965, J. F. Lawrence coll. (Lot No. 1559), ex *Fomes cajanderi* Karsten on *Picea* sp.; deposited in the American Museum of Natural History, New York. Paratypes, 2 ♂ ♂ and

---

[2]Parshley, H. M., 1921. **Essay on the American species of Aradus (Hemiptera).** Trans. Amer. Ent. Soc., 47: 1-106. 7 Pls.

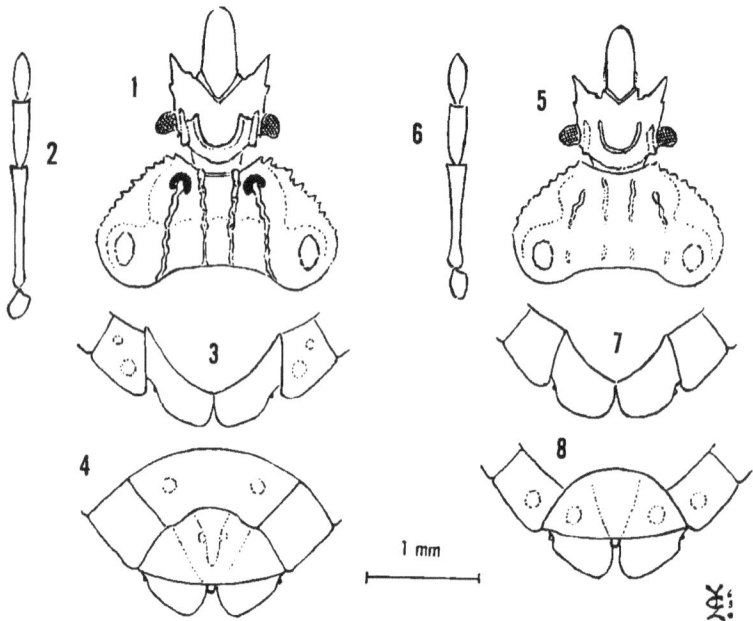

Figs. 1 — 4. *Aradus oviventris* n. sp. Fig. 1, head and pronotum; Fig. 2, antenna; Fig. 3, tip of abdomen (♂); Fig. 4, tip of abdomen (♀).

Figs. 5 — 8. *Aradus lawrencei* n. sp. Fig. 5, head and pronotum; Fig. 6, antenna; Fig. 7, tip of abdomen (♂); Fig. 8, tip of abdomen (♀).

3♀♀, same data; in the Museum of Comparative Zoology (MCZ No. 31202) and the author's collection. One nymph collected with this lot. It is a pleasure to dedicate this species to its collector, Dr. John F. Lawrence.

DESCRIPTION : Male elongate-ovate; pronotum flat; finely granulate. *Head* (Fig. 5) slightly longer than its width through eyes (♂ 29:27, ♀ 32 :31) ; anterior process with parallel sides, but very slightly enlarged at base, reaching a little over 1/5 of antennal segment II; antenniferous spines strong, acute, slightly divergent; lateral tooth minute, sometimes obsolete; eyes subglobose, very prominent; preocular teeth diminutive, acute, the postocular acute (♂) or blunt (♀) ; depressions of vertex moderately deep, slightly convergent posteriorly. *Antennae* (Fig. 6) moderately strong, narrower than fore femora; segment II slightly enlarged at base, more so at apex, its length equal to or slightly greater than interocular space plus one eye; proportions of antennal segments: ♂ 6:24:12:11, ♀ 7:27:13.5:

12; rostrum reaching to middle of prosternum. *Pronotum* (Fig. 5) less than half as long as its maximum width (♂ 20:47, ♀ 25:56); anterior border sinuate; anterolateral borders straight, with moderately strong, irregular teeth; posterolateral borders barely convex, slightly convergent posteriorly; disc flat; interlobal depression sometimes obsolete in middle or very shallow; carenae thin and semiobliterated. *Scutellum* triangular, longer than its width at base (♂ 26:21, ♀ 32:23), shorter than (♂) or as long as (♀) head; lateral borders low, very slightly convex; apex narrowly rounded; basal elevation obsolete. *Hemelytra* narrow, leaving entire connexivum and parts of tergum exposed; reaching genital lobes (♂) or base of tergum VII (♀); corium extending a little beyond (♂) or to (♀) suture between terga IV and V, its basolateral borders expanded, rounded, and moderately reflexed. *Abdomen* ovate, longer than its maximum width across segment IV (♂ 80:66, ♀ 106:84); lateral borders convex, very finely serrate, and slightly notched at PE angles of connexiva; genital lobes (Figs. 7 — 8) slightly convex posteriorly, more so in female. *Color* greyish brown; antennae, head, pronotum, scutellum, and fore half of connexiva slightly darker; lateral borders of pronotum in middle whitish; basolateral expansions of corium, and round, callous spots on connexiva III to VII also whitish; some specimens almost uniformly dark grayish-brown. *Total length:* ♂ 5.75 mm., ♀ 7.20 mm.; width of pronotum: ♂ 1.88 mm., ♀ 2.24 mm.; width of abdomen: ♂ 2.64 mm., ♀ 3.36 mm.

Aradus lawrencei is related to both *Aradus basalis* Parshley and *Aradus oviventris,* n. sp. From the former it differs by the shorter antennal segment II, which is equal in length to the interocular space and one eye only, the much shorter rostrum, reaching only to the middle of the prosternum, the smaller size and different coloration. From the latter species it differs by the shorter rostrum, relatively shorter head (only slightly longer than its width through eyes), relatively shorter antennal segment II, much flatter pronotum, with obsolete, or very shallow interlobal depression, and different coloration.

REVISION OF THE GENERA *GNOSTUS* AND *FABRASIA* (COLEOPTERA: PTINIDAE)

By John F. Lawrence[1] and Hans Reichardt[2]

The species of *Gnostus* and *Fabrasia* are the only myrmecophilous Ptinidae occurring in the New World, although the family is represented in South Africa and Australasia by at least 12 genera of inquilines. *Gnostus* comprises three species ranging from Bolivia and central Brazil to Florida and the Bahamas and all apparently associated with ants of the genus *Crematogaster*. The three species of *Fabrasia* are all South American, and two of these (described below) have been taken with ants of the genus *Camponotus*.

Gnostus formicicola was described by Westwood (1855) from material collected with ants in Brazil. Although the species bore a distinct resemblance to the Paussidae in the structure of the legs, antennae, and prothorax, Westwood concluded, after a thorough comparative study, that it was "most nearly allied to such of the Xylophaga of Latreille as possess five-jointed tarsi . . ." Later authors were more impressed by the specialized features of the species, and it was placed in a distinct family by Gemminger and Harold (1868). Wasmann (1894) and others placed it near the Paussidae, Pselaphidae, Scydmaenidae, or Ectrephidae. *Gnostus* remained a genus of dubious affinities until Forbes (1926) pointed out the similarities in wing venation and wing-folding pattern to members of the family Ptinidae. In the present study, it was found that the male genitalia of *G. formicicola* and *G. floridanus* Blatchley (Figs. 13-14) are of the same general type as that of *Fabrasia, Ptinus, Pseudeurostus, Gibbium,* and several of the Old World Ectrephinae (Hinton, 1941; Sharp and Muir, 1912). The ectrephines have already been placed in the Ptinidae by Wasmann (1916) and will be treated in a forthcoming paper (in preparation).

The genus *Fabia* was proposed by Martinez and Viana (1964) for a Brazilian species *(F. alvarengai)*, but no mention was made of myrmecophilous habits in the species; the name was later changed to *Fabrasia* (Martinez and Viana, 1965) because of homonymy. Last year we found specimens of a second species of *Fabrasia* among the William Morton Wheeler inquiline collection in the Museum of Comparative Zoology, and shortly after this Father Thomas Borg-

[1]Museum of Comparative Zoology, Harvard University, Cambridge, Mass.
[2]Departamento de Zoologia, Secretaria da Agricultura, Sao Paulo, Brazil.
Manuscript received by the editor January 6, 1966

meier presented us with a specimen representing another undescribed species. This led to a comparative study of ptinid myrmecophiles, part of the results of which are presented below.

Since both *Gnostus* and *Fabrasia* have been made the types of subfamilies, it might be well to briefly discuss the classification and possible evolutionary origins of the two groups. *Gnostus* and *Fabrasia* differ considerably from any other group myrmecophilous ptinids in general form and in the presence of fully developed wings and humeral callosities; in this respect they are both similar to certain species of the genus *Ptinus*. They do resemble the Old World myrmecophiles in the modifications of the antennae, presence of glandular areas or trichomes, elongation of the clypeus, and reduction of body hairs or scales, so that the surface appears shiny; most of these similarities probably represent adaptations associated with myrmecophilous habits, and similar trends are found in the Paussidae, the clavigerine Pselaphidae, and other groups of inquilines. Although *Gnostus* and *Fabrasia* are set apart from the other genera,

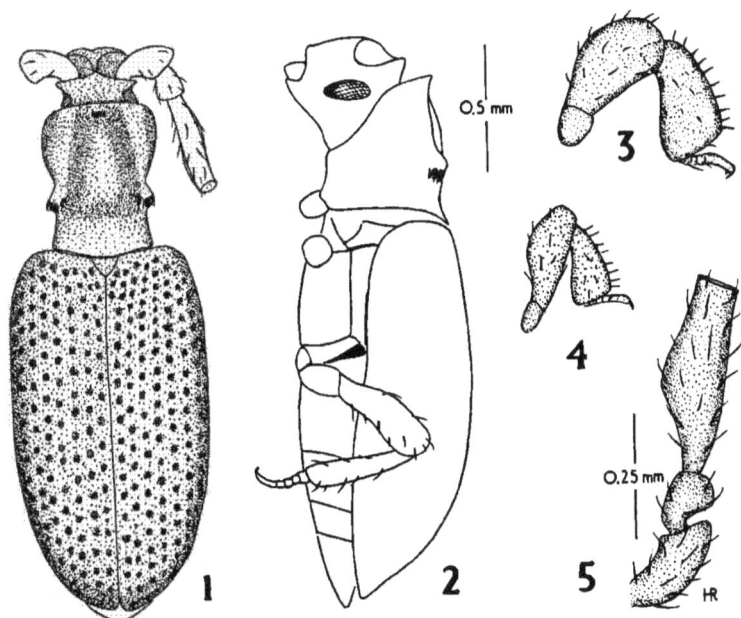

Figs. 1 — 5. *Gnostus floridanus* Blatchley (from Plantation Key, Florida), Fig. 1, dorsal view; Fig. 2, lateral view; Fig. 5, antenna; *Gnostus meinerti* Wasmann (from Barro Colorado Island, Panama), Fig. 3, hind leg; *Gnostus formicicola* Westwood (lectotype), Fig. 4, hind leg.

they are also quite distinct from one another, and it would be difficult to derive them from a common stem. The kinds of adaptive structures occurring in the two groups are entirely different. The glandular structures in *Gnostus* consist of trichomes on the pronotum, while those of *Fabrasia* consist of scattered pores on the elytra and a brush of hairs on either side of the distal articulation of the hind femur. The legs of *Gnostus* may be flattened and expanded like those of certain Paussidae, while the species of *Fabrasia* have peculiarly enlarged and club-like femora, which to our knowledge are unknown in any other beetle group. Characters of the head, antennae, prosternum, abdomen, and genitalia show similar differences. We think that the two genera were probably independently derived from *Ptinus*-like ancestors, perhaps early in the evolution of the family. Since most of the ant host species appear to nest in woody habitats, the beetles may have evolved from subcortical scavengers which had originally been derived from wood-boring ancestors (Crowson, 1955). It appears reasonable to retain the subfamilies Gnostinae and Fabrasiinae for the present, but in a revision of the family they may well be reduced to tribal rank within the Ptininae.

In 1962, Costa Lima described another apparently myrmecophilous ptinid, *Plaumanniola sanctaecatharinae,* which he made the type of another subfamily. The type of this species has been examined, and it was found to belong to the family Scydmaenidae (Lawrence and Reichardt, 1966).

Gnostus Westwood

(Figs. 1 — 5, 13 — 15)

Gnostus Westwood, 1855, Trans. Ent. Soc. London, (2)3: 90. (TYPE SPECIES: *Gnostus formicicola* Westwood, by monotypy).

DESCRIPTION: Form elongate, convex; vestiture of short, suberect, sparsely distributed, fine hairs; surface shiny. *Head* strongly declined, only partly visible from above; vertex concave, forming a broad transverse impression, joined laterally on each side to a deep and narrow, oblique groove extending to the eye below; eyes lateral, relatively small, elongate and carinate; antennal fossae relatively deep, located well above the eyes, separated by a sharp median carina; clypeus subtriangular, almost as long as wide, strongly tumid, and emarginate at apex; labrum inflexed and concave. *Antennae* (Fig. 5) 3-segmented, relatively short (not reaching base of pronotum); segment I elongate, slightly curved, expanded towards apex; II about half as long as I, inserted beneath the latter, terminal segment almost twice as long as I and II together, expanded ventrally at middle and truncate apically, the tip excavate and filled with short hairs.

Pronotum longer than wide, constricted basally; anterior angles rounded; disc somewhat flattened dorsally, with two more or less parallel longitudinal grooves, extending from two anterior pores posteriorly to a broad and deep, transverse impression, which is bordered on each side by two opposing, curved trichomes. *Scutellum* small, semicircular. *Elytra* more than twice as long as pronotum, almost twice as wide at humeri as pronoum at base; sides more or less parallel, expanded and broadly rounded apically; humeral callosities distinct; disc slightly convex dorsally, steeply sloping laterally; each elytron with 9 rows of fine punctures bearing short, suberect, fine, yellow hairs; apices of elytra individually rounded but only barely divergent. *Hindwings* fully developed. *Prosternum* before coxae flat, fairly long, intercoxal process laminate and depressed, so that the elongate coxae are almost touching. *Mesosternum* shorter than prosternum; mesocoxae separated by less than 0.25 times coxal width. *Metasternum* less than 0.50 times as long as wide and slightly longer than mesosternum, convex, median suture absent; metacoxae strongly transverse, separated by less than 0.20 times coxal width. *Abdomen* about as long as wide at base, strongly convex anteriorly; first 3 segments fused, the sutures between them indicated only laterally; 4th segment very narrow. *Legs* (Figs. 2 — 4) relatively short and simple; trochanters elongate-oval; femora and tibiae narrow and slightly flattened *(G. floridanus)* or strongly flattened and expanded *(G. formicicola* and *G. meinerti)*; tarsi short, the first 4 tarsomeres subequal. *Male genitalia* (Figs. 13 — 14) of the general type of *Ptinus* with median lobe articulating dorsally with bases of parameres; basal piece relatively large, parameres very narrow, curved, converging apically. *Total length:* 1.70 — 2.53 mm.

DISTRIBUTION: (Fig. 15): South America (Brazil, Bolivia, and Venezuela), Panama, Florida, and the Bahamas.

The relatively narrow and elongate body form, presence of distinct humeral callosities, and well developed scutellum and hindwings, will distinguish *Gnostus* from the majority of ptinid genera. From *Ptinus* and *Niptinus* it differs by the structure of the clypeus (which is more elongate), the lack of a metasternal suture, narrower pronotum, and the modifications of legs and antennae. *Gnostus* is easily separated from *Fabrasia* by the 3-segmented antennae, position and size of eyes, longer and narrower prothorax, shorter legs, absence of metasternal suture, and partial obliteration of the first two abdominal sutures. The genus is most closely related to *Ptinus* and *Fabrasia.*

All of the species of *Gnostus* appear to be associated with ants of the genus *Crematogaster,* and in the compilation below, at least five species of this genus are involved. To our knowledge, no *Gnostus* has been collected with ants of any other group, and the record of *G. meinerti* from a termite nest needs verification. According to Professor E. O. Wilson (personal communcation), only one specimen of *G. floridanus* was found in a colony of *C. ashmeadi* Mayr on Plantation Key, although the ant is very common at that locality. Bates, on the other hand, as quoted in Westwood (1855), states that the formicaria of *Crematogaster victima* Smith almost invariably contained one, or at most two, *Gnostus formicicola*.

KEY TO THE SPECIES OF GNOSTUS

1. Tibiae only very slightly compressed, about 4 times as long as wide at apex (Fig. 2); longitudinal grooves of pronotum deep; Florida and Bahamas .... *floridanus* Blatchley
    — Tibiae strongly compressed and expanded apically, only 2 times as long as wide at apex (Figs. 3 — 4); longitudinal grooves of pronotum very shallow; South America and Panama 2
2. Posterior tarsus, when retracted, almost completely hidden in apical groove of tibia (only tarsal claws visible); longitudinal grooves of pronotum converging apically; Venezuela and Panama .... *meinerti* Wasmann
    — Posterior tarsus, when retracted, not completely hidden in apical groove of femur (5th tarsomere and claws visible); longitudinal grooves of pronotum subparallel; Brazil and Bolivia
    .... *formicicola* Westwood

Gnostus formicicola Westwood
(Fig. 4)

Gnostus formicicola Westwood, 1855, Trans. Ent. Soc. London, (2)3: 92, pl. 8, figs. 1-21.

TYPE DATA: "Habitat in Brasilia, apud Santarem, in nidis *Myrmicae (Crematogastris) victima*, Smith. D. Bates. In Mus. Britann., &c." Lectotype, by present designation, ♀, with the following labels: 1) "Co-type, Westwood Trans. Ent. Soc. 1855. p. 90. T. 8. Coll. Hope Oxon." (red border), 2) "W Amazon Bates" (diamond-shaped), 3) "Gnostus formicicola Westwood B2 Bates," 4) "Type Col: 235 Gnostus formicicola Westw. Hope Dept. Oxford" (Black border); deposited in the Hope Department of Entomology, Oxford, England.

SPECIMENS EXAMINED: BOLIVIA: *La Paz*, Mapiri, iv — ix. 1925, G. L. Harrington col. (1♀, USNM). BRAZIL: *Mato Grosso*, Utiariti, 325 m, viii.5.1961, K. Lenko col., with *Crematogaster* prope *brasiliensis* Mayr (W. W. Kempf det.) (2 exx., CDZ); *Para*, Santarem, 54 63 (1♀, BM); Villa Nova, 55 75 (1♂, BM); *Amazonas*, Sao Paulo [de Olivenca] (1 ex., BM); "Amazon, Bates" (1♀, BM). This species was previously known only from the several specimens examined by Westwood; the only available specimen which can be assumed to be from the original type series is designated as lectotype above. Four other specimens in the British Museum are apparently not from the Bates material examined by Westwood. *Gnostus formicicola* seems to have a fairly wide distribution south of the Rio Amazonas. It appears to be very closely related to the northern *G. meinerti*, and only a few minor characters separate them. Since the two species are allopatric on the basis of presently known material, it is quite possible that they represent geographical races. Because of the paucity of available specimens, the lack of intermediate forms, and the absence of noticeable variation within either population, we prefer to retain them as distinct species. The original series of *G. formicicola* was taken from the nests of *Crematogaster victima* Smith, but Lenko has recently collected it in the colony of a *Crematogaster* near *brasiliensis* Mayr.

Gnostus meinerti Wasmann
(Fig. 3)

Gnostus meinerti Wasmann, 1894, Kritisch. Verzeich.: 121, 216.

TYPE DATA: "Ein Exemplar von Dr. F. Meinert am Rande des Weges von las Trincheras nach Valencia (Venezuela) im Nest von *Cremastogaster limata* Sm. am 5. Nov. 1891 entdeckt." According to Wasmann the type is deposited in "Collect. Mus. Univ. Hafn.;" not examined.

SPECIMENS EXAMINED: PANAMA: *Canal Zone*, Barro Colorado Island, vii.17.1924, G. C. Wheeler col., with *Crematogaster limata dextella* Santschi (Santschi det.) (2 exx., USNM, CNHM); same locality, vi.1923, R. C. Shannon col., ex stomach of anteater *(Tamandua tetradactyla chiriquensis)* (2♀♀, USNM); Erwin Island, vi.17.1923, R. C. Shannon col. (1 ex., USNM); Gatun Lake, Barro Colorado Island, Wheeler col., with *Coptotermes niger* Snyder (1 ex. USNM).

Although Wasmann's type was not examined, specimens of the Panama population agree well enough with the description to be considered conspecific with *meinerti* from Venezeula. The species seems to be restricted to northern South America, but further records will be needed to ascertain the limits of its distribution. Both of the known populations of this beetle have been collected in associa-

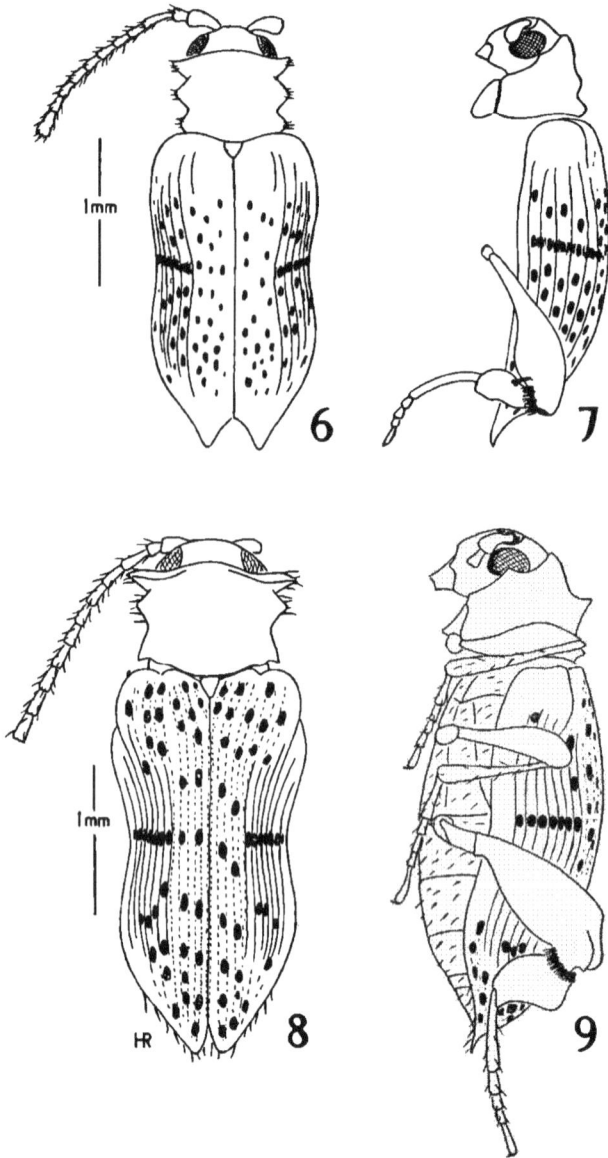

tion with *Crematogaster limata* Smith. The close relationship to *G. formicicola* has been discussed under that species.

Gnostus floridanus Blatchley
(Figs. 1, 2, 5, 13, 14)

Gnostus floridanus Blatchley, 1930, Ent. News, 36: 111-112, fig. 1.

TYPE DATA: "Type a unique (sex undetermined) in the author's collection, taken near Dunedin, Florida, March 7, 1927" Location of type apparently in Blatchley Collection, Purdue University, Lafayette, Indiana; not examined.

SPECIMENS EXAMINED: FLORIDA: Plantation Key, vi.17.58, E. O. Wilson col., with *Crematogaster ashmeadi* Mayr. BAHAMAS: New Providence, Clifton Point, iv.2.65, R. W. Hamilton & B. D. Valentine col., with *Crematogaster sanguinea lucayana* Wheeler (compared with type in the M. C. Z. collection).

Gnostus floridanus was previously known only from the type locality, but the data presented above indicates that it may be more widespread in Florida and the West Indies. Blatchley's specimen was beaten from spanish moss, but this species, like its congeners appears to be found only with ants of the genus *Crematogaster*. It is easily distinguished from *formicicola* and *meinerti* by the characters given in the key, although all three species are fairly similar.

Fabrasia Martinez and Viana
(Figs. 6 — 12, 15)

Fabia Martinez and Viana, 1964, Neotropica, 10(31): 8, not Dana, 1851.
(TYPE SPECIES: *Fabia alvarengai* Martinez and Viana, by original designation).
Fabrasia Martinez and Viana, 1965, Neotropica, 11(34): 18.

DESCRIPTION: Form elongate, strongly convex; vestiture of short, suberect, sparsely distributed bristles; surface shiny. *Head* strongly declined, only partly visible from above; vertex slightly convex, with elongate, narrow, median impression; eyes lateral, well developed, rounded; antennal fossae broad and shallow, located between eyes, separated by a slight tumidity *(F. alvarengai)* or a distinct carina *(F. borgmeieri* and *F. wheeleri)*; clypeus subtriangular, almost as

EXPLANATION OF PLATE 2
Fabrasia borgmeieri. n. sp. (holotype), Fig. 6, dorsal view; Fig. 7, lateral view; *Fabrasia wheeleri*, n. sp. (paratype ♀), Fig. 8, dorsal view; Fig. 9, lateral view.

long as wide, strongly tumid, sharply inflexed and emarginate at apex;
labrum flat. *Antennae* 11-segmented, extending at least to elytral humeri, moniliform to subserrate, the distal segments slightly wider at
apices; segment I oval to oblong, 2 times as long as II which is subglobular, III narrow and elongate, IV — VIII decreasing in length,
IX — XI increasing in length; terminal segment distinctly expanded
and truncate apically, the tip excavate and filled with short hairs.
Pronotum slightly transverse, constricted basally; anterior angles produced laterally forming 2 sharp flanges which partly conceal eyes; disc
with 6 medial tubercles in a transverse row. *Scutellum* small, semicircular. *Elytra* more than 3.50 times as long as pronotum; sides subparallel, but distinctly constricted just anterad of middle; humeral
callosites well developed; disc somewhat flattened dorsally on either
side of suture, steeply sloping laterally; each elytron with 6 or 8 deep
lateral striae and 2 dorsal striae, which may be obsolete except at base;
punctation dual, consisting of small, setiferous punctures, which are
seriate and located in the interstices, and larger, shallow ones, which
contain glandular pores and are located within the striae; glandular
pores in the lateral constrictions larger and closer together, giving
the appearance of a transverse band; apices of elytra slightly to
strongly divergent. *Hindwings* fully developed. *Prosternum* before
coxae tumid, fairly short, intercoxal process long, narrow but not
laminate; procoxae separated by less than 0.25 times coxal width.
Mesosternum subequal to prosternum; mesocoxae separated by about
0.33 times coxal width. *Metasternum* about 0.50 times as long as
wide and 1.50 times as long as mesosternum, strongly convex and
rounded, median suture present; metacoxae transversely oval, separated by 0.50 times coxal width. *Abdomen* 1.25 times as long as
wide at base, strongly convex anteriorly, the sutures all distinct. *Legs*
(Figs. 7, 9) long and highly modified; trochanters elongate-oval;
femora enlarged and club-like distally, the hind femur greatly enlarged and irregularly formed, its tibial articulation with a dense
brush of yellow hairs on each side; front and middle tibiae elongate,
the hind tibia short and formed as in figure; first tarsomere more
than 2 times as long as 2nd in front and middle tarsi, more than 3
times as long in hind tarsus. *Male genitalia* (Figs. 10 — 12) of the
general type of *Ptinus* with median lobe articulating dorsally with

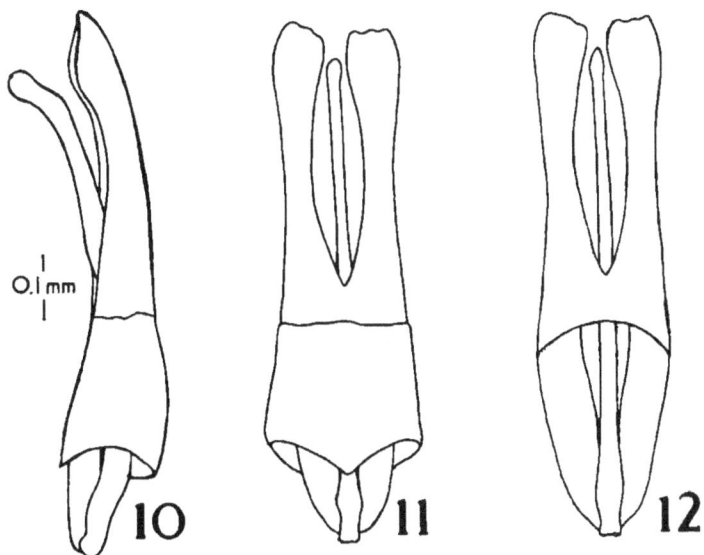

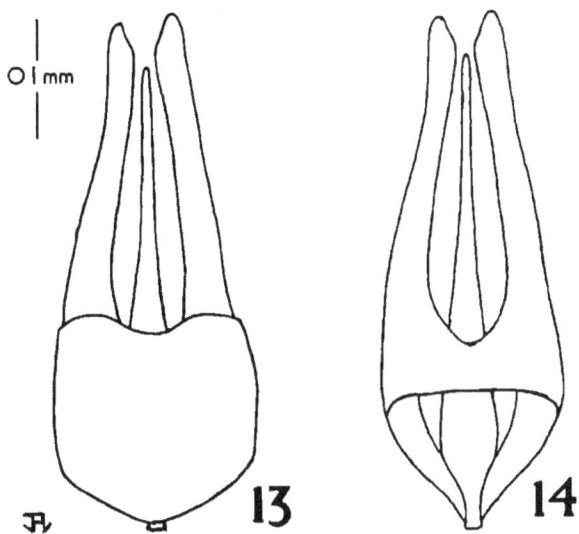

bases of parameres; basal piece relatively small, parameres fairly broad and straight, slightly expanded at apices. *Total length:* 2.87 — 3.32 mm.

DISTRIBUTION (Fig. 15) : South America (Brazil and Colombia).

Fabrasia may be distinguished from the majority of ptinid genera by the body form, distinct humeral callosities, scutellum, metasternal suture, and fully developed hindwings. It differs from *Ptinus* and *Niptinus* by the clypeal structure, elytral constriction, glandular pores, and modifications of legs and antennae. It may be separated from *Gnostus* by the characters given under that genus. This genus, like *Gnostus*, seems to be related to *Ptinus*.

Although the type species has not been collected with ants, both *F. borgmeieri* and *F. wheeleri* have been taken in the nests of species of *Camponotus*. It is interesting to note that the two ant hosts belong to the same subgenus *(Myrmothrix)*, but more material will be needed to consider this anything but an accident of sampling. *Camponotus bugnioni*, the host of *Fabrasia wheeleri*, is known only from near the type locality in northern Colombia, while *C. renggeri*, the host of *F. borgmeieri*, is a common, widespread species, occurring from northern Argentina to northern Brazil. Nothing is known at present of the habits of these myrmecophiles; a study of their behavior might be particularly fruitful, considering the unique specialized structures which they possess.

Key to the species of *Fabrasia*

1. Elytra with 8 lateral striae, 2 dorsal striae visible for their entire lengths; discal tubercles of pronotum conical and sharp; apices of elytra only slightly divergent; hind tibia without pencil of black hairs; elytral bristles very short; larger species (3.17 — 3.30 mm.) ; Colombia .... *wheeleri* n. sp.

— Elytra with 6 lateral striae, 2 dorsal striae obsolete except at base; pronotal tubercles low and rounded; apices of elytra strongly divergent; hind tibia with 1 or 2 pencils of black hairs; elytral bristles longer; smaller species (2.87 — 3.15 mm.) 2

2. Hind tibia with a single pencil of hairs on outer side; clypeus distinctly swollen; antennal fossae joined by a transverse channel; Brazil (Rio Grande do Norte) ....
.... *alvarengai* Martinez and Viana

— Hind tibia with 2 pencils of hairs, one on inner and one on outer side; clypeus not swollen; antennal fossae separated by a median carina; Brazil (Goias) .... *borgmeieri* n. sp.

Fabrasia alvarengai (Martinez and Viana)

Fabia alvarengai Martinez & Viana, 1964, Neotropica, 10(31): 9, figs. 1-3.

Fabrasia alvarengai (Martinez & Viana), 1964, Neotropica. 11 (34): 18.

TYPE DATA: ". . . 1 holotipo de Brasil, Rio Grande do Norte, Natal, VI-1951 (M. Alvarenga-leg.), en la coleccion Moacir Alvarenga de Rio de Janeiro." Holotype examined. This species is represented by a single specimen whose abdomen is missing so that the determination of sex is impossible.

Fabrasia borgmeieri, new species

(Figs. 6 — 7)

DESCRIPTION: Reddish-brown with dark brown spots on elytra; clothed with short yellowish bristles, which are longer on elytra and more concentrated in median constriction, giving the appearance of a transverse band on each side. *Head* with vertex shallowly impressed, post-antennal ridges weakly developed, antennal fossae relatively shallow and separated by a weak, somewhat flattened ridge; clypeus tumid, but not swollen as in *alvarengai;* surface coarsely, densely and shallowly punctate and granulate. *Antennae* almost 3 times as long as pronotum; segment I 1.57 times as long as wide, expanded at apex. *Pronotum* 0.79 times as long as wide at base, anterior angles moderately produced, the sharp flanges only slightly longer than medio-lateral tubercles, which are sharp and conical, the other discal tubercles low and rounded; surface rugosely punctate and granulate, as is scutellum, and clothed with short yellowish bristles. *Elytra* 1.94 times as long as wide at base and 3.81 times as long as pronotum; base with large and rounded humeral callosities and a low rounded elevation on each side between callosity and suture; dorsal striae obsolete except at base, lateral striae 6 in number, very deep in the vicinity of the medial constriction, where the glandular pores are larger and closer together; elytral apices strongly divergent and narrowed, forming 2 triangular processes; surface smooth and shiny, clothed with suberect yellowish bristles, which form brushes laterally in between the pores. *Hind legs* as in *alvarengai,* but the tibia with a longer pencil of black hairs on outer side and a shorter one on inner side. *Abdomen* strongly convex anteriorly, but not impressed mesially. *Total length:* 2.87 mm.; greatest width (across humeral callosities): 1.12 mm.

TYPE DATA: Holotype, probably ♀, Campinas, Goias, Brazil, ii.1964, Schwarzmaier col., with *Camponotus (Myrmothrix) renggeri* Emery

(T. Borgmeier, det.). Holotype deposited in the Departamento de Zoologia, Secretaria da Agricultura, São Paulo, Brazil.

F. borgmeieri is very similar in general appearance to *F. alvarengai,* sharing with it several characters (given in key) which are not found in *F. wheeleri. F. borgmeieri* is easily distinguished from *alvarengai* by the presence of a ridge between the antennal fossae, 2 pencils of hairs on the hind tibia, somewhat shorter antennae, and a less swollen clypeus. Since the specimen of *alvarengai* cannot be sexed, it has occurred to us that the two forms may represent male and female of a single species; the two forms are, however, separated by several characters of the type that are not involved in sexual dimorphism elsewhere in the Ptinidae. The two species are closely related, and when more material is studied, they may prove to be geographic races, which, like *Gnostus formicicola* and *G. meinerti,* occur on either side of the Rio Amazonas.

Fabrasia wheeleri, new species
(Figs. 8 — 12)

DESCRIPTION : Reddish-brown with blackish elytral spots, which are larger and fewer in number than in *borgmeieri;* clothed with very short yellowish elytral bristles; elytra with accumulations of white

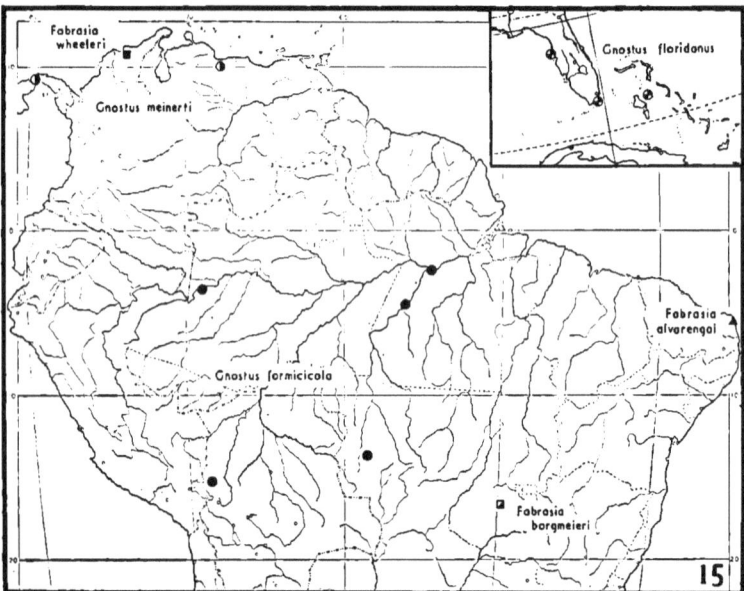

Fig. 15. Geographic distribution of the species of *Gnostus* and *Fabrasia.*

waxy secretion on each side in the constriction, giving the appearance of a transverse band. *Head* with vertex deeply impressed, post-antennal ridges well developed and sharply defined, the antennal fossae deeper and separated by a sharp carina; clypeus tumid but not swollen; more distinctly inflexed than in *borgmeieri;* surface very coarsely, densely, and deeply punctate. *Antennae* about 2.50 times as long as pronotum; segment I 1.33 times as long as wide, subglobular. *Pronotum* 0.76 times as long as wide at base, anterior angles strongly produced, the sharp flanges distinctly longer than the medio-lateral tubercles, which are sharp and conical, the other medial tubercles higher and sharper than in *borgmeieri,* 2 comma-shaped antero-mesal longitudinal ridges bordering a median impression which extends to anterior edge; surface very coarsely and densely punctate, as is scutellum, and clothed with yellowish bristles, which are finer and longer than those on elytra. *Elytra* 1.93 times as long as wide at base and 3.77 times as long as pronotum; base with humeral callosities strongly developed and somewhat carinate, without antero-mesal elevations, but with a deep puncture on either side of the suture; dorsal striae distinct for their entire lengths, lateral striae 8 in number, containing glandular pores as in *borgmeieri,* which are also concentrated in the constriction; elytral apices only slightly divergent and rounded. *Hind legs* as in *borgmeieri,* but lacking a pencil of black hairs on the tibia. *Abdomen* of male with a distinct median impression on the first two visible sternites. *Aedeagus* (of paratype) elongate, basal piece subquadrate, subangulate basally, tegmen deeply cleft apically forming 2 fairly narrow and straight lateral lobes or parameres which are expanded and setose at their tips; median lobe narrow and elongate, curved dorsally at apex and at base, where it is attached to base of tegmen (Figs. 10 — 12). *Total length:* 3.17 — 3.30 mm. (type 3.17 mm.); greatest width (across humeral callosities) : 1.27 — 1.38 mm. (type 1.27 mm.).

TYPE DATA: Holotype, ♂, paratype, ♂, and paratype, ♀, Sevilla, Magdalena, Colombia, vi.12.1927, G. Salt col. (No. N343), with *Camponotus (Myrmothrix) bugnioni* Forel (compared with cotype in the M.C.Z. collection). Holotype and paratype ♀ deposited in the Museum of Comparative Zoology, Cambridge, Mass. M.C.Z. N. 31200; paratype ♂ deposited in the Departamento de Zoologia, Secretaria da Agricultura, São Paulo, Brazil.

Fabrasia wheeleri is easily distinguished from the other two species by its larger size, sharper pronotal tubercles, different clypeal structure, shorter pubescence, and the absence of pencils of hairs on the hind tibia. It certainly seems to be more distantly related to either *alvarengai* or *borgmeieri* than these two are to each other. The species is named in honor of Professor William Morton Wheeler, renowned authority on ants and their inquilines.

ACKNOWLEDGMENTS

The authors would like to express their sincere thanks to the following institutions and individuals for the loan of specimens in their care: J. F. Gates Clarke, T. J. Spilman, and J. M. Kingsolver, United States National Museum (USNM), Washington, D. C.; H. S. Dybas, Chicago Natural History Museum (CNHM), Chicago, Ill.; J. Balfour-Browne, British Museum (Natural History) (BM), London, England; E. Taylor, Hope Department of Entomology, Oxford, England; A. Martinez, Buenos Aires, Argentina; M. A. Vulcano, K. Lenko and W. C. A. Bokerman, Departamento de Zoologia, Secretaria da Agricultura, (CDZ), Sao Paulo, Brazil; R. W. Hamilton and B. D. Valentine, Ohio State University, Columbus, Ohio; M. Alvarenga and T. Borgmeier, Rio de Janeiro, Brazil. For determination of ants and other information, special thanks are given to R. W. Taylor and E. O. Wilson, Harvard University, Cambridge, Mass. and to W. W. Kempf, São Paulo, Brazil.

LITERATURE CITED

BLATCHLEY, W. S.
    1930. On a family of Coleoptera new to the fauna of North America with description of one new species (Gnostidae). Ent. News, 41: 108-112, 1 fig.
COSTA LIMA, A. DA
    1962. Micro-coleoptero representante da nova subfamilia Plaumanniolinae (Col., Ptinidae). Rev. Bras. Biol., 22(4): 413-418, 4 figs.
CROWSON, R. A.
    1955. The natural classification of the families of Coleoptera. Lloyd, London. 187 pp., 212 figs.
DANA, J. D.
    1851. Conspectus crustaceorum quae in orbis terrarum circumnavigatione, Carolo Wilkes e classe Reipublicae Foederatae duce, lexit et descripsit. [part]. Proc. Acad. Nat. Sci. Phil., 5: 247-254, 267-272.
FORBES, W. T. M.
    1926. The wing folding patterns of the Coleoptera. Jour. New York Ent. Soc., 34: 42-68, 91-139, pls. 7-18.
GEMMINGER, M. & E. VON HAROLD
    1868. Catalogus Coleopterorum hujusque descriptorum synonymicus et systematicus. Tom. II. Dytiscidae . . . . Scaphidiidae. Gumm. Monaco. pp. 425-752.
HINTON, H. E.
    1941. The Ptinidae of economic importance. Bull. Ent. Res., 31(4): 331-381, 59 figs.

LAWRENCE, J. F. & H. REICHARDT
  1966. The systematic position of *Plaumanniola* Costa Lima (Coleoptera: Ptinidae) Coleopt Bull. (in press).
MARTINEZ A. & M. J. VIANA
  1964. Una nueva subfamilia de coleopteros (Ptinidae; Fabiinae). Neotropica, 10(31): 7-14, 3 figs.
  1965. Una caso de homonimia en Ptinidae (Coleoptera). Neotropica. 11(34): 18.
SHARP, D. & F. MUIR
  1912. The comparative anatomy of the male genital tube in Coleoptera. Trans. Ent. Soc. London, 1912: 477-642, pls. 42-78.
WASMANN, E.
  1894. Kritisches Verzeichniss der myrmekophilen und termitophilen Arthropoden. Dames, Berlin. xiii + 231 pp.
WASMANN, E.
  1916. Wissenschaftliche Ergebnisse einer Forschungsreise nach Ostindien. . . . V. Termitophile und myrmecophile Coleopteren . . . Zool. Jahrb., 39: 169-210, pls. 4-5.
WESTWOOD, J. O.
  1855. Description of a new genus of coleopterous insects inhabiting the interior of ants' nests, in Brazil. Trans. Ent. Soc. London, (2)3: 90-94, pl. 8.

THE LOWER PERMIAN INSECTS OF KANSAS. PART 11. THE ORDERS PROTORTHOPTERA AND ORTHOPTERA[1]

By F. M. Carpenter
Harvard University

The two preceding papers in this series dealt with representatives of seven closely related families of the Order Protorthoptera occurring in the Elmo limestone. The present paper treats additional families of more diverse relationships within that order and also covers several families of the Order Orthoptera.

The problems involved in the systematics of the Palaeozoic orthopteroids are intrinsically very great, mainly as a result of our fragmentary knowledge of most species but also as a result of the variability of the venation within species. It was my belief more than twenty years ago (1943, pp. 76-77) that the classification of the Palaeozoic orthopteroids as suggested by Handlirsch first and by Martynov later was not realistic in the light of our knowledge at that time. Since then many additional orthopteroids have been described, mostly from the Lower and Upper Permian strata of the Soviet Union. These new fossils have added greatly to our knowledge of the early history of the orthopteroid complex. Through the courtesy of Dr. B. B. Rohdendorf, Arthropod Section, Palaeontological Institute, Academy of Sciences, in Moscow, I had the opportunity in 1961 of studying both the undescribed and described material in the collection of the Institute; and of discussing with Dr. Sharov, Dr. Martynova, Dr. Bekker-Migdisova and other staff members of the Institute various problems of insect evolution. I would be remiss if I did not acknowledge at this time my gratitude to the entire staff of the Institute for their kindness and help during and subsequent to my stay.

During the past decade I have been able to study additional orthopteroids collected at the Elmo locality and especially in the Midco beds in Oklahoma. Two additional trips to the Institute de Paléontologie in Paris have enabled me to make further examination of the Commentry fossils, which I still consider (in spite of the remarkable fossil insects from Tchekarda in the Soviet Union) the foundation on which our understanding of Palaeozoic insects rests.

[1]This research has been supported in part by a National Science Foundation Grant, No. GB 2038.

Part 10 of this series was published in the Proc. Amer. Acad. Arts Sci., 78:185-219, 1950.

In the present state of our knowledge, the classification of the Palaeozoic orthopteroids is necessarily based on the venation of the fore wings, the hind wings and body structures being very little known at best and entirely unknown in by far the majority of species. Since considerable difference of interpretation exists in even the recent literature on the orthopteroid venation, I consider it necessary to present here my own views on the homologies of wing veins in these particular insects and indeed in insects in general. I find that few students of insects have any understanding of the problems of vein homology or of the current status of the subject. The following account is intended to present the background and the nature of my own views used throughout this paper and the subsequent parts in the series.

Although some preliminary attempt was made by Hagen (1870) to homologize the wing veins of insects, Redtenbacher (1886) was the first to make a significant contribution to the subject. He proposed the recognition of six main veins, which he termed the costa, subcosta, radius, media, cubitus and anal. In reaching his conclusions, he considered the general correlation of the positions of the veins, as well as a primitive alternation of topography, i.e., convexity and concavity. The Redtenbacher System of nomenclature was followed by Comstock and is actually the one which has been in general use, although it is commonly referred to as the Comstock-Needham System.[2] Comstock's first publications on wing veins appeared in 1892. In 1895, J. G. Needham, then a graduate student under Comstock, began a new approach to the study of wing vein homology and the ontogenetic development of wings and their veins. Results of these studies were first published in a series of articles under joint authorship of Comstock and Needham in 1898 and 1899. An extensive series of papers, mainly by Needham, appeared in subsequent years and in 1918 Comstock brought together in book form a compilation of what had been done in his and Needham's laboratories. They concluded that the various patterns of wing venation in insects had been derived from a common ancestral type and that the veins of different orders could be homologized. The Redtenbacher System of nomenclature was used by them, although no significance was attached to the convexity or concavity of the veins.

As noted above, the innovation brought into their venational studies was the ontogenetic method. Noting that in such primitive insects

---

[2] Comstock himself pointed out (1918, p. 11) that this nomenclature should be recognized as the Redtenbacher System, not the Comstock-Needham System.

as the Plecoptera only tracheae could be seen in the developing wings, and that the pattern of venation of the adult wing agreed closely with the pattern of tracheation in the wing pad, they concluded that tracheae determined the positions of the veins (Comstock, 1918, p. 12). They also concluded that the ontogenetic history of the tracheal pattern recapitulated the phylogenetic history of the venation in the group of insects concerned. Applying these principles to the Odonata and Ephemeroptera, for example, they reached the unexpected conclusion that a branch of the radius vein had crossed over a branch of the media in the course of the evolution of these groups; the trachea appeared to cross over in the wing pad and this, in their view, meant that the vein had done likewise in previous geologic time. Objections to the tracheation theory of vein determination and especially to the recapitulative conclusions were raised by several students of fossil insects and insect evolution (e.g., Tillyard, Martynov, Carpenter, Fraser) in the period from 1923-1935. In 1935, Needham reiterated his stand on the ontogenetic-phylogenetic relationship of tracheae and veins; and in 1951, he published a more detailed discussion in defense of this thesis, especially as it related to the Odonata, although a substantial part of his paper was an attempt to ridicule in a personal manner all individuals who had disagreed with him.[3]

As Needham himself indicated (1935, p. 129) there had not been undertaken up to that time a thoroughgoing investigation of the development of nymphal wings of any species, at least with respect to the development of tracheae and veins. Shortly after, however, such an investigation was made by Holdsworth (1940, 1941), this consisting of a histological study of the development of wing pads, tracheae and veins, starting with the earliest beginnings of the wing buds. The plecopteran, *Pteronarcys*, was chosen because Comstock and Needham considered the stone-flies as demonstrating most clearly the tracheal determination of veins. Holdsworth's results were strikingly clear: the tracheae did not enter the main area of the wing pads until the blood spaces or lacunae between the blocks of epidermal cells had already established the positions of the veins. The tracheae, as they grew longer, simply entered the lacunae which had already been blocked out, following the lines of least resistance. Variation in the tracheal branching was obvious and usually several

---

[3]One can only regret that this final paper on this subject by Needham was so vindictive. It contributed nothing to science and detracted from Needham's image as a scientist. It also earned a black mark for the American Entomological Society for publishing it.

lacunae received no tracheae. Eventually, the epidermal cells lining
the lacunae, including those without tracheae, secreted the cuticular
materials which finally formed the veins. The obvious conclusion
from this investigation was that the tracheae did not determine the
positions of the veins. What Comstock and Needham had observed
was the entrance of the tracheae into the wing pad, followed by vein
formation, which ultimately closely resembled the tracheal pattern.
What they did not see was that the blood lacunae, along which the
veins would form, were already blocked out, before the development
and extension of the tracheae.

Holdsworth's conclusions have been corroborated by the investigations of Henke (1953) and of Leston (1962) on the inter-relation-
ships of veins and tracheae, demonstrating that the *lacunae* in wing
pads are the precursors of veins, the tracheae merely occupying the
available lacunae. Smart (1961) has shown that the cutting of the
main tracheae in the wing pad of *Periplaneta* resulted in degeneration
of tracheal branches and in retracheation but with an abnormal pattern, which, however, had no effect on the normal venational pattern.
His conclusion was that the pattern of tracheation of the nymphal or
the pupal wing could not be taken as fundamental in determining the
homologies of the veins.[4] As the situation now stands, the Comstock-
Needham method of determining homologies of veins, which dominated investigations of wings for the first half of the present century,
must be regarded as a side issue which actually led nowhere. However, it must also be emphasized that many of the conclusions reached
by Comstock and Needham, not involving their ontogenetic method,
are perfectly valid.

Another approach to the problem of homologies was introduced
by Lameere in 1923, as a result of his extended and important studies
on the Carboniferous insects of Commentry, France. Impressed by
the regularity of the convexities and concavities, he concluded that
there were originally two media veins and two cubitus veins,
one of each being convex (+) and the other concave (−) ; these
he termed the media anterior (MA), media posterior (MP), cubitus
anterior (CUA) and cubitus posterior (CUP). He believed that
some insects had both convex and concave elements, while others
had various combinations of one or the other. Support for his con-

---

[4] I have given this detailed summary of the Comstock-Needham method of
determining wing homologies because their conclusions, based on this technique, have become firmly implanted in American entomological literature
and in current texts. See, for example, the 1963 edition of Borror and
DeLong's "An Introduction to the Study of Insects."

clusions has come from the study of Palaeozoic insects and more primitive groups of living insects with the result that the Lameere view has been generally accepted as a working hypothesis by students of fossil insects and insect evolution. In this connection, one should recall that Redtenbacher in his original account of vein homologies used the alternation of convexities as part of the evidence for his system of homologies. Unfortunately, the convexity or concavity of several veins has been lost in most orders of insects. The subcosta (−), radius (+), radial sector (−), anterior cubitus (+) and posterior cubitus (−) tend to retain their topography in membranous wings, although virtually all veins in thick tegmina or elytra appear to have lost their topographic positions. The anterior media (+) and posterior media (−) have generally come to lie flat in the wing membrane, except in the palaeopterous orders, where they are distinctly different. As a working hypothesis, I am assuming the presence of both of these veins in the early neopterous stock; there is some evidence from the pattern of these two veins in closely related taxa that they have been retained even in the endopterygote line (see, for example, Carpenter, 1940, Adams, 1958). Histological investigations on the development of convex and concave veins are still needed. Holdsworth included some histological observations in his work previously cited, but his studies were limited to one species. Mayfly wings, treated with caustic potash, separate into their original membranes, all the convex veins being on the dorsal membrane and all the concave veins on the ventral membrane (Speith, 1932; Holdsworth, 1941). Holdsworth noted that, although there was not this sharp difference in *Pteronarcys,* most of the cuticular material of the convex veins appeared to be formed in the dorsal epidermal layer and most of that of the concave veins in the lower epidermal layer. It is not improbable that this is generally the case. As noted above, veins have tended to lose the topographic characteristics in tegmina or elytra; and it is possible that a previously concave vein might eventually acquire a convex position secondarily if the tegmen became membranous. However, I regarded the latter occurrence as probably a rare event and consider convexities or concavities of veins as due to the original condition, unless strong evidence exists to the contrary.

In my own work on insect evolution, therefore, I use the following terminology for wing veins: costa (+), subcosta (−), radius (+), radial sector (−), anterior media (+), posterior media (−), anterior cubitus (+), posterior cubitus (−), and anals (+ , − , or flat). The term postcubitus was suggested by Snodgrass for the first anal of Comstock and Needham; however, I see no reason to make this change especially since the new name would almost certainly be confused with Lameere's posterior cubitus mentioned above.

Order Protorthoptera

As noted above, the Palaeozoic orthopteroids present unusual problems in classification. The Blattodea, although part of this phylogenetic complex, are not included in the present discussion, since they are usually regarded as comprising a distinct order. The Manteodea and Phasmatodea are as yet unknown in Palaeozoic strata. We are therefore concerned in this discussion with the living order Orthoptera (i.e., Saltatoria) and with a bewildering variety of orthopteroid fossils, some of which appear to be close to the Orthoptera, but others which are suggestive of the Blattodea, Manteodea, Phasmatodea, Plecoptera, or combinations of two or more of these groups. Unfortunately, our knowledge of about four-fifths of these species is restricted to the fore wings or even to only a part of the fore wings.

Handlirsch (1906) recognized two main extinct orders in the complex, the Protorthoptera and Protoblattoidea, but found it necessary to recognize a third category, "Protorthoptera vel Protoblattoidea" for the species which he could not clearly assign to one or the other. As more Palaeozoic insects became known, a gradual diminution of the distinctions between the Protorthoptera and Protoblattoidea resulted and the number of genera in the "Protorthoptera vel Protoblattoidea" category became nearly as great as the number in the Protoblattoidea itself. In 1937, Martynov suggested the separation of the several non-saltatorial families into a distinct order, Paraplecoptera, leaving in the Protorthoptera only the saltatorial forms. More recently, this proposal has been amplified and somewhat altered by Sharov, who has suggested additional differences between the Protorthoptera, Protoblattoidea, and Paraplecoptera. This involves the transfer of a few species (Oedischiidae) with well developed jumping hind legs into the true Orthoptera, restricting the Protorthoptera to one family, having an incipient saltatorial modification of the legs, with the bulk of the Palaeozoic orthopteroid families going into the Paraplecoptera and Protoblattoidea.

Before considering Sharov's proposed classification, I wish to discuss certain aspects of the venation of the fore wing of these Orthopteroids, at least those features which involve differences in interpretation. Sc, R1, Rs, CuP and the anals present no difficulties in their homologies, but the media (and to some extent CuA) is a different matter. In the orthopteroids, as noted above, the media does not show the clear division into a convex anterior branch and a concave posterior one. It is often deeply forked and the posterior branch may be strongly concave or only slightly concave or even neutral (flat), but I think it can be safely said that there is no orthopteroid known in which the anterior branch of the media is *convex*. We have no way of knowing, therefore, whether in such cases the entire media consists only of MP (with a flattened anterior branch) or of MA and MP, with a flattened MA. The only *positive* criterion by which we can identify a vein in the orthopteroids as homologous with MA of the Palaeoptera is by its *convexity* — which none have. I think there is enough evidence, however, to justify the *probable* determination of the anterior branch of M as MA in some families of orthopteroids, but the determination is only a working hypothesis.[5]

Another area of controversy is the relationship between CuA and M. In the majority of the orthopteroids there is some type of connection between M and CuA, if only a short cross-vein. In others (as Stereopteridae, figures 10-13 of the present paper), CuA curves upwards and fuses with part of M before diverging off as an independent vein. It should be noted that there is marked individual variation in the nature and amount of this coalescence. In others, such as the Blattinopsidae, there is a strongly convex stem of M (see figures 7 and 8 of this paper) which become abruptly flat or concave after the divergence of a short, convex, posterior branch. I think it probable here that the anterior branch of CuA is fused with M from the very base until the point of divergence. A somewhat similar situation appears to occur in the Oedischiidae and related families (these being treated here as true Orthoptera), but I believe the homologies are different (see figure 15). The stem of M, instead of being markedly convex, is flat or even concave. The short vein which diverges towards CuA is rather weak in the Oedischiidae, although it may be stronger in other, related families. In this case,

---

[5]In my own descriptive accounts of the Paleozoic orthopteroids I use the designation MA and MP if the posterior branch is definitely concave and the anterior branch flat; if the posterior branch is flat like the anterior one I use the designation M for the entire system; if all branches of the media are concave, I use the designation MP for all.

EXPLANATION OF PLATE 4

Lemmatophora typa Sellards. Photograph of specimen No. 3539, Museum of Comparative Zoology, showing prothoracic lobes, with hair covering and reticulated pattern. Original.

CARPENTER — PROTORTHOPTERA

I consider the divergent vein as a modified cross vein, which in many cf the orthopteroids appears in diverse forms (e.g., Strephocladidae, figures 1 and 2). It is my opinion, therefore, that the connections between CuA and M are of a diverse nature in the orthopteroids and that these connections have arisen independently many times.

Regarding Sharov's proposed classification of the Palaeozoic orthopteroids, I have previously (1954) adopted Zeuner's suggestion (also accepted by Sharov), that the Oedischiidae are true Orthoptera; Sharov has with good reason made a similar inclusion of a few related families (of which the Permelcanidae, figure 18, is a representative). He then proposed restricting the Protorthoptera to the single family Sthenaropodidae, defining (1960, p. 295) the order as including those orthopteroids with "dorso-ventral flattening of the body, cursorial hind legs, lacking the two rows of spines on the hind margin of the tibia, by the small precostal area lacking the numerous veinlets and by the absence of an undifferentiated concave MA2." This definition I find much too narrow for an *order;* it might well fit a family — a small one — but certainly not an order. The remainder of the orthopteroids which I have previously included in the Protorthoptera, Sharov proposes to divide into the Protoblattodea and the Paraplecoptera. The former order he would restrict to those species having wide coriaceous fore wings, the absence of a clearly defined division of the media stem into two main branches, MA and MP, by large coxae and by general resemblance to Blattodea. In this case, Sharov's characterization seems to be much too broad and generalized. Certainly the coriaceous nature of the fore wings varies greatly within orders (e.g., Orthoptera); in some the fore wings are truly membranous but in others they are definite tegmina or even elytra. So far as the division of the media into MA and MP is concerned, I question that this is clearly divided in any of the orthopteroids; as noted above, there is no orthopteroid that has a convex, and therefore, definite, MA. The coxae are known in very few of the species that Sharov would place in the Protoblattodea and, once again, I cannot see this as an ordinal characteristic. The Paraplecoptera are distinguished by Sharov by the presence of membranous, elongated fore wings, by the clearly defined division of the median into MA and MP and by the general resemblance of the insects to the Plecoptera. On examining the genera which Sharov includes in the Paraplecoptera, as described and figured in the Osnovy (1962), I find many families (e.g., Spanioderidae, Probnidae, Strephocladidae, etc.) in which the fore wings are distinctly coriaceous and as relatively broad and oval as those of the previous order. The condition of MA and MP has already been commented upon.

I can see no justification in Sharov's account for the recognition of the Protorthoptera, Protoblattodea and Paraplecoptera as separate orders, and I propose to place all of these without subgrouping in the order Protorthoptera. Admittedly, the Protorthoptera as thus constituted would be almost certainly polyphyletic. But it seems to me that Sharov's classification would recognize two polyphyletic orders, (Protoblattodea and Paraplecoptera) with the order Protorthoptera itself so narrowly defined as to include only one family. In all probability, the Palaeozoic Orthopteroids were not evolving just in the direction of the living orders Blattodea, Plecoptera, and Orthoptera but, as a result of radial evolution, in many directions. Certainly this is what one would expect from the geological record of other groups of animals. The setting up of the three orders Protoblattodea, Paraplecoptera and Protorthoptera would seem to me to conceal what were almost certainly the real evolutionary lines of these insects. Hence, I prefer to group these orthopteroids into one large complex — the Protorthoptera — until we have enough evidence to indicate what the several lines of evolution have been. I do not believe that we have that now.

I am convinced that Sharov is correct in maintaining that the Lemmatophoridae are not sufficiently different from the Liomopteridae, etc., to justify separation in a distinct order, Protoperlaria. Certainly, as Sharov points out, both fore and hind wings of the Lemmatophoridae and related families can be distinguished from those of other Protorthoptera only with the greatest difficulty. I cannot agree wtih Sharov, however, in his claim that the paranotal lobes in the Lemmatophoridae were continuous and formed a pronotal shield as in Liomopteridae, instead of being independent lobes, as Tillyard and I had described them. Sharov states that his study of the published photographs in Tillyard's (1928) and Carpenter's (1935) papers shows that the lobes unite in front and behind. Although photographs are extremely useful in the study of fossils, they are no substitute for the actual specimens. Tillyard's drawing and mine were based on different specimens and were made several years apart. I have re-examined the material in both the Harvard and Yale collections since the publication of Sharov's paper and I cannot agree with the interpretation which he has made from the published photographs. Photographs of the thoracic region of two specimens of *Lemmatophora typa* Sellards are included here (plates 4 and 5). The first of these shows a specimen which is not quite in a symmetrical

CARPENTER — PROTORTHOPTERA

position; it shows especially clearly the form of the individual lobes. The second specimen, which is the one originally figured by Tillyard, shows the thorax in a more symmetrical position. When Tillyard's original photograph was made, plant fragments and other organic debris covered much of the thorax, obscuring the form of the paranotal lobes posteriorly. Subsequently, as shown in the photograph on plate 5, this debris was removed, presumably by Tillyard himself. The paranotal lobes are reddish-brown in color, like the true wings; the plant fragments and the debris are black, so that the two are more distinctive in the actual fossil than is apparent in a black-and-white photograph. In any event, I do agree that these paranota are not sufficient to justify the separation of the Lemmatophoridae from the Protorthoptera.

In the preceding papers in this series, eight families of Protorthoptera were considered: Lemmatophoridae, Probnidae, Liomopteridae, Chelopteridae, Stereopteridae, Demopteridae, Phenopteridae and Protembiidae. In the present paper three additional families are covered, the Strephocladidae, Blattinopsidae, and Tococladidae, and the Stereopteridae are discussed further, in the light of new material.

Family Strephocladidae Martynov

Strephocladidae Martynov, 1938, p. 100.

Fore wing: coriaceous; precostal area absent; Sc well developed, extending to mid-wing or beyond, with several to many forked branches; Rs arising before mid-wing; R1 extending well towards apex, with several oblique branches leading to margin beyond Sc; Rs very well developed, with several to many long branches, usually without forks except for the branches in the apical part of the wing; M forked before origin of Rs, the anterior branch often touching Rs briefly or connected to it by a short, stout cross vein; M with several long branches, usually simple, independent of R basally, often touching CuA briefly or connected to it by a stout cross vein or possibly by an anastomosed branch; Cu independent of M basally; CuP arising near base; CuA directed longitudinally, giving rise to several long branches, usually simple; branches of Rs, M and CuA parallel and slightly sigmoidal; CuP usually nearly straight, except near its distal end; a distinct furrow posterior to CuA, very close and parallel to it; 1A close and parallel to CuP; other anal veins irregular and

EXPLANATION OF PLATE 5

Lemmatophora typa Sellards. Photograph of specimen No. 5115, Peabody Museum, Yale University.

highly variable; cross veins numerous and regularly arranged over the areas of Rs, M and CuA; an irregular network in costal area and between CuA and CuP and the anal veins. Wing membrane with fine microtrichia between veins; prominent setae or other cuticular derivatives developed to variable degrees on most of the veins of wing, including many cross veins.

Hind wing unknown and body structure unknown, except for part of one leg.

This family has not been given any diagnosis previously, except by generic assignment. In the preceding account I have attempted to bring together venational characteristics of the fore wing present in several Palaeozoic genera which are apparently closely related to *Strephocladus* and which I am placing in the family. However, the strephocladids will probably turn out to be an extensive group and its diagnosis will undoubtedly need modification as other genera become known.

Strephocladus was established in the Order Palaeodictyoptera by Scudder (1885) for a species (*subtilis* Kliver) which was collected in Upper Carboniferous strata of Saarbrücken and which had originally been placed by Kliver in the blattod genus *Petroblattina*. It has subsequently been placed in the order Protoblattoidea, Incertae Sedis, by Handlirsch (1908, 1921); in the order Protorthoptera, family Oedischiidae, by Waterlot (1934) and Guthörl (1936); in a new order Strephocladodea, family (new) Strephocladidae, by Martynov (1938); in the order Paraplecoptera, family Strephocladidae by Sharov (1961); and in the Protorthoptera, family Strephocladidae, by Kukalová (1965), who added another genus, *Spargoptilon* (L. Permian, Moravia), to the family. From my study of the type specimen of *Strephocladus subtilis* and of the several species from Elmo

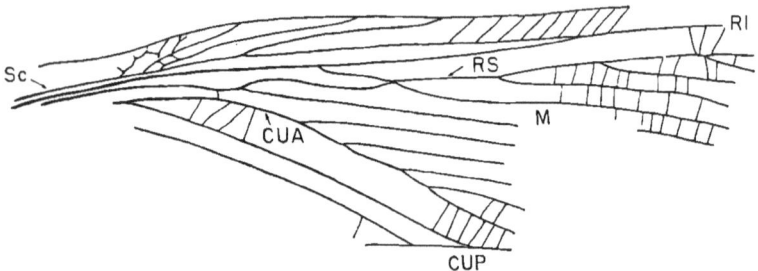

Text-figure 1. *Strephocladus subtilis* Kliver. Original drawing of fore wing, based on holotype, No. D/164, Bergingenieurschule, Saarbrücken.

described below, I consider that the family Strephocladidae fits well within the order Protorthoptera and that Martynov's order Strephocladodea is synonymous with the order Protorthoptera. The relationships of the family Strephocladidae within the Protorthoptera are not so definite. The little-known Strephoneuridae Martynov, from the Lower Permian of URSS, are closest in venational details so far as they are known; but only when the hind wings and body structures have been found can these affinities be worked out satisfactorily.

The most significant features of the Strephocladidae are the presence of long, forked branches on Sc, and the long, parallel and nearly unbranched veins forming Rs, M, and CuA. The identity of most of the main veins is clear; R1 and CuA are strongly convex, and Sc, R1 and CuP are concave. The media does, as usual in the Protorthoptera, present a problem; it shows neither convex nor concave elements and is accordingly being designated here as M. In *Strephocladus, Spargoptilon* and the new genera herein described, CuA either arches anterior, touching M briefly *(Spargoptilon)* or connects with M by a stout cross vein; because of the convexity of all veins included, I agree entirely with Dr. Kukalová's interpretation that no branches of M are, in fact, involved in the CuA complex. The relationship between Rs and the anterior branches of M seems to be similar; in some species *(Spargoptilon)* there is slight anastomosis, but in others the connection is by a cross vein. These variations almost certainly occur as individual fluctuations within species.

Apart from the general venational pattern, there are two features of the fore wings of strephocladids that deserve further comment. (1). Setae on veins. Most orthopteroids possess fine microtrichia on the wing membrane and their presence on the wings of Protorthoptera is well known. The notable feature here is the presence of large *setae* on the veins, these being especially clear in *Homocladus*. These are, of course, represented in the main by setal bases, the setae themselves apparently being broken off in the rock matrix. These setae occur only on that half of the fossil (reverse) which has the impression of the dorsal surface of the wing; the ventral surface of the wing was apparently devoid of such setae. Setae have previously been found on the veins of a few Protorthoptera but they have not previously been noted as occurring so abundantly or regularly. Neither microtrichia nor setae are visible on the type specimen of *Strephocladus subtilis* but this is almost certainly the result of poor preservation of the fossil. (2) The costa, for a variable distance along the anterior margin, is actually sub-marginal for most of its length, there being a narrow but distinct, membranous border. This is a condition which occurs in many Orthoptera. Under low power magnification, this gives the impression that the costa is a much wider vein than it actually is. (See Plate 6).

Since the figures and descriptions of *Strephocladus subtilis* Kliver which have previously been published are not satisfactory, I include here (Text-figure 1) an original drawing of the type, which was placed at my disposal by Dr. G. Kneuper. The length of the preserved part of the wing is 20 mm.; comparison with other Strephocladid wings indicates that the complete wing was about 30 mm. There are three distinctive features of the wing that separate *Strephocladus* from other genera now known in the family: the presence of short, oblique veins from Sc to the costal margin, the definite termination of Sc on R1; and the pectinate origin of the branches of CuA. As can be seen in the figure, the front branch of M is in brief contact with R; CuA is joined by a short cross vein to M. It should be noted that the stem of M is not convex, and that the vein designated CuA is entirely convex. The shallow furrow, directly posterior to CuP, can clearly be seen.

The following are the strephocladids in the Elmo limestone:

Genus **Homocladus,** new genus

Fore wing: costal margin with a distinctly arched border at about the level of the origin of Rs; Sc with numerous long, branched veinlets, directed longitudinally and terminating on costal margin; Rs arising at about one-third the wing-length from the base, giving rise to numerous, long branches, all simple except near the wing apex; M forked just before the origin of Rs, forming several long, simple branches; fork of CuA at least slightly basal of the first fork of M; CuP at its distal end extending parallel and close to the wing margin, this marginal vein being continuous basally by extensions of the

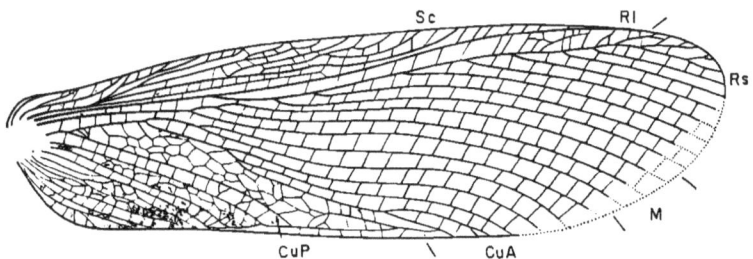

Text-figure 2. *Homocladus grandis,* **n.** sp. Drawing of fore wing (holotype).

anal veins; branches of CuA arising dichotomously, more curved than those of Rs and M; apex of wing much nearer the anterior wing margin than the posterior. Area between CuA and CuP with a coarse reticulation of cross veins. Hind wing unknown.

Type-species: *Homocladus grandis*, n. sp.

This genus differs from *Strephocladus* in lacking the straight, oblique branches to the costa, and in having the branches of CuA arising dichotomously, instead of pectinately; it differs from *Spargop-tilon* by its more slender wing shape, the pectinate, instead of dichotomous, branching of Rs, and in the position of the distally extended part of CuP.

Homocladus grandis, n. sp.
Text-figures 2, 3, 4 and Plate 6

Length of fore wing (holotype): 43 mm.; width, 11 mm. Costal area with only a slight broadening before mid-wing; several rows of cells between CuA and CuP; wing without markings; setae

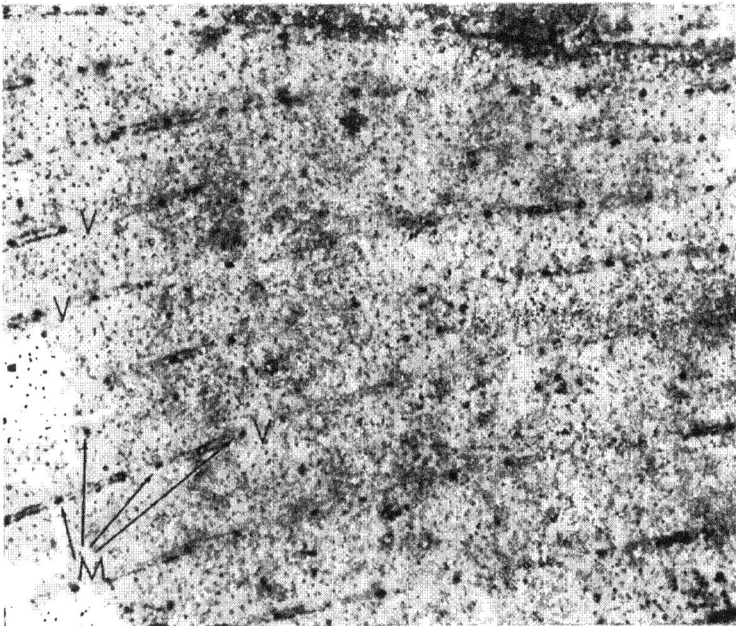

Text-figure 3. *Homocladus grandis*, n. sp. Photograph of wing surface of holotype, showing veins (V) and setal bases (M) on veins and membrane; and microtrichia on membrane.

numerous and well developed on main veins and some cross veins. The venational details of the holotype are shown in figure 2.

Holotype: No. 5874ab, Museum of Comparative Zoology; collected by F. M. Carpenter, in the lower layer of the Elmo limestone in 1927. The specimen consists of a very nearly complete fore wing, lacking only the distal wing margin. A second specimen (No. MCZ 5875ab), with the same collecting data, consists of the proximal two-thirds of a fore wing; a drawing is included here to show the apparent fluctuation in the venation. Also on this piece of rock, only 2 or 3 mm. from the wing, is part of a femur and tibia of a leg; the proximity and size of this leg indicate that it is from the same insect as the wing. The tibia is armed with two rows of heavy spines and the femur bears a few smaller ones.

Homocladus ornatus, n. sp.
Text-figure 5

Fore wing: length, as preserved, 20 mm.; width, 7 mm.; estimated complete wing length, 30 mm. Costal area with a more prominent broadening than in *grandis;* area between CuA and CuP with fewer cells; wing at least four transverse bands. Venational details are shown in figure 5.

Holotype: No. 15584, Peabody Museum, Yale University; collected in Elmo limestone by C. O. Dunbar, 1921.

This species differs from *grandis* mainly by the wing markings and smaller size.

Genus **Paracladus**, new genus

Fore wing: costal margin almost smoothly curved; Sc with several oblique veinlets, mostly branched, but generally much less developed than in *Homocladus;* Sc apparently terminating either on

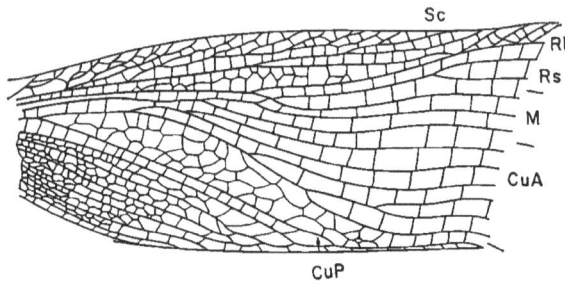

Text-figure 4. *Homocladus grandis,* n. sp. Drawing of fore wing (paratype no. 5875ab).

margin or R1; origin of Rs at or slightly beyond mid-wing, its branches arising dichotomously; CuP only very slightly curved distally, without the terminal extension as in *Homocladus*. Microtrichia on wing membrane more numerous than in *Homocladus;* setae on veins apparently less developed and less numerous.

Type-species: *Paracladus retardatus*, n. sp.

This genus, though clearly related to *Homocladus*, differs by the late origin of Rs, and especially by the absence of the marginal extension of CuP; in the latter respect, it resembles *Strephocladus*.

Paracladus retardatus, n. sp.
Text-figure 6

Length of fore wing, as preserved, 20 mm.; width, 7 mm.; estimated complete wing length, 30 mm. Subcosta space distinct and rather wide, with a few cross veins; relatively few cells between CuA and CuP; 1A connected to CuP distally by a strong, longitudinal cross vein. Wing markings absent. Venational details are shown in figure 6.

Holotype: No. 5877ab, Museum of Comparative Zoology; collected in the lower layer of Elmo limestone in 1932 by F. M. Carpenter.

Family Blattinopsidae Bolton

Blattinopsidae Bolton, 1925, p. 23.
Oryctoblattinidae Handlirsch, 1906, p. 705 (*Oryctoblattina* is a junior objective synonym of *Blattinopsis*).

Fore wing: membrane apparently thin, at most weakly coriaceous; wing generally oval but often very short; Sc extending at least to mid-wing, often considerably beyond; area between Sc and R1 at least

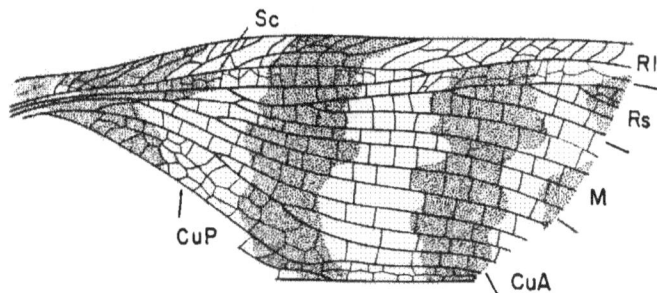

Text-figure 5.   *Homocladus ornatus*, n. sp. Drawing of fore wing (holotype).

as wide as the costal space; R1 usually slightly sigmoidal; Rs usually arising at about one-quarter of the wing length from R1 and giving rise to several branches either dichotomously or pectinately; M apparently independent of R at the base, although very close to it in some species; M almost always with at least two terminal branches; CuA1 apparently anastomosed with the stem of M for a considerable distance, diverging posteriorly from it just before the level of the origin of Rs, then coalescing for a variable distance with CuA2; CuP arising from the stem of Cu near the base of the wing and continuing as a nearly straight, strongly concave vein; the posterior margin of the wing is usually strongly indented at the termination of CuP; 1A usually very close to CuP and in some species apparently anastomosed with it; usually at least two other distinct anal veins present; cross veins highly variable in form, usually numerous and often forming a reticulation over the central and posterior portions of the wing; a curved transverse line, starting from R1 at about the level of the end of Sc and terminating on CuA at about the level of the first definite fork of CuA, is visible on the wings of most members of the family.

The hind wings and body of the blattinopsids are almost entirely unknown; a short, stout ovipositor apparently existed in some species (Kukalová, 1959). A fragmentary wing, probably a hind wing, is the basis of the description of *Blattinopsis elegans* Handlirsch (1906, p. 160), from the Upper Carboniferous of Germany; however, since this wing is not associated with a fore wing and since the venation of the remigium is distinctly different from that of the fore wing, there is no real basis for considering this to be a member of *Blattinopsis*. Laurentiaux (1950, p. 66) has established *Blattinopsis incerta* (Upper Carboniferous of France) for a specimen consisting of

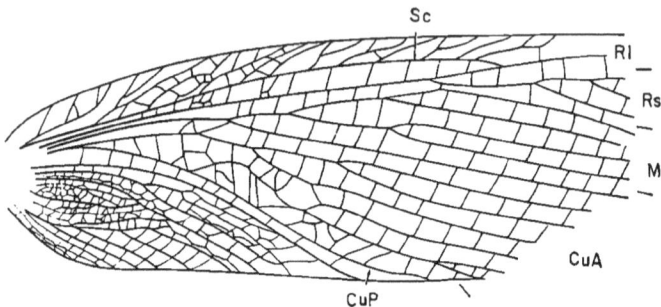

Text-figure 6. *Paracladus retardatus*, n. sp. Drawing of fore wing (holotype).

a fore wing and part of a hind; however, venational details of the fore wing, such as the proximity of Sc to R1, eliminate this species from *Blattinopsis;* it is herein assigned to the genus *Stephanopsis* Kukalová, which was erected as a subgenus of *Blattinopsis* in 1958 (p. 131), with *incerta* as the type species of the subgenus. This is the only species, apart from the very dubious *elegans* Handlirsch, previously mentioned, which can be assigned at the present time to *Stephanopsis*. It is highly doubtful, in my opinion, that *Stephanopsis* actually belongs to the Blattinopsidae.

The venation of the fore wings of the blattinopsids presents some difficulties, at least with respect to homologies of M and CuA. In all members of the family which have been described, the basal portion of M is strongly convex and the remainder concave or at least neutral. The change in the topography of this veins occurs as a strongly convex branch diverges obliquely, fusing with what is obviously part of the anterior cubitus, as shown in figure 7 and in the numerous illustrations of blattinopsids given by Kukalová (1959, 1965). The venation of the blattinopsids, in this respect, is different from that of the carcurgids (i.e., *Heterologus*) and the oedischiids in having no concave vein between CuP and CuA. It seems most likely to me that CuA1 is coalesced with M basally and that it then diverges off as the oblique vein and anastomoses with CuA2. Sharov (1962) is of the opinion that MP is the oblique vein that coalesces with CuA. This interpretation, however, does not explain the strong convexity of the base of M, the convexity of the oblique vein itself, or the change in the topography of the rest of M beyond the divergence of the oblique vein.

In some genera of blattinopsids (i.e., *Glaphyrophlebia*) distinct grooves extend longitudinally between the branches of Rs and M. They have been represented in some figures (Handlirsch, 1906) as actual veins but examination of these wings under high magnification and optimum illumination fails to show any sign of cuticular lines along the grooves. Actually, these structures seem to be shallow depressions in the membrane bordered by low ridges of membrane; similar surface features are found in the wings of various genera of orthopteroid insects, including the Blattodea.

The most notable structure in the blattinopsid fore wings is a curved line which runs transversely from R1 at about the middle of the wing to CuA or even slightly beyond. Kukalová (1959) has pointed out that this resembles the line in the fore wings of some Recent cockroaches of the family Polyphagidae, in which it is apparently formed by spreading and folding of the wings. Others have noted the similarity of this line to the transverse mark that occurs in the fore wings of some Homoptera, and Haupt (1941, p. 88) has actually established a new order, Protofulgorida, for the Blattinopsidae, which he regards as closely related and ancestral to the Homoptera. All available evidence, however, indicates that the blattinopsids are undoubtedly orthopteroid. For example, the details of venation are surely like those in other Protorthoptera and the anal area is clearly orthopteroid, not homopterous.

Previous accounts of the blattinopsids (Bolton, 1925, Kukalová, 1959) have noted the fragmentary nature of all specimens of fore wings. So far as I am aware only one species, *Glaphyrophlebia speciosa* (Sellards), is known from a complete wing. In most specimens, either the apical region or the anal area has been broken away. This is true even of such relatively large species as *Blattinopsis kukalovae,* described below, and it is in marked contrast to the frequency of occurrence of undamaged wings of such small and delicate insects as the Homoptera and Psocoptera in the Elmo limestone. This circumstance seems to indicate that the fore wings of the blattinopsids were unusually thin and delicate.

Genus *Blattinopsis* Giebel

Blattinopsis Giebel, 1867, Zeitschr. Ges. Naturw. 30:417; Kukalová, 1959, Rozpravy. Ceskos. Acad. Ved. 69:(1):5.
Oryctoblattina Scudder, 1895, Bull. U.S. Geol. Surv. 124:133 (jr. obj. syn.).

Fore wing: costal area and area between Sc and R1 with numerous oblique veinlets, very close together and often branched; area between branches of Rs, M and Cu with similar cross veins, those in the

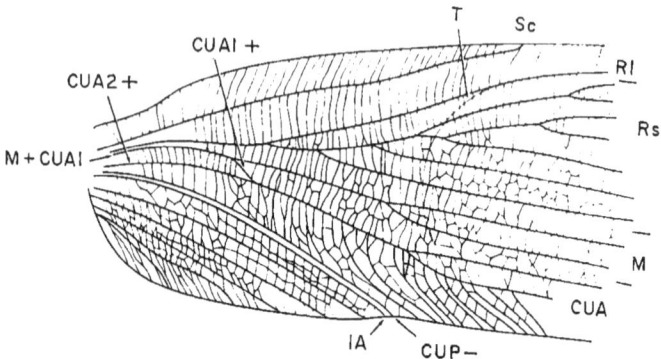

Text-figure 7. *Blattinopsis kukalovae,* n. sp. Drawing of fore wing (holotype). M+CUA1 is the convex base of these coalesced veins; T is the transverse line.

Homocladus grandis, n. sp. Photograph of paratype, No. 5875, Museum of Comparative Zoology, showing membrane extension in front of costa. Setal bases are also visible on the membrane of most of the wing.

distal part forming a fine reticulation; area between CuA and CuP with numerous oblique, parallel branches, mostly slanted towards the posterior margin and parallel to CuP; anal area with numerous cross veins forming a reticulation.

Generic limits of *Blattinopsis* are very difficult to make because of the obvious variation in the venation within species. I consider it advisable to treat this genus broadly, as was done by Kukalová. The type-species, *Blattina reticulata* Giebel, is not so well known as several others, but there is no question about its basic venation. The genus has been recorded from Upper Carboniferous and Lower Permian strata of both Europe and North America. The probable generic synonomy has been discussed by Kukalová (1965).

Blattinopsis kukalovae, n. sp.
Text-figure 7

Fore wing: incompletely known; estimated length, 22 mm.; holotype (basal half of wing), 12 mm.; width 7 mm. Costal margin nearly straight, not conspicuously arched; costal area narrowed at wing base; venation typical of the genus; Rs arising from a single stem; M (in holotype and paratypes) with a deep fork; cross veins in costal area and between R1 and Sc, and R1 and Rs very close together and parallel, almost without cellules; reticulation between branches of Rs, M and CuA.

Holotype: No. 6301ab, Museum of Comparative Zoology; consisting of basal half of a wing; collected by F. M. Carpenter in the upper layer of the Elmo limestone.

Paratype: No. 6302ab, Museum of Comparative Zoology; consisting of a more distal portion of the wing, lacking the apex; paratype No. 15582ab, Peabody Museum, Yale University; collected by C. O. Dunbar; middle portion of the wing, not so well preserved. A third specimen, No. 15633b, Peabody Museum, is a small fragment which probably belongs to this species.

This species has the wing form and size of the type-species of the genus, but it lacks the reticulation in the area between R1 and Sc, and the subcosta is considerably shorter than in *reticulata*. It differs from most of the species described by Kukalová from the Permian of Czechoslovakia in having (1) the costal margin smoothly curved, (2) less reticulation of the cross veins and (3) a much less conspicuous lobation of the anal area.

The species is named for Dr. Jarmila Kukalová of Charles University in Prague, in recognition of her achievements in both collecting and studying the Permian insects of Moravia.

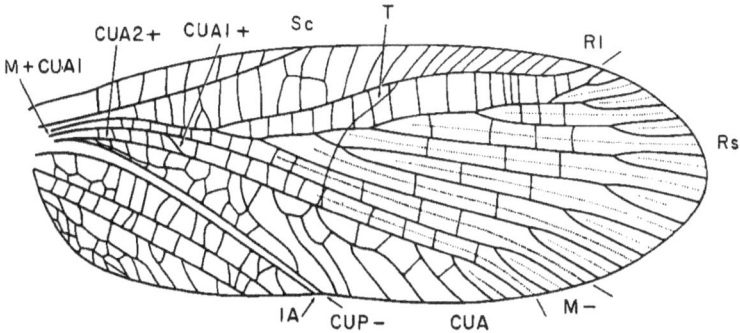

Text-figure 8. *Glaphyrophlebia speciosa* (Sellards). Drawing of fore wing, based on neotype.

Genus *Glaphyrophlebia* Handlirsch

Glaphyrophlebia Handlirsch, 1906, Proc. U.S.N.M. **29**:707.
Sindon Sellards, 1909, Amer. Journ. Sci., **27**:154.
Pursa Sellards, 1909, ibid. **27**:153.

Fore wing: membranous or weakly tegminous; Sc terminating at or slightly beyond mid-wing; costal and subcostal areas with few cross veins; Rs arising at or slightly before mid-wing, with numerous branches, most of them forked distally; M and Cu as in *Blattinopsis,* but usually with fewer branches leading from CuA to the hind margin distally; areas of Rs and M with a few, widely scattered distinct cross veins, not forming a reticulation; curved line across middle of wing, much as in *Blattinopsis;* space between branches of Rs and M with a prominent groove or grooves parallel to the veins. Hind wing unknown.

Type-species: *Glaphyrophlebia pusilla* Handlirsch, from Grove County, Pennsylvania, Illinois; Upper Carboniferous. The type-specimen of *pusilla* consisted of the distal two-thirds or half of a fore wing;[6] although it is well preserved, Handlirsch did not distinguish between the actual forks of the branches of Rs and the grooves in the intervening membranes. Almost certainly the veins had two distal forks, as in the other species now known in the genus.

---

[6]The type and only known specimen of *pusilla* was contained in the Daniels Collection at the time of Handlirsch's description. This collection was supposedly turned over to the U.S. National Museum (Handlirsch, 1906, p. 662) but apparently it was not; none of the specimens originally in the Daniels Collection are in the National Museum.

This genus is undoubtedly close to *Blattinopsis* but differs from it by having (1) distinctly few cross veins over the wing in general and especially in the distal portion and (2) clearly defined grooves in the wing membrane between the branches of Rs and M. *Sindon* Sellards and *Pursa* Sellards seem to me to be inseparable from *Glaphyrophlebia;* as shown below, the type-species of both of these genera possess the venational characteristics of Handlirsch's genus. *Glaphyrophlebia* is represented by one species (*clava* Kukalová) from the Lower Permian of Moravia and two species (*uralensis* Martynov and *rossicum* Martynov) from the Permian of USSR, both originally described in *Sindon*.

Glaphyrophlebia speciosa (Sellards)

Text-figure 8

Sindon speciosa Sellards, 1909, Amer. Journ. Sci., 23:154, fig. 1.

Fore wing: length, 8 mm., width, 3.8 mm. (neotype). Sc terminating at mid-wing; R1 strongly sigmoidal; Rs with seven main branches, each forked distally; M (in type, probably variable) forked only near wing margin; oblique part of CuA slightly basal to the origin of Rs; CuA with only about six branches leading to the hind margin; costal veinlets unbranched (in type), separated by spaces about equal to their length; cross veins in the area of the subcosta and R1 with similar spacing; veinlets from R1 to the costal margin beyond the end of Sc somewhat more numerous and closer together; cross veins in the area of Rs, M and CuA widely spaced; no reticulation between CuA and CuP, although two rows of cells occur in that area basally; anal area without a reticulation.

The holotype specimen, No. 85 in the Sellards collection, was studied by me in 1927, at Austin, Texas. Since this fossil has subsequently been lost, I designate as the neotype specimen No. 6303, in the Museum of Comparative Zoology. This was collected at Elmo, by F. M. Carpenter in 1927; it consists of a complete and well preserved fore wing. Sellards figure of the original type was slightly in error in showing Sc too long and in showing too many branches from CuA to the wing margin. The neotype is very close to the original type except that in the latter the fork of M was much deeper. As pointed out by Kukalová (1965), the branching of M is subject to much fluctuation within the species of Blattinopsidae.

The venational details of this species are shown in text-figure 8. So far as I am aware, this is the only species of the Blattinopsidae known from a *complete* wing.

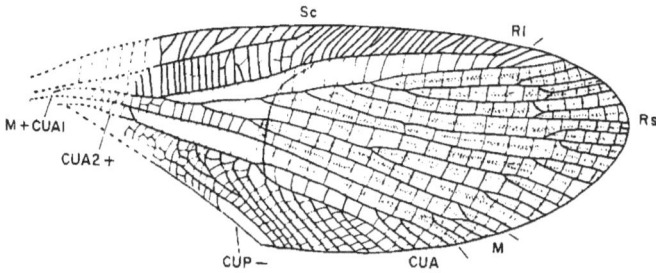

Text-figure 9.   *Glaphyrophlebia ovata*   (Sellards).   Drawing based on neotype.

Glaphyrophlebia ovata (Sellards)
Text-figure 9

Pursa ovata Sellards, 1909, Amer. Journ. Sci., 27:156, fis. 4.

Fore wing: length 8 mm.; width, 3.5 mm. (neotype). Sc terminating at mid-wing; R1 slightly sigmoidal; Rs with 9 branches, each forked distally (neotype); M forked only at wing margin (neotype); costal veinlets and those between R1 and Sc much closer together than in *speciosa;* cross veins between R1 and anterior margin numerous and close together; cross veins between R1 and Rs and between branches of Rs much as in *speciosa;* CuA with about 13 branches leading to hind margin, close together and parallel; area between CuA and CuP with a reticulation basally.

The holotype specimen, No. 1126 in the Sellards collection was studied by me in 1927; since that has subsequently been lost, I designate as the neotype specimen No. 4965ab, Museum of Comparative Zoology; this was collected by F. M. Carpenter, at Elmo, in 1927. It consists of a very well preserved fore wing, lacking the anal area. The species is similar to *speciosa* but has the veinlets in the costal and subcostal areas much more numerous; it also has more branches of Rs and of CuA. The grooves of the membrane between the branches of Rs and M are more complicated than in *speciosa,* each one apparently being composed of 2 or 3 fine grooves.

Sellards figure of *ovata,* based on a poorly preserved wing, confused the branches of Rs with grooves between them and also incorrectly represented the structure of M. This species has the relatively small number of cross veins and lack of reticulation characteristic of *Glyphrophlebia* but has more cross veins and veinlets from CuA to the hind margin than *speciosa* does; in these respects it suggests the condition in *Blattinopsis* more than the latter.

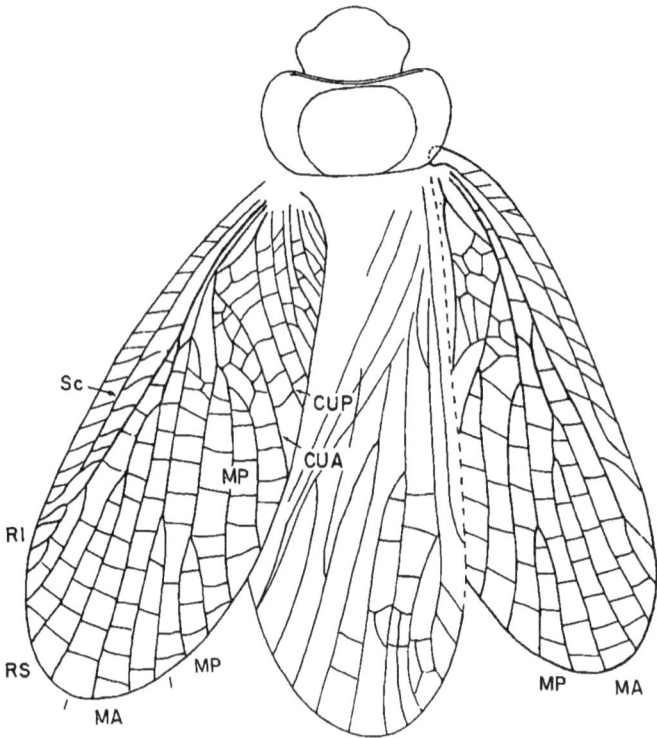

Text-figure 10. *Stereopterum breve,* n. sp. Drawing based on holotype.

Family Stereopteridae Carpenter
Stereopteridae Carpenter, 1950, p. 201.

This family was established on a single species, *Stereopterum rotundum* Carpenter, from the Elmo limestone. Several additional specimens of this insect have subsequently been found as well as representatives of two other species, described below. In one of the latter (*S. breve,* n. sp.) the prothorax is seen to be broad, with the pronotum extended laterally, but truncate anteriorly and posteriorly. Nothing further is known of the body structure in this family.

The stereopterids were probably related to the Euryptilontidae, known from the Lower Permian of the USSR. The prothorax seems to be quite differently formed in these two groups and until the hind wings are known, it seems advisable to recognize the families as distinct.

Stereopterum rotundum Carpenter
Text-figures 11, 12

Stereopterum rotundum Carpenter, 1950, Proc. Amer. Acad. Arts Sci. **78**: 202.

Six additional specimens have been collected in the Elmo limestone since 1950, these bearing numbers 4959, 5253, 5254, 5258, 5259, 5260; all were collected in the lower layer of the limestone (F.M.C.). The species has not yet been recorded from the upper layer. A survey of all of these fossils shows a greater variation in the venational pattern of the fore wing than has previously been realized. The subcosta and R_1 remain fairly constant. Rs in several specimens (4959, 5880, 5885) has a deep fork; in another (5887) it has three branches instead of 2 and in a third (5879) it is unbranched. In the type specimen (4922) it has a shallow, distal fork. In a few specimens (5886, 5879, 5885) MA_1 is anastomosed for a short distance with Rs; in others, as well as the type, it is free from Rs. The weak condition of the basal part of CuA_2, as seen in the type, is apparently unusual; in most specimens (e.g., 5887, 5879) it arises distinctly from the stem of CuA; in one specimen (5886) it arises from $CuA + M$, i.e., before the separation of CuA from M. The pattern of cross veins is variable but essentially as shown in the type; beyond the end of Sc the oblique veinlets from R_1 to the margin are somewhat closer together than elsewhere; this seems to be consistent in all specimens. The distinctive cluster of hairs on MA and MP near the middle of the wing can be seen in several specimens in addition to the type (e.g., 5879); few smaller setae are visible on some other veins but they do not form a definite patch.

All of the fossils which show the base of the wing have a distinct lobe which resembles a heavily sclerotized fold of the costal area extending backwards of the base of Sc and R (see text-figure 11). Having noted this in several specimens, I attempted to chip away the very base of the type specimen, which turns out to have the lobe present also. This lobe was probably concerned with the fitting of the tegmen against the pronotum when the wings were in the resting position; a variety of sclerotized structures, which occur at the wing bases in many living orthopteroids, seem to have a similar function.

Drawings of two specimens are included here (text-figures 10 and 11) to show the extreme variation in some of the features mentioned. It should be noted that in one of the specimens (5886) there is no basal connection between CuP and CuA, although the latter produces both CuA1 and CuA2 directly from M. In the other specimen (4958) both CuA1 and CuA2 arise from MP, not from the stem of M.

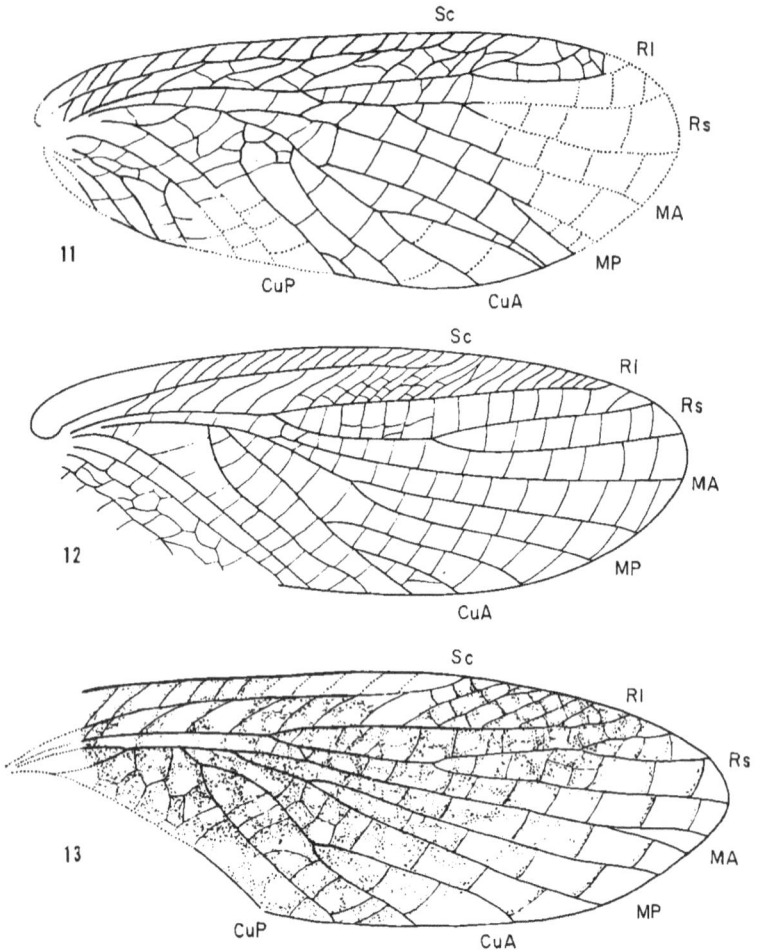

Text-figure 11. *Stereopterum rotundum* Carpenter. Drawing of specimen no. 5886, M. C. Z.

Text-figure 12. *Stereopterum rotundum* Carpenter. Drawing based on specimen no. 4958, M. C. Z.

Text-figure 13. *Stereopterum maculosum*, n. sp. Drawing based on holotype.

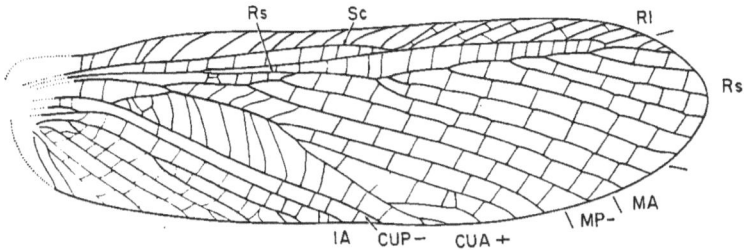

Text-figure 14. *Tococladus rallus*, n. sp. Drawing of fore wing (holotype).

Stereopterum maculosum, n. sp.
Text-figure 13

Fore wing: length, 8.5 mm., width, 3.2 mm. (holotype); more slender than that of *rotundum;* Rs usually with some coalescence between Rs and MA1; CuA or CuA1 anastomosed with stem of M; cross veins in area between CuA and CuP forming a very coarse network; wing distinctly coriaceous, with numerous irregular maculations, preserved as reddish-brown spots.

Holotype: No. 15653, Peabody Museum of Natural History, Yale University; collected in the Elmo limestone by C. O. Dunbar. This consists of a nearly complete wing, lacking the anal area and portions of the wing base and anterior margin.

Paratypes: No. 5257, Museum of Comparative Zoology; collected in the lower layer of the Elmo limestone by F. M. Carpenter; this consists of a nearly complete fore wing, lacking only the basal part; a plant fragment rests near mid-wing, obscuring the veins in a small area. No. 4958, Museum of Comparative Zoology, collected in Elmo limestone, lower layer, by F. M. Carpenter. This consists of a nearly complete fore wing lacking the apical quarter and parts of the hind margin and anal areas. This is the only specimen of *maculosum* which shows the basal part of the wings; the peculiar lobe at the base of the costal area is not present, although there are several prominent spines along the costal margin basally, much as in *rotundum.*

Apart from its shape, maculations, and more pronounced coriaceous texture, this wing differs from that of *rotundum* by the more widely spaced cross veins and the coarser network between CuA and CuP.

Stereopterum breve, n. sp.
Text-figure 10

Fore wing: length, 7.5 mm.; width, 3.5 mm.; Sc extending nearly to the termination of R1; only 1 or 2 veinlets from R1 to costal margin beyond Sc; costal space forming the basal, posterior lobation as in *rotundum;* R1 with one or more distal branches; CuA2 absent as a distinct vein; area between CuA and CuP small; cross veins much as in *rotundum.* Pronotum broad, with curved lateral extensions; anterior border concave; with very little extension; no posterior extension. Head of moderate size.

Holotype: No. 2137, Museum of Comparative Zoology, collected in lower layer of the Elmo limestone by F. M. Carpenter. This consists of a complete insect, showing both fore wings and parts of the body. Unfortunately, the hind wings are overlapped and rest on the abdomen in such a way that their venation cannot be untangled.

This species differs from *rotundum* and *maculosum* by its much smaller size, broader fore wing, relatively longer Sc, the apparent loss of CuA2 and the presence of a smaller space between CuA and CuP.

The preservation of both fore wings enables a comparison of the venation of the two wings in this one specimen. As can be seen' in figure 10, there are differences in the branching of all main veins in the two wings, especially of MA, MP, and CuA. In all probability the coalescence of MA with Rs is subject to similar fluctuation, although it occurs in both wings. The prothorax is clearly preserved, showing the pronotum proper and the thin, lateral extensions. As shown in the figure, the extensions are absent posteriorly and are scarcely present anteriorly, although they are well developed laterally. This is in contrast to the structure in the liomopterids as well as in the euryptilontids, in both of which the extensions are well developed posteriorly.

The head is preserved in a dorsal view and shows no structural details, apart from indications of small compound eyes.

Family **Tococladidae**, new family

Fore wing: costal marginal; wing margin very nearly straight, narrowed basally; Sc extending to about mid-wing, with oblique, unbranched veins leading to margin; similar branches from R to margin beyond Sc; Rs arising well before mid-wing, with several long branches; M independent of R basally; MA with long, simple branches; MP unbranched; area between CuA and CuP traversed by numerous, strong cross-veins, not forming a reticulation; CuP nearly straight, not extending markedly along posterior margin; no separate vena dividens; anal veins numerous and well defined; cross veins distinct and simple over virtually all the wing, including the anal area. Microtrichia and setae absent. Hind wing and body unknown.

This family is probably related to the Ischnoneuridae and Protokollaridae. The very base of the wing is known; a precostal area may have been present. The wing is made distinctive by the extensive development of the radius and the parallel arrangement of the branches of Rs and M. The basic structure Cu is different from that of the Oedischiidae and related groups in that all the branches of Rs are markedly convex, without the basal concave vein present in the Oedischiidae and the Carcurgidae. The stem of M is flat and very weak, not strong and convex as in the Blattinopsidae.

Genus **Tococladus**, new genus

Fore wing: slender, costal area moderately narrow; Sc ending on R1, with numerous oblique veinlets; Rs remote from R1 near midwing but approaching it distally; anterior branch of M forked shortly after origin of Rs, its branches long and simple; several anal veins or main branches.

Type-species: *Tococladus rallus,* n. sp.

Tococladus rallus, n. sp.
Text-figure 14

Fore wing: length, 24 mm.; width, 7 mm. Rs with six branches; front branch of M coalesced with Rs for a short distance before diverging posteriorly (possibly an individual fluctuation); 1A apparently with three long branches; cross veins widely spaced over most of wing.

Holotype: No. 5866ab, Museum of Comparative Zoology, collected in the lower layer of the Elmo limestone by F. M. Carpenter. This consists of a complete fore wing, well preserved but lacking the very base. The wing, which is preserved with fine wrinkles, was apparently thin and membranous, not coriaceous.

Order Orthoptera

The Palaeozoic families Oedischiidae, Tcholmanvisiidae and Permelcanidae are now generally regarded as orthopterous, rather than protorthopterous, this view being based mainly on the saltatorial modification of the hind legs and the probable lateral flattening of the body. Of these, only the Oedischiidae are known from the Upper Carboniferous. These early Orthoptera are not extensively repre-

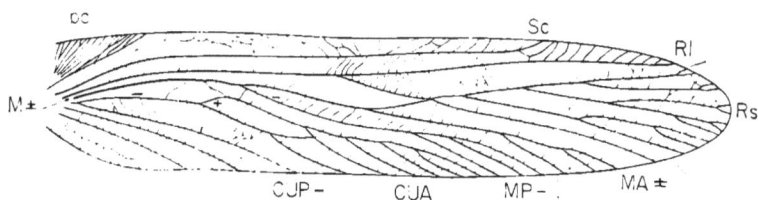

Text-figure 15. *Oedischia williamsoni* Brongniart. Original drawing, based on type in Inst. Paléont., Paris. pc is the precostal area.

sented in any Permian deposit. In the Elmo limestone there is one genus which appears to belong to the Oedischiidae and which is close to *Metoedischia* from the Permian of the Soviet Union. There are also representatives of three other families, two of them new.

It should be noted that there are many additional orthopteroids present in the Yale and Harvard collections from the Elmo limestone, almost all of them undescribed. But none of them, so far as can be determined now, belong to the Orthoptera. They will be treated in the next part of this series of papers.

Family Oedischiidae Handlirsch

Oedischiidae Handlirsch, 1906, p. 700.

Fore wing: usually thin, only slightly coriaceous; precostal space well developed; Sc extending well beyond mid-wing, with several branches; M dividing at about a third of the wing-length from the base into MA, which is not clearly convex, and MP, which is markedly concave; MA usually anastomosed with Rs; Cu forked near the base, the posterior branch, CuP, strongly concave; the anterior branch (CuA) forking at least once, in part coalescing with a cross vein leading from M, and eventually forming several branches which lead to the hind margin; CuP unbranched; at least three anal veins; cross veins numerous, in some species forming a reticulation in certain parts of the wing. (See text-figure 15)

Hind wing unknown. Body unknown, except for legs; hind legs long and modified for jumping.

This family is known from the Upper Carboniferous of France (Commentry) and Germany and the Permian of USSR and possibly Czechoslovakia. The species described below constitutes the first record of the family in North American deposits.

Unfortunately, almost all specimens of Oedischiids consist of isolated wings. The type-species of *Oedischia* (*williamsoni* Brongniart) is represented by two fragmentary specimens showing the fore

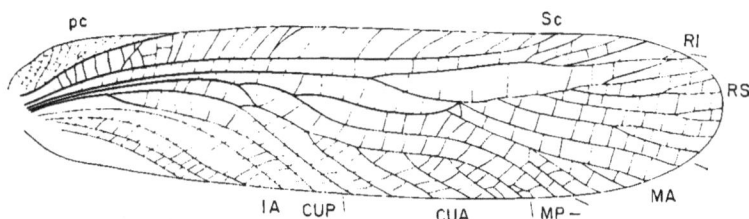

Text-figure 16. *Paroedischia recta*, n. sp. Drawing based on the holotype (middle part of wing), paratype No. 15638 (base of wing) and paratype no. 15757 (apex of wing).

wings and legs. As noted above, the hind wings are unknown in the family[7]; a small and apparently distorted fragment of a hind wing is preserved in the type of *Permoedischia moravica* Kukalová, from Czechoslovakia, but this genus can only doubtfully be referred to the Oedischiidae. It has been assumed, probably correctly, that the oedischiid hind wings had an expanded and folded anal area. I have discussed above the peculiarities of the topography of the venation of *Oedischia* and have given reasons for my present belief that in this family, at least, the short vein connecting the stem of M to CuA is a modified cross vein, not a branch of M or a part of CuA.

Genus **Paroedischia**, new genus

Fore wing: shape much as in *Metoedischia*. Sc extending well beyond mid-wing, longer than in *Metoedischia;* Rs arising at about mid-wing, free piece of Rs (before anastomosis with M) longer than in *Metoedischia;* separation of CuA and CuP much later than in *Metoedischia;* cross veins as in *Metoedischia*, but without formation of reticulation. Hind wing unknown.

Type-species: *Paroedischia recta*, n. sp.

On the basis of the fore wing, which is all that is known, this genus seems to be close to *Metoedischia* but differs in the several respects already noted.

Paroedischia recta, n. sp.
Text-figure 16 and Plate 7

Fore wing: Length of holotype fragment, 20 mm.; width 7 mm.; estimated complete length of wing, 37 mm.; width 7 mm. Precostal space with a series of nearly parallel veinlets, connected by short

---

[7]The restoration of the oedischiid genus *Metoedischia* given by Martynov (1938, p. 49) was based on specimens of two species, one of which is now placed in the genus *Pinegia* of the family Tcholmanvissiidae.

cross veins; costal area with a series of straight or nearly straight veinlets, only very rarely branched; R1 with several branches distally; Rs with several main branches, each forked; M dividing well before origin of Rs; MP sigmoidally curved; CuA with 6 terminal branches; space between 1A and 2A widened distally; cross veins as shown in figure .

Holotype: No. 5897ab, M.C.Z., collected by F. M. Carpenter, in lower insect layer at Elmo, Kansas; this consists of the middle part of a well preserved fore wing. Several additional specimens almost certainly belonging to this species are as follows: No. 15757, Peabody Museum, Yale University (collected by C. O. Dunbar), consisting of a distal third of a fore wing; No. 15638ab, Peabody Museum (collected by C. O. Dunbar); consisting of the basal quarter of a fore wing; No. 5900, M.C.Z. (collected by F. M. Carpenter), distal half of fore wing; No. 5898, M.C.Z. (collected by F. M. Carpenter), basal third of fore wing; No. 5899, M.C.Z. (collected by F. M. Carpenter), distal fragment of fore wing; No. 5896, M.C.Z. (collected by F. M. Carpenter), distal fragment of fore wing.

The fragmentary nature of these specimens is strongly indicative of unusually delicate wings, almost certainly membraneous, rather than coriaceous. A composite drawing of the fore wing of *recta* is included in figure 16; the central part of the wing is drawn from the holotype; the basal and distal portions are based on specimens numbered 15638 and 15757, respectively.

The venation of this insect is clearly subject to much variation, the number and precise arrangement of branches being different to some degree in all specimens.

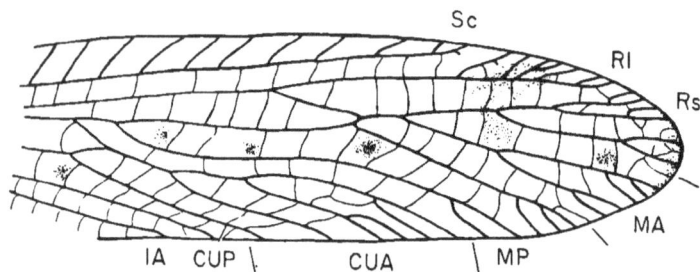

Text-figure 17. *Paroedischia maculata*, n. sp. Drawing of fore wing (holotype).

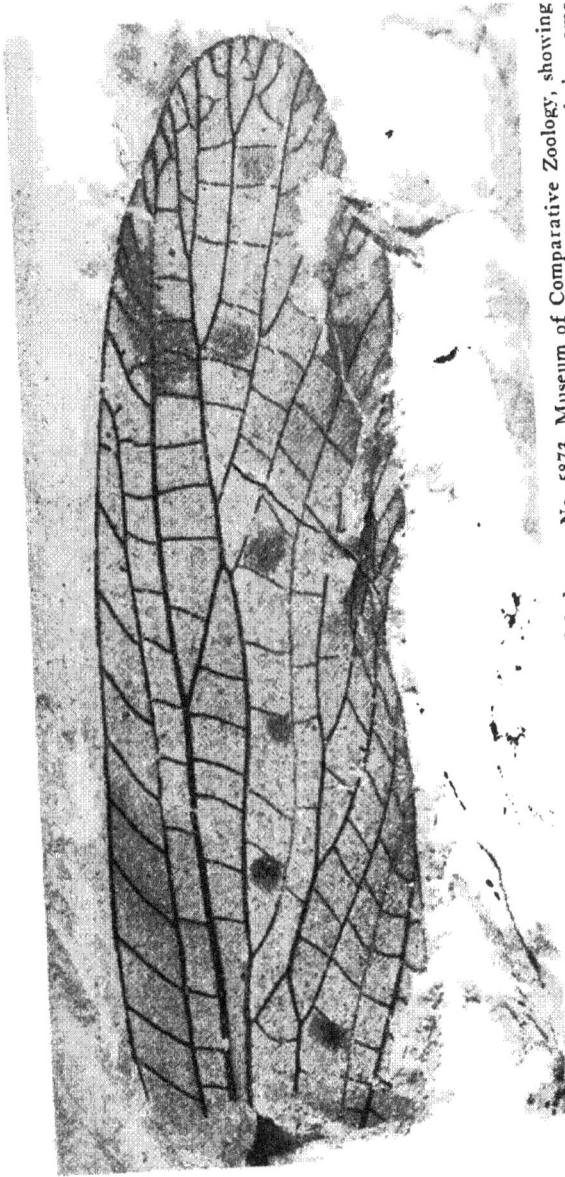

Paraoedischia maculata, n. sp. Photograph of holotype, No. 5873, Museum of Comparative Zoology, showing wing markings. This photograph is a composite one, made up of the obverse and reverse halves of the same specimen.

Paroedischia maculata, n. sp.
Text-figure 17

Fore wing: length, as preserved, 20 mm. width, 7 mm.; estimated complete length, 30 mm. Venation so far as known like that of *recta*, except that the main veins are almost consistently forked at the wing margin, the branching of R is less, the main veins are thicker, and the cross veins are thinner and more irregular. In addition the wing has several distinct maculations, as shown in the photograph, plate 4. The wing of *recta* shows no signs of markings of any kind.

Holotype: No. 5873ab, Museum of Comparative Zoology (Collected by F. M. Carpenter), in the lower layer of the Elmo limestone; this consists of a distal two-thirds of a wing, which is somewhat wringled along the posterior border but otherwise very well preserved.

Family Permelcanidae Sharov
Permelcanidae Sharov, 1962, p. 112.

Fore wing: membranous or very weakly coriaceous. Precostal area well developed but not forming a prominent bulge, extending about one-fourth wing length from base; Sc extending slightly beyond mid-wing; R distinct from Sc basally; Rs arising near or just beyond mid-wing, usually anastomosing with a branch of MA for at least a short distance; Rs and M with at least two terminal branches; CuA as in the Oedischiidae, with several terminal branches; CuP close to 1A; 1A with several veinlets leading to the hind margin; 2A and 3A much shorter. Cross veins much fewer than in the Oedischiidae, not forming a true reticulation.

Specimens showing both fore and hind wings have not been found, but isolated portions of hind wings, consisting mainly of the remigium in each case and probably belonging to this family, have been described by Sharov. In these hind wings the costa is short and submarginal; Sc, R1, Rs and M are essentially as in the fore wing; an anal area was presumably present although only a suggestion of one is visible in the fossils. The body structure is unknown.

Three previously described genera belong here: *Promartynovia* Tillyard, from the Elmo limestone, Kansas; and *Permelcana* Sharov and *Proelcana* Sharov, from upper and lower Permian deposits, respectively, in the USSR.

Genus *Promartynovia* Tillyard
Promartynovia Tillyard, 1937, Amer. Journ. Sci., 33:99.
Permelcana Sharov, 1962, Paleont. Journ. 2:114.

Fore wing: costa usually consisting of two or more distinct

branches arising from the wing base; Rs arising just before the end of Sc; CuA with several terminal branches; 1A extending well beyond 2A and sending several short branches to the hind margin; cross veins usually straight, only rarely branched. Pterostigmal and apical areas of wing pigmented.

Type-species: *Promartynovia venicosta* Tillyard.

I have been unable to find sufficient differences between *Promartynovia* Tillyard and *Permelcana* Sharov to justify generic separation. *Promartynovia* was very incompletely known to Tillyard, who placed it in the order Neuroptera, and his description of *P. venicosta* was unsatisfactory, for the reasons given below. The type-species (*sojanense* Sharov) of *Permelcana* Sharov is known by a nearly complete fore wing, which lacks only the apical region. Sharov had little reason to associate his fossil from the Upper Permian of the USSR with *Promartynovia,* although I had pointed out in 1943 (p. 61) that the latter genus was orthopteroid not neuropteroid. I strongly suspect, also, that *Proelcana* Sharov, based on an apical fragment (*uralica* Sharov) from Lower Permian deposits of Tchekarda, USSR, will turn out to be a synonym of *Promartynovia;* the amount of anastomosis between Rs and M, and the detailed arrangement of the branches of these veins, used by Sharov as generic characters, are highly variable within this group of orthopteroids.

Promartynovia venicosta Tillyard
Text-figure 18

Promartynovia venicosta Tillyard, 1937, Amer. Journ. Sci., 33:100; fig. 6 (Order Neuroptera, family Martynoviidae).

Fore wing: length 11 mm.; width 2.6 mm.; front margin apparently slightly concave; costa consisting of two main branches leading from wing base, the posterior one simple, the other forming

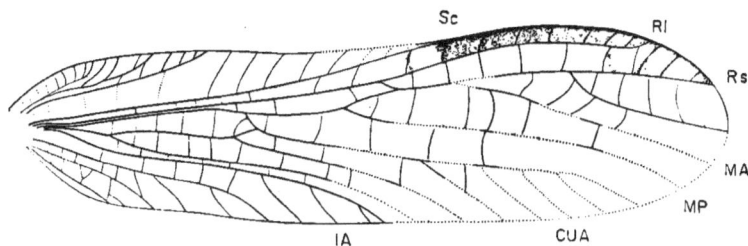

Text-figure 18. *Promartynovia venicosta* Tillyard. Drawing of fore wing, based on holotype in Peabody Museum, Yale University.

a complex of several branches; costal veinlets oblique, long, unbranched; Rs with two branches; MA anastomosed with Rs for a short distance; MP apparently unbranched.

Holotype: No. 15594, Peabody Museum, Yale University. This specimen, when studied by Tillyard, had not been completely cleaned; it was known to him only by the base of the wing. Removal of matrix has revealed the greater part of the rest of the wing, as shown in figure 18; some parts of the posterior margin of the wing are missing but they are not critical for the determination of the species.

In his figure of the fossil, Tillyard omitted the weakly developed CuP, which arises from Cu basally and runs closely parallel to 1A. It can be seen clearly in the specimen, however, with the aid of low-angle illumination. Tillyard's assignment of *Promartynovia* to the Neuroptera (Sialoidea) was made with some doubt; actually he placed the genus in the family Martynoviidae, now included in the extinct order Diaphanopterodea. The similarity of the fore wing of *venicosta* to that of *sojanense* Sharov is really striking. They are of comparable size, have a similar venation and even possess the identical pigmentation of the pterostigmal area.

Family **Parelcanidae**, new family

Fore wing: more coriaceous than in Oedischiidae; precostal area forming a prominant bulge; Sc apparently extending well beyond mid-wing; Rs (so far as known) arising slightly beyond mid-wing, anastomosed with a branch of M for a short distance; CuA and CuP as in Oedischiidae; 1A nearly straight; cross veins about as numerous as in Oedischiidae. Hind wing and body unknown.

This family, which is apparently more closely related to the Oedischiidae than to the Permelcanidae, is characterized mainly by the prominance of the precostal area and by the coriaceous nature of the fore wing.

Genus **Parelcana**, new genus

Fore wing: costa usually consisting of two distinct branches, the anterior one giving rise to a series of radiating veins, the posterior one forked; at the level of end of precostal area, the costal space is about as wide as the space between R and Sc; termination of 1A close to end of 2A; cross veins close together, uniformly distributed; no reticulation formed (at least in basal half of wing).

Type-species: *Parelcana dilatata*, n. sp.

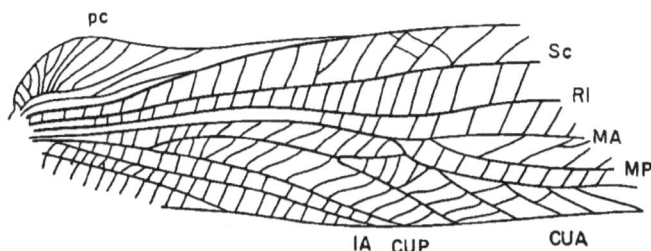

Text-figure 19. *Parelcana dilatata*, n. sp. Drawing of fore wing (holotype).

Parelcana dilatata, n. sp.
Text-figure 19

Fore wing: length of preserved part 19 mm.; width, 5 mm.; estimated length of complete wing, 36 mm.; costal veinlets slightly oblique, mostly unbranched; branches of CuA short. Details of venation shown in figure 19.

Holotype: No. 6304 ab, Museum of Comparative Zoology (collected by F. M. Carpenter in lower layer of Elmo limestone). This type consists of a well preserved basal half of a fore wing.

The precostal area of this wing is unusually prominent. Although the wing is incomplete, that part which is preserved seems to be definitely coriaceous; the cross veins are preserved as distinct ridges, which are especially prominent when observed under oblique light.

Genus Petrelcana, new genus

Fore wing: distinctly coriaceous; slender. Precostal area not so long or so broad as in *Parelcana,* but projecting beyond the line of the anterior margin of the wing; costa little-known, irregularly formed; R1 with several oblique, almost longitudinal veinlets beyond the end of Sc; at level of end of precostal area, costal space much wider than space between Sc and R; termination of 1A well beyond the end of 2A; cross veins more widely separated than in *Parelcana* and more irregular, forming a coarse reticulation in parts of the anal area.

Type-species: *Petrelcana elongata,* n. sp.

Petrelcana elongata, n. sp.
Text-figure 20

Fore wing; length, as preserved, 33 mm.; width 7 mm.; estimated complete length, 40 mm.; veinlets widely separated and irregular in

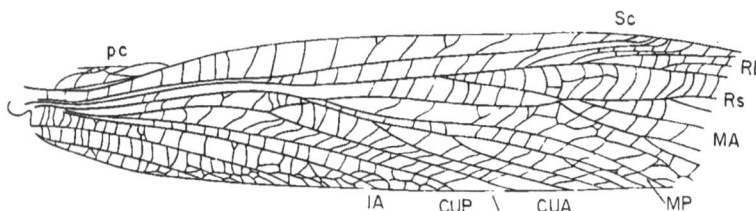

Text-figure 20. *Petrelcana elongata*, n. sp. Drawing of fore wing (holotype).

most of costal area; cross veins between R1 and Rs sigmoidal and parallel; branches of CuA long, extending beyond the level of anastomosis of Rs with M.

Holotype: No. 6306, Museum of Comparative Zoology, collected by F. M. Carpenter in the lower layer of the Elmo limestone. This consists of a nearly complete fore wing, lacking only the apical region. The fossil is very well preserved and shows definite indications of pigmentation along almost the entire length of R and R1, the pigmentation broadening out to include surrounding areas after the origin of Rs. The precostal area is not entirely known, although in the specimen it clearly projects beyond the rest of the wing margin; whether or not it forms as noticeable a bulge as in *Parelcana* cannot be determined. The family assignment of this genus may need to be changed when the form of the costa is known.

REFERENCES

BOLTON, H.
    1925. Insects from Coal Measures of Commentry. Brit. Mus., Fossil Insects, 2:1-56.
CARPENTER, F. M.
    1935. The Lower Permian insects of Kansas. Part 7. The Order Protoperlaria. Proc. Amer. Acad. Arts Sci. 70:103-146.
    1943. The Lower Permian insects of Kansas. Part 9. The Orders Neuroptera, Raphidiodea, Caloneurodea and Protorthoptera, with additional Protodonata and Megasecoptera. Proc. Amer. Acad. Arts Sci. 75:55-84.
    1950. The Lower Permian insects of Kansas. Part 10. The Order Protorthoptera: the Family Liomopteridae and its relatives. Proc. Amer. Acad. Arts Sci. 78 (4):185-219.
    1954. Key to extinct families of insects. In Brues, C. T., A. L. Melander and F. M. Carpenter, Classification of Insects. Bull. Mus. Comp. Zool. 108:777-827.
COMSTOCK, J. H.
    1918. The Wings of Insects. Comstock Publ. Co.

COMSTOCK, J. H. AND NEEDHAM, J. G.
  1898-99. The Wings of Insects. Amer. Nat. vols. 32, 33. (A series of
    23 papers).
FRASER, F. C.
  1931. A note on the fallaciousness of the theory of pretracheation of the
    wing venation of Odonata. Proc. Roy. Ent. Soc. London, 13:
    60-70.
GUTHÖRL, P.
  1936. Neue Beiträge zur Insekten-Fauna des Saarcarbons. Sencken. 18:
    Zlb. 72:1-51.
HAGEN, H. A.
  1870 Ueber rationelle Benennung des Geäders in den Flügeln der
    Insekten. Stett. Ent. Zeitung 31:316-320.
HAUPT, H.
  1941. Die ältesten geflügelten Insekten und ihre Beziehungen zur Fauna
    der Jetztzeit. Z. Naturw. 94: 60-121.
HENKE, K.
  1953. Die Musterbildung der Versorgungssystem in Insektenflügel. Biol.
    Zlb. 72:1-51.
HOLDSWORTH, R.
  1940. Histology of the wing pads of the early instars of *Pteronarcys
    proteus* Newman. Psyche, 47:112-120.
  1941. The wing development of *Pteronarcys proteus* Newman. Journ.
    Morphology, 70:431-461.
KUKALOVÁ, J.
  1959. On the family Blattinopsidae Bolton, 1925. Roz. ceskosl. acad.
    véd., 69 (1): 1-27.
  1965. Permian Protelytroptera, Coleoptera and Protorthoptera (Insects)
    of Moravia. Sborník geol. véd. pal. 6:61-98.
LAMEERE, A.
  1922. Sur la nervation alaire des insectes. Bull. Class Sci. Belgium,
    1922:138-149 (transl. Psyche 30:123-132, 1930).
LESTON, D.
  1962. Tracheal capture in ontogenetic and phylogenetic phases of in-
    sect wing development. Proc. R. Ent. Soc. Lond. (A) 37:135-144.
MARTYNOV, A. V.
  1924. Sur l'interpretation de la nervuration et de la tracheation des
    ailes des Odonates et des Agnathes. Rev. Russe d'Ent., 18:145-174.
    (transl. Psyche 37:245-280, 1930).
  1937. Permian fossil insects from Kargala and their relationships. Trav.
    Inst. Paléont. Acad. Sci. URSS, 7:1-92.
  1938. Etudes sur l'histoire géologique et de phylogénie des ordres des
    insectes (Pterygota). Trav. Inst. Paléont. Acad. Sci. URSS 7:
    1-150.
NEEDHAM, J. G.
  1935 Some basic principles of insect wing-venation. Journ. N. Y. Ent.
    Soc. 43:113-129.
  1951. Prodrome for a manual of the dragonflies of North America, with
    extended comments on wing venation systems. Trans. Amer. Ent.
    Soc. 77:21-62.

88 *Psyche* [March

REDTENBACHER, J.
1886. Vergleichende Studien über das Flügelgeäder der Insekten. Ann. des k.k. nat. Hofmuseums 1. (3): 153-232.
ROHDENDORF, B. B., ET AL.
1962. Osnovy Paleontologii. Insecta. pp. 1-373. Akad. Nauk. SSSR.
SCUDDER, S. H.
1885. Palaeodictyoptera: or the affinities and classification of Paleozoic Hexapoda. Mem. Bost. Soc. Nat. Hist. 3:319-351.
SELLARDS, E. H.
1909. Types of Permian insects. Part 3. Amer. Journ. Sci. 27:151-173.
SHAROV, A. G.
1960. On the system of the Orthopterous Insects. Internat. Cong. Ent., Wien, 1960 (1): 295-296.
1962. A new Permian family Permelcanidae (Orthoptera). Pal. Journ. 2:112-116.
SMART, J.
1956. A note on insect wing veins and their tracheae. Quart. Jour. Micros. Sci. 97 (4): 535-539.
SPEITH, HERMANN.
1932. A new method of studying the wing veins of the mayflies and some results obtained therefrom. Ent. News, 43:103.
TILLYARD, R. J.
1923. The wing-venation of the order Plectoptera or mayflies. Journ. Linn. Soc. Zoology, 35:143-162.
1927. Kansas Permian insects. Part 17. The Order Megasecoptera and additions to the Palaeodictyoptera, Odonata, Protoperlaria, Copeognatha and Neuroptera. Amer. Journ. Sci. 33:82-110.
1928. The new order Protoperlaria. Amer. Journ. Sci. 16:185-220.
WATERLOT, G.
1934. Bassin houiller de la Sarre et de la Lorraine. ii. Faune fossile. Etudes Gites Min. Fr: 1934. 111-221; 269-273.

CAMBRIDGE ENTOMOLOGICAL CLUB

A regular meeting of the Club is held on the second Tuesday of each month October through May at 7:30 p.m. in Room B-455, Biological Laboratories, Divinity Ave., Cambridge. Entomologists visiting the vicinity are cordially invited to attend.

The illustration on the front cover of this issue of Psyche is a reproduction of a drawing of a female bethylid wasp, *Pseudisobrachium terresi* Mann, from Haiti (Psyche, vol. 22, p. 165, 1915).

BACK VOLUMES OF PSYCHE

The Johnson Reprint Corporation, 111 Fifth Avenue, New York 3, N. Y., has been designated the exclusive agents for Psyche, volumes 1 through 62. Requests for information and orders for such volumes should be sent directly to the Johnson Reprint Corporation.

Copies of issues in volumes 63-72 are obtainable from the editorial offices of Psyche. Volumes 63-72 are $5.00 each.

F. M. CARPENTER
Editorial Office, Psyche,
16 Divinity Avenue,
Cambridge, Mass., 02138.

FOR SALE

4

PSYCHE

A JOURNAL OF ENTOMOLOGY

Vol. 73   June, 1966   No. 2

CONTENTS

PSYCHE is published quarterly by the Cambridge Entomological Club, the issues appearing in March, June, September and December. Subscription price, per year, payable in advance: $4.50 to Club members, $5.00 to all other subscribers. Single copies, $1.25.

Checks and remittances should be addressed to Treasurer, Cambridge Entomological Club, 16 Divinity Avenue, Cambridge, Mass.

Orders for back volumes, missing numbers, notices of change of address, etc., should be sent to the Editorial Office of Psyche, Biological Laboratories, Harvard University, Cambridge, Mass.

IMPORTANT NOTICE TO CONTRIBUTORS

Manuscripts intended for publication should be addressed to Professor F. M. Carpenter, Biological Laboratories, Harvard University, Cambridge, Mass.

Authors contributing articles over 4 printed pages in length may be required to bear a part of the extra expense, for additional pages. This expense will be that of typesetting only, which is about $10.00 per page. The actual cost of preparing cuts for all illustrations must be borne by contributors: the cost for full page plates from line drawings is ordinarily $12.00 each, and the full page half-tones, $18.00 each; smaller sizes in proportion.

AUTHOR'S SEPARATES

Reprints of articles may be secured by authors, if they are ordered at the time proofs are received for corrections. A statement of their cost will be furnished by the Editor on application.

The March, 1966 Psyche (Vol. 3, no. 1) was mailed August 31, 1966.

PSYCHE

Vol. 73   June, 1966   No. 2

PROTELYTROPTERA FROM THE UPPER PERMIAN OF
AUSTRALIA, WITH A DISCUSSION OF THE PROTO-
COLEOPTERA AND PARACOLEOPTERA[1]

By JARMILA KUKALOVÁ
Charles University, Prague

In the Tillyard collection of Upper Permian insects from Belmont,
New South Wales (now in the British Museum of Natural History
in London), there is a remarkable series of extinct elytrophorous insects of the order Protelytroptera. The specimens belong to four
families, all endemic to Australia so far as known. Some of the
genera, however, have formerly been referred to the "orders" Protocoleoptera and Paracoleoptera, which were supposed to represent the
ancestors of true Coleoptera.

The order Protelytroptera, one of the most diversified groups of
hemimetabolous insects of extensive geographical distribution, has
been found so far in Permian strata of North America, Czechoslovakia, U.R.S.S. and Australia. Because of the striking similarity of
their fore wings to those of beetles, the remarkable Australian fossils,
Protocoleus and *Permophilus,* were described by Tillyard (1924) as
primitive coleopteroids, *Protocoleus* being placed in a new order,
Protocoleoptera, and *Permophilus* in the Coleoptera. Their phylogenetic position has been repeatedly discussed in the literature.
Although the protelytropterous character of *Protocoleus* was pointed
out later by Tillyard (1931) and Carpenter (1933), the systematic
position of *Permophilus* has remained uncertain and in 1953 it was
assigned by Laurentiaux to another new order, Paracoleoptera. Numerous and well preserved specimens in the Tillyard collection in
the British Museum have enabled me to recognize the orders Proto-

[1]Much of this research was done while the author was at the Biological
Laboratories, Harvard University, 1964, under a National Science Foundation Grant (NSF GB-2038) to Professor Carpenter, to whom I am grateful
for help in the preparation of this paper. I am much indebted to Dr. E. I.
White and Mr. R. Baker of the British Museum (Natural History) for the
opportunity of studying these Australian insects. A grant-in-aid of research
from the Society of the Sigma Xi has covered part of the cost of publication.

coleoptera and Paracoleoptera as synonyms of the Protelytroptera
and to describe additional members of Australian Protelytroptera.[2]

ORDER PROTELYTROPTERA TILLYARD

Family Protocoleidae Tillyard, 1924

Protocoleidae Tillyard, 1924, Proc. Linn. Soc. N.S.W. 49:(4):434. Lameere,
1932, Soc. ent. Br., Liv. Cent.: 596; Forbes, 1928, Psyche, 35:33; Tillyard,
1931, Amer. Journ. Sci. 21:234; Peyerimhoff, 1934, Bull. Soc. ent. Fr. 39:39;
Richter, 1936, Rev. d'ent. URSS, 26:31; Lameere, 1938, Bull. Ann. Soc.
ent. Belg. 78:355; Jeannel, 1949, Traité de Zool. 9:63; Laurentiaux, 1953,
Traité de Paleont. 3:475; Carpenter, 1954, Classification of Insects, p. 789;
Rohdendorf, 1962, Osnovy paleont., p. 268.

Diagnosis: The following diagnosis of the family is based on the
description and photograph of *Protocoleus mitchelli* Tillyard, as well
as on a study of the topotypical material of Protocoleidae in the
British Museum.

Fore wings: large, tegminous, little sclerotized, only slightly convex; sutural margin bordering the whole posterior margin; wing
surface covered with dense granulation and larger flat tubercles, apparently on both dorsal and ventral surfaces; a cluster of setae present
in the subcostal area; costal expansion large, projecting, rounded;
anterior margin strongly convex; venation richly branched, especially
the radius; Sc long, dividing into several parallel branches; R sending off a series of branches anteriorly; Rs short or missing; M and
CuA variable in form; CuP slightly concave or flat, often branched;
anal veins directed anteriorly, 3-5 in number; cross veins numerous,
regular or irregular, sometimes connected by anastomoses.

Relationship. In 1924 Tillyard described a remarkable fossil fore
wing as *Protocoleus mitchelli* and referred it to his new order Protocoleoptera. In his opinion this order was intermediate between the
Carboniferous Protoblattoidea and the Coleoptera. Subsequently,
much discussion has centered on the phylogenetic and systematic position of *Protocoleus*. Many authors (e.g., Lameere, 1926, Forbes,
1928, Peyerimhoff, 1933, Carpenter, 1933, Richter, 1935, Jeannel,
1949) doubted the relationship of *Protocoleus* to the true Coleoptera.
Tillyard himself in 1931 (p. 264) stated that the Protocoleidae could
not have been the real ancestors of the Coleoptera but were more
probably an archaic remnant of the older Protelytroptera. Laurentiaux (1953, p. 475) put this genus in the distinct order Protocoleoptera but agreed with its proximity to Dermaptera and

---

[2]For a general account of the Protelytroptera, see Carpenter and Kukalová,
1964, and Kukalová, 1965.

Protelytroptera. Carpenter (1954, p. 798) referred the family to the Protelytroptera, which he considered to be a highly specialized order, resembling the Coleoptera but actually related to the Blattodea. Rohdendorf (1962) referred the family to the Coleopteroidea, incertae sedis.

In the Tillyard collection at the British Museum there are 7 complete fore wings of the family Protocoleidae well preserved enough to confirm the correctness of Carpenter's conclusion (1954). The specimens show the prominent, typical costal expansion (not preserved in the holotype of *P. mitchelli*), a well developed sutural margin, a distinct patch of setae and, in spite of the unusual richness of branches, a protelytropterous pattern of venation.

The family Protocoleidae includes the largest forms among Protelytroptera and is well removed from all other families, excepting the Permophilidae, which also have the wing surface covered with both granulation and tubercles, a similar outline of the wing and a broad subcostal area.

Two other species of elytrophorous insects were described by Tillyard from the Permian of New South Wales: *Permofulgor belmontensis* Tillyard (1917) and *Permofulgor indistinctus* Tillyard (1922). The family Permofulgoridae was established for the genus *Permofulgor* by Tillyard in 1917 and was placed in the order Hemiptera. Subsequently (1926, p. 186), Tillyard became convinced that these fossils were related to *Protocoleus* and assigned them to the Protocoleoptera. They are presumably protelytropterous, also, but because of poor preservation and the fragmentary nature of these fossils, generic and family diagnoses cannot be made.

Since the venation of the Protocoleidae is both complicated and indistinct, drawings are unusually difficult to make. Fortunately, venational details are very variable and of little use at the specific level.

Geological occurrence of the family: Upper Permian of Australia (N.S.W.)

Genera included: *Protocoleus* Tillyard, 1924; *Phyllelytron*, new genus; *Austrelytron*, new genus.

Genus *Protocoleus* Tillyard

Protocoleus Tillyard, 1924, Proc. Linn. Soc., N.S.W. 49(4):434; Tillyard, 1931, Amer. Journ. Sci. 21:234.

Diagnosis. Fore wing: tegminous, darkly pigmented; wing surface covered by flat, regularly arranged tubercles (not occurring on veins) and by fine granulation; costal expansion unknown; wings relatively broad and short, apical part prolonged and narrow; anterior margin strongly convex, posterior margin slightly concave apically; branches of main veins nearly parallel, distinct; Sc sending off several parallel branches, almost reaching apex; R sending off a series of long branches towards Sc; Rs hardly distinguishable from the other branches of R; M and CuA with a variable number of irregular branches; CuP long, branched, slightly concave; anal veins about 5 in number, some directed anteriorly; cross veins numerous, regular.

Relationship. *Protocoleus* Tillyard, 1924, differs from the related new genus *Phyllelytron* in the more distinct venation, in the more regularly and parallel-arranged veins and cross veins, and in the regularly arranged tubercles, distinct on the whole wing surface. From *Austrelytron*, n. gen., it differs in the more richly branched main veins, the presence of many cross veins and absence of regular series of pointed tubercles on the veins.

Stratigraphic occurrence: Upper Permian of Australia (N.S.W.).

Type-species: *Protocoleus mitchelli* Tillyard, 1924

Protocoleus mitchelli Tillyard

Protocoleus mitchelli Tillyard, 1924, Proc. Linn. Soc., N.S.W. 49(4):432; pl. 46, fig. 3.

Fore wing: about 27-29 mm. long and 7-9.3 mm. broad, sutural margin broader in the proximal half, narrowing abruptly in the distal half; tubercles densely arranged, often bordering veins in regular rows; fore wing very narrow in the apical third; anterior margin very convex, in the distal third slightly concave; branches of R distinct, very oblique and regular; cross veins mostly straight.

Discussion. Since Tillyard had at his disposal only the reverse of *Protocoleus* for study, he considered the surface of the elytron to be covered by pits. Actually, the tubercles and interspaces between them are so much alike that the reverse and obverse sculpturing does not show much difference. The fine granulation, on the other hand, appears in the reverse half of the fossil as small, dense pits. The granulation, which is extraordinarily fine in *Protocoleus*, was not mentioned in Tillyard's original description. It is very probable that both tubercles and granulation were present on both dorsal and ventral surfaces of the tegmina.

Holotype: specimen (reverse), figured by Tillyard (1924) on plate 46, fig. 3; collected in Upper Permian beds of Belmont, N.S.W. (Not seen).

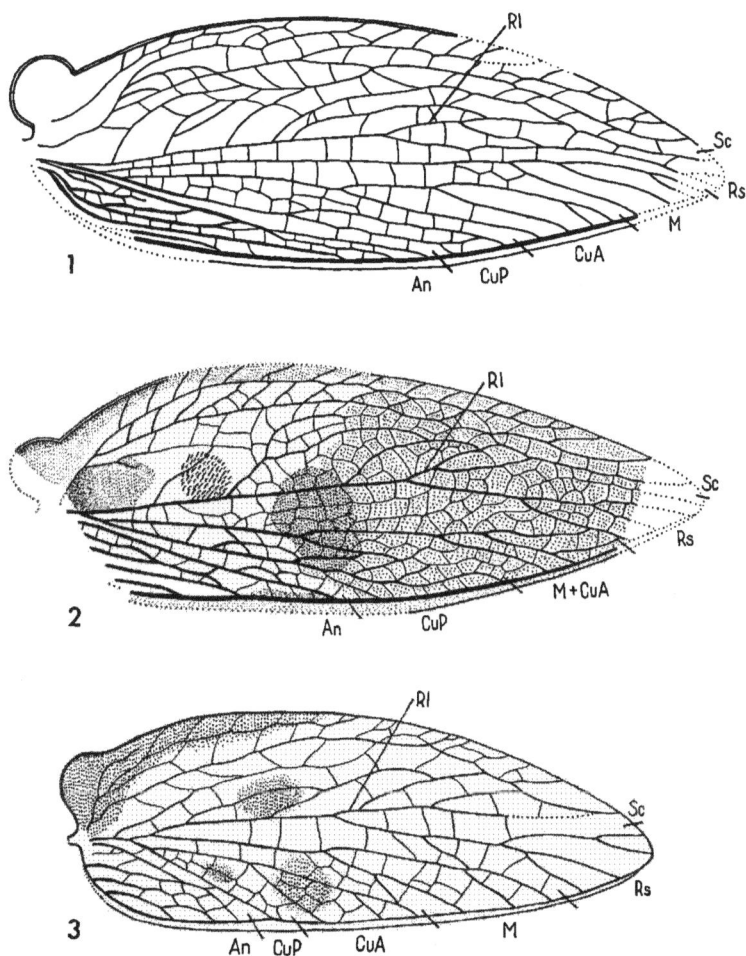

Text-figure 1. *Phyllelytron folium* n. sp. Drawing of holotype, No. In 45364, Brit. Mus.; fore wing, Upper Permian, Australia (original). Lettering: Sc, subcosta; R1, radius; Rs, radial sector; M, media; CuA, anterior cubitus; CuP, posterior cubitus; A1, first anal vein; An, anal area.
Text-figure 2. *Phyllelytron petalon* n. sp. Drawing of holotype, No. In 45703, Brit. Mus.; fore wing, Upper Permian, Australia (original).
Text-figure 3. *Phyllelytron granulatum* n. sp. Drawing of holotype, No. In 38115, Brit. Mus.; fore wing, Upper Permian, Australia (original).

Genus **Phyllelytron**, new genus

Fore wing: tegminous, darkly pigmented; sutural margin narrow; tubercles distinct in the anal area or in the whole posterior part of the wing, flat; granulation dense, distinct on the whole wing surface; costal expansion of circular shape, strongly projecting; apex directed posteriorly, pointed, apical part only little prolonged; anterior margin convex; veins not running parallel, branches of R, M and CuA usually indistinct; Sc sending off 2 or more long parallel branches, with numerous veinlets; R sending off anteriorly a series of irregular, slightly oblique, weak branches; M and CuA of various forms, branched; CuP long, slightly concave, usually branched; anal veins broad, 4-5 in number, some of them directed anteriorly; cross veins numerous, irregular.

Relationship. *Phyllelytron,* n. gen., differs from *Protocoleus* Tillyard in the less prolonged apex, more irregular branches of veins (mainly R), less distinct veins, less numerous tubercles restricted mainly to the posterior half of the wing, not regularly arranged; granulation more coarse and cross veins more irregular. *Phyllelytron,* n. gen., differs from *Austrelytron,* n. gen., in the more richly branched veins and more numerous cross veins, smaller number of anal veins and flat tubercles, which are absent on the veins.

Stratigraphic occurrence: Upper Permian of Australia (N.S.W.)

Type-species: *Phyllelytron folium* n. sp.

Phyllelytron folium, n. sp.
Text-figure 1

Fore wing: 21-24 mm. long, 6.2-7.8 mm. broad; sutural margin relatively narrow; tubercles distinct in the anal area, in the other parts of the wing almost missing; granulation fine, costal expansion markedly projecting, circular; anterior margin strengthened; posterior margin slightly concave, with small concavity in the anal part; branches of R indistinct, irregular, connected with few cross veins;

Relationship. *Phyllelytron folium,* n. sp., differs from *P. petalon,* n. sp., in the more regular, less numerous cross veins, in the absence of dark color spots in the proximal half of the wing and in the equally dark-pigmented veins. In comparison with *P. granulatum,* n. sp., it has a more projecting costal expansion, smaller and less coarse granulations, more distinct tubercles and no dark spots. From *P. melinum,* n. sp., it differs in its shorter, broader and probably thinner tegmen, narrower sutural margin and more projecting costal expansion.

Holotype: No. In 45364 (reverse). Specimens No. In 45529 and In 45504 are apparently the same species. British Museum (N.H.), London. Collected in Upper Permian, Belmont, Australia (N.S.W.).

Phyllelytron petalon, n. sp.
Text-figure 2

Fore wing: 19 mm. long, 6.5 broad; sutural margin considerably narrow; tubercles well developed on the whole posterior half of the wing; granulation medium coarse; costal expansion projecting, circular; branches of R slightly oblique, irregular, connected with many cross veins; cross veins numerous, very irregular; veins and cross veins not pigmented, interspaces between them darkly pigmented before all in the distal half of the wing; darker spot before the middle of the wing, along the basal part of the anterior margin and round the base.

Relationship. *Phyllelytron petalon*, n. sp., is related to *P. granulatum*, n. sp., by darkly colored tegmina with unpigmented veins. It differs from this species in its finer granulation, distinct tubercles and relatively large, different pattern of colored spots and irregular cross veins.

Holotype: No. In 45703 (obverse). Specimens No. In 45528 and 45734 are probably this species. British Museum (N.H.), London. Collected in Upper Permian, Belmont, N.S.W.

Phyllelytron granulatum, n. sp.
Text-figure 3

Fore wing: 15.2 mm. long and 5.3 mm. broad; sutural margin narrow; tubercles indistinct; granulation coarse; costal expansion projecting; anterior margin strengthened, pigmented in the proximal half; branches of R indistinct, irregular, connected with cross veins; cross veins not very numerous, irregular; veins not pigmented, three dark colored spots in the proximal half of the wing.

Relationship: *Phyllelytron granulatum*, n. sp., differs from all species of the same genus in smallest dimensions, coarsest granulation and indistinct tubercles.

Holotype: No. In 38113 (reverse). Specimens No. In 45513 and In 45519 are the same species. British Museum (N.H.), London. Collected in Upper Permian, Belmont, N.S.W.

Phyllelytron melinum, n. sp.
Text-figure 4

Fore wing: about 28 mm. long, 6.8 mm. broad, uniformly dark-colored; sutural margin broad; tubercles well developed only in the

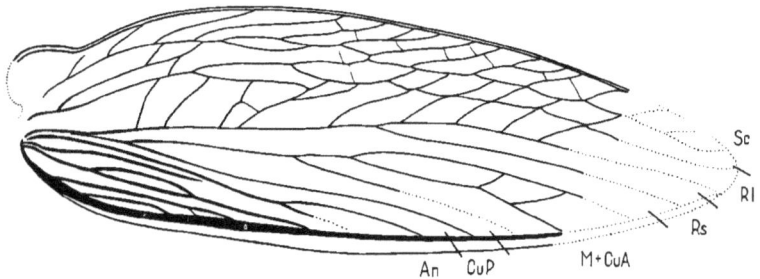

Text-figure 4. *Phyllelytron melinum* n. sp. Drawing of holotyye, No. In 45510, Brit. Mus.; fore wing, Upper Permian, Australia (original).

anal area; granulation fine; costal expansion not very projecting; branches of R indistinct, irregular, connected with few cross veins; R1, M and CuA very indistinct; cross veins faintly visible, few, mostly regular.

Relationship. *Phyllelytron melinum,* n. sp., differs from all species of the genus in largest, relatively narrowest and apparently thickest tegmina with broadest sutural margin and very indistinct R1, M and CuA.

Holotype: No. In 45510 (obverse). British Museum (N.H.), London. Collected in Upper Permian, Belmont, N.S.W.

Genus **Austrelytron**, new genus

Fore wing: tegminous, relatively small; sutural margin narrow; wing surface covered by dense granulation and isolated, pointed tubercles, which also form rows on the veins; costal expansion not very projecting; wings broadest before the middle of the wing, narrowing quickly towards the apex; anterior margin convex, posterior margin slightly concave; main veins with few branches; Sc with two or more branches parallel to each other, terminating well before apex; R sending off several irregular branches towards Sc; Rs distinct, originating after the middle of the wing; CuP long, concave; about three unbranched anal veins; cross veins few, simple.

Text-figure 5. *Austrelytron tillyardi* n. sp. Drawing of holotype, No. In 45525, Brit. Mus.; fore wing, Upper Permian, Australia (original).

Text-figure 6. *Permophilus hirtus* n. sp. Drawing of holotype, No. In 46014, Brit. Mus.; fore wing, Upper Permian, (original).

Text-figure 7. *Permophilus capulus* n. sp. Drawing of holotype, No. In 45518, Brit. Mus.; fore wing, Upper Permian, Australia (original).

Text-figure 8. *Elytrathrix hirsuta* n. sp. Drawing of holotype, No. In 45503, Brit. Mus.; fore wing, Upper Permian, Australia (original).

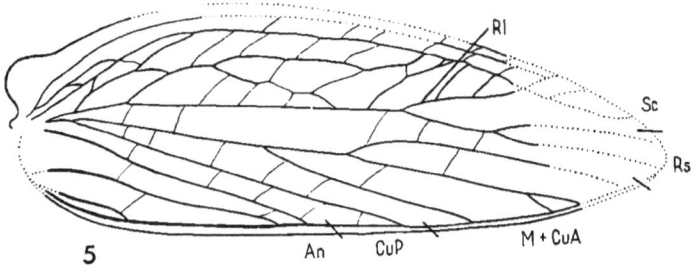

5

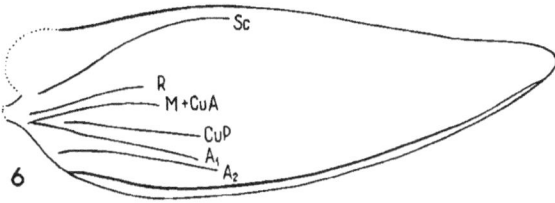

6

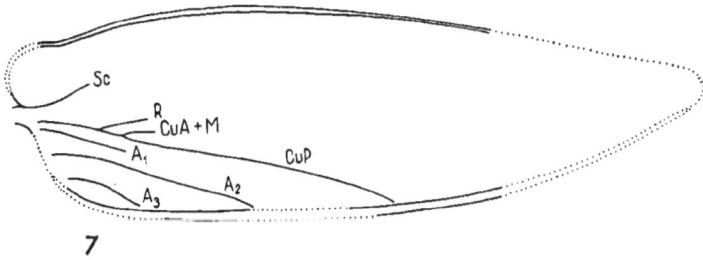

7

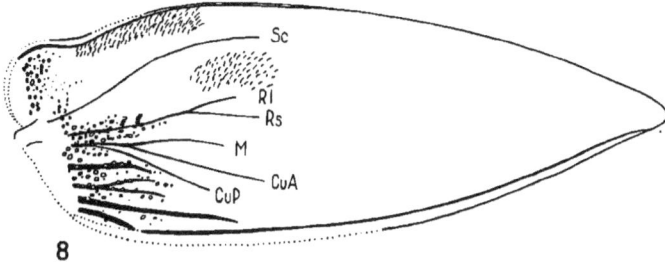

8

Relationship. *Austrelytron,* n. gen., differs from the genus *Proto-coleus* and *Phyllelytron,* n. gen., by having fewer branches on veins, less numerous cross veins and by the nature of the tubercles, which are not flat and numerous, but pointed and isolated, and also arranged in rows on the veins.

Stratigraphic occurrence: Upper Permian of Australia (N.S.W.).

Type-species: *Austrelytron tillyardi* n. sp.

Austrelytron tillyardi, n. sp.

Text-figure 5

Fore wing: 11 mm. long, 4 mm. broad; sutural margin narrow; tubercles pointed, forming regular rows on the veins; the areas between the veins covered by dense granulation and very isolated, irregularly distributed tubercles; costal expansion projecting only a little; branches of R very irregular, distinct, connected with few cross veins; all main veins distinct; R straight, R1 directed anteriorly towards costal margin well before apex; Rs well developed; M branched, fused for a long distance with the simple CuA; CuP long, straight, concave; anal veins simple, of irregular form.

Holotype: No. In 45525 (obverse). British Museum (N.H.), London. Collected in Upper Permian, Belmont, N.S.W.

Family Permophilidae Tillyard, 1924

Permophilidae Tillyard, 1924, Proc. Linn. Soc., N.S.W. 49:434 (Coleoptera) ; Laurentiaux, 1953, Traité de paléont. 3:475 (Paracoleoptera) ; Carpenter, 1954, Classification of Insects, p. 824 (Coleoptera).

Diagnosis. Fore wing: tegminous, only slightly convex; sutural margin well developed; wing surface covered on both dorsal and ventral surfaces by dense granulation and isolated, more or less distinct tubercles, sometimes more frequent in the basal part; setae present in a distinct patch; costal expansion projecting, circular; wings narrowed abruptly before the pointed apex; venation much reduced, restricted to the basal part of the wing, in the distal part completely missing.

Relationship. Tillyard (1924) established the new family Permophilidae, which he considered to be coleopteroid, ancestral to recent Hydrophilidae. According to his description, the type-species, *Permophilus pincombei* Tillyard, 1924, is large in size (21 mm.) with pointed apex, without definite longitudinal striae, but with traces of delicate, branching venation here and there, with the surface furnished in several places with very weakly formed, flattened tubercles.

In the Tillyard collection of the British Museum (N.H.) in London, I found 4 specimens, corresponding to this description. One of them (No. In 45518) is designated by the label, attached to the fossil and in Tillyard's hand-writing, as *"Permophilus?"*. For that reason, there is little doubt that the fossils belong to the family Permophilidae. They are clearly protelytropterous, showing the costal expansion (interpreted by Tillyard as an allula), distinct sutural margin, the setae in patches, and, in spite of its reduction, a protelytropterous pattern of the venation. Laurentiaux, it should be noted (1953, p. 475), referred the Permophilidae to a new order Paracoleoptera, which is not distinct from the Protelytroptera. The wing surface of Permophilidae (dense granulation and tubercles), as well as the form of the wings, resembles that in the family Protocoleidae. It is not impossible that they might have originated from a common ancestor.

Geographical occurrence of family: Upper Permian of Australia (N.S.W.).

Genera included: *Permophilus* Tillyard, 1924; *Elytrathrix*, new genus.

Genus *Permophilus* Tillyard

Permophilus Tillyard, 1924, Proc. Linn. Soc., N.S.W. 49:434; Jeannel, 1949, Traité de zool. 9:64; Laurentiaux, 1953, Traité de paléont. 3:476.

Fore wing: tegminous, slightly convex, darkly pigmented; sutural margin relatively narrow; wing surface covered by dense granulation and isolated, indistinct tubercles; costal expansion projecting; apical part narrowed and prolonged; main veins strongly developed in the basal third, but absent completely in the distal part of the wing.

Relationship. Not having at my disposal the type for study, I am not able to decide definitely the generic position of Specimens No. In 46014 and In 45518. According to the original diagnosis given by Tillyard, they differ from the holotype of *P. pincombei* only in the smaller size. For this reason, I refer them to the same genus, but they might also be considered as representing a separate genus. Specimen No. In 45517 (fragment) corresponds to about the size given for the type of *Permophilus,* but it is too poor for any conclusion. Specimen No. In 45503, which I refer to a new genus *Elytrathrix,* has very distinct, large tubercles concentrated at the basal part of the fore wing, which would presumably have been mentioned in Tillyard's description of *Permophilus pincombei* if they had been present.

Stratigraphic occurrence: Upper Permian of Australia (N.S.W.)

Type-species: *Permophilus pincombei* Tillyard, 1924

Permophilus hirtus, n. sp.
Text-figure 6

Fore wing: 6.8 mm. long and 2.2-2.4 mm. broad; granulation dense and small, covering the whole wing surface, tubercles very flat and sparse, indistinct; costal expansion unknown; apical part of wing narrow, prolonged, the apex placed in about the longitudinal axis of the wing; anterior margin convex, slightly concave before the apex, strengthened in the basal half; posterior margin slightly concave; Sc well developed, narrowing distally to the anterior margin, reaching almost the middle of the wing length; subcostal area very broad; R, M+CuA, A_1 and A_2 strong veins in the basal third, but completely reduced in the more distal part of the wing; CuP concave, indistinct.

Relationship. *Permophilus hirtus,* n. sp., differs from *Permophilus capulus,* n. sp., in its smaller dimensions, more abruptly narrowing wing distally, indistinct, shortened CuP and probably more sclerotized wings and veins. From *Permophilus pincombei* Tillyard it differs by its smaller dimensions.

Remarks. In the anal area of the holotype (No. In 46014, obverse) a small piece of the dorsal fore wing membrane is missing so that the sculpturing of the inner side of the ventral fore wing membrane is visible. It is covered by punctations, which correspond to the small granulation on the outer surface of the ventral membrane. This fortunate breaking away of the wing membrane shows that both sides of the tegmina of Permophilidae were covered by projecting sculpturing, even the ventral surface. The only punctate sculpturing on the wing surface is the small trace at insertion of setae, arranged in patches, as is to be expected in the case of good preservation in the subcostal area and along the anterior margin in the basal part of the wing.

Holotype: No. In 46014 (obverse), British Museum (N.H.), London. Specimen No. In 45805 is the same species. Collected in Upper Permian, Belmont, N.S.W.

Permophilus capulus, n. sp.
Text-figure 7

Fore wing: about 15 mm. long and 3.9 mm. broad, little sclerotized; granulation small, dense on the whole wing surface, tubercles flat and indistinct; costal expansion unknown; anterior margin slightly convex, strengthened only in the basal part; Sc, R, M+CuA and A1 strong, ending in the basal third; CuP concave, distinct, running its whole course; A2 and A3 also complete.

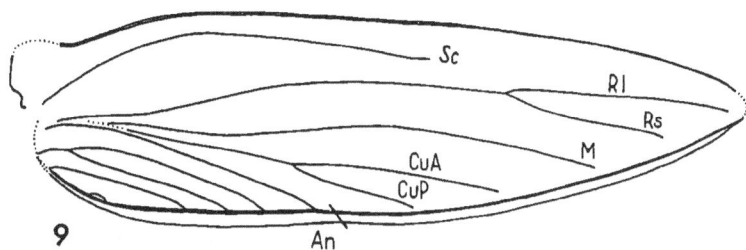

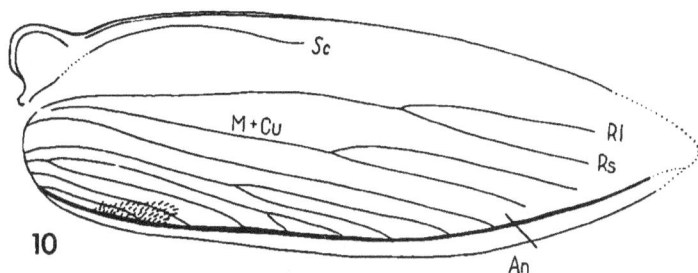

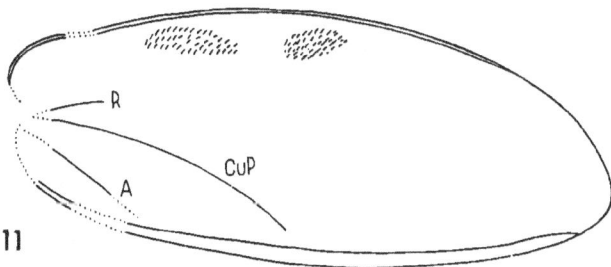

Text-figure 9. *Stenelytron enervatum* n. sp. Drawing of holotype, No. In 45958 (obverse) and In 45515 (reverse), Brit. Mus.; fore wing, Upper Permian, Australia (original).
Text-figure 10. *Xenelytron ligula* n. sp. Drawing of holotype, No. In 45526, Brit. Mus.; fore wing, Upper Permian, Australia (original).
Text-figure 11. *Dermelytron conservativum* n. sp. Drawing of holotype, No. In 45725, Brit. Mus.; fore wing, Upper Permian, Australia (original).

Relationship. *Permophilus capulus,* n. sp., differs from *Permophilus hirtus,* n. sp., in its larger, less sclerotized, relatively longer and narrower tegmina, with well developed CuP. From *Permophilus pincombei* Tillyard it differs in its smaller dimensions.

Holotype: No. In 45518 (obverse), British Museum (N. H.), London. Collected in Upper Permian, Belmont, N.S.W.

Genus **Elytrathrix**, new genus

Fore wing: tegminous, darkly pigmented; sutural margin narrow; wing surface covered by dense granulation and sparse tubercles, which become very conspicuous in the basal part; setae bordering the yard in the presence of conspicuous, large tubercles, developed in the costal area; costal expansion projecting, covered by large tubercles; main veins strong in the basal third, but completely lacking in the more distal part of the wing.

Relationship. *Elytrathrix,* n. gen., differs from *Permophilus* Tillyard in the presence of conspicuous, large tubercles, developed in the basal third of the wing and on the costal expansion.

Stratigraphic occurrence: Upper Permian of Australia (N.S.W.).

Type-species: *Elytrathrix hirsuta* n. sp.

Elytrathrix hirsuta, n. sp.
Text-figure 8

Fore wing: about 15 mm. long and 5 mm. broad; granulation dense, coarse; tubercles at the base numerous, large, pointed, irregularly covering the veins, the areas between veins, and costal expansion; setae distinct, strong, especially near the anterior margin; costal expansion projecting, circular; apex in the longitudinal axis of the wing; anterior margin strengthened in the basal third, not concave before apex; posterior margin very strong; veins reduced but very strong, especially in the anal area; 4 anal veins.

Holotype: No. In 45503 (obverse), British Museum (N.H.), London. Collected in Upper Permian, Belmont, N.S.W.

Stenelytridae, new family

Diagnosis. Fore wing: tegminous, almost flat, darkly pigmented; sutural margin bordering the whole posterior margin; wing surface covered with dense, fine granulation; setae forming a patch in the subcostal area and perhaps also along the proximal part of the posterior margin; costal expansion large, projecting; apical part narrowed and prolonged; anterior margin strengthened; venation of normal protelytropterous pattern; Rs originating late; subcostal area unusually broad.

Relationship. The family Stenelytridae is closer, on the basis of

Photograph of holotype of *Stenelytron enervatum*, n. sp. Length of elytron, 14 mm. Original.

its venation, to the European and American Protelytroptera (especially to the family Protelytridae) than to other Australian groups.
Nevertheless, in spite of the differences in venation of Protocoleidae,
Permophilidae and Stenelytridae, there are some remarkable features
in common, the complex of which differentiates the Australian forms
from those of the Northern Hemisphere: flat tegmina of large size,
covered by fine granulation, the very prominent and circular costal
expansion, and the very broad subcostal area.

Geological occurrence of family: Upper Permian of Australia
(N.S.W.)

Genera included: *Stenelytron*, new genus; *Xenelytron*, new genus.

Genus **Stenelytron**, new genus

Fore wing: tegminous, sutural margin long, not broad; costal
expansion sub-circular, straight on the proximal side; setae forming
a patch in the subcostal area; apex directed anteriorly; anterior margin more or less convex; posterior margin slightly concave before the
end of the anal area; Sc distinct, shortened, not reaching the anterior
margin, approaching it in the basal third; subcostal area broad; R
usually slightly convex, directed towards apex; Rs originating beyond
middle of wing, usually simple and weak; M of variable form, mostly
simple; Cu usually divided into short CuA and slightly concave
CuP; anal veins broad, strong, 3-5 in number, simple or forked.

Relationship. *Stenelytron*, n. gen., differs from *Xenelytron*, n. gen.,
in the narrower sutural margin, free M (not in close proximity to
CuP) and in the much smaller anal area, not reaching far beyond
the middle of the wing.

Stratigraphical occurrence: Upper Permian of Australia
(N.S.W.)

Type-species: *Stenelytron enervatum*, n. sp.

Stenelytron enervatum, n. sp.
Text-figure 9; plate 8

Fore wing: about 14 mm. long and 3.5-4.4 mm. broad; sutural
margin narrow; setae in the patch in the very proximal part of the
subcostal area; apex directed slightly anteriorly; Sc relatively long,
terminating beyond middle of wing; subcostal area broad; M free;
the stem of Cu concave near the base; CuA separating from CuP
late; anal area not large, with 3-4 mostly simple, strong veins.

Holotype: No. In 45958 (reverse), In 45515 (obverse). Specimens No. In 45523, In 45508, In 45930, In 45704, In 45520, In

45505, In 45516, In 45512, are also this species. British Museum (N.H.), London. Collected in Upper Permian, Belmont, N.S.W.

Genus Xenelytron, new genus

Fore wing: tegminous, almost flat; sutural margin broad; costal expansion large, subcircular, straight on the proximal side; apex on about the axis of wing; anterior margin little convex; R1 directed towards apex; Rs originating late, weak; M usually in close proximity to Cu, simple or forked; Cu long, terminating far behind the middle of the wing; anal veins broad, strong, 3-5 in number, simple or forked.

Relationship. *Xenelytron*, n. gen., differs from *Stenelytron*, n. gen., in its broader sutural margin, the close proximity of M to CuP, and in the large anal area, terminating far beyond the middle of the wing.

Stratigraphic occurrence: Upper Permian of N.S.W., Australia.

Type-species: *Xenelytron ligula* n. sp.

Xenelytron ligula, n. sp.
Text-figure 10

Fore wing: 10.1-11.5 mm. long and 3-3.8 mm. broad; sutural margin broad excepting the proximal part; anterior margin strengthened; M in close proximity to CuP, detaching from it at about the middle of the wing.

Holotype: No. In 45526 (obverse). Specimen No. In 38113 is perhaps the same species. British Museum (N.H.), London. Collected in Upper Permian, Belmont, N.S.W.

Dermelytridae, new family

Diagnosis. Fore wing: small, convex, but weakly sclerotized, with dark pigmentation; sutural margin well developed; wing surface rugose; setae forming patches; costal expansion projecting only a little; veins much reduced, missing or partially indicated at the base.

Relationship. Among the Protelytroptera there are three families, the venation of which is very reduced: Blattelytridae Tillyard, Permophilidae Tillyard and Dermelytridae, n. fam. I am convinced that they represent three separate lines of evolution, with no closer phylogenetic relationships. As pointed out already by Carpenter (1938) in the Blattelytridae the fore wings are very convex and sclerotized, the whole venational pattern is obsolescent, but completely represented and much similar to that of Protelytridae. In the Permophilidae, the fore wings are tegminous and their shape, sculpturing, as well as the remnants of the veins, recall the Protocoleidae. In Dermelytridae, n. fam., the venation is the most reduced in the Protelytroptera, so far known. The veins are only weakly indicated at most, never showing the whole venational pattern. The fore wings are elytra-like in shape and convexity, but with very little sclerotization. The origin of Dermelytridae, n. fam., remains uncertain so far because of its great specialization.

Probably belonging to the Dermelytridae is the specimen designated (without figure) by Tillyard (1924) as *Permophilus* (?) *minor*.

Genera included: *Dermelytron*, new genus; *Psychelytron*, new genus; *Chanoselytron*, new genus.

Genus Dermelytron, new genus

Fore wing: more or less oval, convex but very little sclerotized; sutural margin broad; costal expansion projecting only very little; setae making patches in the subcostal area; apex directed posteriorly; anterior margin strengthened, convex, very slightly concave beyond the costal expansion; posterior margin slightly concave; CuP and one of the anal veins sometimes weakly indicated.

Relationship. *Dermelytron*, n. gen., differs from *Chanoselytron*, n. gen., by the smaller costal expansion and oval shape of the fore wings. From *Psychelytron*, n. gen., it differs in posteriorly directed apex.

Stratigraphic occurrence: Upper Permian of Australia.

Type-species: *Dermelytron conservativum*, n. sp.

Dermelytron conservativum, n. sp.
Text-figure 11

Fore wing: 5.5-7.2 long and 2.5-3.1 mm. broad, uniformly darkly colored; setae making two small patches in the subcostal area; apex rounded.

Relationship. *Dermelytron conservativum*, n. sp., differs from *Dermelytron pigmentatum*, n. sp., in the uniformly dark pigmentation of the fore wing, without darker spots, and in the rounded apex.

Holotype: No. In 45725 (reverse). Specimens No. In 45514, In 45768, In 45522, In 32758 are also the same species. British Museum (N.H.), London. Collected in Upper Permian, Belmont, N.S.W.

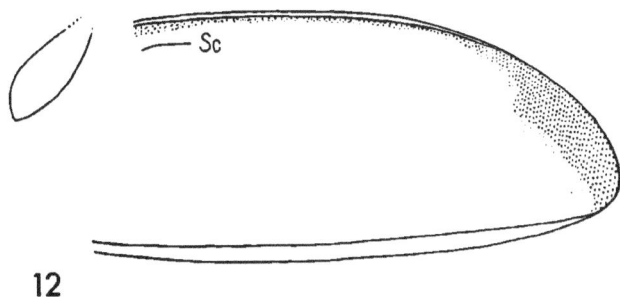

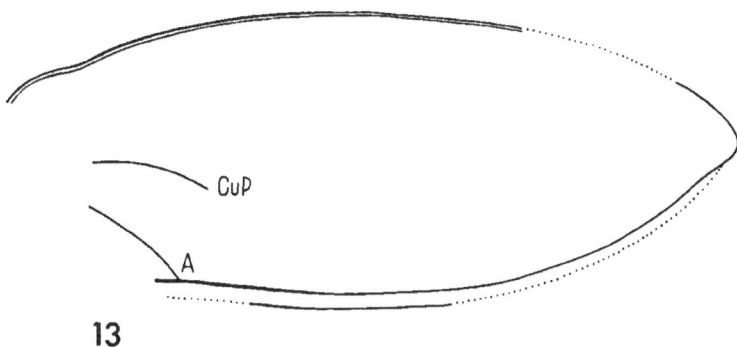

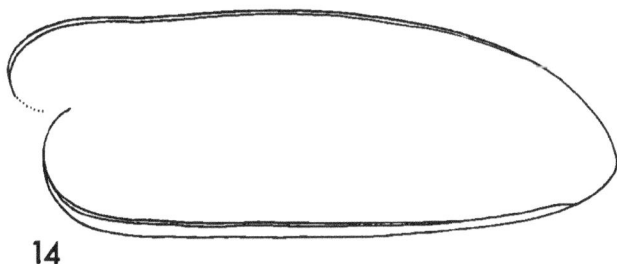

Text-figure 12. *Dermelytron pigmentatum* n. sp. Drawing of holotype, No. In 45474, Brit. Mus.; fore wing, Upper Permian, Australia (original).
Text-figure 13. *Psychelytron progressivum* n. sp. Drawing of holotype, No. In 45900, Brit, Mus.; fore wing, Upper Permian, Australia (original).
Text-figure 14. *Chanoselytron gingiva* n. sp. Drawing of holotype, No. In 45493, Brit. Mus.; fore wing, Upper Permian, Australia (original).

Dermelytron pigmentatum, n. sp.

Text-figure 12

Fore wing: about 6.3 mm. long and 2.4 mm. broad, with a darker spot in the apical part, and along the anterior margin; apex pointed.

Relationship. *Dermelytron pigmentatum*, n. sp., differs from *D. conservativum*, n. sp., in the presence of the darker spot, less oval shape and pointed apex.

Holotype: No. In 45474 (obverse), British Museum (N.H.) London. Collected in Upper Permian, Belmont, N.S.W.

Genus **Psychelytron**, new genus

Fore wing: convex, but thin, very weakly sclerotized; sutural margin narrow; costal expansion unknown; apex directed anteriorly; anterior margin strengthened, convex; posterior margin concave.

Relationship. *Psychelytron*, n. gen., differs from *Dermelytron*, n. gen., and *Chanoselytron*, n. gen., by the presence of the anteriorly directed apex.

Stratigraphic occurrence: Upper Permian of Australia (N.S.W.).

Type-species: *Psychelytron progressivum*, n. sp.

Psychelytron progressivum, n. sp.

Text-figure 13

Fore wing: about 8 mm. long and 2.8 mm. broad, uniformly dark-colored; apex pointed, placed about in the longitudinal axis of the wing; posterior margin slightly concave in the anal area.

Holotype: No. In 45900 (obverse). British Museum (N.H.), London. Collected in Upper Permian, Belmont, N.S.W.

Genus **Chanoselytron**, new genus

Fore wing: only slightly convex, thin, relatively narrow; sutural margin narrow; costal expansion relatively large, rounded, extending beyond the wing proximally; anterior and posterior margins almost parallel; apex directed distally.

Relationship. *Chanoselytron*, n. gen., differs from *Dermelytron*, n. gen., in the larger costal expansion and relatively narrow wing with anterior and posterior margins almost parallel. From *Psychelytron*, n. gen., it differs by the posteriorly directed apex.

Stratigraphic occurrence: Upper Permian of Australia (N.S.W.).

Type-species: *Chanoselytron gingiva*, n. sp.

Chanoselytron gingiva, n. sp.

Text-figure 14

Fore wing: 7.5 mm. long and 2.9 mm. broad; costal expansion separated by a very slight concavity from the rest of the anterior margin; apex rounded.

Holotype: No. In 45493 (reverse). British Museum (N.H.), London. Collected in Upper Permian, Belmont, N.S.W.

DISCUSSION

Because of the remarkable convergence with the Coleoptera, the Protelytroptera have been often regarded as true beetles or their ancestors. As to the marked morphological convergence of the fore wings, the number of diagnostic features is, above all in view of some archaic beetles, restricted. For the Protelytroptera, the patches of setae are very characteristic, but their presence in specimens depends on the nature of the preservation. A more reliable morphological feature is the vein Sc, which is usually weak and more or less shortened, never reaching apex, and never running along close to and parallel to the anterior margin, as it is in the case of some primitive beetles. A further distinctive feature is the course of CuA, which is mostly oblique in Protelytroptera, of "orthopteroid" type, but which in many Paleozoic Coleoptera is more or less parallel with the posterior margin. The costal expansion and sutural margin in their usual form and in combination with the typical form of Sc and CuA are very characteristic for Protelytroptera. Nevertheless, the individual features are often not developed typically, or are completely missing, or may be similar to those of beetles. The surface of the fore wings is very variable, including a reticulation (Protelytridae), granulation (Stenelytridae), cross veins (Archelytridae), tubercles (Protocoleidae), rugosity (Dermelytridae), dense hairs (Megelytridae), etc., much as in the beetles.

A comparison of the Australian endemic families of Protelytroptera with those of the Northern Hemisphere is very interesting. There is no doubt that all Protelytroptera have been derived from a common ancestor. The Protocoleidae and Permophilidae are likely to show some closer phylogenetic relationship to each other, in spite of the differences in venation; they are well removed from all the Northern forms so far known. The Stenelytridae of the Australian series suggest mostly the typical Northern family, Protelytridae, by its venation, but not by form of elytra, degree of sclerotization and sculpturing.

The Australian Protocoleidae, Permophilidae and Stenelytridae have some characteristic features in common — large or very large, little sclerotized, flat tegmina of blattoid type with original archedictyon reduced to dense granulation (eventually with tubercles added), a rounded and very projecting costal expansion, and an extremely broad subcostal area. It is very hard to say at present whether these morphological features are due to phylogenetic relationship, or due to functional adaptation to similar environmental conditions. The difficult problem is the position of Dermelytridae, because of the specialized outline, and the practically complete reduction of venation. Still, even this very remote family has "Australian" features, as tegminous (though convex in this case only) fore wings and rugose wing surfaces, the Dermelytridae lack the typical, rounded, projecting costal expansion. Relationship with European and American Blattelytridae, which also possess the reduced venation, is not apparent.

It appears that the Australian Protelytroptera have been derived from very archaic protelytropterous ancestors with tegminous fore wings, rich in branches, during the Carboniferous. They radiated in different lines, with a general trend to strengthen their tegmina more by sculpturing (granulation, tubercles, rugosity) than by sclerotization.

REFERENCES

CARPENTER, F. M.
  1933. The Lower Permian Insects of Kansas. Part 6. Delopteridae, Protelytroptera, Plectoptera, and a new collection of Protodonata, Odonata, Megasecoptera, Homoptera and Psocoptera. Proc. Amer. Acad. Arts Sci. 68 (11) :411-503.
  1938. The Lower Permian Insects of Kansas. Part 8. Additional Megasecoptera, Protodonata, Odonata, Homoptera, Psocoptera, Protelytroptera, Plectoptera and Protoperlaria. Proc. Amer. Acad. Arts Sci. 73 (3) :29-70.
  1954. Keys to Extinct Families of Insects, in: Brues, C. T., Melander, A. L., Carpenter, F. M., Classification of Insects. Bull. Mus. Comp. Zool. 108 :777-826.
CARPENTER, F. M. AND J. KUKALOVÁ
  1964. The structure of the Protelytroptera, with description of a new genus from Permian strata of Moravia. Psyche 71 (4) :183-197.
FORBES, W. T. M.
  1928. The Protocoleoptera. Psyche, 35 :32-35.
JEANNEL, R.
  1949. Les insectes fossiles, in: Grassé, P., Traité de Zoologie, 9 :1-85.

KUKALOVÁ, J.
   1965. Permian Protelytroptera, Coleoptera and Protorthoptera (Insecta)
         of Moravia. Sborník geol. ved., paleont. 6:61-98.
LAMEERE, A.
   1932. Un peu de systematique. Soc. ent. Fr., Liv. de Cent. 593-596.
   1938. Evolution des Coléoptères. Bull. Ann. Soc. Ent. Belg. 78:355.
LAURENTIAUX, D.
   1953. Insects, in: Piveteau, J., Traité de Paléontologie 3:397-527.
RICHTER, A. A.
   1935. On the elytral venation of Coleoptera. Rev. d'ent. U.R.S.S.,
         26:25-58.
ROHDENDORF, B. B.
   1962. Osnovy paleontologii, Coleoptera: 241-268.
PEYERIMHOFF, P.
   1934. Les Coléoptères remontent-ils au Permien? Bull. Soc. ent. Fr.,
         39:37-44.
TILLYARD, R. J.
   1917. Permian and Triassic Insects from New South Wales, in the
         collection of Mr. John Mitchell. Proc. Linn. Soc. N.S.W. 42(4):
         720-756.
   1924. Upper Permian Coleoptera and a new order from the Belmont
         Beds, New South Wales. Proc. Linn. Soc. N.S.W. 49(4):429-435.
   1926. The Insects of Australia and New Zealand. (Angus and Robert-
         son, Sydney), pp. 1-560.
   1931. Kansas Permian Insects. Part 13. The New Order Protelytrop-
         tera, with a Discussion of its Relationships. Amer. Journ. Sci.
         21:232-266.

NEW SPECIES OF *MEXISPHODRUS* FROM MEXICAN CAVES (COLEOPTERA: CARABIDAE)[1]

By Thomas C. Barr, Jr.

Department of Zoology, University of Kentucky

The first true sphodrine known from North America was collected in a cave in Veracruz, Mexico, in 1964. I described it as *Mexisphodrus veraecrucis* (Barr, 1965), emphasizing the sharply truncate, triangular base of the prosternum, which appears to be the most reliable sphodrine character. Straneo (1957) had previously assigned another interesting anchomenine genus, *Bolivaridius* Straneo, to the true sphodrines because of a superficial resemblance to *Sphodropsis* Seidlitz, but *Bolivaridius* lacks the characteristic prosternal feature so clearly exhibited in *Mexisphodrus* and the Palearctic sphodrines, and in my opinion does not belong in this group.

Mr. James R. Reddell and the members of the Association for Mexican Cave Studies have recently sent me additional specimens referable to *Mexisphodrus*, rather obviously specifically distinct from *M. veraecrucis*. These insects were collected in deep pits in San Luis Potosi and Tamaulipas, respectively. I am indebted to Mr. Reddell and to Messrs. David McKenzie, John Fish, L. E. Gilbert, and Orion Knox for this unusual material. Holotypes of both species are deposited in the Museum of Comparative Zoology, Harvard University.

Mexisphodrus tlamayaensis Barr, new species

Distinguished from *M. veraecrucis* Barr by smaller size, larger eyes, presence of functional wings, and other features. Length 11.3 mm. Head and pronotum rufocastaneous, shining; elytra darker castaneous, slightly iridescent, shining, polished; elytral disc with microsculpture finely transverse. *Head* as wide as long, not including outstretched mandibles; greatest width across eyes; eye diameter a little more than length of scape, eyes pale, very convex; antenna 3/5 the total body length. *Pronotum* 7/8 as long as wide, width of apex and width of base subequal and about 3/4 the maximum width, which occurs at apical 1/3; anterior angles prominent; hind angles large and slightly obtuse, rather blunt; margin broadly re-

[1]This investigation was supported in part by a grant from the National Science Foundation (GB-2011).

Manuscript received by the editor April 7, 1966

flexed; sides rounded, shallowly sinuate in basal 1/5; basal fossae broad with gentle lateral slopes but with impressed line at bottom. *Elytra* 1 1/2 times as long as wide, elongate-oval; apices conspicuously sinuate, individually finely but distinctly truncate; striae regular and distinctly impressed, intervals subconvex; 3rd interval with 3 discal punctures, anterior against 3rd stria, middle and posterior against 2nd stria; functional metathoracic wings present. *Aedeagus* elongate, slender, 2.25 mm (about 1/5 the total body length) in holotype, very similar in form to that of *M. veraecrucis* but smaller; median lobe narrowly keeled ventrally and anterior to apex; parameres conchoid, right slightly smaller and apically more pointed than left; internal sac completely folded, bearing several dense patches of small scales.

Holotype male (a unique), Sótano de Tlamaya, near village of Tlamaya, municipality of Xilitla, San Luis Potosi, Mexico, 30 January 1966, John Fish leg.

This species is obviously less conspicuously "spelean" in appearance than *M. veraecrucis* or the species described below. The type cave, Sótano de Tlamaya, is the deepest known cave in the western hemisphere, with a total depth of 1354 feet. It is entered through pits at the south edge of the Tlamaya doline. Bell and Raines (1965) have recently described the cave and given an account of its exploration.

Mexisphodrus profundus Barr, new species

Similar to *M. veraecrucis* in the small eyes, elongate pronotum, uniform color, and vestigial metathoracic wings, but distinguished by the smaller size, smaller aedeagus, the rounded elytral apices, and the finely transverse microsculpture of the elytral disc. Length 12.1-12.9 mm. Reddish-ferrugineous, shining; elytra polished-shining, the microsculpture finely transverse, the meshwork slightly denser than in *M. tlamayaensis* and less noticeably iridescent. *Head* as wide as long, not including the outstretched mandibles; greatest width across the eyes; eye diameter about 2/3 length of scape; antenna 2/3 the total body length. *Pronotum* a little more than 9/10 as long as wide, width of apex and width of base subequal and about 4/5 the maximum width, which occurs at apical 1/3; anterior angles very prominent; hind angles large, sharp, very slightly more than right; margin broadly reflexed; sides feebly rounded, sinuate at basal 1/5, then subparallel to the hind angles; basal fossae broad and deep. *Elytra* 1.9 times as long as wide, elongate-elliptic; apices sinuate and individually narrowly rounded; striae moderately impressed and regular, intervals subconvex; intervals without discal punctures; metathoracic wings vestigial. *Aedeagus* about as in *M. tlamayaensis*, 2.12 mm in holotype.

Holotype male, Sótano de la Joya de Salas, 25 km west of Encino, elevation 1600 meters, Tamaulipas, Mexico, 3 June 1965, David McKenzie, John Fish, and Orion Knox leg. Three paratypes from the same cave, two on 3 June and one taken 23 January 1965 by D. McKenzie. A fourth paratype, "30 ft. down in sinkhole", Rancho del Cielo, 6 km NW Gomez Farias, Tamaulipas, 1 July 1965, L. E. Gilbert.

Like *M. veraecrucis*, this species seems to be an incipient troglobite, with an elongate body, very small eyes, and vestigial metathoracic wings. Mr. James R. Reddell provided the following information: "The three *Mexisphodrus* were found in the same vicinity of the first specimen — within a well-illuminated area of about 4 square yards on the floor of the entrance shaft. Decaying animal carcasses were near-by. This was also a very wet portion of the rocky floor area, which was 20 feet by 75 feet. All of the beetles had apparently burrowed to positions beneath shoe-sized rocks partially embedded in mud. When uncovered and disturbed they ran rather rapidly. The dry season may be limiting their activity in this locale; the area is well ventilated and subject to drying. But none were discovered in the moist lower portions of the cave where other troglobites were common."

TABLE 1

MEXISPHODRUS SPP., HOLOTYPES,
COMPARATIVE MEASUREMENTS (Millimeters)

	M. veraecrucis Barr	M. tlamayaensis n. sp.	M. profundus n. sp.
Total length	18.1	11.3	12.1
Head length	3.2	2.1	2.1
Head width	2.0	2.1	2.1
Antenna	10.6	6.8	8.0
Eye diameter	0.6	0.7	0.4
Pronotum length	3.4	2.1	2.3
Pronotum max. width	3.4	2.4	2.5
Pronotum apex width	2.4	1.8	2.0
Pronotum base width	2.8	1.8	1.9
Elytra length	10.0	6.1	7.0
Elytra width	5.5	4.0	3.7
Aedeagus	3.3	2.2	2.1

Comparative measurements of the holotypes of the three known species of *Mexisphodrus* are given in the accompanying table. The three species may be separated by the following key.

Key to Known Species of *Mexisphodrus*

1 Eyes small and flat, their diameter less than length of scape; pronotum elongate, the sides only feebly rounded; color uniformly rufotestaceous or ferrugineous; metathoracic wings vestigial 2

   Eyes large and convex, their diameter greater than length of scape; pronotum distinctly wider than long, sides conspicuously rounded; head and pronotum rufocastaneous, elytra darker, shining; metathoracic wings functional; San Luis Potosi .... *M. tlamayaensis* Barr, n. sp.

2 Size larger (16-18 mm); aedeagus larger (3.3 mm); apices of elytra individually acuminate, dehiscent; elytral disc dull shining, microsculpture rather coarsely isodiametric, granular; Veracruz .... *M. veraecrucis* Barr

   Size smaller (12-13 mm); aedeagus smaller (2.1 mm); apices of elytra individually rounded; elytral disc polished shining, microsculpture a transverse meshwork; Tamaulipas ....
   .... *M. profundus* Barr n. sp.

LITERATURE CITED

BARR, THOMAS C., JR.
  1965. A new cavernicolous sphodrine from Veracruz. Mexico (Coleoptera: Carabidae). Coleopt. Bull., 19(3): 65-72.
BELL, BILL, AND TERRY RAINES.
  1965. The exploration of Sótano de Tlamaya. Nat. Speleol. Soc. News, 23(5): 62-65.
STRANEO, S. L.
  1957. Due nuovi carabidi del Messico (Col. Carab.). Ciencia (Mex.), 17(4-6): 81-84.

STUDIES ON NEOTROPICAL POMPILIDAE
(HYMENOPTERA)
II. GENUS *ARIDESTUS* BANKS*

By HOWARD E. EVANS
Museum of Comparative Zoology

Banks (1947, Bull. Mus. Comp. Zool., 99: 432) based the genus *Aridestus* on a single female from Paraguay. This specimen was identified as "*bergi* Brèthes" although in fact *bergi* is a Holmberg species, described in 1881 from a single female from the province of Buenos Aires, Argentina. I have before me fifteen females and six males which I consider to be congeneric with *bergi*, and it seems appropriate to present a fuller description of the genus *Aridestus* on the basis of this additional material.

In his generic description, Banks emphasized the transverse striae on the propodeum. As a matter of fact these striae are absent in the male *bergi* and in both sexes of a Chilean species which is exceedingly similar to *bergi* in all other respects, including the male terminalia. I therefore find it desirable to define *Aridestus* somewhat differently than did Banks. I consider *Evagetes, Aridestus,* and the African genus *Asthenoctenidia* Pate (=*Asthenoctenus* Arnold) to form a closely knit generic complex characterized by the thickened and slightly flattened antennae, by the reduced pulvillar pad and comb, by having the clypeus no wider than the lower front, and by several other common features. *Evagetes* is known to be a cleptoparasite of other Pompilini, and it seems to me very likely that the other two genera behave similarly.

The known species of *Aridestus* are black with the abdomen mostly or entirely red, and they are especially similar to those species of *Evagetes* having the abdomen partly rufous and the pronotum subangulate behind (e.g. *crassicornis* Shuckard). The species of *Aridestus* differ in having the clypeus, front, and vertex narrow, the middle interocular distance not exceeding .58 times the transfacial distance in either sex, the clypeus not more than 2.5 times as wide as high in the female, 2.2 times as wide as high in the male. The pronotum is also short medially and in the female somewhat swollen anterolaterally, there is an unusually distinct median groove on the front, and the marginal cell is far removed from the wing-tip (at least

*Published with the aid of a grant from the Museum of Comparative Zoology.

Manuscript received by the editor May 15, 1966.

by 1.6 times its own length). From *Asthenoctenidia, Aridestus* differs in having a much shorter and more angulate pronotum as well as a complete postnotum which is at least nearly half the length of the metanotum. The male terminalia of the three genera show only minor differences.

As noted above, the citation of the type species of *Aridestus* should be corrected to read: *Pompilus bergi* Holmberg, 1881 (monobasic). The following is a redescription of the genus.

Small wasps, 5-12 mm in length; known species black with abdomen rufous except often fuscous at extreme base and apex (apical fourth sometimes fuscous in males); males usually with an interrupted pale yellow band along the posterior margin of the pronotum and always with the apical abdominal tergite in large part pale yellow or whitish. Mandibles with a single tooth on the inner margin; clypeus truncate, its width equal to or slightly less than the lower interocular distance; front narrow, middle interocular distance not exceeding .58 times transfacial distance; front with a median linear impression from the antennal bases to the anterior ocellus; vertex passing nearly straight across between tops of eyes. Antennae short and in the female slightly incrassate, the flagellar segments somewhat flattened on the outer surface; third antennal segment in the female 2.5-3.5 times as long as thick, .50-.65 times upper interocular distance; third antennal segment in male shorter than fourth segment, 1.4-1.9 times as long as thick; apical antennal segment of male obliquely truncate at tip. Pronotum along midline very much shorter than mesoscutum, in the female somewhat bulging anterolaterally; posterior margin broadly subangulate or subarcuate; post-

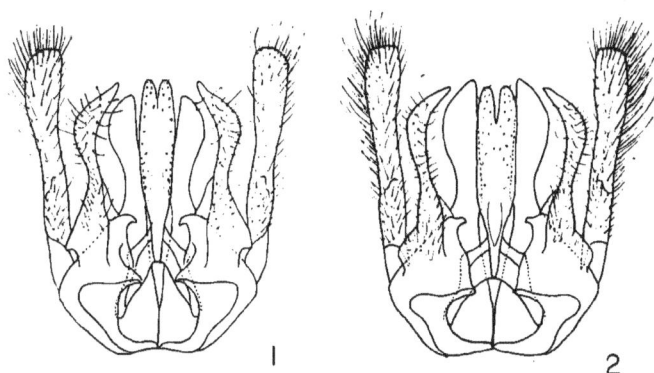

Figs. 1 and 2. Male genitalia of species of *Aridestus*, ventral aspect. Fig. 1. *A. bergi* (Holmberg). Fig. 2. *A. jaffueli* (Herbst).

notum a complete transverse band at least nearly half as long as the
metanotum; propodeum relatively short and strongly convex, with
the median line impressed basally, the posterior slope with or without
transverse rugae. Middle and hind tibiae with sparse but fairly
strong spines above; front tibiae not at all spined above; female with
a strong tarsal comb, the spines very long and slender, the apical
basitarsal spine longer than the second segment; apical tarsal segments at least weakly spined beneath in the females; claws slender,
dentate except inner claws of front tarsi of males strongly curved,
somewhat bifid, this tarsal segment weakly lobed on the inner margin;
pulvillar pad very small, giving rise to 2-6 minute setae. Wing
venation essentially as in *Evagetes* (see Evans, 1950, Trans. Amer.
Ent. Soc., 75: 162, Figs. 12, 13); marginal cell 1.6-2.1 times its
own length from the wing tip; second and third submarginal cells
small, both narrowed above. Male subgenital plate simple, its sides
tapering to a broadly rounded or subtruncate apex; male genitalia
with the basal hooklets single, the aedoeagus simple, bearing a few
minute apical setae; parameres fairly broad, strongly setose (Figs. 1,
2).

Key to species

Females

1. Propodeum without transverse rugae; inner orbits more strongly
    convergent at the top, upper interocular distance .84-.90 times
    lower interocular (Chile, Patagonia) .... 3. *jaffueli* (Herbst)
    Propodeum with fairly strong transverse rugae; upper inter-
    ocular distance .93-1.00 times lower interocular 2
2. Transverse rugae reaching the extreme side margins of the
    propodeum; pubescence of head and thorax wholly dark; scape,
    head, and front coxae with rather strong dark setae; length
    12 mm (Peru) .... 2. *porteri* n. sp.
    Transverse rugae stopping well short of side margins of pro-
    podeum; pubescence silvery at least on the clypeus, parts of
    the front, coxae, thoracic pleura, and propodeum, often ex-
    tensively silvery; front coxae without dark setae, scape with
    at most a few setae; length 5.7-9.0 mm (northern Argentina,
    Paraguay, southern Brazil) .... 1. *bergi* (Holmberg)

Males

Abdomen more or less fuscous beyond the fourth segment; clypeus
    and scape with only a few setae; inner orbits divergent above,
    upper interocular distance 1.13-1.20 times lower interocular;

parapenial lobes shorter than aedoeagus and digiti (Fig. 1) ....
.... 1. *bergi* (Holmberg)
Abdomen almost wholly rufous, the subgenital plate contrastingly
black; clypeus and scape with rather dense, black setae; inner
orbits subparallel, upper interocular distance 1.00-1.05 times
lower interocular; parapenial lobes large, slightly exceeding
aedoeagus and digiti (Fig. 2) .... 2. *jaffueli* (Herbst)

1. *Aridestus bergi* (Holmberg)

Pompilus bergii Holmberg, 1881, Anales Soc. Cient. Argentina, 12: 142.
    [Type: ♀, ARGENTINA: Prov. Buenos Aires (C. Berg) (Mus. Arg. Cienc.
    Nat.)].
Aridestus bergi Banks, 1947, Bull. Mus. Comp. Zool. Harvard, 99: 432.

Female. — Length 5.7-9.0 mm; fore wing 5.0-7.0 mm. Head and
thorax black, the pubescence silvery at least on the clypeus, lower
front, anterior and posterior parts of the pronotum, parts of the
pleura and leg-bases, and posterior slope of the propodeum, often
almost wholly silvery-sericeous, the band along the pronotal margin
especially heavy; abdomen rufous except black at extreme base, apex
sometimes weakly infuscated, wholly covered with fine, pale pubescence; wings subhyaline or lightly infuscated, with a broad darker
band along the outer margin of the fore wing. Temples and propleura with some erect hairs, body otherwise barely hairy except for
dark hairs on the clypeus, front, vertex, and scape in occasional
specimens. Clypeus 2.1-2.4 times as wide as high, truncate or slightly
concave apically. Front narrow, middle interocular distance .52-.58
times transfacial distance; upper interocular distance .95-1.00 times
lower interocular; POL subequal to or slightly exceeding OOL.
Third antennal segment 2.8-3.5 times as long as thick, equal to .50-
.63 times upper interocular distance. Posterior slope of propodeum
with transverse rugae, but the rugae not nearly reaching the extreme
lateral margins. Front basitarsus with three comb-spines, the basal
one usually shorter than the others. Third submarginal cell triangular or subtriangular.

Male. — Length 5.5-6.0 mm; fore wing 4.8-5.1 mm. Head and
thorax black except posterior margin of pronotum with a pale band;
abdomen rufous except extreme base black, fifth and sixth segments
fuscous, apical tergite whitish; body very extensively clothed with
silvery pubescence, the pubescence dark on the vertex, most of the
mesoscutum and scutellar disc, and base of the fifth abdominal segment; wings hyaline, with a broad brownish band along the outer
margin of the fore wing. Temples and propleura with abundant
pale hairs; scape, front, and vertex with short, dark setae. Clypeus

2.0 times as wide as high. Front narrow, middle interocular distance
.55-.57 times transfacial distance; middle interocular distance 1.25-
1.30 times lower interocular distance, upper interocular distance 1.13-
1.20 times lower. POL:OOL about as 6:5. Third antennal segment 1.5-1.9 times as long as thick, sometimes barely shorter than
fourth segment. Subgenital plate roundly elevated medially; genitalia as shown in Fig. 1.

Distribution. — Northern Argentina, Paraguay, southern Brazil.

Specimens examined. — 10 ♀♀, 4 ♂♂. ARGENTINA: 1 ♀, Volcan,
Jujuy, 2500 meters, 4 Dec. 1964 (C. C. Porter) [MCZ]. PARA-
GUAY: 1 ♀, Villa Rica (F. Schade) [MCZ]. BRAZIL: 8 ♀♀, 4 ♂♂,
Nova Teutonia, Santa Catarina, Oct. — March (F. Plaumann)
[MCZ, Coll. G. R. Ferguson].

Remarks. — The specimen from Jujuy is from a considerably
higher altitude from the others, and is the only female studied which
has black hairs on the scape and on the front and vertex; this specimen also has the pale pubescence somewhat reduced, that on the
front tending to form streaks along the sides and along the median
sulcus, as in the Chilean species *jaffueli*. With respect to pubescence
and pilosity, this specimen seems to occupy an intermediate position
among the three species (as it does geographically), but in all structural characters it agrees very well with specimens of *bergi* from
lower and more easterly localities.

2. **Aridestus porteri** new species

Holotype. — ♀, PERU: Cuzco, 3800 meters, Sept. 20 — Oct. 2,
1964 (C. C. Porter) [MCZ, No. 31,182].

Description of female type. — Length 12 mm; fore wing 9 mm.
Head and thorax black, rendered somewhat bluish by the wholly
dark pubescence; abdomen rufous, only the extreme base of the first
segment and extreme tip of the apical segment infuscated; wings
fuscous, violaceous, fore wing distinctly darker in a broad band along
the outer margin. Head rather densely dark-haired, including the
scape; propleura hairy; pronotum, front coxae, and lower part of
mesopleura (in front of middle coxae) with a few dark setae. Clypeus
2.2 times as wide as high. Front of moderate breadth, middle interocular distance .58 times transfacial distance; upper interocular
distance .93 times lower interocular; POL and OOL subequal.
Third antennal segment 3.0 times as long as thick, equal to .56
times upper interocular distance. Transverse rugae of propodeum
strong, the more posterior ones extending all the way to the ridge
separating the propodeum from the metapleura. Fore basitarsus with

three long comb-spines and a shorter one basad of these. Marginal
cell removed from wing tip by a distance equal to 1.85 times the
length of the marginal cell; third submarginal cell narrowed by
three-fourths above, but not triangular.

Remarks. — This large and well characterized species is known
only from the type. It was collected at the same time and place as
a long series of *Pompilus (Arachnospila) dichromorphus* (Rohwer),
to which it bears a strong superficial resemblance.

3. *Aridestus jaffueli* (Herbst) new combination

Pompilus jaffueli Herbst, 1923, Revista Chilena Hist. Nat., 25: 150. [Type:
♀, CHILE: Marga Marga, Prov. Valparaiso, Jan. 15, 1919 (F. Jaffuel)
(MCZ, No. 17,184)].

Female. — Length 7-9 mm; fore wing 6-7 mm. Head and thorax
black, the dorsum rendered somewhat bluish by the pubescence, with
an extensive pattern of silvery pubescence as follows: sides of clypeus,
a streak along the inner orbits and also up the median frontal sulcus,
temples, all coxae, propleura, pronotum anteriorly and along the
posterior margin, posterior margin of mesoscutum, sides of scutellum,
metanotum, and most of the propodeum and pleura; abdomen rufous,
extreme tip sometimes infuscated, clothed with fine, pale pubescence;
wings lightly infuscated, with a broad darker band along the outer
margin of the fore wing. Front with short, dark hairs; clypeus and
scape with a few hairs; temples and propleura clothed with pale
hairs. Clypeus 2.3-2.5 times as wide as high, truncate apically.
Front narrow, middle interocular distance .53-.55 times transfacial
distance; upper interocular distance .84-.90 times lower interocular,
the inner orbits thus somewhat more distinctly convergent above than
in *bergi*. POL subequal to or slightly exceeding OOL. Third antennal segment 2.5-3.0 times as long as thick, equal to .55-.64 times
upper interocular distance. Median impression of propodeum nearly
complete, the propodeum completely without transverse rugae. Front
basitarsus with three strong comb-spines, sometimes with a weak
fourth spine basad of these. Third submarginal cell subtriangular.

Male. — Length 5.0-7.5 mm; fore wing 4.2-6.0 mm. Coloration
of body, wings, and pubescence much as in the female except for
the usual pale yellow markings on the pronotum and tip of the
abdomen; abdomen almost wholly rufous and covered with a fine,
pale pubescence; subgenital plate black; scape with some dark hairs
beneath, clypeus, front, and vertex also more conspicuously hairy than
in the female. Clypeus 2.1-2.2 times as wide as high. Front narrow, middle interocular distance .56 times transfacial distance; middle interocular distance 1.15-1.20 times lower interocular; upper

interocular 1.00-1.05 times lower. POL:OOL about as 4:3. Third antennal segment 1.4-1.6 times as long as thick. Subgenital plate with a strong median keel; genitalia differing from those of *bergi* only in having more heavily setose parameres, a more deeply cleft aedoeagus, and slightly longer and broader parapenial lobes (Fig. 2).

Distribution. — Central Chile, Patagonia.

Specimens examined. — 4 ♀♀, 2 ♂♂. CHILE: 1 ♀, 1 ♂, Marga Marga, Prov. Valparaiso, Jan. 15, 1919 (F. Jaffuel) [type and allotype, MCZ]; 1 ♀, 1 ♂, Valle los Piuquenes, Rio Blanco, Prov. Aconcagua, Feb. 7-12, 1964 (L. Peña) [MCZ]; 1 ♀, Pichinahuel, Prov. Arauco, 1400 meters, Jan. 31, 1954 (L. Peña) [Coll. G. R. Ferguson]. ARGENTINA: 1 ♀, Chubut, Patagonia (W. F. H. Rosenberg) [USNM].

Remarks. — The close similarity of the male genitalia of *jaffueli* and *bergi* indicates conclusively that the presence or absence of rugae on the female propodeum should not be regarded as a generic character. The description and drawing of the genitalia of *jaffueli* were made from the specimen from Valle los Piuquenes. The genitalia of the allotype were extracted some years ago by R. R. Dreisbach, but the slide which he prepared contains only a broken fragment of the subgenital plate, the genitalia presumably having been lost.

AMERICAN SPIDER GENERA *THERIDULA* AND *PARATHERIDULA* (ARANEAE: THERIDIIDAE)[1]

BY HERBERT W. LEVI

Museum of Comparative Zoology

Since my revision (1954) of the genus *Theridula* in North America, no additional species have been found. In the meanwhile, however, I have been able to examine the types of South American species (except that of *Theridula polita,* which appears to be lost). Additional records of *Paratheridula perniciosa* have been obtained since I described the genus (1957), but no additional species. That *Paratheridula perniciosa* is a pantropical species is suggested not only by its wide distribution in the Americas, but also by the absence of related species. Its small size, inconspicuous appearance, and the fact that its epigynum is always covered by a secretion (which has to be removed to examine it), suggest that it may have been overlooked in collections.

I would like to thank Dr. G. Owen Evans and his staff at the British Museum (Natural History) for making the Keyserling types available for study. A National Science Foundation grant (G-4317) permitted initial examination of theridiid types in European museums. The further researches were supported in part by Public Health Service Research Grant AI-01944 from the National Institute of Allergy and Infectious Diseases.

MISPLACED SPECIES: *Theridula polita* Mello-Leitão, 1947, Papéis Avulsos, Dept. Zool., São Paulo, 8(11): 127, fig. 1, ♀. Female holotype from Santa Cruz, Est. Paraná, Brazil, apparently lost, is probably a *Dipoena* judging by coloration, shape, and proportions of the species. The black stripe on the legs and the illustration of the epigynum suggest that it is *D. militaris* Chickering. The holotype of *Theridula polita* is not in the Mello-Leitão collection in Rio de Janeiro nor in São Paulo. Some Mello-Leitão types are alleged to be in the Museum Paranaense, but according to Mr. P. de Biasi it is not there either. The illustration of Mello-Leitão has been copied (Fig. 6).

Theridula Emerton

Theridula Emerton, 1882, Trans. Connecticut Acad. Sci. 6:25. Type species *Theridion sphaerula* Hentz, 1850 [=*T. opulenta* (Walckenaer)], however Emerton misidentified the specimens which he examined; they belong to *T. emertoni.*

[1]*Manuscript recived by the editor May 11, 1966*

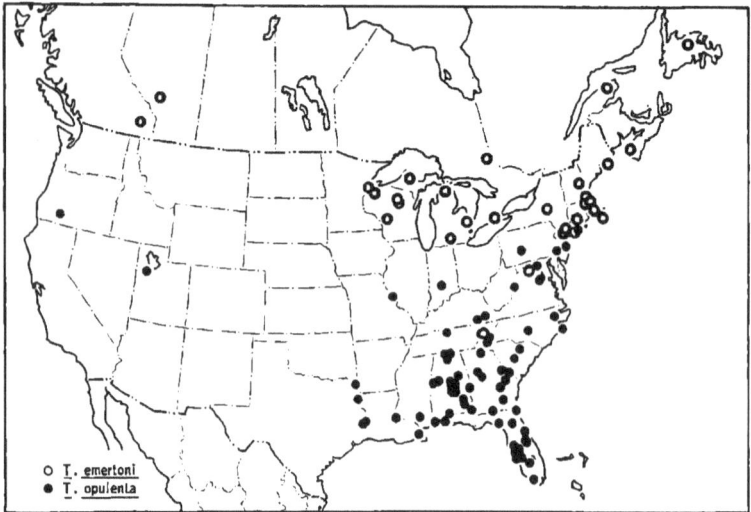

Map 1. Distribution of *Theridula emertoni* Levi and *Theridula opulenta* (Walckenaer).

Carapace as in *Theridion*, not modified. Chelicerae with two teeth on anterior margin, none posterior. First leg longest with patella and tibia 1.2 to 1.5 times carapace length. Abdomen wider than long in females, and lacking a colulus. Male palpus very simple, without conductor, median apophysis or radix. Haematodocha fastens both ends of tegulum to cymbium.

Key to *Theridula* species in the Americas

References to "figures" in lower case signify illustrations in Levi 1954, to "Figures" in upper case signify the ones in this paper.

1a. Females..2
1b. Males...9
2a. Epigynum with two distinct circular openings (Figs. 2, 5)........
....3
2b. Epigynum with humps or otherwise no distinct opening visible
....5
3a. Connecting duct with one loop (fig. 19)............... *gonygaster*
3b. Connecting ducts not looped (Figs. 1, 4)...............................4
4a. Openings connected by a posterior lip (Fig. 2).... *multiguttata*
4b. Openings on a hump not connected by a lip (Fig. 5)...............
.... *nigerrima*

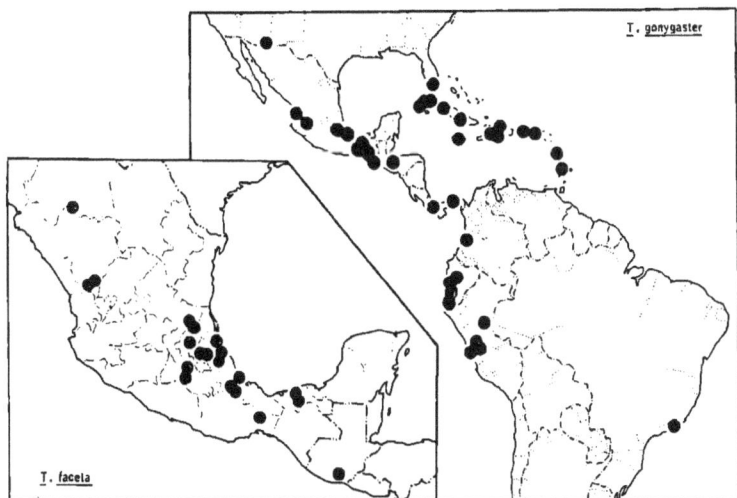

Map 2. Distribution of *Theridula faceta* (O. P.-Cambridge) and *Theridula gonygaster* (Simon).

Theridula emertoni Levi
Map 1

Additional record. Newfoundland. Junction Pond, Notre Dame Camp, 13 July 1961, ♀ (C. P. Alexander).

Theridula opulenta (Walckenaer)
Map 1

Additional record. United States. Oregon: Crater Lake Natl. Park, 15 June 1947, ♀ (B. Malkin and S. Sargent).

Theridula faceta (O. P. - Cambridge)
Map 2

Additional record. Mexico. Tabasco: 3.2 km NE of Comalcalo.

Theridula puebla Levi
Map 3

Additional records. Panama. Canal Zone: Madden Dam, 8 Aug. 1939 (A. M. Chickering); Barro Colorado Island, several records (A. M. Chickering). Boquete, several records (A. M. Chickering).

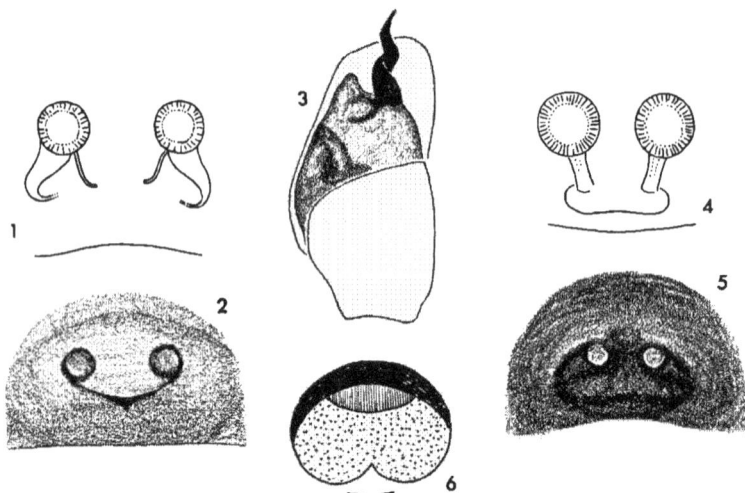

Figs. 1, 2. *Theridula multiguttata* Keyserling. 1. Female genitalia, dorsal view. 2. Epigynum.

Figs. 3-5. *T. nigerrima* (Petrunkevitch). 3. Left palpus. 4. Female genitalia, dorsal view. 5. Epigynum.

Fig. 6. *T. polita* Mello-Leitao, epigynum after Mello-Leitão.

Theridula gonygaster (Simon)
Map 2

Theridium gonygaster Simon, 1873, Mém. Soc. Roy. Sci. Liège, (2)5:109. Male lectotype designated by Levi, 1954, in the Muséum National d'Histoire Naturelle, Paris.

Theridula gonygaster,—Levi, 1954, Trans. Amer. Microscop. Soc., 73:340, figs. 18-22, ♀ ♂.

Distribution. Worldwide tropical. In America from Arizona, southern Florida, eastern Mexico, West Indies to Rio de Janeiro, Brazil.

Additional records. United States. Arizona: Cochise Co. Cave Creek Canyon. *Columbia. Valle:* Buenaventura, 4 Nov. 1950 (E. I. Schlinger, E. S. Ross). *Ecuador. Guayas:* Milagro (H. E., D. L. Frizzell); Guayaquil (Landes, H. E., D. L. Frizzell). *El Oro:* 5 km above Pasaje (R. Walls). *Peru. Piura:* Sulana, banana grove (H. E., D. L. Frizzell); Higuerón, Las Lomas (H. E., D. L. Frizzell). *Lima:* San Antonio (E. I. Schlinger, E. S. Ross).

Theridula nigerrima (Petrunkevitch)
Figures 3-5, Map 3

Diporna nigra Keyserling, 1886, Die Spinnen Amerikas, Theridiidae, 2(2): 43, pl. 12, fig. 158, ♀ ♂. Female lectotype here designated from Pumamarca [?Pumamanta, Junin], Peru, in the Polish Academy of Sciences, Warsaw; examined. Name preoccupied by *D. nigra* Emerton, 1882.

Diporna nigerrima Petrunkevitch, 1911, Bull. Amer. Mus. Nat. Hist., 29: 174. New name for *D. nigra* Keyserling, preoccupied.

Diagnosis. The openings of the epigynum are on the anterior edge of a sclerotized plate (Fig. 5), quite different from *T. gonygaster* which lacks this plate. The connecting canals seem straight and short (Fig. 4). The shape of the narrow pointed embolus (Fig. 3) separates *T. nigerrima* from *T. gonygaster.*

Records. Ecuador. Azuay: Cuenca, 3 Apr. 1942, ♀ (H. E., D. L. Frizzell). *Peru. Cuzco:* Machu Picchu, 3000 m elev., 6 Mar. 1947, 2 ♂ (J. C. Pallister).

Theridula multiguttata Keyserling
Figures 1, 2. Map 3

Theridula multiguttata Keyserling, 1886, Die Spinnen Amerikas, Theridiidae, 2: 258, pl. 21, fig. 306, ♀. Female holotype from Blumenau, [Santa Catarina], Brazil, in the British Museum (Natural History); examined.

The shorter straight connecting ducts (Fig. 4) separate this species from *T. gonygaster.*

Map 3. Distribution of *Theridula puebla* Levi, *T. casas* Levi, *T. nigerrima* (Petrunkevitch), and *T. multiguttata* Keyserling.

Record. Brazil. Pernambuco: Recife (in the Senckenberg Museum).

Paratheridula Levi

Paratheridula Levi, 1957, Trans. Amer. Microscop. Soc., 76:105. Type species by original designation, *Mysmena quadrimaculata* Banks [=*Paratheridula perniciosa* (Keyserling)].

Carapace as in *Theridion*, not modified. Chelicerae with two teeth on anterior margin, a small tooth on posterior of female. First leg longest, patella and tibia 1.3 to 1.4 times carapace length. Abdomen subspherical and without colulus. Male palpus very simple without conductor, median apophysis or radix, and having only a basal hematodocha.

The single species known is widely distributed; it is suspected that it is introduced.

Paratheridula perniciosa (Keyserling)
Map 4

Theridium perniciosum Keyserling, 1886, Die Spinnen Amerikas, Theridiidae, 2(2): 233, pl. 20, fig. 288, ♀. Female type from Blumenau, [Est. Santa Catarina], Brazil, in the British Museum (Natural History); examined.

Map 4. Distribution of *Paratheridula perniciosa* (Keyserling).

Mysmena quadrimaculata Banks, 1896, Trans. Amer. Entomol. Soc., 23: 66.
Female holotype from Punta Gorda, Florida, in the Museum of Comparative Zoology.
Paratheridula quadrimaculata,—Levi, 1957, Trans. Amer. Microscop. Soc., 74: 106, figs. 1-6, map.

Distribution. Gulf states, Mexico, Central America, West Indies, South America to Chile, possibly pantropical.

Additional records. Mexico. San Luis Potosí: Valles, July 1956 (W. J. Gertsch, V. Roth). *Cuba. Villas:* Soledad. *Bahama Island.* New Providence (J. Greenway). *Ecuador. Napo-Pastaza:* Río Topo, June 1943 (H. E., D. L. Frizzell). *Peru. Junín:* San Ramón, 800 m (H. W. Levi). *Brazil. Pernambuco:* Recife. *Chile. Osorno:* Valley Forest, 18 km W of Purranque, Jan. 1951 (E. S. Ross, A. E. Schlinger); 10 km E of Puyehue, Jan. 1951 (E. S. Ross, A. E. Schlinger).

REFERENCES CITED

LEVI, H. W.
1954. The spider genus *Theridula* in North and Central America and the West Indies. Trans. Amer. Microscop. Soc. 73: 331-343.
1957. The North American spider genera *Paratheridula, Tekellina, Pholcomma,* and *Archerius. Ibid.* 76: 105-115.

COLONIZING FLIGHTS AND ASSOCIATED ACTIVITIES OF TERMITES.
I. THE DESERT DAMP-WOOD TERMITE *PARANEOTERMES SIMPLICICORNIS* (KALOTERMITIDAE)[1]

By W. L. NUTTING
Department of Entomology, University of Arizona

INTRODUCTION. — The swarming period provides the only occasion when observations can be made undisturbed on many species of termites. Flights involving large numbers of alates, apparently synchronized with particular seasons, are a conspicuous phenomenon in many parts of the world and well known to local inhabitants. Yet only the most limited information is available on the flights of a small percentage of the commoner species, *i.e.*, the months and time of day during which flights are staged, and perhaps an association with rainfall. Not until recent years have many real efforts been made to correlate the dispersal flights of termites (Snyder, '61) or the nuptial flights of ants (Kannowski, '59; Talbot, '56; '64) — which appear to be similarly related to definite weather patterns — with even the most obvious environmental factors. The difficulties involved in gathering more detailed intelligence, however, become apparent after a season or two of field study.

The following account is the result of an increasingly successful series of observations made on one of twelve different species in a single area over a period of seven years. It summarizes field notes on 78 separate flights together with a preliminary analysis of accompanying weather data. The ultimate objective of such a study should be the elucidation of the physical and physiological factors which trigger the flights of a species, both seasonally and daily, over its entire range. At present the bulk of the data is climatological and far outweighs that on the behavior of the termite itself; the study is thus perforce largely descriptive. Succeeding papers in this series should gain in significance from data being gathered concomitantly on additional species in the families Kalotermitidae, Hodotermitidae, Rhinotermitidae and Termitidae. Although the actual flight stimuli may eventually prove very different from those which suggest themselves from time to time, this descriptive state should provide a starting point for other more profitable approaches to the subject.

[1]Arizona Agricultural Experiment Station Journal Article No. 1112.
Manuscript received by the editor February 25, 1966

Paraneotermes simplicicornis is apparently unique among the dry-wood termites (Kalotermitidae) for, although the reproductive center has never been found, it is fundamentally subterranean in habit. Over its known range in the deserts from southern California and northern Baja California to southern Nevada, southwestern Texas and northern Sinaloa, Mexico, it typically attacks moist wood in or on the ground in washes and canyons. Small living trees are even cut off just beneath the soil on occasion. A detailed account of the biology, distribution and taxonomic relations of this most interesting termite was published by Light in 1937. At that time swarming had never been observed, nor has it been reported since.

STUDY AREA AND METHODS. — Nearly all the flights were observed within an area of less than an acre in north-central Tucson, Arizona, at an altitude of 2400 ft. This part of the valley floor is now about equally divided between creosote bush desert *(Larrea tridentata)* and small residential developments. Three to four feet of fine-textured alluvium overlies a narrow zone of friable caliche or hardpan. The mean annual precipitation of 10.9 inches is almost equally divided between a summer (July-Sept.) and a winter (Dec.-March) rainy season, characteristic for most of the Sonoran Desert. Although the mean annual temperature is 19.6°C, it is of little significance unless it is realized that daily fluctuations of 15° are common and of 21°C not unusual. In 62 years the highest recorded temperature was 44.4° (July, 1953, and several other dates), the lowest −14.4°C (Jan., 1913) (Sellers, '60).

Considering our scant knowledge of the types of sense organs with which the various castes of termites are equipped, much less the information which they are collecting, it is still far from clear what environmental factors should be measured, to say nothing of the necessary degrees of accuracy. Hence, many of the methods used here are admittedly exploratory and probably crude. Certain refinements have already been made and others are continually suggesting themselves. For example, it would probably be desirable to measure many microclimatic parameters; however, their usefulness will depend upon a much greater knowledge of the termites and their pre-flight activities within and near the nest than is now available.

Starting in January, 1960, continuous records of air temperature and relative humidity have been made in the study area with a Bendix-Friez Hygrothermograph, Mod. 594 (maintained to an accuracy within approximately ±1°C from −12 to +43°C and ±5% from 0 to 100% RH). The instrument is sheltered six feet above the ground. Weekly mean temperatures and relative humidities were figured from the hygrothermograph records with the aid of a planimeter (Cutright, '27). Evaporation data are available (U. S. Department of Commerce, '62; '63) from measurements made daily at 5:00 PM on the campus of the University of Arizona, Tucson, 2.5 mi. SSW of the study area. Saturation deficit was calculated for time of sunset plus 15 minutes at Tucson, and for certain other times, on the basis of hygrothermograph records. Rainfall was measured daily with a simple plastic collecting gauge near the center of the area from midnight to midnight. Illumination at the zenith was measured several different times with a Weston photographic exposure meter (Master II, Mod. 735). During 1962 barometric pressure was continuously recorded on a temperature-compensated Taylor recording barometer. Some observations were made on flights from a laboratory colony in an 8 × 8-foot walk-in refrigerator which was equipped with a Partlow recording temperature program control (Mod. RCS) capable of providing any desired daily or weekly temperature pattern. All times are Mountain Standard and based on the 24-hour clock.

DEVELOPMENT OF ALATES AND PRE-FLIGHT BEHAVIOR. — Light ('37) termed the large aggregations of nymphs and soldiers of this species "temporary outposts" or "foraging subcolonies"; no reproductives of any form, eggs or small nymphs have yet been found in them. Samples from 19 subcolonies collected in or within 25 miles of Tucson have revealed subimaginal nymphs (with large wing pads) to be present between August 30 (1962) and May 20 (1961). On the latter date an entire subcolony was removed from a large timber beneath the steps of a farm building and set up in a laboratory observation nest. It contained 39 soldiers and 760 nymphs, many of them pre-alates. Between June 2 and 15, all of these had developed into 130 alates at laboratory temperatures only slightly less variable than, and averaging a few degrees below, those outside. By a most fortunate coincidence another subcolony was found on June 14, 1961, in the roots of a dead palo verde tree *(Cercidium microphyllum)*. It contained 104 soldiers, at least 1100 nymphs (no pre-alates) and 190 alates. No flights were observed in the Tucson area in 1961 until July 5, although it is likely that this was not the first flight of the season. The above evidence shows an abrupt and rapid mass development of alates within three weeks, probably less, of the first flight. Although no local soil temperature records are available it seems reasonable to assume that this maturation is a direct result of the intense heating of the soil which occurs during the very clear, dry months of May and June. Monthly mean air temperatures increase rapidly from 18.1°C in April to 22.4° in May, 27.6° in June and 30.1° in July (Sellers, '60).

Light ('37) reported alates in colonies in California from late October into November and in Nevada during May. Snyder ('54) noted that alates were taken from a colony in Texas in mid-April. In the absence of flight records from these regions speculation is unprofitable, although flight schedules are probably shifted in conformity with local weather patterns which result from altitudinal and latitudinal differences over its entire range.

Once alates are present in a colony, the influence of biological factors on the initiation of flights must also be considered. Although the behavioral interactions among the members of a colony have only begun to be fathomed, the feverish activity exhibited within a colony at the onset of conditions favoring flight has probably been noted many times (*e.g.,* in *Kalotermes* [=*Incisitermes*] *minor* Hagen by Harvey, '34, p. 221). In this connection some early attempts were made to induce flights from a large sub-colony which had been in the laboratory for about a month. It was confined in an observation nest of seven plastic petri dishes interconnected with polyethylene

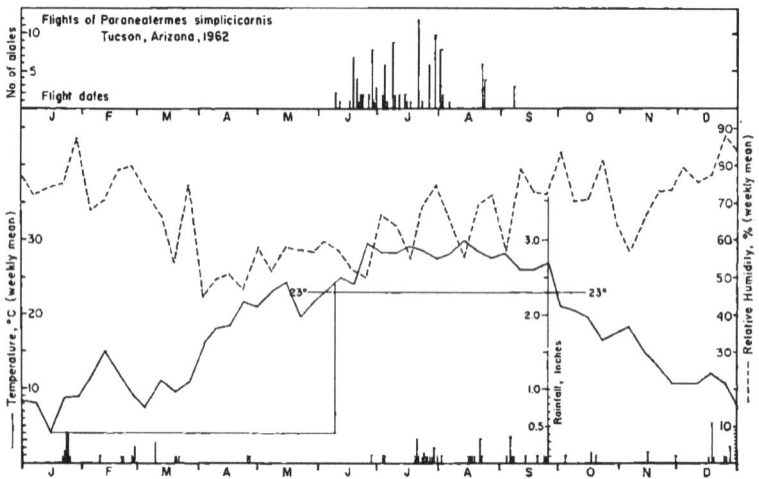

Figure 1. Flight season of *Paraneotermes simplicicornis* in relation to rainfall, weekly mean temperature and relative humidity at Tucson, Arizona, in 1962. Dates showing 0.1″ actually indicate amounts from a trace to 0.1″ of rain. Flights began when mean temperature remained above about 23°C. The upper section shows the numbers of alates observed on each date during the flight season from June 9 to Sept. 7.

tubing and placed on a large tray of moist soil. (*Paraneotermes* has been maintained for more than a year in this type of nest with the petri dishes containing a layer of 4% agar and thin slices of wood.) The colony was held in the dark, walk-in refrigerator for about a week at 27°C and 30% RH prior to a brief, simulated flight season. Observations were made with the program control set to duplicate the temperature cycle of five consecutive days of typical summer weather. Daily temperatures varied between 22° and 43°C, relative humidities between 28 and 78%. Temperature peaks occurred between 1500 and 1600 each day. During the middle of these days the temperature sometimes rose at a rate of about 3.3°C per hour and fell later by as much as 9°C per hour for short periods. No measurements were made within the nest, although it is certain that the relative humidity was continuously at or close to saturation. Most of the observations were made under a red light.

Under such conditions and below about 34°C, activity in the colony appeared to be normal, with the alates remaining almost motionless in one or more tightly packed clusters. As the temperature rose between about 34° and 36°C, the general activity gradually increased; the alates began to run about and the clusters broke up. Above about 36°C the entire colony became more and more agitated and the alates leaped and fluttered their wings in frenzied excitement. As the temperature dropped this behavioral sequence was reversed. In the range from 38° to 36°C, the alates again became gregarious — in one instance within 15 minutes from their peak of activity.

On three days, small numbers of these excited alates (15, 13, 2) actually emerged from the nest through a small hole drilled in the cover of one petri dish as well as from under the edge of the cover. In the latter case two soldiers were obviously and attentively stationed near the point of emergence although they did not appear to be regulating the exit of the alates as suggested for *Kalotermes (=Incisitermes) minor* by Harvey *(loc. cit.)*. The emerging alates rapidly gained high points on the soil and small stones in the tray, then took flight after much moving of heads from side to side and waving of antennae. The door of the chamber was opened and observations were terminated after the alates had made rapid, erratic flights into the day-lighted room outside.

These limited observations show that the phases of flight activity, even within the colony, are amenable to laboratory study. Although the preceding manipulations did not duplicate the environmental conditions under which this essentially subterranean termite stages its flights, they do suggest that high temperature (probably reached later in the day near the soil surface) may provide an important cue for the initiation of daily flight periods. As more data become available further refinements in this type of experimentation are planned with several other species of termites in Arizona.

FLIGHT SEASON. — According to legend in the Sonoran Desert, the summer rainy season begins on San Juan's Day, June 24. The rains are also believed to initiate the swarming season of the termites in this region; indeed, in many Latin American localities with a similar weather pattern, the swarming alates are called "Palomitas de San Juan" (Light, '34). Legend and meager published information led to some early and rather casual observations which resulted in one flight record for *Paraneotermes* on August 12, 1956; three in 1957, on July 10, 14 and 16; and one on July 17, 1959. More persistent observation, still within the rainy season, yielded 11 flights from July 5 through 29, 1961. Guided by experience of previous seasons and new knowledge that alate production may begin in early June, intensive observations were made from mid-May to mid-September in 1962 and, with the exception of six weeks of June and July, again in 1963. Thirty-one flights were thus recorded from June 9 through Sept. 7, 1962 (fig. 1), while the first and last flights in 1963 were recorded on June 15 and August 19 (fig. 2). These records spanning 91 and 66 days attest to a considerably protracted flight season for this species, beginning well in advance of the rainy season. A flight on May 29, 1965, further expands the cumulative seasonal record to 102 days within five consecutive months. T. E. Snyder has informed me ('64, *in litt.*) that the U. S. National Museum contains alates caught by light trap on July 6 and August 15, 1947, at Blythe, Riverside Co., California.

INFLUENCE OF ENVIRONMENTAL FACTORS ON TIME OF FLIGHT. — The flights of termites are considered to provide for the foundation of new colonies and hence the maintenance and dispersal of the species. Extensive observations on the termite fauna in Mexico and the southwestern United States have led the writer to conclude that matings between sexes from different colonies, in synchronous flights over limited areas, are presumably usual. The idea that sibling matings are the rule has been advanced by several authors (Weesner, '60, p. 161) although, admittedly, either position would be equally difficult to prove. Since alates of *Paraneotermes* have never been observed emerging from a nest in nature, the following factors actually describe the conditions under which flights are known to have occurred. A more refined analysis does not yet seem warranted on the basis of such data, limited as they are to only two seasons. A

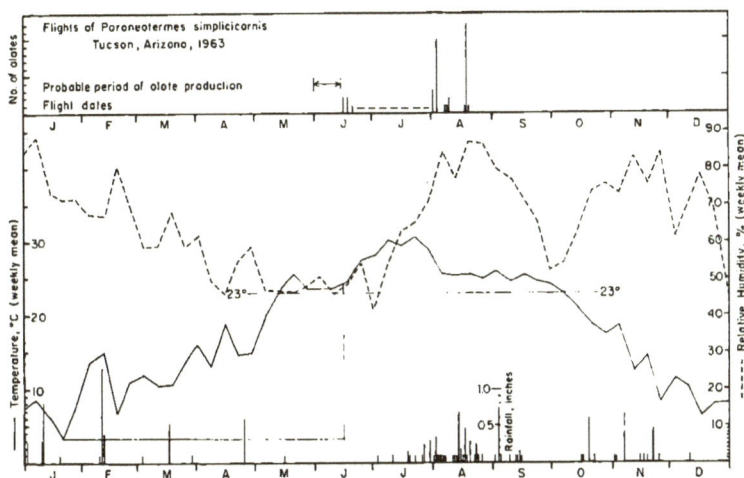

Figure 2. Flight season of *Paraneotermes simplicicornis* in relation to rainfall, weekly mean temperature and relative humidity at Tucson, Arizona, in 1963. Dates showing 0.1″ actually indicate amounts from a trace to 0.1″ of rain. Flights began when mean temperature remained above about 23°C. The upper section shows the numbers of alates observed on each date during the flight season from June 15 to Aug. 19. No observations were made between June 24 and August 1. Data on the maturation of alates were obtained from two colonies, one in the laboratory and one in the field.

few simple correlations are apparent, however, and may provide a basis for determining the cues which are actually used by *Paraneotermes* for initiating both its annual flight season and daily flight periods.

Temperature

The timing of the flight season in relation to weekly mean temperature and relative humidity for two years is plotted in figures 1 and 2. Flights began when the weekly mean temperature remained consistently above about 23°C, while later in the season means reached as high as 29.9° ('62) and 30.6°C ('63). The seasons ended during weekly means of 25.9° ('62) and 25.4°C ('63), leaving three and seven weeks in these years before falling to 23°C. At this point it might be mentioned that the areas under the curves for the two years studied — taken arbitrarily from the lowest weekly mean of the winter to the date of the first flight (figs. 1 and 2) — are very close as measured with a planimeter. This has suggested that it might eventually be profitable to explore modifications of the temperature-summation method in connection with alate development both in nature and in controlled environments, and then to relate results to the initiation of the flight season. However, the list of unknowns concerning this species is so great — location and environment of the nest, favorable temperature ranges for the development of any caste, etc. — that meaningful calculations are hardly possible at present. The simplest and perhaps most plausible explanation for the termination of the flight season might lie in the fact that all alates had flown.

Figure 3 shows the flight periods in relation to the following daily temperatures during the season in 1962; minimum, maximum and temperature 15 minutes after sunset. Daily flight periods (29 in 1962, 11 in 1963) occurred on days with a mean minimal temperature of 20.1° (range, 12.0 — 24.8) in 1962, and 19.0° (range, 13.7 — 22.0) in 1963. The mean maximal temperature for the same days was 33.3° (range, 26.9 — 37.6) in 1962, and 32.3° (range, 29.5 — 36.7) in 1963. Flights began each day at approximately 15 minutes after sunset; the mean temperature for this time, on the days when flights occurred, was 28.2° (range, 23.4 — 32) in 1962, and 26.0° (range, 23.7 — 29) in 1963. Within these limits there is no readily apparent relation to daily temperature patterns.

The temperature cycle of a "typical day," together with curves

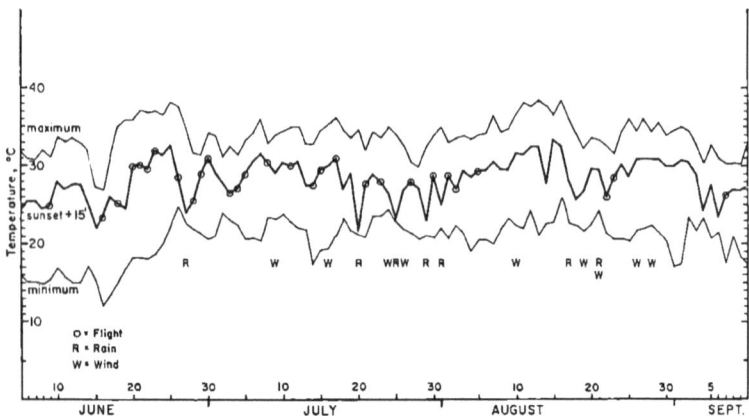

Figure 3. Flight dates of *Paraneotermes simplicicornis* in relation to daily temperature fluctuations in Tucson, Arizona, in 1962. Flights began at approximately 15 min. after sunset. Rain or wind may have prevented flights on at least 15 evenings.

for relative humidity and saturation deficit, is presented in figure 4. The combinations of temperature and relative humidity at the time of sunset plus 15 minutes are plotted in figure 6. Daily flights almost always begin while temperature is falling steadily and generally near or shortly after the low in humidity for the day.

Moisture

Rainfall and Soil Moisture. — The relation of the flight season and the daily flights to rainfall for 1962 and '63 is shown in figures 1 and 2. For these years, where the first and last flights were established with reasonable certainty, the flight season began well in advance of the summer rains. In 1962 the first flight was staged 81 days after the last measurable rain of 0.09" was recorded on March 20. Eight flights had occurred before the next measurable rain (0.02") had fallen 99 days later. The next year, 51 days elapsed between the last measurable rain of 0.58" on April 25 and the first flight, with at least three flights occurring before the first measurable rain (0.01") in 69 days. In 1965 the first flight took place 17 days after 0.01" was measured on May 12. These records established beyond any doubt that *Paraneotermes* does not begin swarming in response to seasonal rainfall. This is apparently the case with many dry-wood termites, such as *Cryptotermes* (Weesner, '60, p. 160).

Although a few of the larger flights have taken place on days following substantial rains, the general pattern seems to be one in which rain is actually avoided (figs. 1 and 2). Of 29 flights observed in the study area during 1962, only eight occurred on rainy days, and on each of these days only 0.05" or less was measured. Further, flights did not take place if any rain occurred within an hour before or after flight time. A similar pattern is evident for other years, although the data are much less complete.

No measurements of soil moisture have been made in connection with the flights of this termite. It is certain, however, that the general floor of the desert is hard-packed and that the soil is extremely dry to a depth of many feet during the early part of the season. The matter of the selection of nesting site is briefly covered under *Post-Flight Behavior.*

Relative Humidity. — Figures 1 and 2 show the relation of the total flight season to the weekly mean relative humidity for two years. The seasons took place within means of 50.1 and 79.1% ('62) and 40.6 and 86.9% relative humidity ('63). These ranges include very nearly the extremes for each year, and cover the summer trend from very low to high mean humidities.

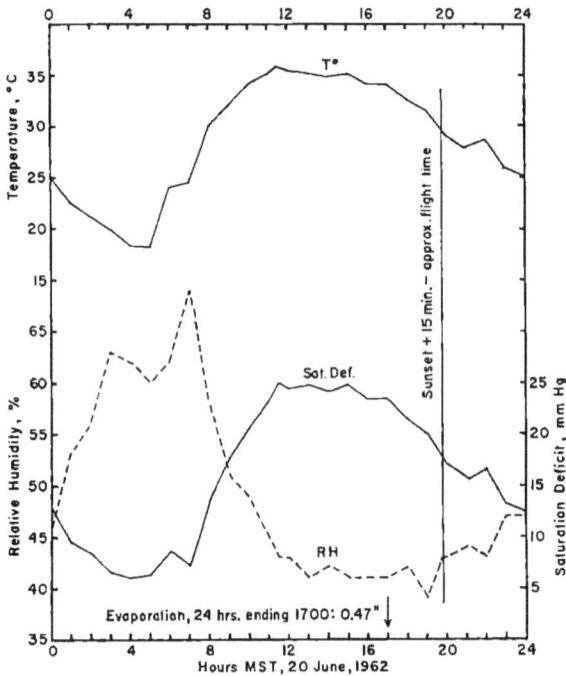

Figure 4. Relationship between approximate flight time (sunset plus 15 min.) of *Paraneotermes simplicicornis* and temperature, relative humidity, saturation deficit and evaporation. June 20 was taken as a typical day during the 1962 flight season in Tucson, Arizona.

In relation to daily fluctuations of relative humidity, individual flight periods (29 in 1962, 11 in 1963) occurred as follows: on days with a mean minimum humidity of 45.8% (range, 37 — 65) in 1962, and 47.4% (range, 30 — 65) in 1963; on days with a mean maximum humidity of 85.9% (range, 62 — 100) in 1962, and 91.4% (range, 65 — 100) in 1963. Mean humidity at flight time (sunset plus 15 minutes) was 56.8% (range, 38 — 92) in 1962, and 71.3% (range, 36 — 100) in 1963.

When the rains begin, usually in July, fluctuations in relative humidity vary widely during each day as well as from day to day. There were several days during the two years studied when the relative humidity at the time of sunset was at or close to 100%. Daily flights of *Paraneotermes* almost never occurred on such days; indeed, probably as a result of its avoidance of rain, it rarely flew when the relative humidity was as high as 80 or 90%. It is hardly necessary to point out that the relative humidity at the time of flight, generally well below 60%, is closely correlated with the high temperatures during afternoon and evening (fig. 4).

Evaporation and Saturation Deficit. — Since evaporation was measured 2.5 miles from the study area, the following figures are included only as a general indication of the evaporative power of the atmosphere in a region occupied by *Paraneotermes*. Figure 5 shows that flights occur during the season with the highest evaporation rate of the entire year. The mean daily evaporation rate for 29 flight days in 1962 and 11 in 1963 was 0.36" (range, 0.10 — 0.51) in 1962, and 0.30" (range, 0.10 — 0.56) in 1963 (U. S. Department of Commerce, '62; '63). The overriding influence of high temperature at this time of year insures a high level of evaporation in spite of the moderating effect of the rains which are, at best, sporadic and only infrequently heavy.

The saturation deficit at the study site provides another measure of the dryness of the atmosphere which the alates encounter during their brief period of actual flight. Also closely dependent on temperature, this factor varies about a very high level during the flight season. The weekly mean saturation deficit for the approximate time of flight (sunset plus 15 minutes) is plotted in figure 5. In 1962 the 29 daily flights began at a mean saturation deficit of 12.8 mm. Hg (range, 2.1 — 20.7 mm. Hg). The typically wide daily variation in saturation deficit is shown in figure 4. Although this information may be of little value at present, laboratory experiments might be designed to determine whether the alates respond to differences in relative humidity or in evaporation (or saturation deficit), and thus provide a means for evaluating the effect of these factors on flight behavior. For example, perhaps the contrast between a relatively dry atmosphere and the higher moisture levels in microclimates at the level of the soil provides gradients which are used by the alates, first in leaving the colony and later in seeking out suitable nesting sites.

Light

The rather consistent appearance of alates at lights in the early evening for several seasons suggested that light intensity might be a cue for the initiation of daily flight periods. The times of "first sightings" of alates during 1962 are shown in relation to time of sunset for Tucson in figure 7. Starting in 1963, measurements of light intensity at the zenith have been made with a photographic light

meter on a number of evenings during each flight season. *Para-*
neotermes has never been observed in flight until the light intensity
has thus registered approximately 0.5 lumen per square foot (foot
candles) or less. As with *Neotermes tectonae* Damm. (Kalshoven,
'30) and probably other evening fliers, a few observations have shown
that flight time is earlier on cloudy evenings. Considering the handi-
cap of unknown nesting sites, the correlation between the beginning
of the flight period and the time of sunset, or light intensity, is close.
Whatever other advantages there may be, it is certain that many
predators must be avoided by swarming at dusk.

These few notes indicate the desirability of continuous and more
sensitive measurements of light intensity in the vicinity of the emergence holes, whenever they can be found. The subject of rhythms
and other aspects of behavior in the alates, nymphs and soldiers should
also be studied in laboratory colonies under controlled illumination.
Indeed, a most encouraging find has been made in this connection
with certain species of ants. McCluskey ('65) has shown that en-
dogenous activity rhythms of the males correspond to the timing of
mating flight in the field.

FLIGHT BEHAVIOR. — Considering the relative scarcity of evidence
for *Paraneotermes* in the vicinity of Tucson and the numbers of
alates appearing at lights, it is probable that there were no more than
one or two colonies in or near the study area. On any basis, the
number of alates involved in each daily flight would be very small.
Assuming that most of the alates in 71 flights were from a single
colony and visited the lights (front and back of house), the average

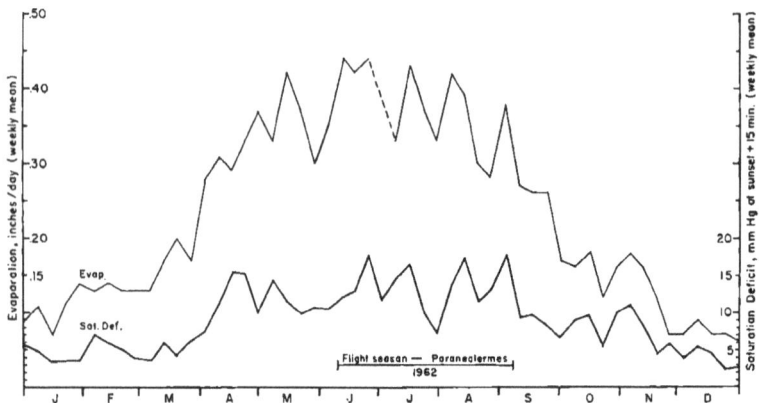

Figure 5. Relationship between flight season of *Paraneotermes simplicicornis* and evaporation rate and saturation deficit in Tucson, Arizona, 1962.

number per flight was approximately five. The usual number seen during a flight was between one and 12, but on three occasions in seven years, the numbers were 23, 48 and 57. Both sexes have been taken in single flights, although no record of the distribution was made. Concurrent flights have been recorded five times: At 1.8, 2.6, 2.8, 12 and 13 miles from the study area.

Paraneotermes was observed in natural flight only as it flew in rapidly, between two and six feet above the ground, to lighted areas. After alighting on walls or pavement, individuals frequently leaped and flew about very erratically. Light ('37) and Light and Weesner ('48) briefly described flights under what were probably abnormal conditions, and Light termed the species a strong and rapid flier. Although in a dry container alates will die in less than a day after capture, presumably of desiccation, they have been held for as long as two weeks in petri dishes containing 4% agar. Alates have been noted to remain in the vicinity of lights up to 80 minutes after their arrival.

POST-FLIGHT BEHAVIOR. — Alates of this species were observed to lose their wings much more readily than many other members of

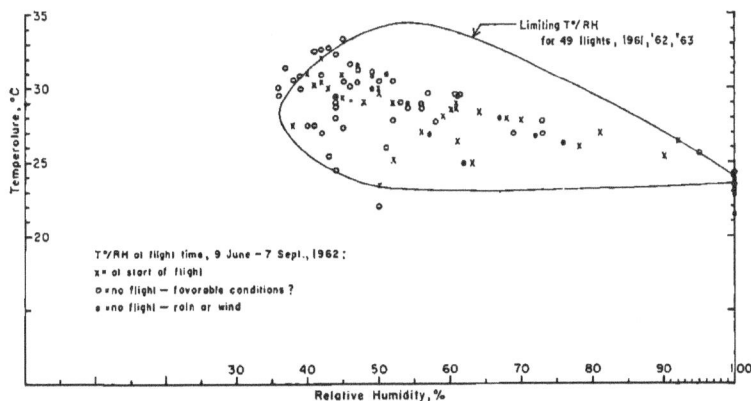

Figure 6. Combinations of temperature and relative humidity at approximate flight time (sunset plus 15 min.) for *Paraneotermes simplicicornis* at Tucson, Arizona. The limits of these conditions for 49 flights are shown by the closed curve. Conditions for the 91 evenings in the 1962 flight season are plotted as follows: x, at the start of 29 flights; solid circles, at flight time on 15 evenings when flights may have been prevented by rain or wind; open circles, at flight time on 47 evenings when no flights were observed. In the latter case these conditions could have been limiting on 13 evenings where they fell outside the curve.

the Family Kalotermitidae. However, it is strongly suspected that the environment under which the following observations were made (residential area with irrigated plantings) is far more suitable for the rapid entrainment of normal post-flight behavior than for that of other local, but strictly dry-wood species such as *Incisitermes* (=*Procryptotermes*) *hubbardi*. The de-alation of many adults around lights usually occurs within a few minutes to a half hour of their first appearance. This is accomplished through the usual bodily contortions and, frequently, by lunging forward and backward and rubbing the wings against the edges of cracks or protrusions. Similar behavior was also observed by Light ('37). Using several groups of alates of both sexes taken at lights, it was found that alates would eventually die in possession of their wings when confined in a dry environment. In contrast, and even after such confinement for several hours, alates rid themselves of their wings within one to five minutes upon being released in a petri dish containing agar and decaying wood. Further, both sexes were observed to lose their wings within as little as 30 seconds after being placed in a dish containing de-alated individuals. (In similar manipulations with *Amitermes emersoni* [*Termitidae*], alates lost their wings on an agar surface which had recently been occupied by de-alated individuals.) The readiness with which these alates divested themselves of their wings in the presence of others, albeit in a suitable environment, suggests that a pheromone may be released by the de-alated forms which provokes, or at least facilitates, de-alation. Since a strict accounting of the sexes was not kept, it is possible that the female odor (either in calling or shortly before) may also stimulate this behavior in the males, or even in both sexes.

Female alates frequently assumed the calling attitude soon after alighting on vertical or horizontal surfaces. The abdomen is typically raised at an angle of about 25° from the horizontal with the tip slightly downturned and thus roughly parallel with the surface. Under the artificial conditions provided in a petri dish containing agar and wood, a single, de-alated female assumed the calling attitude many times during three days' confinement. On the third evening a winged male responded to her presence by dropping his wings and following her within one minute. These disconnected observations on *Paraneotermes* are strongly suggestive of the post-flight behavior of *Neotermes tectonae* described by Kalshoven ('30): either sex may locate a suitable nesting site where it then survives, apparently capable of attracting a mate, for some weeks or months. In species such as these where small numbers fly rather frequently over a long season,

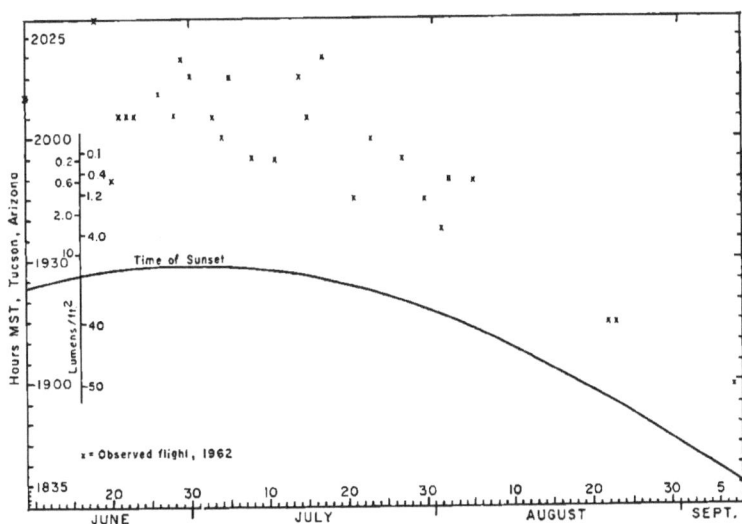

Figure 7. Relationship between observed time of flight of *Paraneotermes simplicicornis* and time of sunset in Tucson, Arizona, in 1962. Inset scale gives approximate light intensity (in lumens per square foot) in the study area on a cloudless evening early in the flight season. No flights have ever been observed earlier than 15 min. after sunset or at a light intensity greater than approximately 0.5 lumen per square foot.

the ability to survive and to attract a mate from succeeding flight periods is an obvious asset.

Alates often formed tandem pairs on walls and on pavement shortly after their arrival at lights. In situations involving several members of both sexes, de-alated pairs were soon formed and these generally left the lighted area within a half hour. This movement appeared to result from the unsuitability of the featureless pavement in the vicinity of the lights, and perhaps from a preference for more humid areas of soil nearby, for they seemed to be completely indifferent to light.

Light ('37, pp. 431 - 4) showed that colonizing pairs were able to dig into fine, damp soil, and did so in preference to wood, although they frequently dug in close to pieces of wood. In the present study, pairs isolated in petri dishes (containing 4% agar and a piece of decayed wood) readily dug into the agar and formed small cells partly in the agar and partly in the wood. These attempts to set colonies from primary pairs have been generally unsuccessful. All pairs started in dishes of agar and wood died within two months without producing any eggs. On the other hand, pairs of replacement reproductives have appeared in large laboratory subcolonies of 1000 - 2000 individuals, and these have produced dozens of eggs which hatched successfully over the course of a year or more. Colonizing pairs have been found a few hours after flights under pieces of dead wood in the study area. In the desert where the soil is hard and dry during much of the flight season, pairs may find points suitable for digging in next to, or beneath, dead wood. The sequence of post-flight behavior thus appears to bear certain similarities to that of many subterranean termites.

PREDATORS. — It has been assumed that most of the diurnal reptiles would find no opportunity for feeding on *Paraneotermes*. It was, therefore, a surprise when Asplund ('64) found 24 alates in one, and 10 in another, stomach of the tree lizard, *Urosaurus ornatus*. Such numbers suggest that the alates may have been taken at their emergence holes.

Observations in the study area and surrounding desert have established that most of the common birds have ceased their feeding activities and final vocal chorus shortly before the daily flight periods of *Paraneotermes* begin. Both Nighthawks and bats have been seen patrolling the area as early as five minutes before sunset and until no longer visible, approximately 25 minutes after sunset. Although no stomachs from any birds in the area have been examined, many stomachs of several species of bats have been carefully studied. Undetermined fragments of termite wings were found in the stomachs of three specimens of the Hoary Bat, *Lasiurus cinereus,* taken either in southern Arizona or New Mexico (Ross, '64).

DISCUSSION. — In the preceding presentation a variety of problems have arisen and possible approaches to their solutions have been suggested by the evidence at hand. A few additional questions of a more general nature are included here. During the long flight season of *Paraneotermes* there are many evenings when no flights are staged. In 1962 flights were recorded on only 29 out of 91 evenings between the inclusive dates July 9 — Sept. 7. On at least 15 of these evenings rain or moderate to strong winds occurred which are probably valid deterrents to flight. In this connection it should be worth determining the temperature limits within which the alates are capable of sustained flight. For example, on 13 evenings, the combinations of temperature and relative humidity (at sunset plus 15 minutes) were outside the range determined for a total of 49 flights in the study area (fig. 6). Allowing for a few flights which may have been missed, this still leaves 34 evenings, or over one-third of the total, when no flights took place. There are no other environmental factors which might obviously have prevented flights on these days. The most reasonable explanation which can be advanced at present — and which would also explain the long flight season characteristic of many termites — is a progressive production of alates. Evidence from the two subcolonies taken in 1961 does not support this idea, for large numbers of alates were produced within a short time, just prior to the flight season. It is still possible, however, that the pre-alates develop deep within the colony and migrate to the more superficial out posts to complete their development as the season progresses. Herfs ('51) found that *Reticulitermes lucifugus* (Rossi) (maintained in 13 large groups under constant conditions) produced alates over a period varying from 0.25 to 3.5 months.

During their flight season, and not always at the time of flight, one or more castes of the following genera in Arizona have been noticed at emergence ("observation"?) holes: *Incisitermes, Zootermopsis, Heterotermes, Amitermes* and *Gnathamitermes*. This habit, which has probably been noted by many other observers, has led to the suspicion that termites may not be so much the "dwellers in darkness" as generally believed. It further suggests that many termites may thus have considerable, and perhaps rather continuous, information on the photoperiod and other external environmental factors, either through actual openings to the outside or through the walls of superficial galleries in wood or soil. The behavior of alates, or of an entire colony, might then be readily imagined to be adjusted to the approximate frequency of one or more points in the daily photoperiod. Data on the flight behavior of *Paraneotermes* strongly suggest that the alates are initially stimulated by high temperatures, but that the daily flights may be finally triggered in response to a definite level of diminishing light intensity on otherwise favorable evenings. The flights of many termites and of several other insects have been shown to be closely correlated with dusk or to decreased light intensity (*e.g.,* Myers, '52; Bates, '49).

Field studies in progress on a variety of other termites in Arizona and Mexico are aimed at providing a basis for the comparative study of termite flight behavior. Thus far, limited experience has shown that it may be possible to resolve certain behavioral problems by the manipulation of captive colonies in the laboratory. It is anticipated that a balanced combination of field and laboratory studies may eventually permit the forecasting of both flight seasons and daily flight periods of the species within limited geographic areas.

SUMMARY. — Weather data have been collected and studied in

conjunction with field observations on 78 flights of the desert damp-wood termite, *Paraneotermes simplicicornis,* in southern Arizona. Its flight behavior is characterized by a large number of generally small flights occurring over a prolonged season and over a rather wide range of environmental conditions. Alates appear in the colonies about three weeks in advance of the flight season. As many as 31 flights have been observed in one season which may extend from late May into early September. Flights begin when weekly mean temperatures remain consistently above 23°C. They are staged during evening twilight and begin at a mean temperature of 27.6°C. (range, 23.4 — 32) and a mean relative humidity of 60.8% (range, 36 — 100). Mean saturation deficit at the start of 29 flights in one season measured 12.8 mm. Hg and ranged between 2.1 and 20.7 mm. Records clearly indicate that this termite does not begin swarming, nor stage its daily flights, in response to rainfall. Since the summer rains occur in the form of sporadic thunderstorms, the mean daily evaporation rate remains high: 0.36 inches (0.10 to 0.51) for the flight days in 1962. The sequence of post-flight behavior is described and bears certain similarities to that of subterranean termites.

REFERENCES CITED

ASPLUND, KENNETH K.
    1964. Seasonal variation in the diet of *Urosaurus ornatus* in a riparian community. Herpetologica, 20:91-94.
BATES, M.
    1949. The Natural History of Mosquitoes. Macmillan Co., New York, pp. 54-55.
CUTRIGHT, C. R.
    1927. Notes on the computing of mean temperatures for biological use. Ann. Ent. Soc. Amer., 20:255-261.
HARVEY, P. A.
    1934. The distribution and biology of the common dry-wood termite, *Kalotermes minor.* II. Life history of *Kalotermes minor,* p. 221. *In* Kofoid, C. A., *et al.* [eds.] Termites and Termite Control, 2nd ed., Univ. Calif. Press, Berkeley.
HERFS, A.
    1951. Der Schwarmflug von *Reticulitermes lucifugus* Rossi. Zeitschr. Angew. Ent., 33:69-77.
KALSHOVEN, L. G. E.
    1930. (Bionomics of *Kalotermes tectonae* Damm. as a base for its control.) Mededeel. Inst. plantenziekt., Buitenzorg, 76:1-154.
KANNOWSKI, PAUL B.
    1959. The flight activities and colony-founding behavior of bog ants in southeastern Michigan. Insectes Sociaux, 6:115-162.

LIGHT, S. F.
    1934. The southern and mountain dry-wood termites, *Kalotermes hubbardi* and *Kalotermes marginipennis*, p. 268. *In* Kofoid, C. A., *et al.* [eds.] Termites and Termite Control, 2nd ed., Univ. Calif. Press, Berkeley.
    1937. Contributions to the biology and taxonomy of *Kalotermes (Paraneotermes) simplicicornis* Banks (Isoptera). Univ. Calif. Publ. Ent., 6 :423-464.

LIGHT, S. F. AND FRANCES M. WEESNER.
    1948. Biology of Arizona termites with emphasis on swarming. Pan-Pacific Ent., 24: p. 56.

MCCLUSKEY, E. S.
    1965. Circadian rhythms in male ants of five diverse species. Science, 150:1037-1039.

MYERS, K.
    1952. Oviposition and mating behavior of the Queensland fruit-fly, *Dacus (Strumeta) tryoni* (Frogg.) and the *Solanum* fruit-fly, *Dacus (Strumeta) cacuminatus* (Hering). Australian J. Sci. Res., B, 5 :264-281.

ROSS, ANTHONY.
    1964. Ecological aspects of the food habits of some insectivorous bats. Ph.D. Thesis, Univ. Arizona, pp. 33, 35.

SELLERS, W. D., ED.
    1960. Arizona Climate. Univ. Ariz. Press, Tucson, v + 60 pp. + climatological summaries.

SNYDER, T. E.
    1954. Order Isoptera, the termites of the United States and Canada. Nat. Pest. Control Assoc., New York, Tech. Bull., pp. 38, 40.
    1961. Supplement to the annotated, subject-heading bibliography of termites, 1955 to 1960. Smithsonian Misc. Coll., 143: p. 27.
    1964. Personal communication.

TALBOT, MARY.
    1956. Flight activities of the ant *Dolichoderus (Hypoclinea) mariae* Forel. Psyche, 63 :134-139.
    1964. Nest structure and flights of the ant *Formica obscuriventris* Mayr. Animal Behaviour, 12 :154-158.

U. S. DEPARTMENT OF COMMERCE. WEATHER BUREAU.
    1962. Climatological Data, Arizona, v. 66.
    1963. Climatological Data, Arizona, v. 67.

WEESNER, FRANCES M.
    1960. Evolution and biology of termites. Ann. Rev. Ent., 5: pp. 160-162.

CHEMICAL RELEASERS OF SOCIAL BEHAVIOR.
X. AN ATTINE TRAIL SUBSTANCE IN THE VENOM OF A NON-TRAIL LAYING MYRMICINE, *DACETON ARMIGERUM* (LATREILLE)[1].

BY M. S. BLUM[2]
and
C. A. PORTOCARRERO[2, 3]

Although the poison gland secretion may provide species in several myrmicine genera with a readily available source of odor trail pheromone, this venom does not represent a highly species-specific secretion. It has been demonstrated recently that odor trails prepared from extracts of the poison gland are non-specific even among unrelated genera, although specificity may be absolute when these extracts are tested on species in the same genus (Blum and Ross, 1965). The lack of specificity of the poison gland extracts appears to be due to the fact that trace constituents, which are common to different venoms, are employed by different genera as odor trail releasers. Thus, although members of two genera may be employing different trail substances, they will follow trails prepared from each other's poison glands because their odor trail compounds are present in both venoms. Since some of the trace compounds in the venoms synthesized by unrelated trail-laying myrmicines appear to be similar, it would not be surprizing if the venom of a non-trail laying species contained a trace constituent which was the same as the odor trail pheromone employed by trail-laying members of this subfamily. The purpose of this present paper is to report on the occurrence of just such a case. *Daceton armigerum* (Latreille) a primitive member of the tribe Dacetini, contains in its venom a powerful releaser of trail following for members of three attine genera as well as for an inquiline cockroach which is associated with one of these genera.

The biology of *Daceton* has been studied in detail by Wilson (1962). *Daceton* workers hunt singly and no evidence of trail laying or recruitment was observed either in the field or in the laboratory. The large eyes of *Daceton* workers appear to endow them with

[1]This work was supported in part from two grants from the University Council on Research of Louisiana State University

[2]Department of Entomology, Louisiana State University, Baton Rouge, Louisiana.

[3]Present address: Department of Communications, Michigan State University, East Lansing, Michigan.

Manuscript received by the editor June 29, 1966.

Table 1. Response of attine species and a species of *Attaphila* to
artificial trails prepared from extracts of the poison gland of
Daceton armigerum.

Test species	No. of workers tested	No. of workers responding
Daceton armigerum	100	0
Trachymyrmex septentrionalis	100	90
Acromyrmex coronatus	100	87
Acromyrmex nr. *coronatus*	100	94
Sericomyrmex urichi	60	0
Atta texana	100	73
Atta cephalotes	100	82
Attaphila sp.	30	28

exceptional vision and they are able to pursue their prey for considerable distances (Wilson, 1962).

The two colonies of *Daceton* that Wilson studied were strictly aboreal and in no instance did he see workers move from the trees to the ground. However, in the single *Daceton* colony which we observed we noted three workers on the leaf litter adjacent to the base of their nest tree, making no apparent effort to forage on the leaves, and two other workers some distance from their colonial tree. Under the nest tree there were two small shrubs separated from the overhanging tree by at least three feet. A *Daceton* worker was resting on each shrub. These workers only could have reached these shrubs by walking across the leaf litter under their nest tree or by falling from the tree onto the shrubs. These observations suggest that under certain conditions *Daceton* workers may not be totally arboreal.

METHODS AND MATERIALS

A nest of *Daceton* was located in a large tree in a nursery at Buenos Aires, 25 kilometers south of Pucallpa, Peru, near the Rio Ucayalli. The colony consisted of three fragments in two branches of the tree. Approximately 600 workers were collected from the nest and were transported to Pucallpa for odor trail studies. Their poison glands were extracted in absolute ethanol. These ethanolic extracts were employed for preparing circular trails (Moser and Blum, 1963) and *Daceton* and *Atta cephalotes* (L.)[4] workers were tested on these trails. The living *Daceton* workers were transferred

[4]Collected at Pucallpa, Peru.

to Tingo Maria, where further artificial trail testing was performed using chloroform solutions of the *Daceton* poison glands. The following species were also tested on the trails: *Acromyrmex coronatus* (F.)[5], *Acromyrmex* nr. *coronatus* (F.)[5], and a cockroach, *Attaphila* sp.[5], which was found in the fungus garden of *A. coronatus*.

The *Daceton* workers then were frozen and packed in dry ice for air transport to the United States. Workers of *Trachymyrmex septentrionalis* (McCook)[6], *Sericomyrmex urichi* Forel[7], and *Atta texana* (Buckley)[8] were tested on artificial trails prepared from methylene chloride solutions of poison glands dissected from the frozen *Daceton* workers.

RESULTS

Although *Daceton* workers do not follow artificial trails prepared from their own poison gland secretion, these trails release strong trail following in attine members of the genera *Trachymyrmex, Acromyrmex,* and *Atta* (Table 1). On the other hand, workers of *Sericomyrmex urichi* did not follow trails prepared from the venom of *Daceton.* The concentration of the attine odor trail pheromone in the venom of *Daceton* appears to be the same as it is in the venoms of the attines. Extracts which were prepared from *Daceton* and *Atta* poison glands of equivalent size exhibited about the same odor trail potencies after serial dilution.

It is quite likely that the *Attaphila* are responding to the same compound in the venom of *Daceton* as are the attines. Moser (1965) has shown that *Attaphila fungicola* Wheeler will follow artificial trails prepared from the venom of both *A. texana* and *T. septentrionalis.* Although Moser reported that *A. texana* workers were more sensitive to the odor trail pheromone than the cockroaches, we noted that the *Attaphila* held to the artificial trails much more tenaciously than the ant workers in any of the genera.

Since *Sericomyrmex urichi* did not follow artificial trails prepared from the venom of *Daceton,* we wished to determine whether or not this attine would respond to artificial trails prepared from the poison glands of other attines and *vice versa.* Assuming that the venom of *Daceton* contains a compound which is similar to those employed by several of the attine genera as trail substances, then

[5]Collected at Tingo Maria, Peru.
[6]Collected at Baton Rouge, Louisiana.
[7]Collected at Trinidad by Prof. Neal A. Weber, Department of Biology, Swarthmore College, Swarthmore, Pa.
[8]Collected at Pineville, Louisiana.

Table 2.   Numbers of *Sericomyrmex*, *Trachymyrmex*, and *Atta* workers responding to the poison gland secretion in the artificial test. Number of replications in parentheses[9].

Test species

Source species	Sericomyrmex urichi	Trachymyrmex septentrionalis	Atta texana
Sericomyrmex urichi	78(8)	0 (8)	40(10)
Trachymyrmex septentrionalis	10(8)	90(8)	91(10)
Atta texana	0(8)	88(8)	96(10)

the failure of *Sericomyrmex* to follow *Daceton* trails would indicate that its trail pheromone was different from those of the other attines. Circular trails were prepared from extracts of the poison glands of *S. urichi*, *T. septentrionalis* and *A. texana*, and the response of workers of each species to the trails was determined. The results, presented in Table 2, demonstrate that *S. urichi* does not follow the odor trails of *A. texana* or *T. septentrionalis*. Similarly, the trail substance in the poison gland secretion of *Sericomyrmex* releases virtually no trail following in workers of *T. septentrionalis* and is only slightly active when tested with workers of *A. texana* (Table 2).

DISCUSSION

Although *Daceton armigerum* does not lay odor trails, its venom contains a substance which is either similar or identical to the trail pheromones employed by attines in the genera *Trachymyrmex*, *Acromyrmex*, and *Atta*. In all probability this substance is a trace constituent of the poison gland secretion produced by *Daceton*. The venom of *Daceton* is rich in proteins which solidify when the poison vesicle is ruptured in the air. An attine odor trail pheromone can be readily extracted from the solidified venom without a measurable weight loss occurring and it is probable that a trace component is being removed during the extraction process. Similarly, the odor trail pheromones can be extracted from the solidified attine venoms without causing any detectable weight loss in the venomous residues. The attine venoms, like that of *Daceton*, are rich in proteins but in addition, the poison gland secretions of the attines contain large series of free amino acids which cannot be detected in the venom of *Daceton*.

More evidence that the venom of *Daceton* contains an attine odor trail pheromone is derived from the fact that the *Attaphila* follow

[9]Ten workers per replicate.

the artificial *Daceton* trails. Moser (1965) has demonstrated that another cockroach species, *Attaphila fungicola,* follows artificial attine trails, and Echolls (1965) has seen this cockroach on trails of *A. texana* in the early morning (1 a.m.) Obviously these blattids can maintain a close association with their *Atta* hosts because of their ability to follow the odor trails of the ants. Thus, since members of the genus *Attaphila* appear to be following the same trail substance as the attines employ, these cockroaches would be expected to follow artificial *Daceton* trails if their venom contained an attine trail pheromone. It should be added that the *Attaphila* also follow artificial trails of both *Acromyrmex* species, as they would be expected to do.

The evidence concerning *Sericomyrmex* is also circumstantial but is equally persuasive. Previously it had been shown that there was no specificity in the trail substances produced by four attine genera which encompassed the broad phylogenetic spectrum of the tribe Attini (Blum et al., 1964). Since these attines follow each other's odor trails, then they would be expected to follow the artificial *Daceton* trails if these trails contained a substance which was chemically similar to their apparently common odor trail pheromones. On the other hand, if an attine produced a trail substance which was different from the one being employed by these several attine genera, then this attine would respond neither to the artificial trails of these other attine genera nor to the *Daceton* trail. *Sericomyrmex urichi* is the first member of an attine genus which has been shown not to respond to the artificial trails prepared from the poison gland secretions of other attine genera. Weber (1966) considers *Sericomyrmex* a somewhat aberrant member of the higest genera and it is certainly distinguished from at least two of the other higher attine genera by this apparent employment of a different trace constituent as an odor trail pheromone.

The other gland associated with the sting, Dufour's gland, also has been shown to be an unexpected source of a myrmicine trail pheromone. Wilson and Pavan (1959) reported that the Dufour's gland secretion of the dolichoderine *Monacis bispinosa* (Olivier) contained a powerful trail substance for the fire ant *Solenopsis saevissima* (Fr. Smith) which produces its trail substance in Dufour's gland. However, *M. bispinosa* synthesizes its own trail pheromone in Pavan's gland, a special organ which lies on the sixth abdominal sternite. Thus the function of the Dufour's gland secretion in *M. bispinosa* is completely unknown but it is obviously not employed for laying odor trails. It seems eveident that *M. bispinosa,* like *Daceton,* produces some natural products in its sting-associated glands which are also produced by members of the Myrmicinae. It is not unlikely that the natural products' chemistry of the glands associated with the ant sting will continue to be characterized by the presence of common products, some of which are employed as trail substances. Under these circumstances we may anticipate that the Formicidae will continue to be a rich source of unsuspected trail substances whose specificities will be at best, unpredictable.

SUMMARY

Artificial trails prepared from the poison gland of *Daceton armigerum* (Latreille), a myrmicine which does not lay odor trails, cause trail following in attine species in the genera *Trachymyrmex, Acromyrmex,* and *Atta.* An inquiline cockroach, *Attaphila* sp., also follows trails prepared from the venom of *Daceton.* The poison gland secretion of *Daceton* apparently contains a trace constituent which is similar or identical to the odor trail pheromone used by these attine genera. An attine species in the genus *Sericomyrmex* responds neither to artificial *Daceton* trails nor the odor trail pheromones of *Atta* or *Trachymyrmex.*

REFERENCES

BLUM, M. S., J. C. MOSER, and A. D. CORDERO.
    1964. Chemical releasers of social behavior. II. Source and specificity of the odor trail substances in four attine genera. (Hymenoptera: Formicidae). *Psyche* 71: 1-7.
BLUM, M. S. and G. N. ROSS.
    1965. Chemical releasers of social behaviour. V. Source, specificity and properties of the odour trail pheromone of *Tetramorium guineense* (F.). Formicidae: Myrmicinae). *J. Insect Physiol.* 11: 857-868.
ECHOLLS, W. H.
    1965. Private communication.
MOSER, J. C.
    1964. Inquiline roach responds to trail-marking substance of leaf-cutting ants. *Science* 143: 1048-1049.
MOSER, J. C. and M. S. BLUM.
    1963. Source and potency of the trail marking substance of the Texas leaf-cutting ant. *Science* 140: 1228.
WEBER, N. A.
    1966. Private communication.
WILSON, E. O.
    1962. Behavior of *Daceton armigerum* (Latreille) with a classification of self-grooming movements in ants. *Bull. Mus. Comp. Zool.* 127: 403-421.
WILSON, E. O. and M. PAVAN.
    1959. Glandular sources and specificity of some chemical releasers of social behavior in dolichoderine ants. *Psyche* 66: 70-76.

CAMBRIDGE ENTOMOLOGICAL CLUB

A regular meeting of the Club is held on the second Tuesday of each month October through May at 7:30 p. m. in Room B-455, Biological Laboratories, Divinity Ave., Cambridge. Entomologists visiting the vicinity are cordially invited to attend.

The illustration on the front cover of this issue of Psyche is a reproduction of a drawing of a female bethylid wasp, *Pseudiso-brachium terresi* Mann, from Haiti (Psyche, vol. 22, p. 165, 1915).

BACK VOLUMES OF PSYCHE

The Johnson Reprint Corporation, 111 Fifth Avenue, New York 3, N. Y., has been designated the exclusive agents for Psyche, volumes 1 through 62. Requests for information and orders for such volumes should be sent directly to the Johnson Reprint Corporation.

Copies of issues in volumes 63-72 are obtainable from the editorial offices of Psyche. Volumes 63-72 are $5.00 each.

F. M. Carpenter
Editorial Office, Psyche,
16 Divinity Avenue,
Cambridge, Mass., 02138.

FOR SALE

CLASSIFICATION OF INSECTS, by C. T. Brues, A. L. Melander and F. M. Carpenter. Published in March, 1954, as volume 108 of the Bulletin of the Museum of Comparative Zoology, with 917 pages and 1219 figures. It consists of keys to the living and extinct families of insects, and to the living families of other terrestrial arthropods; and includes 270 pages of bibliographic references and an index of 76 pages. Price $9.00 (cloth bound and postpaid). Send orders to Museum of Comparative Zoology, Harvard College, Cambridge, Mass. 02138.

PSYCHE

A JOURNAL OF ENTOMOLOGY

Vol. 73   September, 1966   No. 3

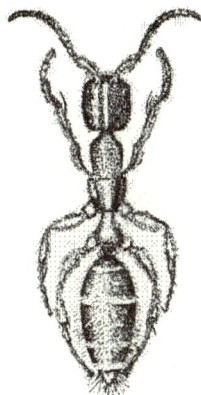

CONTENTS

PSYCHE is published quarterly by the Cambridge Entomological Club, the issues appearing in March, June, September and December. Subscription price, per year, payable in advance: $4.50 to Club members, $5.00 to all other subscribers. Single copies, $1.25.

Checks and remittances should be addressed to Treasurer, Cambridge Entomological Club, 16 Divinity Avenue, Cambridge, Mass.

Orders for back volumes, missing numbers, notices of change of address, etc., should be sent to the Editorial Office of Psyche, Biological Laboratories, Harvard University, Cambridge, Mass.

IMPORTANT NOTICE TO CONTRIBUTORS

Manuscripts intended for publication should be addressed to Professor F. M. Carpenter, Biological Laboratories, Harvard University, Cambridge, Mass.

Authors contributing articles over 4 printed pages in length may be required to bear a part of the extra expense, for additional pages. This expense will be that of typesetting only, which is about $10.00 per page. The actual cost of preparing cuts for all illustrations must be borne by contributors: the cost for full page plates from line drawings is ordinarily $12.00 each, and the full page half-tones, $18.00 each; smaller sizes in proportion.

AUTHOR'S SEPARATES

Reprints of articles may be secured by authors, if they are ordered at the time proofs are received for corrections. A statement of their cost will be furnished by the Editor on application.

The June, 1966 Psyche (Vol. 73, no. 2) was mailed October 21, 1966.

THE LEXINGTON PRESS. INC., LEXINGTON, MASSACHUSETTS

PSYCHE

Vol. 73   September, 1966   No. 3

THREE NEW SPECIES OF *ACCOLA*
(ARANEAE, DIPLURIDAE)
FROM COSTA RICA AND TRINIDAD, W. I.*

By Arthur M. Chickering
Museum of Comparative Zoology

The genus *Accola* Simon was established in 1889 on the basis of an immature specimen of *A. lucifuga* Simon from Venezuela. During the next thirty-six years eight additional species were recognized. Three of these were from Luzon and New Guinea and all were described from females alone. The remaining five were from St. Vincent, W. I., Panama, Chile and Venezuela. Two of these, one from Venezuela and one from Panama, were described from immature individuals. The remaining three species were all described from females alone. In 1945 I was able to describe the male of *A. spinosa* Petrunkevitch together with mature females. In 1964 I was able to describe both sexes of *A. petrunkevitchi* from Puerto Rico and both sexes of *A. lewisi* from Jamaica, W. I. During the past few months I have been able to recognize a new species of this genus taken in a recent collection in Costa Rica and two new species in a collection made in Trinidad, W. I. in April, 1964. These last-mentioned three species are described in the following pages of this brief paper. The present status of the Genus *Accola* Simon, 1889 may, therefore, be stated as follows: fourteen species are now recognized; six of these are known from both sexes; two are known only from immature specimens; the remaining six species are known only from females. I think it safe to predict that numerous additional species will become known as soon as careful collecting is carried out in South America and the West Indies. The greater portion of my collection of this genus has come from weed and hay debris with leaf debris considerably less productive.

All specimens relating to the new species described in this paper will be deposited in the Museum of Comparative Zoology at Harvard University. In my study of the genus *Accola* I have noted irregu-

---

Manuscript received by the editor February 24, 1966.

larities in the outline of certain of the eyes; there seem to be differences in the relative positions of certain of the eyes in some individuals and, apparently, noticeable differences in size of corresponding eyes in certain individuals. When eyes are oval in outline, as they usually appear, the long axis is used in measurements.

The collections from Costa Rica and Trinidad, W. I. from which the three new species of *Accola* were obtained were made possible by Grant GB-1801 from the National Science Foundation. My gratitude and appreciation are also again expressed for the privilege of working in the Museum of Comparative Zoology at repeated intervals over a period of many years. Publication and library privileges together with continued encouragement from directors and staff members have been indispensable for the continuation of my studies.

Genus *Accola* Simon, 1889
Accola downeyi sp. nov.
Figures 1-5

The species is named after Dr. John C. Downey, Professor of Zoology, Southern Illinois University, Carbondale, Illinois.

Male holotype. Total length from clypeus to posterior end of abdomen 3.9 mm; from anterior border of porrect chelicerae to posterior end of abdomen 4.29 mm. Carapace 1.67 mm long; 1.32 mm wide opposite second coxae where it is widest; .44 mm tall; dorsal striae moderately well developed; dorsal median fovea a well defined pit opposite third coxae; stiff bristles along broad posterior border as usual in the genus; with a recurved row of stiff bristles shortly behind the median fovea; with numerous hairs and stiff bristles elsewhere. Eyes: six only; essentially as in *A. lewisi* Chickering, 1964 from Jamaica, W. I.; all compactly grouped on a low tubercle (Fig. 1); viewed from above, posterior row strongly recurved as usual; all eyes white; ratio of eyes ALE : PME : PLE = 11 : 5 : 11. ALE separated from one another by a little less than one fourth of their diameter; PLE separated from one another behind by slightly less than their diameter; PME separated from one another by about 3/10 of their diameter and from PLE by about one fifth of their diameter. Chitinized clypeus almost non-existent; membranous region below chitinized portion quite conspicuous. Chelicerae: paraxial, parallel, porrect as usual in the genus; fairly robust; with a well developed coat of stiff bristles; fang long, slender, evenly curved; promargin of fang groove with a row of ten teeth; a cluster of very minute teeth, irregularly arranged along the obscure retromargin opposite the last four promarginal teeth (teeth observed on a para-

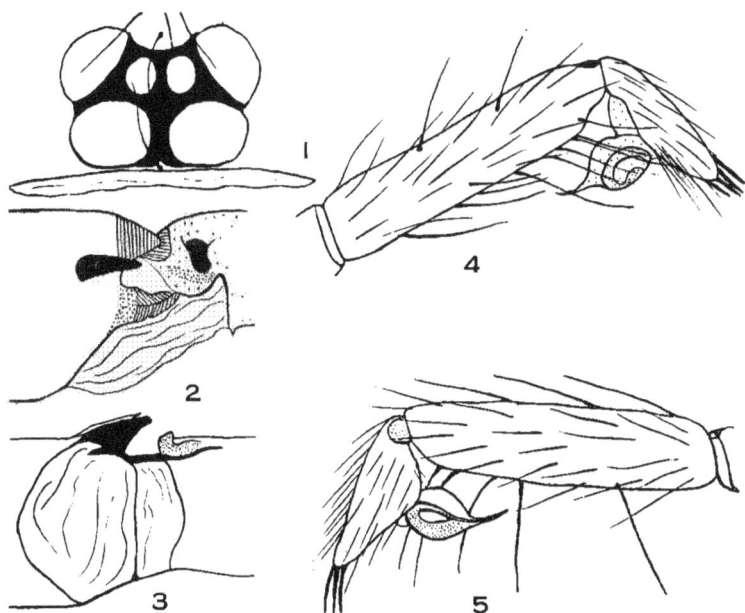

Figs. 1-5. *Accola downeyi* sp. nov. Fig. 1. Eyes of male as seen from above. Figs. 2-3. Spines and associated parts at articulation of first tibia and metatarsus of male holotype; prolateral and ventral views, respectively. Figs. 4-5. Left palpal tibia and tarsus of male holotype; prolateral and retrolateral views, respectively.

type to avoid injury to fragile holotype); retromargin with a well developed scopula of long, slender hairs or bristles. Lip and sternum: essentially typical of the genus. Legs: 4123; tibial index of first leg 10, of fourth leg 12. Spines: all legs bear numerous spines essentially as described for *A. petrunkevitchi* Chickering, 1964 from Puerto Rico; special spines or cusps at articulation of first tibiae and metatarsi shown in Figures 2-3; numerous trichobothria observed on tibiae, metatarsi and tarsi. Palp: essential features shown in Figures 4-5; coxa with a rudimentary maxillary lobe. Abdomen and color in alcohol: both essentially as described for *A. spinosa* Petrunkevitch (1945); anterior spinnerets very fragile.

Female paratype. Total length from clypeus to posterior end of abdomen 5.33 mm; from distal end of porrect chelicerae to posterior end of abdomen 5.92 mm. Carapace 2.05 mm long; 1.52 mm wide opposite second coxae where it is widest; .61 mm tall; otherwise essentially as in male. Eyes: six; essentially as in male. Chelicerae: in general as in male holotype; promargin of fang groove with eleven small but clearly defined teeth; the cluster of very minute teeth along obscure retromargin has about 19 or 20 in the group. Lip and sternum: essentially as in male holotype. Legs: 4123; tibial index of first and fourth legs 12; spines essentially as in male; trichobothria observed on tarsi, metatarsi, tibiae and patellae as well as on palpal segments; palpal claw finely dentate. Abdomen: typical of females of the genus; second pair of lungs clearly delineated. Epigynum: with a well defined plate; posterior margin procurved; typical of females of the genus.

Type locality. The male holotype and the described female paratype are from Turrialba, Costa Rica, July 25 to August 15, 1965. Four male paratypes and about three dozen females and immature specimens were taken in the same general locality and during the same period. In 1945 when I described the mature male and mature female of *A. spinosa* Petrunkevitch I also had a few mature females from Boquete, Panama with only six eyes. These six-eyed specimens were then regarded as deviates of *A. spinosa* Petrunkevitch as explained in a footnote, page 1. Since that time numerous females and three mature males from Boquete and El Volcan, Panama have been collected. These are all six-eyed and agree well with my specimens of *Accola downeyi* sp. nov. For this reason they are, therefore, transferred to this species.

Accola simla sp. nov.
Figures 6-8

The name of the species is a noun used in apposition after the type locality.

Male holotype. Total length from clypeus to posterior end of abdomen 3.38 mm; from anterior border of porrect chelicerae to posterior end of abdomen 3.64 mm. Carapace 1.52 mm long; 1.1 mm wide opposite second coxae where it is widest; 0.4 mm tall; other features typical of males of the genus. Eyes: eight essentially as in *A. petrunkevitchi* Chickering from Puerto Rico; all arranged on a low tubercle (Fig. 6); viewed from above, posterior row strongly recurved; AME dark and difficult to distinguish; all others white; ratio of eyes AME : ALE : PME : PLE = 2 : 11 : 6.5 : 10.5; AME separated from one another by about their diameter; only slightly separated from ALE; ALE separated from one another in front by about one sixth of their diameter; PME separated from one another by about one sixth of their diameter; PME separated

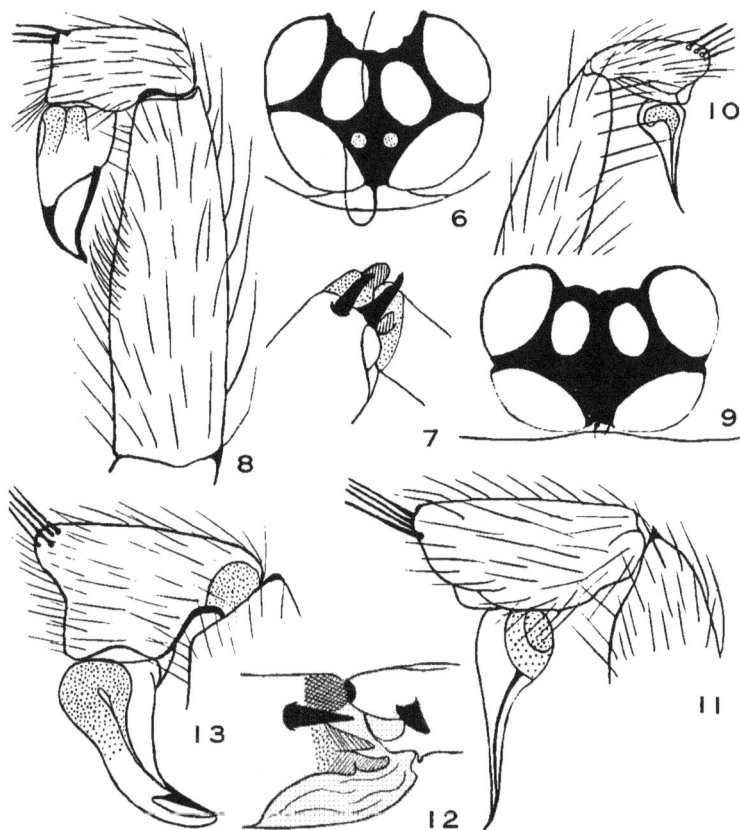

Figs. 6-8. *Accola simla* sp. nov. Fig. 6. Eyes of male holotype as seen from above. Fig. 7. Spines and associated parts at articulation of first left tibia and metatarsus of male holotype; prolateral view. Fig. 8. Left palpal tibia and tarsus of male holotype; retrolateral view.

Figs. 9-11. *Accola barona* sp. nov. Fig. 9. Eyes of male holotype as seen from above. Figs. 10-11. Left palpal tibia and tarsus of male holotype; prolateral and retrolateral views, respectively.

Figs. 12-13. *Accola spinosa* Pet. Fig. 12. Spines and associated parts at articulation of first left tibia and metatarsus of male; prolateral view. Fig. 13. Left palpal tibia and tarsus; retrolateral view.

from PLE by about one fourth of their diameter; PLE separated from one another behind by about four fifths of their diameter. Chitinized height of clypeus very low and irregular; membranous portion much higher. Chelicerae paraxial, parallel, porrect as usual in the genus; fairly robust; with a well developed supply of stiff bristles; fang long, slender, evenly curved; promargin of fang groove with a row of ten small teeth; along the obscure retromargin, as seen on a paratype, is a row of about 7-8 very minute denticles; retromargin with a well developed scopula of long, slender hair or bristles. Lip and sternum: essentially typical of the genus. Legs: 4⋅12=3; tibial index of first and fourth legs 11. Spines: all legs bear numerous spines essentially typical of the genus; special spines at articulation of first tibiae and metatarsi shown in Figure 7; the most ventral of the tibial spines is probably divided but the two parts are so closely apposed that they appear as one. Palp: essential features shown in Figure 8; bulb terminates in two spines. Abdomen: typical of the genus; with a heavy coat of dark hair. Color in alcohol: as usual in the genus; a unicolorous yellowish.

Female paratype. Total length of female paratype, selected for description, from clypeus to posterior end of abdomen 4.03 mm; from anterior border of porrect chelicerae to posterior end of abdomen 4.42 mm. Carapace 1.78 mm long; 1.32 mm wide; .45 mm tall; otherwise essentially as in male. Eyes: essentially as in male. Chelicerae: promargin of fang groove with nine small teeth; retromargin with about eleven minute denticles somewhat irregularly arranged; otherwise essentially as in male. Lip and sternum: essentially typical of the genus. Legs: 4132; tibial index of first and fourth legs 12; spines on legs essentially as usual in the genus. Abdomen: typical of females of the genus; with the usual heavy coat of hairs. Epigynum: with the usual swollen plate, typical of females of the genus. Color in alcohol: as in male.

Type locality. Male holotype and female paratype selected for description taken at Simla, Arima Valley, Trinidad, W. I., April 15th, and 11th, 1964, respectively. Fourteen male paratypes and several dozens of what are believed to be females and immature specimens belonging to this species were taken in same general locality from March 31st to April 26th, 1964.

Accola barona sp. nov.
Figures 9-11

The name of the species is an arbitrary combination of letters. *Male holotype.* Total length from anterior border of ALE to posterior end of abdomen 3.71; from anterior border of porrect chelicerea to posterior end of abdomen 3.9 mm. Carapace: 1.69 mm long; 1.21 mm wide opposite second coxae where it is widest; .34 mm tall; slightly the highest just behind median thoracic pit; other features typical of the genus. Eyes: six only; no traces of the AME observed; viewed from above, posterior row quite strongly recurved; all six eyes white; ratio of eyes ALE : PME : PLE = 10.5 : 5 : 9; ALE separated from one another by about one fifth of their long axis; PME separated from one another by about 3/10 of their long axis and separated from PLE by somewhat less than this; PLE separated from one another behind by a little less than their long axis. Height of clypeus equal to about 1/7 of the long axis of ALE. Chelicerae: essentially as described for *A. simla* sp. nov.; teeth and denticles along fang groove seem to be much as in *A. simla* sp. nov. but they have not been closely observed because of the fragility of the holotype and absence of male paratypes. Lip and sternum: essentially typical of the genus. Legs: 41?23; tibial index of fourth leg 12. Spines: ordinary spines on legs appear typical of the genus; first legs missing and, hence, no record possible in respect to the special spines at articulation of first tibiae and metatarsi. Palp: essential features shown in Figures 10-11. Abdomen: typical of males of the genus. Color in alcohol: as usual, unicolorous yellowish throughout.

Female paratype. Total length of female paratype selected for description 4.23 mm from clypeus to posterior end of abdomen; from anterior border of porrect chelicerae to posterior end of abdomen 4.68 mm. Carapace 1.63 mm long; 1.17 mm wide opposite second coxae where it is widest; about .46 mm tall; other features as usual in females of the genus. Eyes: six as in male holotype; ratio of eyes ALE : PME : PLE = 8 : 4 : 6.5; other features essentially as in male holotype. Chelicerae: general features as usual in the genus; the second female shows promargin of fang groove with about twelve teeth, those in 11th and 12th places the largest; the retromargin has a well developed scopula and a row of a dozen or more very minute denticles irregularly arranged. Legs: 412=3; tibial index of first leg 11, of fourth leg 12; with many spines as usual; tarsal claws finely and multidentate. Abdomen: as usual in the genus. Epigynum: with the usual somewhat thickened plate and the procurved posterior border. Color in alcohol: unicolorous yellowish as usual.

Type locality. Male holotype and described female paratype together with one additional somewhat damaged female all taken from grass and weed debris in the immediate vicinity of the William Beebe Tropical Research Station, Simla, Arima Valley, Trinidad, W. I., April 23, 1964.

Accola spinosa Petrunkevitch
Figures 12-13

As pointed out in the last paragraph of my description of *A. downeyi* sp. nov., all six-eyed specimens now in my collection of the genus *Accola* from Boquete and El Volcan, Panama are transferred to *A. downeyi* sp. nov.

Since the publication of my paper on this species in 1945 I have collected a large number of both sexes in the Panama Canal Zone and, especially, on Barro Colorado Island. Females as expected, far outnumber males. In order to make the distinction clearer between this species and other eight-eyed forms such as *A. petrunkevitchi* Chickering from Puerto Rico and *A. simla* sp. nov. from Trinidad I am including Figures 12-13. Special attention is directed to Figure 12 which shows the division of the most ventral of the spines at the distal end of the first tibia. This division was noted in my 1945 description. There is some variation in the appearance of these spines among males of this species; apparently in some specimens the two spines overlap to such an extent as to obscure one of them. Disarticulation of the first tibia and metatarsus reveals the division more clearly.

SELECTED BIBLIOGRAPHY

BONNET, P.
    1955. Bibliographia Araneorum. Toulouse, Vol. 2 (2).
CHICKERING, ARTHUR M.
    1945. Hypotypes of *Accola spinosa* Petrunkevitch (Dipluridae) from Panama. Trans. Connecticut Acad. Arts and Sciences, 36: 159-167.
    1964. Two New Species of the Genus Accola (Araneae, Dipluridae). Psyche, 71(4): 174-180.
PETRUNKEVITCH, A.
    1925. Arachnida from Panama. Trans. Connecticut Acad. Arts and Sciences, 27: 51-248.
ROEWER, C. FR.
    1942. Katalog der Araneae. 1: 1-1040.
SIMON, EUGENE
    1892- Histoire naturelle des Araignées. Deuxième Edition.
    1903. 2. Librarie Encyclopédique de Roret, Paris.

DISTRIBUTION AND BIOLOGY OF THE PRIMITIVE DRY-WOOD TERMITE PTEROTERMES OCCIDENTIS (WALKER) (KALOTERMITIDAE)[1]

By W. L. Nutting

Department of Entomology, University of Arizona, Tucson

This summary of recent studies on *Pterotermes* is part of an irregular series of contributions to the biology and ecology of the relatively rich termite fauna of southwestern North America. The fact that such a large and primitive termite has been known from about a dozen rather poorly documented collections is indicative of the need for such knowledge in this rapidly developing region. Indeed, very little additional information on this species has beeen published since the important summary by Banks and Snyder in 1920. Most of the 25 new records have been accumulated by members, students and friends of the Department of Entomology at the University of Arizona, largely within the last ten years. The most extensive additions were made during a trip through Baja California in the late summer of 1959 by Floyd G. Werner and Keith W. Radford. Their almost nightly collections of this termite in a light trap indicate that their schedule must have coincided closely with the peak of the flight season. Although most of the records consist of alates taken in light traps, in seven instances one or more colonies have been found which have added much new biological information.

DISTRIBUTION. This species has long been included in the large, cosmopolitan genus, *Kalotermes*. On the basis of careful morphological and taxonomic considerations, Krishna (1961) removed it to a previous place in the genus *Pterotermes*. Because of its probable key position in arising directly from ancestral kalotermitids and its apparent rarity, all readily available records have been brought together in Table 1 and plotted in Figure 1. Those in Mexico, particularly from the generally unfamiliar geography of Baja California, have been numbered to facilitate their location.

The distribution is thus found to conform closely to the Sonoran Desert as it has been delimited on the basis of the vegetation. A few marginal localities in southeastern Arizona and southern Baja California might be considered as local extensions of the region. A brief characterization of this, the richest of the four areas comprising the

[1]Arizona Agricultural Experiment Station Journal Article No. 1149.
Manuscript received by the editor June 22, 1966

North American Desert, is pertinent to the discussions which follow. The physical features, vegetation and flora of this desert have been well reviewed by Shreve (1951). The Sonoran Desert lies in a region of plains, hills and mountains, and extends in elevation from approximately 3500 feet in eastern Arizona and northern Sonora to sea level on the coasts of Sonora and Baja California, and to below sea level in the vicinity of the Salton Sea in southern California. The Colorado River is the only permanently flowing stream in the entire region. A fairly uniform, continental type of climate prevails, in which the temperature varies from some of the highest records for North America to occasionally heavy frosts in the northern and eastern sections. Annual rainfall generally increases in amount from west to east, with less than 5 inches falling in the lower Colorado Valley and much of Baja California to slightly more than 15 inches in eastern Arizona and Sonora. The seasonal distribution of rainfall also varies importantly, with the extreme western areas receiving virtually all of their moisture during the winter from December to March. Going eastward the pattern shifts so that the eastern borders of the desert receive their major rainfall during a well-defined summer season from July to September.

In Arizona where more precise information is available, *Ptero-termes* has been found from approximately 4000 feet on the lower slopes of a few mountain ranges, across the bajadas and onto the adjacent valley floors. It is apparently restricted to the more open foothills and bajadas rather than to the recesses of deep canyons. Here it is found in the larger woody plants of the desert scrub or spinose desert plant communities (Figs. 2 and 3). It is hardly necessary to point out that nearly all the collections from Baja California have been made in the lower, less rugged areas which are more readily accessible, either by sea or by the few passable roads over the peninsula.

Emerson (1955) has mentioned that temperature and moisture are the major physical factors limiting termite dispersal, largely by their effects in determining vegetation types. *Pterotermes* is a primitive, monotypic genus, apparently endemic to the hot, dry Sonoran Desert. Although almost pure speculation, it may be of interest to suggest that *Pterotermes* is so restricted not so much by high temperature and low moisture as by the higher rainfall of the surrounding regions. Approximately 12 vigorous and healthy colonies have been personally examined in extremely desiccated wood. A single large colony was completely removed from a dead palo verde tree in February, 1966, after a series of unusually heavy rains. This colony contained a high percentage of individuals which had apparently succumbed in large terminal chambers to drowning and attack by fungi, bacteria, or both.

There is also limited evidence that *Pterotermes* may occupy a very narrow niche in this region where it only rarely comes into contact with other dry-wood termites. Two colonies have been found in wood previously or concurrently attacked by *Marginitermes hubbardi* (Banks). *Marginitermes* is itself a rather primitive, monotypic genus which is endemic to the southwestern United States and western Mexico. However, from the above evidence and wider field experience with the latter, it is my impression that *Pterotermes* is able to occupy even hotter and dryer situations than *Marginitermes*.

Comparative studies on water loss and cuticular structure (Collins and Richards, 1966) should provide a basis for explaining the adaptations of various species of termites to their particular environments. Indeed, Collins (1966, *in litt.*) has found that older and larger nymphs of *Pterotermes* have a comparatively low rate of water loss. She feels that the cuticular cement layer, which is particularly well developed in these forms, may be largely responsible for the ability of this species to conserve water and, hence, to occupy the severely dry environment of the Sonoran Desert.

As a result of very inadequate collecting there are a few broad discontinuities in the distribution. Further field work should be conducted to determine whether or not this termite has an essentially uninterrupted distribution generally within the Sonoran Desert. It may actually be absent over many of the intermont plains which are dominated by smaller and lower plants such as *Larrea* and *Franseria*. However, it is a strong flier and may well be able to cross narrowed valleys between adjacent mountain ranges — if not in one generation, then in several by way of relatively isolated trees and cacti, essentially as in island-hopping. After all, it does occupy a region where hosts are of necessity very widely spaced.

HOST TREES AND NESTING SITE. According to the meager records, *Pterotermes* has thus far been recorded nesting in the dead wood of only three plants: in the ribbed, woody skeletons of the giant or saguaro cactus, *Cereus giganteus* Engelm. (Fig. 2); one species of the green-stemmed palo verde tree, *Cercidium floridum* Benth.; and in the dead, flowering stalk of the non-arborescent Spanish bayonet, *Yucca Whipplei* Torr.

In the foothill areas of the Santa Rita Range Reserve and south of Oracle Jct., several colonies were discovered in dead palo verdes of this species from which the bark had long since slipped off. A

TABLE 1. Distributional and flight data for *Pterotcrmes occidcntis*. Localities in Mexico are numbered for reference on map in figure 1.

LOCALITY	ELEVATION	DATE	NO. TAKEN IN FLIGHT	COLLECTOR OR REFERENCE
ARIZONA: COCHISE CO.				
"near Douglas"	ca. 4000'			Light, '29
PINAL CO.				
B. Thompson Arboretum (+ mi. W. Superior)	2400'	VIII-6-55	2	B. Benson
Oracle Jct, 3 mi. S, Hwy. 80-89	3200'		Colony	J. M. Nelson
PIMA CO.				
Sta. Rita Range Res. (10 mi. SE Sahuarita)	3600'	III-21-66	6 Colonies	W. L. Nutting
Sabino Can., Sta. Catalina Mts.	ca. 2800'	I-7-17	Colony	Banks and Snyder, '20
	2800'	VII-26-48	3	F. Werner, W. Nutting
Oracle Jct, 8 mi. S, Hwy 80-89	3000'	III-26-65	2 Colonies	R. Rush, W. Nutting
Tucson Mts., N. Slope	2450'	III-5-61	Colony	F. G. Werner
Tucson Mts., W. Slope (Desert Museum)	2800'	VIII-28-55	3	G. Butler, F. Werner
		VIII-1-16-62	1-45	W. Nutting, S. Oman
Coyote Mts.		VIII-4-7-17	"flights"	Banks and Snyder, '20
Baboquivari Mts.		VIII-7-9-17	"flights"	Banks and Snyder, '20
Baboquivari Can., Baboquivari Mts.	3550'	VII-17-49	4	F. Werner, W. Nutting
Ajo, 15 mi. S	1760'	VIII-24-49	4	F. Werner, W. Nutting
Alamo Wash, Organ Pipe Cactus Nat. Mon.	1960'	III-7-64	Colony	J. F. Burger
Ajo Mts., W. slope	2400'	II-15-59	Colony	F. G. Werner

TABLE 1. (Continued)

LOCALITY	ELEVATION	DATE	NO. TAKEN IN FLIGHT	COLLECTOR OR REFERENCE
MEXICO: SONORA				
1 Guaymas, 5 mi. N		VIII-16-59	Colony	F. Werner, W. Nutting
"Westkuste von Centroamerika"			Colony	Hagen, 1858
BAJA CALIFORNIA DEL NORTE				
2 Can. del Tajo, E. slope Sierra Juarez (ca. 30 mi. S. Rumorosa)	ca. 3000'	III-30-53	Colony	J. A. Powell, '66
3 San Felipe	ca. 30'	VIII-23-59	2	F. Werner, K. Radford
4 I. Angel de la Guarda				Banks and Snyder, '20
5 I. San Esteban		IV-19-20-21	Colony	Light, '33
6 Mezquital	ca. 1600'	VIII-25-59	8	F. Werner, K. Radford
7 Puerto de Sto. Domingo (S.D. Landing)		VI-1-27	Colony	Light, '29
BAJA CALIFORNIA DEL SUR				
8 Bahia San Bartolomé		VI-1-3-25	Colony	Light, '33
9 San Ignacio, + mi. W	ca. 300'	VIII-26-59	2	F. Werner, K. Radford
10 Mulegé, 1 mi. S		VIII-27-59	+	F. Werner, K. Radford
11 Canipole, 10 mi. SW		VIII-28-59	3+	F. Werner, K. Radford
12 I. Cármen, Bahia Marquer		V-23-21	Colony	Light, '33
13 I. Monserrate		V-24-21	Colony	Light, '33
14 I. San José				Krishna, '61
15 Pénjamo, 22 mi. NW	ca. 200'	VIII-29-59	26	F. Werner, K. Radford
16 La Paz, 25 mi. W	ca. 300'	VIII-30, IX-1	34, 8	F. Werner, K. Radford
17 La Paz		XII-28	Colony	Light, '29
18 Todos Santos, + mi. N		IX-2-59	448	F. Werner, K. Radford
19 Santiago, 6 mi. SW	ca. 450'	VIII-31-59	+	F. Werner, K. Radford
20 Santa Rosa				Snyder, '66, in litt.
21 San José del Cabo, 10 mi. SW	ca. 100'	IX-1-59	Colony	F. Werner, K. Radford
22 Cabo San Lucas			2	Banks and Snyder, '20

few colonies were also noted in dead branches, down to one inch in diameter, on living trees in the same areas. An incipient colony was found by George Hofer in the sapwood of a dead palo verde (*Cercidium* sp.?) in Sabino Canyon (Banks and Snyder, 1920). The fairly large colony from Guaymas, Sonora, was from a short branch, one inch in diameter, on a living palo verde (species?). Burger took a very large colony in a fragment of palo verde (species?) trunk, about six feet long and 10-12 inches in diameter, partly buried in the sand of Alamo Wash. A colony in a "palo verde stump" was sampled by C. C. Lamb at La Paz, Baja California del Sur (Light, 1929).

There are three or four species of *Cercidium,* one or more of which are very abundant and characteristic trees in various parts of the Sonoran Desert. In the Arizona Upland, and probably elsewhere in their ranges, *C. floridum* is more abundant on upper bajadas and along drainageways, while *C. microphyllum* prefers hills, outwash slopes and plains. There seems to be no reason why *Pterotermes* should not utilize the wood of all these species wherever they occur.

In the Tucson Mts. Werner collected specimens from a colony in a disintegrating saguaro skeleton. The only other association with this wood was the small colony in a single rib, about one inch in diameter and a few feet long, found on the open desert floor in the Ajo Mts., also by Werner. *Cereus giganteus* is prominent over most of the Arizona Upland and the Plains of Sonora, but it is absent from the Foothills of Sonora and Baja California. Extensive collecting has been done in southern Arizona for termites and other xylophagous insects for many years. Since *Pterotermes* has not been found in any other wood (mesquite, *Prosopis juliflora,* and ironwod, *Olneya tesota,* for example) it is not improbable that the palo verdes and saguaro provide the most suitable nesting sites in this part of the desert.

In the remaining subdivisions of the Sonoran Desert, however, there is a different and even wider selection of woody plants which should be searched for *Pterotermes;* for example, the dead skeletons of other large, columnar cacti in the genera *Cereus* and *Pachycereus.* The only additional host data accompany the collection made by J. A. Powell from Canyon del Tajo, Sierra Juarez, in northern Baja California. "These specimens were taken in dry (1952) flowering stalks of *Yucca whipplei* on the trail down into the canyon probably at an elevation of about 3000 feet." Powell also added that "I have subsequently examined stalks of this host over a wide range in California from perhaps 40 or 50 localities in connection

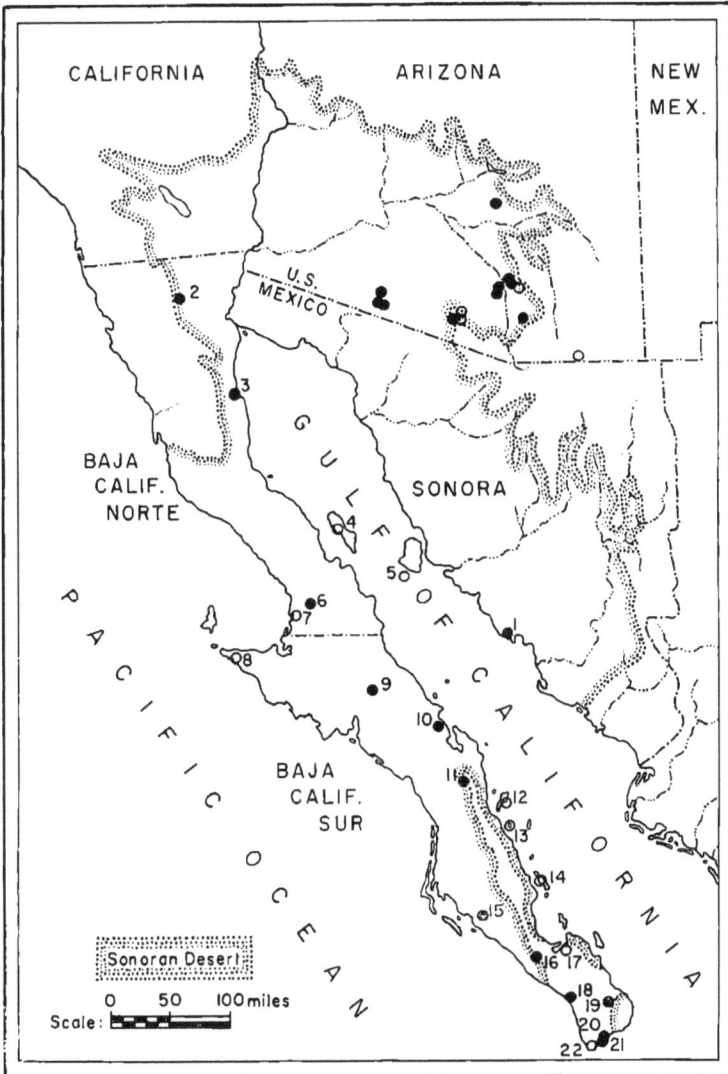

Figure 1. Map of the Sonoran Desert showing distribution of *Pterotermes occidentis:* open circles, previous records; solid circles, new records. See Table 1 for key to numbered localities in Mexico.

with studies of the moths associated with it and have never seen termites in the stalks elsewhere" (Powell, 1966, *in litt.*). A collection of nymphs was taken "in Yucca" by C. C. Lamb at Santo Domingo Landing, Baja California del Sur (Light, 1929). The fibrous or pithy tissues of yuccas would seem to be a rather unusual situation for the nest of a dry-wood termite.

The haphazard system of tunnels and chambers made by a colony of approximately 3000 individuals is shown in the longitudinal section of a dead palo verde in figure 4 B. In this and in one other standing palo verde, the colony had penetrated wood a few inches below ground level. The rough-surfaced galleries of *Pterotermes* could not be mistaken for those of any other termite in the desert. Although in a quite different environment, the workings of a large colony are nearly as large and extensive as those of *Zootermopsis* (Nutting, 1965). Galleries are generally driven in sound wood, although many palo verdes have been found where 50 to 75 percent of the wood has been previously tunneled by wood-boring beetle larvae. In this case the termites work through the tightly packed sawdust and even use the cleared tunnels for short distances. Since the soldier head is approximately 4 mm. wide and the abdomen of a large nymph may be nearly 5 mm. in diameter, the tunnels and access holes between chambers seldom measure less than 3 × 5 mm. Active galleries are nearly free of fecal spottings and pellets, but large dumps of loose pellets are found in abandoned chambers. In a caged palo verde colony, large quantities of fecal pellets were dumped from an old borer exit a few inches from the ground. Considerable use is made of semi-liquid fecal material in walling off old galleries and in plugging lateral tunnels made by borers to the outside.

COLONIZING FLIGHTS. Previous flight records from Arizona had suggested that *Pterotermes* flies on a relatively few nights during late July and August. Alates from Baja California were taken in light traps in late August and early September by Werner and Radford (Table 1). Apparently the only observations on a flight in nature were made by the author on the night of August 7, 1963, in the Tucson Mts. A lantern was operated from dusk until midnight, and between 2235 and 2330 hrs. four males and four females flew rapidly in to the light on the ground. It was impossible to tell from what altitude or direction they had come. They were very active under the light but did not leave. The evening was quiet and nearly cloudless with the temperature between 22 and 23°C. The moon had risen about an hour before the flight and was just past full.

As part of a long-term study, flight and meteorological data were collected from June through September, 1965, in Tucson, Arizona. A six-foot section of dead palo verde, containing what was probably a single colony of *Pterotermes,* was set in a field cage (6x12x6 feet) of 20-mesh Saran screen. Observations were made at various times nearly every night as well as for the entire period from dusk to dawn on a few other nights. A small black light trap was run each night in a corner of the cage so that there was reasonable assurance that practically all alates were captured.

The colony staged 40 separate flights during the 43 days beginning July 22 and ending Sept. 2. The smallest flight consisted of one alate, the largest 199, and roughly equal numbers of males and females were trapped. Twenty-five alates were later found to have escaped the trap and established themselves in cells within the same tree from which they flew. These plus those from the trap gave a total of 1688 alates produced by the colony. Nearly six months later the entire colony was removed from the tree and found to contain 4055 nymphs (Table 2, No. 3). Assuming that there were approximately 5600 nymphs in the colony during the spring of 1965 (number of nymphs produced since then not counted, but probably less than 200), this means that an impressive 30 percent of them developed into alates. It should be stated that it was impossible to determine whether this was actually a single colony or perhaps two, since a queen and a pair of replacement reproductives were found widely separated in the tree.

Although accompanying data have not yet been analyzed, a few generalizations may be made relating weather conditions to the flight season and the daily flight periods. The flight season began about three weeks after the highest weekly mean temperature of the year (30.5°C) was reached and continued for approximately six weeks with weekly means between 26.8 and 29.5°C. Individual flight periods took place with nighttime temperatures ranging from approximately 19 to 29°C. The flight season occurred while some of the highest weekly mean relative humidities of the year were recorded: 48-74%. Individual flight periods took place with nighttime relative humidities ranging between 39 and 100%. Flight periods began at temperature-relative humidity combinations between 29°C/39% RH and 24°C/100% RH. Nearly two inches of rain had fallen during the summer rainy season (June-September) prior to the flight season, and four significant rains (0.3 to 1.5 inches) occurred during the season itself. No flights took place on three nights during the 43-day season, apparently because of rain or considerably cooler temperatures. All flights were staged during dark-

Nutting — Pterotermes

ness, from two hours or more after sunset until three-quarters of an hour or more before sunrise. A complete account of these flight studies on *Pterotermes,* including behavior of the alates, will appear as part of a separate series on the colonizing flights and associated activities of termites.

Table 2. Composition of five colonies of *Pterotermes occidentis* from Arizona. It was impossible to determine whether colonies No. 4 and 5 were fragments of a single colony in the same log, or whether No. 3 was actually made up of two colonies in the same tree. K and Q represent primary reproductives; Rep., replacement reproductives.

No.	Nymphs	Soldiers	Reproductives	Eggs
		Oracle Jct., 8 mi. S.		
1	721	37	K + Q	79
2	2867	42	K + Q	
3	4055	82	Q + 2 Rep.	ca. 30
		Alamo Wash		
4	591	21	2 Rep.	
5	1082	28	1 Rep.	

FOUNDING OF THE COLONY. About 30 incipient colonies have been collected in dead palo verdes in the vicinity of Tucson. Several were found 6 to 10 feet above the ground. Observations on these and on post-flight behavior of caged alates indicate that the alates use cracks and borer exits as primary points of attack. The initial chamber, or copularium, (Fig. 4 A) is usually hollowed out of sound wood less than one inch from the surface. A few captive pairs have been maintained in petri dishes containing a slice of wood on a layer of plaster of Paris, with a few drops of water occasionally added to the wood or plaster. Shrunken reproductives and nymphs become excited in the presence of moisture and will readily drink to repletion from free droplets or a cotton wick. However, laboratory colonies may die within two weeks where free moisture or even moderate humidities prevail. The pairs were kept in a study from September through May where temperatures varied from 13 to 27°C.

EXPLANATION OF PLATE 9

Figure 2. Scene in the foothills of the Santa Catalina Mts. north of Tucson, Arizona. To the left is the ribbed, woody skeleton of a saguaro cactus, *Cereus giganteus;* to the right, a palo verde tree, *Cercidium microphyllum. Pterotermes* has been found in these skeletons and in the dead wood of *Cercidium.*

Figure 3. *Cercidium — Cereus* association on the western slopes of the Tucson Mts. west of Tucson, Arizona. *Pterotermes* has been taken in this area which is typical of the Sonoran Desert in southern Arizona. Photograph by Peter J. Mehringer, Jr.

Perhaps because they were already enclosed, many of the pairs worked intermittently for as long as a month to construct the copularium: irregular grooves in wood beneath the cover of the dish or chambers within the wood, measuring roughly $5 \times 10 \times 6$ mm. Semiliquid fecal material was used freely between wood and cover to encircle the grooves or to plug the chamber entrance. Some pairs produced up to six eggs within the first two or three weeks, while others produced no eggs during ten months of observation. The eggs are opaque, pinkish white and ultimately measure approximately 0.7×1.7 mm. Both sexes occasionally manipulated or cleaned the eggs with their mouthparts, but the eggs were not kept together in any particular place. No detailed observations were made on the progress of these incipient colonies, although most of the eggs had not hatched at the end of six months. Replacement reproductives of both sexes have been found in fragments of colonies in the laboratory and in natural colonies. In the latter case it has not always been possible to determine whether they were heading distinct colonies or were associated with remote parts of colonies headed by primary reproductives. They are pale yellowish-brown and possess very short wing pads. As would be expected, these preliminary observations show that captive colonies of *Pterotermes* provide good material for many types of biological studies.

COLONY SIZE AND OTHER BIOLOGICAL NOTES. Incipient colonies, probably within their first year, have been found consisting of barren pairs and pairs with as many as eight nymphs and five eggs. One colony, presumed to be in its second year, consisted of 13 nymphs, one small soldier and one egg. Another pair, perhaps in their second or third year, had produced 29 nymphs, 2 soldiers and 5 eggs. Data on the size of five older colonies are presented in Table 2. Assuming that all were single colonies, the soldier-nymph ratio varied from 1 to 20 in one of the smaller colonies to 1 to 68 in one containing nearly 3000 nymphs.

It should be of interest to mention the extremely high temperatures which *Pterotermes* must commonly meet in its exposed nesting sites. Temperature records were kept in connection with the flight studies made on the caged colony in Tucson from July through September, 1965. Temperatures were noted several times each day from a remote-reading thermometer, accurate to approximately $\pm 1°C$. The bulb was fixed within the central galleries of the palo verde trunk, three feet above the ground. Brief excursions above $38°$ were common in the late afternoon and on one day reached $41.8°$; the maximum air temperature (shade) on that day was $38°C$. The

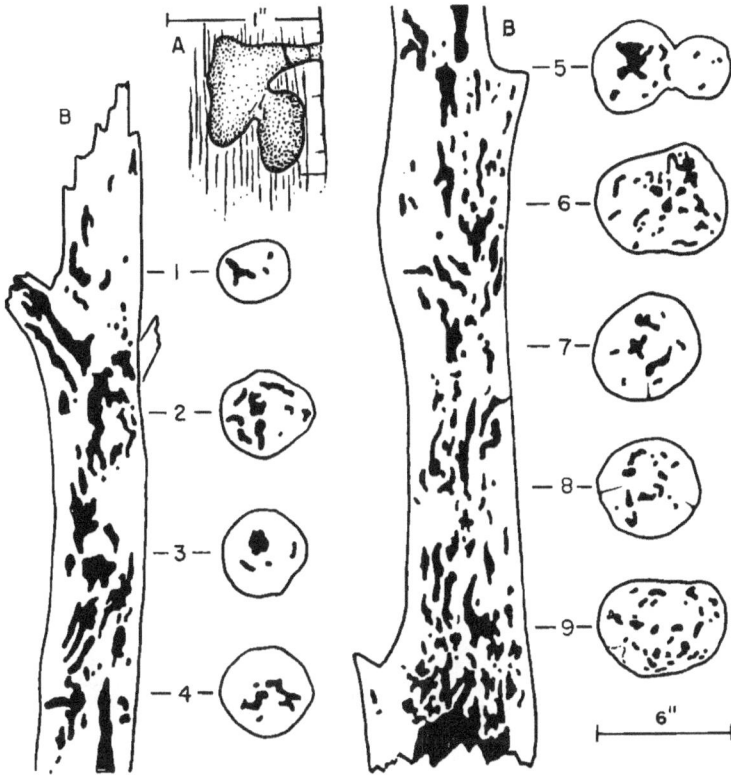

Figure 4. A. Longitudinal section through a copularium of *Pterotermes occidentis* in outer wood of a dead palo verde tree. This chamber contained a primary pair and four small nymphs. B. Longitudinal section showing the galleries of *Pterotermes* in a dead palo verde from the vicinity of Oracle Jct., Arizona. Cross sections 1-9 represent tracings of the galleries in adjacent cuts.

temperature rarely fell below 24°C in the early morning shortly after sunrise during the entire period. This tree received somewhat more than 50 percent shade for most of the day and complete shade early and late each day. Since colonies in nature are rarely in such shaded situations, these figures are certainly conservative. Further, for most colonies in branches and trunks from one to ten inches in diameter, there is no apparent escape from such temperatures.

ASSOCIATION WITH OTHER TERMITES AND INSECTS. In southern Arizona, *Marginitermes hubbardi* (Banks) has been found in palo verde logs, and on two occasions in the same wood with *Pterotermes*. *Paraneotermes simplicicornis* (Banks) is the only other kalotermitid which is known to attack the palo verde. This unusual termite, which is essentially subterranean, generally infests the roots and stumps of dead trees in the desert. Both of these termites probably begin their attacks before wood has dried to the point where it is most favorable for *Pterotermes*. They are much more common in the skeletons of the saguaro cactus, where they appear shortly after the flesh has rotted and fallen off. They have never been found in saguaros inhabited by *Pterotermes*.

Heterotermes aureus (Snyder) is one of the most common subterranean termites in the Sonoran Desert region of southern Arizona. It commonly works in dead saguaros, particularly during periods of higher soil moisture following the winter and summer rains. On the north slopes of the Tucson Mts. its abandoned galleries were obvious in the saguaro stump containing *Pterotermes*. The only other insects commonly found in wood attacked by *Pterotermes* are buprestid and cerambycid larvae which are often very numerous in palo verde.

REFERENCES CITED

BANKS, N., AND T. E. SNYDER.
  1920. A revision of the nearctic termites (Banks) with notes on biology and geographic distribution (Snyder). U. S. Nat. Mus. Bull. No. 108, 228 pp.
COLLINS, MARGARET S.
  1966. Personal Communication.
COLLINS, MARGARET, AND A. GLENN RICHARDS.
  1966. Studies on water relations in North American termites. II. Water loss and cuticular structure in eastern species of Family Kalotermitidae (Isoptera). Ecology, in press.
EMERSON, ALFRED E.
  1955. Geographical origins and dispersions of termite genera. Fieldiana: Zoology, 37: pp. 473-475.
HAGEN, H. A.
  1858. Monographie der Termiten. Part 2. Linn. Entomol., 12: pp. 77-78.
KRISHNA, KUMAR.
  1961. A generic revision and phylogenetic study of the family Kalotermitidae (Isoptera). Bull. Amer. Mus. Nat. Hist., 122: 303-408.
LIGHT, S. F.
  1929. New termite records for Lower California. Pan-Pacific Ent., 6: pp. 67, 69-70.
  1933. Termites of western Mexico. Univ. Calif. Publ. Ent., 6: pp. 85-86.

NUTTING, W. L.
    1965. Observations on the nesting site and biology of the Arizona damp-wood termite *Zootermopsis laticeps* (Banks) (Hodotermitidae). Psyche, 72: pp. 119-121.
POWELL, JERRY A.
    1966. Personal communication.
SHREVE, FORREST.
    1951. Vegetation of the Sonoran Desert. Carnegie Inst. Washington Pub. 591, xii + 192 pp. + 37 pls.
SNYDER, T. E.
    1966. Personal communication.

POSTEMBRYOLOGICAL DEVELOPMENT OF SPIDERLINGS FROM TWO PERUVIAN *LATRODECTUS* POPULATIONS

By John D. McCrone, Florida Presbyterian College

AND

Herbert W. Levi, Harvard University

It is becoming increasingly clear that the solution of the complex taxonomic problems presented by the black widow genus *Latrodectus* will require more basic biological data than are now available. Of particular importance in this regard is information on the postembryological development of color pattern. Many *Latrodectus* populations show marked interpopulation differences in color pattern particularly of the immature stages. It is difficult to assess the taxonomic significance of these differences without reliable information on the development of these patterns in various populations.

Little such information has been published. The most extensive study was that done by Smithers (1944) with *Latrodectus mactans indistinctus*. He raised spiderlings from three different areas in South Africa and recorded the rate of development and the changes in color pattern after each molt. Unfortunately he confined his observations on color pattern to the females.

Recently we were able to obtain egg sacs from two different areas in Peru, Lima and Cuzco. We have reared 54 adults from these sacs and have recorded the changes in their color pattern after each molt. Morphologically these adults all appear to be *Latrodectus mactans*, probably the same as *Latrodectus* species "no. 3" of Abalos' cultures from Santiago del Estero Province in Argentina.

The spiders were raised in the laboratory in St. Petersburg, using a technique previously described (McCrone and Levi, 1964). A record was kept for each developing spider of the number of molts to maturity, the duration of the stadia, and the color pattern of each post-emergent instar. These data are presented in Table 1 and Figs. 1-19. The color patterns figured are the basic patterns found in each population. There were slight individual differences in pattern; however, these did not obscure the basic color patterns.

From the illustrations it can be seen that some instars are more polymorphic than others (Fig. 2, 15, 16) even though the adults end up with more or less similar patterns in females (Fig. 9, 18, 19),

---

Manuscript received by the editor June 28, 1966.

TABLE I — RATE OF DEVELOPMENT OF SPIDERLINGS FROM TWO PERUVIAN LATRODECTUS POPULATIONS

	No. of molts to maturity	No. of individuals	Average No. and Range of Days Elapsed to Each Molt (Measured from time of emergence from egg sac)					
			1*	2	3	4	5	6
Lima males	3	3	20.0 (18-22)	33.0 (28-38)	66.0 (55-83)			
	4	16	20.3 (17-31)	33.9 (23-53)	57.4 (45-90)	91.4 (56-117)		
Cuzco males	3	2	28.5 (24-32)	44.0 (43-56)	83.0 (67-84)	97.1 (89-105)		
	4	10	29.3 (24-32)	48.2 (43-56)	77.9 (67-84)	97.1 (89-105)		
Lima Females	6	10	18.4 (17-21)	31.4 (24-42)	54.4 (44-66)	96.5 (65-123)	133.8 (122-160)	181.3 (161-194)
Cuzco Females	6	13	22.6 (13-33)	44.2 (33-63)	78.6 (73-91)	108.0 (100-119)	141.2 (120-164)	180.8 (164-194)

* First molt after emergence from egg sac.

and quite different ones in males (Fig. 5, 13). The adult male is lighter than in the previous instar and the adult female is darker than in the penultimate stage. The individual variation of adult males is greater than that of adult females.

The spiderlings from Cuzco went through different color phases than did the Lima spiderlings although the adults are similar. Smithers (1944) reported the same phenomenon in South Africa. Adult females from the Little Karroo and Port Elizabeth were identical, but the color patterns of the immatures were quite different in the two groups. Considering the geographical proximity of the two Peruvian populations the differences in color pattern are remarkable.

Males from the Peruvian population were mated with *L. mactans mactans* from Florida. Although they readily mated and egg sacs were produced, none of the eggs hatched. Unmated *Latrodectus* do not produce an egg sac at all. Similar results were obtained when female *L. mactans tredecimguttatus* from Israel were mated with Florida *L. mactans*. The significance of this reproductive isolation is unclear because we have made no crosses with geographically intermediate populations. Members of different sympatric Florida species can not be mated with each other in the laboratory. The same observation has been made in Argentina (Abalos, pers. comm.).

The marked intra- and interpopulational differences in the color patterns of the immature and adult spiders from the two Peruvian populations studied show that the use of color pattern as a diagnostic species character must be done with great caution. For example, that some collections of juveniles from Texas were almost white, others black, seems to be of little significance. Both colorations were found after one molt (Fig. 2) from the same egg sac. Color pattern differences have significance only when they can be correlated with other morphological and biological characters (e.g. *L. bishopi*).

EXPLANATION OF PLATE 10

Figures 1-9. *Latrodectus mactans* from Lima, Peru; coloration diagrammatic. Left venter, right dorsum with legs. Molts counted from after leaving egg-sac; there is one molt within egg-sac.
Fig. 1. After hatching (males and females). Fig. 2. After first molt (males and females); at right, variant pattern of about 10%. Fig. 3. After second molt (males and females); at right, variant pattern. Fig. 4. After third molt (penultimate male). Fig. 5. After fourth molt (adult male). Fig. 6. After third molt (female). Fig. 7. After fourth molt (female). Fig. 8. After fifth molt (female). Fig. 9. After sixth molt (adult female).
White: white; crosshatch: light brown; double crosshatch: dark brown; light stipple: orange; dark stipple: red; black: black. There may be a yellow fringe around the red in areas marked white.

McCRONE AND LEVI — LATRODECTUS

Another variable, not yet investigated, is the different number
of molts to adulthood of females. While Turnbull (1960, 1965)
found that different amounts of food do not change the number of
molts in *Linyphia triangularis* (Linyphiidae) *and Agelenopsis potteri*
(Agelenidae), it is known that the number of instars is variable in
Nephila madagascarensis, examined by Bonnet (1930) and Gerhardt
(1933), and in *Latrodectus mactans,* studied by Deevey (1949).

The spiderling molts once within the egg-sac. Herms *et al.* calculated that spiders remain between 14 and 30 days in the egg-sac;
Lawson calculated a minimum of 15 days, but usually 3 to 4 weeks.
Probably the temperature determines the length of this period. The
second instar includes only the period after emergence. According
to Herms, females from California molt 6 to 8 times, males 3 to
6. Blair reports that females from Alabama molt 6 times, males 5.
Lawson found that in Kansas females undergo 7 to 8 molts, males
4. Burt *et al.* reported 8 to 9 molts for Hawaiian females. Thorpe
and Woodson recorded 6 to 9 molts for females and 3 to 6 for males.
Deevey recorded that in southeastern Texas the females molt 7 to
9 times, the males 4 to 8. Despite uniform conditions, in only one
series did all the males and all the females from a single egg-sac
mature at the same molt. All seven females fed maximally matured
at the seventh molt. Deevey also recorded considerable variation in
length of time to maturity. *Latrodectus variolus* and *L. mactans*
may have been confused in some of these observations, although
most probably apply to the much more common *L. mactans.* Unfortunately, it seems that none of the authors recorded differences in
coloration of adults after different molts, although some poor photographs show change in patterns.

Deevey (1949), in a useful table, summarized the work of pre-

---

EXPLANATION OF PLATE 11

Figures 10-19. *Latrodectus mactans* from Cuzco, Peru; coloration diagrammatic. Fig. 10. After hatching (males and females). Fig. 11. After first
molt (males). Fig. 12. After second and third molts (male). Fig. 13.
After fourth molt (adult male). Fig. 14. After third molt (female). Fig. 15.
After fourth molt (female). Fig. 16. After fourth molt, variant coloration
(female). Fig. 17. After fifth molt (female). Fig. 18. After sixth molt
(mature female). Fig. 19. After sixth molt, variant pattern (mature female).

(Molts are counted from after leaving egg-sac; there is one molt within
egg-sac.)

White: white; crosshatch: light brown; double crosshatch; dark brown;
light stipple: orange; dark stipple: red; black: black. There may be a
yellow fringe around the red in areas marked white.

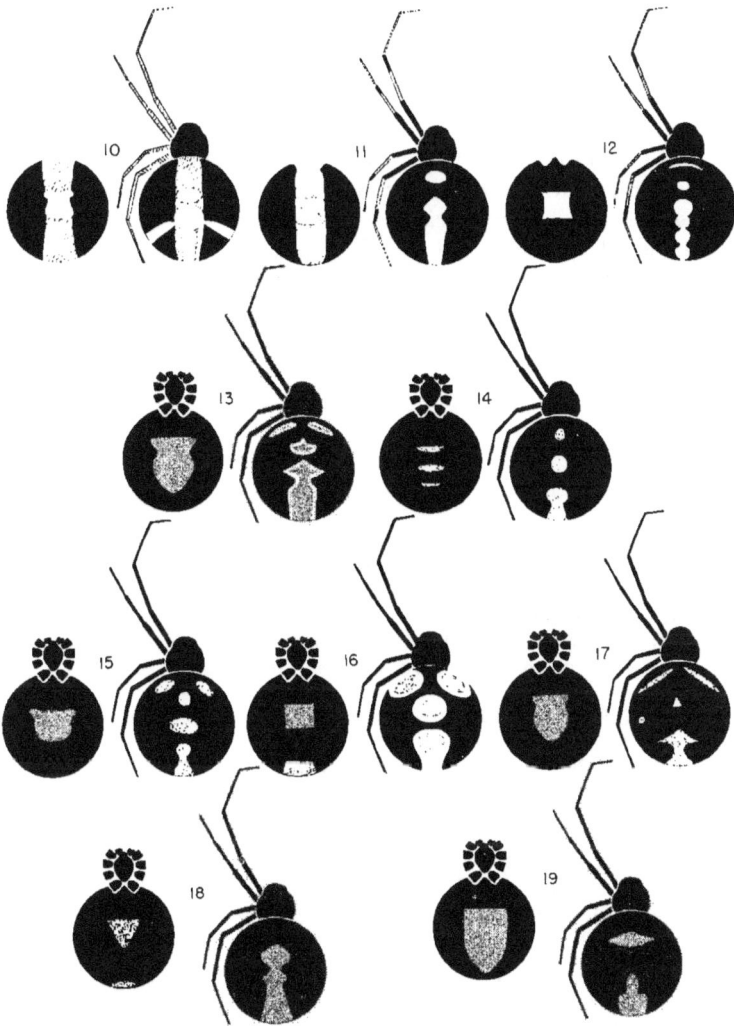

McCRONE AND LEVI — LATRODECTUS

vious authors, especially Bonnet, on the number of molts observed in spiders reared and the variation in number of instars. In addition, Deevey (1949) observed differences in color of eggs. Some eggs were pink, and out of them pink spiderlings hatched; most of the eggs were creamy white in color.

Acknowledgements: This investigation was supported in part by Public Health Service Research Grant AI-01944 from the National Institute of Allergy and Infectious Diseases, and Public Health Service Research Grant GM 11206 from the National Institute of General Medical Sciences. We wish to thank Paul C. Dell for technical assistance and Dr. F. Carrasco Z. of the University of Cuzco for help in obtaining specimens from the area.

LITERATURE CITED

BLAIR, A. W.
    1934. Life history of *Latrodectus mactans*. *Arch. Internal Med.* 54:844-850.
BONNET, P.
    1930. Le Mue, l'autotomie et la régéne ration chez les Araignées. *Bull. Soc. Hist. Natur. Toulouse* 59: 237-700.
DEEVEY, G. B.
    1949. The developmental history of *Latrodectus mactans* at different rates of feeding. *Amer. Midland Natur.* 42: 189-219.
GERHARDT, U.
    1933. Neue Untersuchungen zur Sexualbiologie der Spinnen. *Z. Morphol. Ökol. Tiere* 27: 1-75.
HERMS, W. B., BAILEY, S. F., AND McIVOR, B.
    1935. The black widow spider. *Bull. Calif. Agr. Exp. Sta.* 591: 1-30.
LAWSON, P. B.
    1933. Notes on the life history of the hour-glass spider. *Ann. Entomol. Soc. Amer.* 26: 568-574.
McCRONE, J. D. AND LEVI, H. W.
    1964. North American widow spiders of the *Latrodectus curacaviensis* group (Araneae: Theridiidae). *Psyche,* 71: 12-27.
SMITHERS, R. H. N.
    1944. Contribution to our knowledge of the genus *Latrodectus* in South Africa. *Ann. South African Mus.* 36: 263-312.
THORP, R. W. AND WOODSON, W. D.
    1945. Black Widow, America's most poisonous spider. Univ. of North Carolina Press.
TURNBULL, A. L.
    1960. Prey of *Linyphia triangularis*. *Canadian J. Zool.* 38: 859-873.
    1965. Prey abundance and the development of the spider *Agelenopsis potteri*. *Canadian Entomol.* 97: 141-147.

THE REDISCOVERY OF
CAMPONOTUS (MYRMAPHAENUS) YOGI WHEELER
(HYMENOPTERA: FORMICIDAE)

BY WM. S. CREIGHTON, CITY COLLEGE, NEW YORK[1]
and ROY R. SNELLING, LOS ANGELES COUNTY MUSEUM[2]

No North American ant has been more of an enigma than Wheeler's *Camponotus yogi*. Much of this is due to the fact that the two types of *yogi* were misplaced when a part of the Wheeler Collection was transferred from the Museum of Comparative Zoölogy to the American Museum of Natural History in 1938. For the next twenty-six years Wheeler's description of *yogi* was the only source of information on this species (1). Of necessity this description was the basis for the treatment of *yogi* in *The Ants of North America* (2). Unfortunately, one of the key features chosen (the length of the antennal scape) was incorrectly described by Wheeler; hence the key for *yogi* in the above publication is confusing rather than helpful. It appears that *yogi* has been saved from even greater confusion only because so little additional material has been taken. In 1958 F. Raney found a few specimens at the Oak Creek Ranger Station in San Diego County, California. In 1963 the junior author took three colonies of *yogi* at Etiwanda, in San Bernardino County, California. The senior author at first refused to believe that this material could be *yogi* because it so obviously failed to agree with Wheeler's description. Then, in 1964, the two types of *yogi* were discovered in the collection of the American Museum of Natural History. These established the fact that the Oak Creek and Etiwanda specimens are *yogi*.

Several of the shortcomings of Wheeler's description can be attributed to his attempt to relate *yogi* to the subgenus *Colobopsis*. Whether he realized it or not, Wheeler described important features of the head of the major of *yogi* from a position where it most closely resembled that of a *Colobopsis* major. That is to say, the head was not viewed in full face but tilted forward until the truncated anterior portion and the mandibles were barely visible. There is no possible doubt about this for the "broadly excised posterior border" which Wheeler described for the head of the *yogi* major

[1]Emeritus Professor, Department of Biology
[2]Senior Preparator, Department of Entomology
Published with a Grant-in-Aid of Research from the Society of the Sigma Xi. *Manuscript received by the editor May 9, 1966*

cannot be seen unless the head is tilted forward. In conventional full face view the occipital border of the major of *yogi* is flat or very slightly convex (See Plate 12, Fig. 2). Precisely the same explanation applies to Wheeler's statement that the scapes of the major of *yogi* "reach the posterior corners of the head". When the head of the major is tilted far enough forward to show the excavated rear border of the occiput, it is true that the scapes appear to reach the occipital corners. But in conventional full face view they extend beyond the occipital corners. It is obvious that tilting the head would not greatly affect the configuration of the frontal carinae and, if one is willing to unravel the description that both Wheeler and Forel customarily applied to lyrate carinae, then these were accurately described. In the writer's opinion this is the only feature in the description of *yogi* which enabled Emery to allocate the species to the subgenus *Myrmaphaenus* for, with strongly lyrate frontal carinae, it cannot belong to *Colobopsis*.

Finally, there is the matter of pilosity. Wheeler recognized that some of the cephalic pilosity of the major of *yogi* is notably different from that on other parts of the body. He gave an accurate description of the short, blunt, reclinate hairs that arise from the foveolae of the clypeus and the adjacent parts of the genae. But he failed to mention the erect hairs which occur on the sides of the head from the rear border of the eye to the mandibular insertion. These hairs also occur on the lateral parts of the gula and over an area extending inward toward the antennal fossa. Although short, they are quite numerous and form a conspicuous fringe on the anterior half of the head. Their structure is unusual for, although each hair is of uniform thickness throughout most of its length, many of them have enlarged tips. The enlarged tip is often spherical and such hairs look remarkably like the upper ends of insect pins.

One of the most characteristic features of *yogi* is the sculpture on the front of the head of the major. The surface is rough and covered with coarse elevations and depressions which are too broad and ill-defined to be called rugae. The roughened areas on the clypeus have no fixed direction but those on the genae approximately parallel the long axis of the head. Among these roughened ridges are scattered oval foveolae from which flattened hairs arise, but these are difficult to see because the entire roughened surface is evenly covered with very fine, densely set, oval punctures which give the area a

EXPLANATION OF PLATE 12

Camponotus (Myrmaphaenus) yogi Wheeler. Figure 1. Head of female. Figure 2. Head of major. Both figures drawn to the same scale.

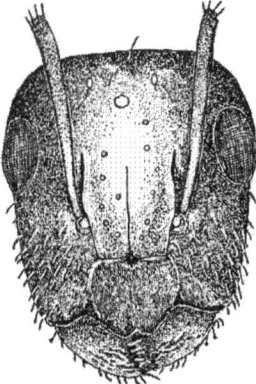

1

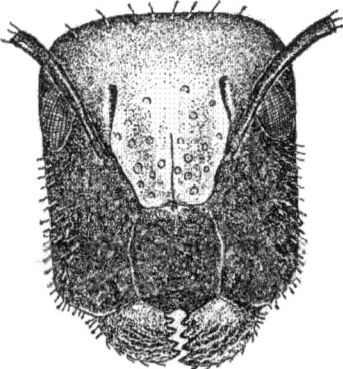

2

CREIGHTON AND SNELLING — CAMPONOTUS

granular appearance. The sculpture just described is confined to the anterior half of the head. The frontal lobes are heavily shagreened, the middle of the occiput more feebly shagreened and the sides of the head and the occipital angles are smooth and shining. There are conspicuous circular punctures on the frontal lobes, smaller oval ones on the sides of the head and very small and obscure punctures on the occiput. No other North American species of *Camponotus* has a comparable cephalic sculpture and *yogi* may be recognized by this feature alone.

There is nothing in Wheeler's treatment of *yogi* more exasperating than his statement that this species is related to *Colobopsis*. In 1896 Emery listed the distinguishing features of *Colobopsis* (3). When Wheeler monographed our North American forms in 1904 he repeated Emery's criteria and added two of his own (4). According to Wheeler's summary the female and major worker of *Colobopsis* have a head in which the truncated portion is circular in outline and sharply separated from the remainder of the head (marginate). There are conspicuous, umbilicate punctures on the sides of the head immediately behind the truncation. The mandibles have an external ridge or angle which separates the anterior face from the equally large latero-ventral face. Medias are rare or lacking and the pupae are not enclosed in cocoons. Because of the limited type material of *yogi* Wheeler could not know that in this species medias are present and the larvae are enclosed in cocoons. Nor could he know anything about the structure of the female. Nevertheless, Wheeler was aware that the truncated portion of the head of the major of *yogi* is neither circular in outline nor marginate. He was aware that there is no external ridge on the major's mandible. Since he described the dense, granular, sculpture which obscures the foveolae on the sides of the head of the major of *yogi*, Wheeler must have realized that these foveolae are scarcely comparable to the distinct, umbilicate, punctures of the *Colobopsis* major. In short, not a single feature of the major of *yogi* agreed with the major of *Colobopsis* as that caste was defined by Wheeler in 1904.

These contradictions are annoying but they are not inexplicable. Wheeler's initial views on *Colobopsis* were based almost entirely on species in the *truncatus-impressus* complex, as were the views which Emery had expressed earlier. By 1907, due to the many identified exotics which he had received from Forel, Wheeler was prepared to expand his original views on *Colobopsis*. It is regrettable that when he described *yogi* Wheeler failed to make it clear that some of the Asiatic and South Pacific species assigned to *Colobopsis* are more aberrant than *yogi* when compared to species in the *truncatus-impressus* complex. With this in mind the question is not whether Wheeler was justified in placing *yogi* in *Colobopsis* but whether Emery was any better off when he transferred it to *Myrmaphaenus*. At present no final answer can be given for both subgenera are unusually heterogeneous. Nevertheless we prefer Emery's treatment for the following reasons:

(1) It is quite impossible to relate *yogi* to the *truncatus-impressus* complex in *Colobopsis*.

(2) If *yogi* is assigned to *Colobopsis* it will have to be placed in one of the Old World groups which are, at present, too ill-defined to permit certainty of assignment.

(3) There is no feature of *yogi* which would prevent its inclusion in *Myrmaphaenus* and it possesses several features which indicate that it fits better in that subgenus than in *Colobopsis*.

Most of these features have been mentioned above but one of them merits a more detailed discussion. The head of the female of *yogi* resembles that of the media rather than that of the major. In full face view the head of the major is as wide (in some specimens slightly wider) at the level of the rear of the clypeus as it is at the anterior border of the eyes. This gives the head a distinctly rectangular outline, for the sides turn in toward the mandibular insertions abruptly below the level of the middle of the clypeus. In the female and media the sides of the head converge gradually from the level of the anterior border of the eyes to the mandibular insertions. Thus in full face view the anterior half of the head is distinctly narrower than the posterior half (See Plate 12, Fig. 1). There are sculptural differences as well, for the female and the media lack the roughened areas on the clypeus and its surface, as well as that of the truncated parts which flank it, is granulo-shagreened only. The roughened ridges are present on the sides of the head but they are feebler than those of the major and the oval foveolae show more plainly.

A comparable condition is found in *C. (Myrmaphaenus) andrei* Forel, which occurs on the Mexican plateau. Moreover, the major of *andrei* is remarkably like that of *yogi*, both in the anterior truncation of the head and in the structure of the clypeus.[3] Since *andrei* has a strongly polymorphic worker caste it would appear that we are reaching some uniformity in the species assigned to *Myrmaphaenus*. At least we have in *yogi, andrei* and *ulcerosus* three species where

---

[3]The insect which Forel described as the major of *andrei* is actually a media. Neither he nor Wheeler ever saw the major of *andrei*, which is a very distinct caste.

the worker caste is polymorphic, the front of the head of the major is truncated, the clypeus of the major is flat and ecarinate or nearly so, the anterior border of the clypeus of the major is distinctly (often deeply) impressed and the head of the female resembles that of the media. These three species form a reasonably compact geographic group, since *yogi* occurs in southern California, *ulcerosus* in western Texas, southern Arizona and northern Chihuahua and *andrei* in Durango, Zacatecas and Hidalgo. It seems best to recognize the common structural and geographical affinities of these species and we believe that Emery's assignment of *yogi* to the subgenus *Myrmaphaenus* is the correct procedure.

The meager biological data which we can present at this time are as tantalizing as the taxonomic history of *yogi* has been confusing. The type specimens were taken, according to Wheeler, "from a hollow twig of manzanita . . . on Point Loma, near San Diego." The senior author has examined considerable manzanita and live oak in coastal southern California without successfully relocating the species. Quite by accident the junior author was led to an examination of the living stems of *Haplopappus pinifolius* (Gray) Hall.

This shrub occurs in the foothill chaparral of the San Gabriel, San Bernardino and San Jacinto Mountains south to San Diego County. Although this species does not occur on Point Loma (the type locality of *yogi*), a related species, *H. palmeri* (Gray) Hall, is found there. It is possibly significant that all the records of *yogi* thus far are from areas where one or the other of these species of *Haplopappus* is known to occur.

To date, the junior author has taken six colonies of *yogi*, all from stems of *H. pinifolius*. The most unusual point of this association is that all six colonies were taken from living stems. Numerous dead stems were examined, but only traces of former occupancy by *yogi* were found in these. So far as is known the ant does no excavation of the living tissues; all galleries are merely appropriated burrowings of buprestid larvae, apparently of one or two species of *Acmaeodera*. The manner in which the founding queen initially gains entry into the beetle burrows is not known.

Attempts to discover something of the foraging activities of *yogi* have so far been futile. No foraging individuals have been seen during the day or at night. However, observations on a captive

---

EXPLANATION OF PLATE 13

Camponotus (Myrmaphaenus) yogi Wheeler. **Fig. 1.** Male. **Fig. 2.** Minor. **Fig. 3.** Major. **Fig. 4.** Female. All figures drawn to the same scale.

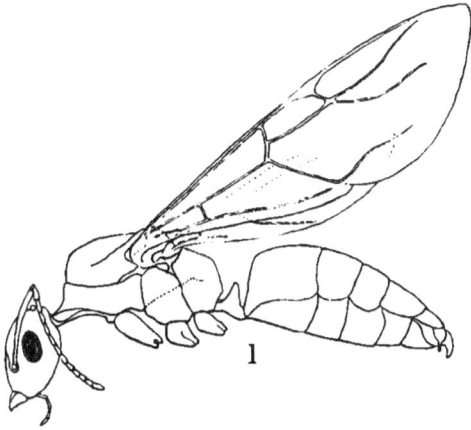

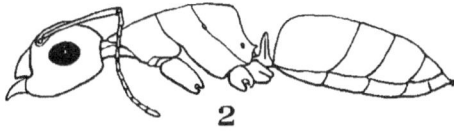

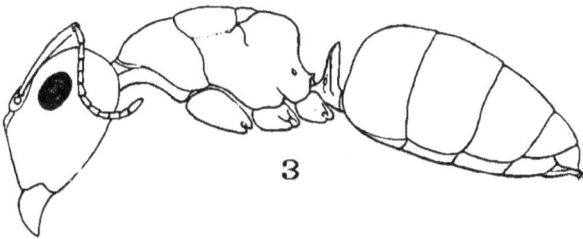

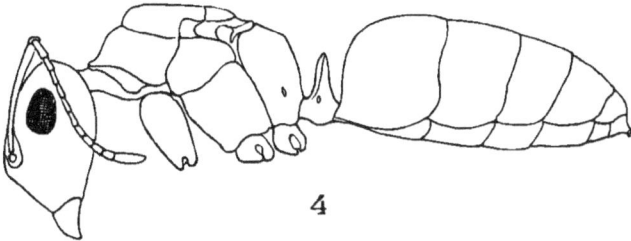

CREIGHTON AND SNELLING — CAMPONOTUS

colony suggest that this species regularly forages at night. During the day, members of the captive colony normally remained crowded within galleries cut into a wood block; with the coming of darkness they moved out of the tunnels to the surface of the block to feed on a honey-water solution provided for them.

The captive colony showed no interest in dead insects nor in various vegetable foods (seeds, bran, wheat germ, pollen, etc.). The primary food source seems to be the sweet exudates of several species of Pseudococcidae. Species of mealybugs are: *Puto* sp.[4], (immatures only), *Humococcus inornatus* McKenzie[5], *Anisococcus crawii* (Coquillett)[5] and *Chorizococcus abroniae* McKenzie?[5]. The first two species were taken from the galleries occupied by the ant, and were feeding on the plant within these galleries. In the case of the two latter species there is some confusion, since both were mixed in a single vial; some of the specimens are known to have come from the galleries while others were taken feeding on the outer surface of the stems and crowns. Whether or not the ants actually moved the mealybugs into the galleries remains to be determined. However, that ants do transport mealybugs to advantageous feeding sites is well known, and it would not be amiss to suggest that *yogi* does so.

Two ant species have been found living in a plesiobiotic relationship with *yogi*. There are *Solenopsis (D.) molesta validiuscula* Emery and *Leptothorax andrei* Emery. Each of these was found only once, and little can be said here regarding their relationship with *yogi*. The former species is commonly associated with larger ants, and the latter has been taken several times from colonies of various species of *Camponotus* and *Formica*.

One colony was apparently being attacked at the time it was collected. The attacker was *Formica (F.) pilicornis* Emery, a common and aggressive species in the lower chaparral region. The *Formica* had gained entrance into the galleries of the *Camponotus*, and workers of the former were seen carrying off the larvae and pupae of *yogi*. The remainder of the *yogi* colony, soldiers, workers, the queen and some brood, were crammed into three upper galleries, the majors lowest and receiving the brunt of the attack. The majors of *yogi* were massed together, with antennae extended forward; when a *pilicornis* worker touched the antennae the *yogi* major lurched forward and attempted to fasten its jaws to an appendage of the attacker. Several such encounters were noted; when the defender's

[4]determined by H. L. McKenzie
[5]determined by R. F. Wilkey

jaws closed over the appendage of a *pilicornis*, the *yogi* major jerked back into the original position; at the same time the head was snapped up and down. This frequently resulted in severing or severely mangling the appendage of the attacker.

It was noted that the *Formica* so attacked usually retreated in a highly agitated manner. Closer observation of the process revealed that when the jaws of the *yogi* major clamped over an attacker's appendage a grayish-white exudate oozed forth from the lower part of the major's head. Creighton (5) noted a similar occurrence in the case of *C. (Colobopsis) papago*, with the remark that the fluid came from the mouth. Subsequent examination of the *yogi* majors suggested that in the case of this species, it is exuded from the mandibular bases; individuals which had the hardened material quite conspicuous on the mandibles and lower portions of the face showed no traces of it in the immediate vicinity of the mouthparts. This fluid, when in contact with the integument of ants of other species, causes considerable excitation of the individual affected, and, in the case of the *pilicornis*, an immediate retreat from the conflict. That this fluid serves as a defensive repellent seems obvious; whether or not it is toxic as well is not yet known.

The colonies of *yogi* thus far collected have been rather small; it is doubtful if colonies exceed three hundred individuals. Colony no. 1, collected on May 11, contained 27 majors and 165 media and minor workers; the queen was not located, but is presumed to have been overlooked during the collecting. Colony no. 4, collected on September 29, contained 1 queen, 8 males, 54 majors, 90 media and minor workers, 51 larvae and 7 pupae (5 ♂ ♂, 2 ♀♀); colony no. 5, also taken on September 29, consisted of 1 queen, 1 alate female, 3 males, 12 majors and 36 media and minor workers, and is the smallest colony taken to date.

The mating flight evidently takes place during late summer. Winged sexuals have been taken in the nests in late August and September; winged females have been attracted to lights at night in Glendale, Los Angeles County, on October 14.

LITERATURE CITED

1. **Wheeler, W. M.**, Bull. Amer. Mus. Nat. Hist., 34: 420 (1915)
2. **Creighton, W. S.**, Bull. Mus. Comp. Zoöl., 104: 401 (1950)
3. **Emery, Carlo**, Mem. Acad. Sci. Bologna, 5: 761-780 (1896)
4. **Wheeler, W. M.**, Bull. Amer. Mus. Nat. Hist., 20: 140 (1904)
5. **Creighton, W. S.**, Psyche, 59, 4: 161 (1952)

TWO NEW GENERA OF SOUTH AMERICAN COCKROACHES SUPERFICIALLY RESEMBLING *LOBOPTERA*, WITH NOTES ON BIONOMICS (DICTYOPTERA, BLATTARIA, BLATTELLIDAE).

BY ASHLEY B. GURNEY* AND LOUIS M. ROTH**

All cockroaches initially extrude the oötheca with the keel or the micorpylar ends of the eggs facing dorsally, but some species rotate the egg case before depositing it (Roth and Willis, 1954, 1958). According to McKittrick (1964), one of the important characters for separating the Plectopterinae from the Blattellinae (both are in the Blattellidae) is the position in which the oötheca is carried just before it is deposited by the female. In the Plectopterinae, the keel of the egg case remains upright until deposition; in the Blattellinae, the oötheca is rotated so the keel and micropylar ends of the eggs face laterally, behavior characteristic of the Ectobiinae and Nyctiborinae (Blattellidae) as well as of all the Blaberidae (ovoviviparous and viviparous species). The new genera here described were recognized as a result of studies stimulated by observing the lack of rotation by a species which formerly had been assumed to be one of the Blattellinae. Therefore, in addition to presenting descriptions and biological notes, this paper provides an application of the higher categories in the classification of McKittrick (1964).

On June 11, 1965, one of us (L.M.R.) received some living specimens of *Loboptera thaxteri* Hebard from Buenos Aires, Argentina.[1] When we found that the females of *thaxteri* do not rotate the oötheca before its deposition, we investigated the taxonomic position of *Loboptera* Brunner. McKittrick (1964) had reported the rotation of the oötheca by *Lobopterella dimidiatipes* (Bolivar),[2] and as a result of this and other observations she placed it in the Blattellinae. [*Loboptera decipiens* (Germar) also rotates its oötheca before deposition (Lefeuvre, 1959; Roth, unpublished observations).] We

*Entomology Research Division, Agr. Res. Serv., U. S Department of Agriculture, Washington, D. C.

**Pioneering Research Division, U. S. Army Natick Laboratories, Natick, Massachusetts.

Manuscript received by the editor September 21, 1966.

[1]The species has been cultured easily on Purina laboratory chow. However, individuals of *thaxteri* were heavily parasitized by the fungus *Herpomyces lobopterae* Thaxter.

[2]For many years authors referred *dimidiatipes* to *Loboptera*, and McKittrick did so. Princis (1957) based the genus *Lobopterella* upon it.

therefore sent specimens of *thaxteri* to Dr. McKittrick without identifying the material, and she placed it in the Plectopterinae. She wrote, "When I looked at it, I thought '*Loboptera*' and was thoroughly surprised when I checked the genitalia."

In the past years, various species seeming to belong to the Old World genus *Loboptera* Brunner [type species, *L. decipiens* (Germar),[3] an Old World species] have been described from the New World. Such generic assignment of New World species has been based primarily on superficial appearance. Two South American species, in particular *thaxteri* Hebard and *insularis* R. S. Albuquerque and Gurney, have a general appearance that is so similar to *decipiens* that Hebard (1932) assumed *thaxteri* to be an introduction from the Old World. In fact, no previously described genera appear adequate for the inclusion of *thaxteri* and *insularis*. Therefore in order to assign these species in a manner consistent with current generic concepts in the Blattaria, we are describing a separate genus for each. Although the two seem congeneric in general appearance, the differences noted in the generic key following to distinguish *Agmoblatta*, new genus, from *Isoldaia*, new genus, are fundamental.

Agmoblatta, new genus

This genus closely resembles *Loboptera* in general external appearance; it differs as noted in the following key. Its closest relative is *Isoldaia*, also known from eastern South America.

Generic description: Size medium for Blattellidae. Body with sparse slender setae slightly shorter than 1st antennal segment; moderately glossy. Head very broad; interocular distance a little greater than distance between antennal sockets; vertex smooth; antennae unspecialized; maxillary palpus of moderate length, apical segment narrowly triangular. Pronotum hemispherical, moderately vaulted, posterior margin straight except near simply rounded lateral angles. Tegmen a narrow, subtriangular lateral pad; wings absent. Front femur with anteroventral margin (Fig. 8) bearing a few strong spines, 1 or 2 of which toward knee of decreasing length, followed by about 5 piliform spines and 3 strong apical spines of increasing length; posteroventral margin with 3 or 4 spaced, strong, short spines in apical half, a slightly longer apical spine. Middle and hind femora with strong spines on both ventral margins. Middle and hind tibiae spined in 3 series on dorsal surface. Basal tarsomere of hind tarsus slightly more than one-half length of tarsus, ventral

---

[3]Hebard (1922, p. 332) indicated the type species.

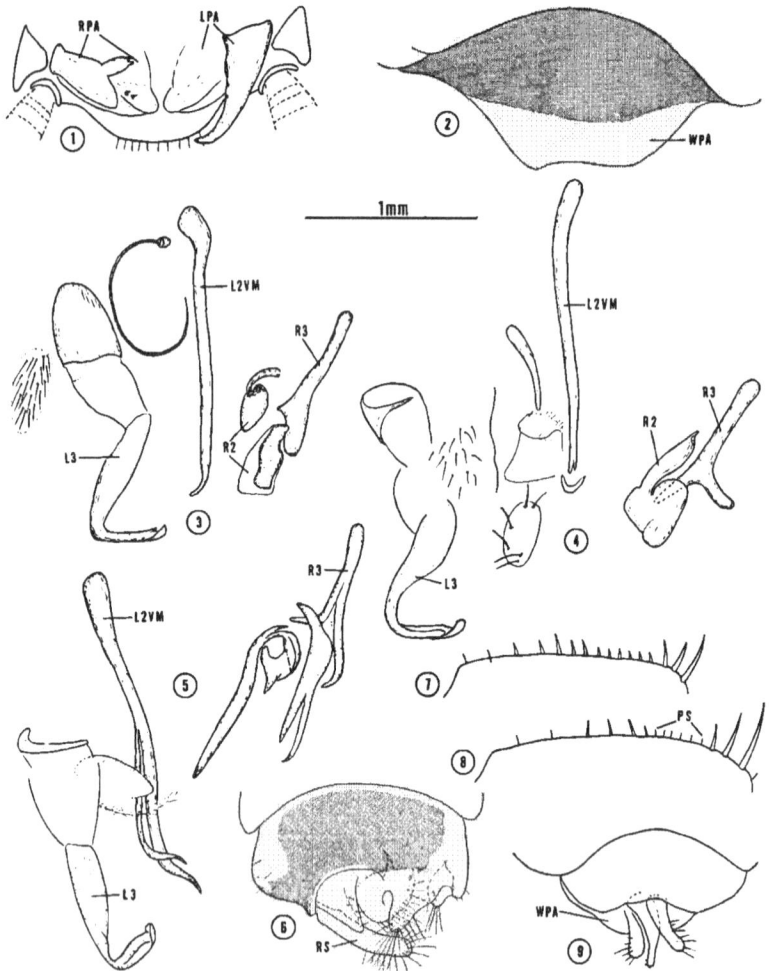

Figs. 1-9. Male genitalia of *Loboptera*, *Lobopterella*, and *Agmoblatta* (All figures except no. 2 drawn from KOH preparations)

1-3. *Loboptera decipiens* (Germar), male from culture at MacDonald College, originating in the Azores. 1. Ventral view of paraprocts and associated structures. 2. Ventral view of subgenital plate. 3. Dorsal view of phallomeres.

4. *Loboptera maroccana* Bolivar, male from Tangiers. Dorsal view of phallomeres.

5-6. *Lobopterella dimidiatipes* (Bolivar), male from Fiji. 5. Dorsal view of phallomeres. 6. Ventral view of subgenital plate.

surface with double row of closely set, strong, short setae, pulvillus occupying apical 10th of ventral surface: small pulvilli on tarsomeres 1-4; claws simple, equal; arolium of moderate size.

Abdomen smooth (Figs. 15, 16); lateroposterior angles of terga simple; tergum 7 of male with a wide median depression in which a tuft of hairlike setae arises (Figs. 15, 20); cercus with about 9 segments. Male genitalia: Supra-anal plate broadly triangular, unspecialized; subgenital plate (Fig. 9) with specialized posterior margin, with styli; paraprocts without conspicuous specialization; phallomeres (Fig. 10) of plectopterine type, 1st sclerite of left phallomere (L1) a conspicuous framework, median sclerite (L2VM) slender and elongate; 2nd sclerite of right phallomere (R2) a conspicuous hook. Female supra-anal plate triangular, simple; subgenital plate broad, posterior margin weakly cleft medially and bent dorsad (Fig. 19).

Type-species: *Loboptera thaxteri* Hebard.

The name *Agmoblatta* is derived in part from the Greek word "Agnos," meaning a break or fracture and has reference to the cleft of the female subgenital plate.

Hebard (1932) described only the female of *A. thaxteri* and erred in suggesting that it is parthenogenetic; he based this suggestion on the fact that all his specimens were females. The male markings strongly resemble those of the female (Figs. 15, 16). The female genitalia of *A. thaxteri* and *Loboptera decipiens* are shown in Figs. 22 and 24. The female genitalia of *Lobopterella* are illustrated by McKittrick (1964, p. 161). *Agmoblatta thaxteri* has one pair of spermathecae, but each spermatheca has a double terminal bulb (Fig. 25). *Loboptera decipiens* also has only one pair of spermathecae (Fig. 23), but each has many amber-colored tubules or branches. Sixteen of these branches terminate in rounded colorless bulbs in which the sperm are stored. Among the species studied by Mc-Kittrick (1964), only members of the Blattidae and Cryptocercidae have "forked" (i.e., branched) spermathecae; none of the Blaberoi-

---

7. *Loboptera decipiens* (Germar), male from Madeira. Spines on antero-ventral margin of front femur.

8-9. *Agmoblatta thaxteri* (Hebard). 8. Female paratype, spines on anteroventral margin of front femur. 9. Male from Natick culture originating in Buenos Aires, Argentina. Ventral view of subgenital plate.

Abbreviations: L2VM=median sclerite (second or ventromedial sclerite of left phallomere); L3 = 3rd sclerite of left phallomere; LPA = left paraproct; PS = piliform spines; R2 = 2nd sclerite of right phallomere; R3 = 3rd sclerite of right phallomere; RPA = right paraproct; RS = right stylus; WPA = weakly pigmented area of subgenital plate.

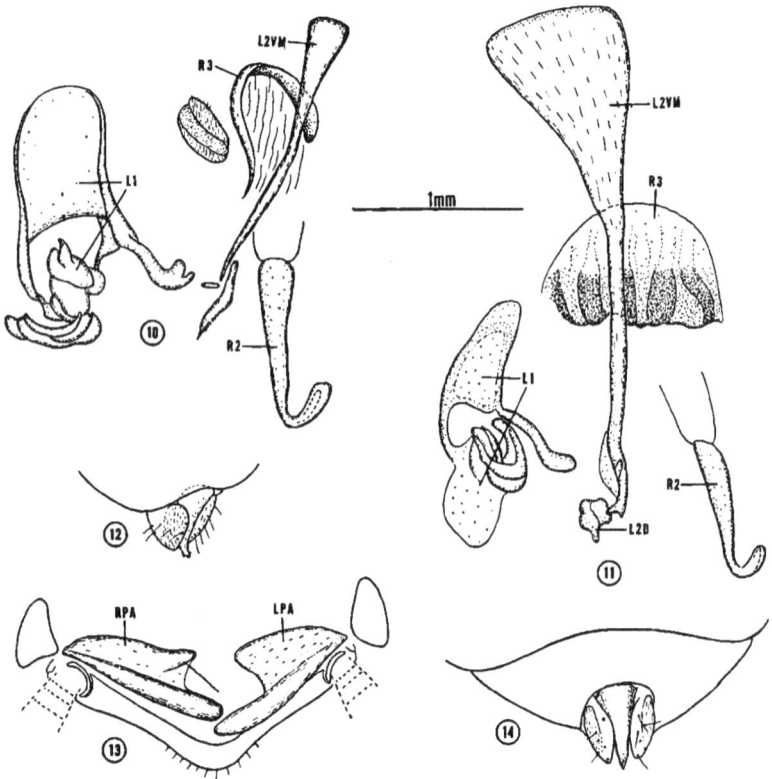

Figs. 10-14. Male genitalia of *Agmoblatta* and *Isoldaia* (All drawn from KOH preparations)

10. *Agmoblatta thaxteri* (Hebard). Male from Natick culture originating in Buenos Aires, Argentina. Dorsal view of phallomeres.

11-14. *Isoldaia insularis* (R. S. Albuquerque and Gurney), male holotype. 11. Dorsal view of phallomeres. 12. Ventrolateral view of apical portion of subgenital plate. 13. Ventral view of paraprocts and associated structures. 14. Ventral view of subgenital plate.

Abbreviations: LI = 1st sclerite of left phallomere; L2 = second dorsal sclerite of left phallomere; other abbreviations as in figs. 1-9.

dea have this type of spermatheca. She believes that the branched spermatheca is a primitive condition. The many branched spermatheca in *Loboptera dicipiens* is unique for the Blattellidae and may represent a relic character. *Lobopterella dimidiatipes* has 2 pairs of spermathecae (McKittrick, 1964, p. 153).

The oötheca (Fig. 17) of *A. thaxteri* has a deep groove ventrally along the midline (Fig. 18) made by the upturned medial cleft (Fig. 19) of the subgenital plate; the cleft serves as a mold as the oötheca is formed and extruded posteriorly. The oötheca remains upright until deposition, and its keel rests in the medial marginal indentation of the supragenital plate. The eggs require water for development, and the females usually deposit their oöthecae on the moist cotton of the water vials.

Observations were made on the courtship behavior of *Agmoblatta*. A newly emerged female was placed with 2 old males. Initially, the males showed only mild interest in the female, but within an hour they were actively pursuing and courting her. The males antennated and palpated the female and turned with their backs toward her, stretching and arching their abdomens and fully exposing the gland on the 7th terga. However, the female did not respond by mounting and palpating the gland, and the males did not extend their phallomeres and attempt to grasp her genitalia. This behavior is similar to that of *Blattella germanica* (L.) (Roth and Willis, 1952), *Nauphoeta cinerea* (Olivier), and other genera in which the male will not attempt to seize the female until she mounts or palpates his tergum (Roth and Barth, 1964). The male of *Agmoblatta* relies on antennal contact in pursuing the female; if he loses this contact, he seems to wander about haphazardly until he again makes contact, turns his back, and courts. Also, the male can discriminate between contact with a female and a male; males on touching each other did not court. This behavior is very similar to that shown by *B. germanica* (Roth and Willis, 1952).

The female we used had not mated 2 hours after the start of observations. However, females do mate soon after emergence since a pair was seen *in copula* in the typical opposed position (heads facing in opposite directions) though the female was still very light in color and less than a day old. Subsequently, on days 13, 20, 25, 31, and 39, she deposited egg cases. Thereafter she deposited no more oöthecae though she was kept until 62 days after emerging.

Isoldaia, new genus

This genus is similar superficially to *Agmoblatta,* from which it differs primarily in the lack of tergal specialization in the male and in the uncleft posterior margin of the female subgenital plate.

Generic description: Agrees with *Agmoblatta* except as follows: About 10 to 12 piliform spines in apical half of anteroventral margin of front femur, in contrast to about 5 to 6 in *Agmoblatta;* maxillary

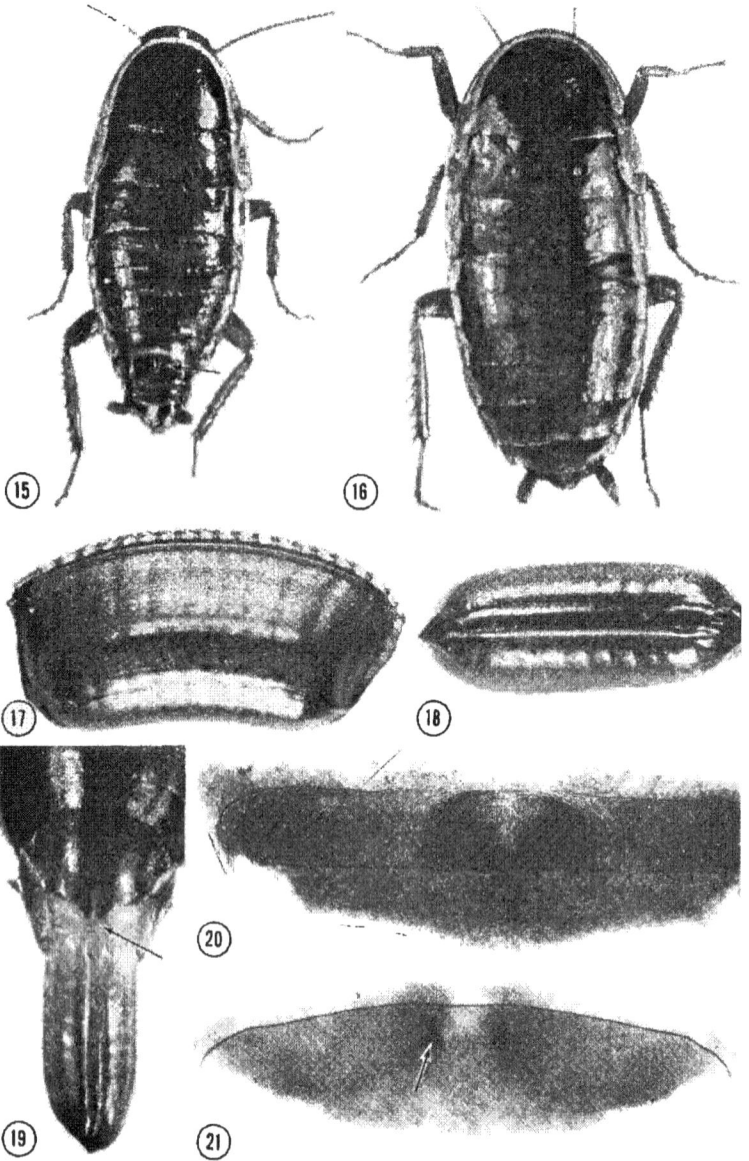

GURNEY AND ROTH — COCKROACHES

palpus longer, exemplified by antepenultimate segment clearly more than half as long as width of interocular space (palpus shorter in *Agmoblatta,* antepenultimate segment decidedly less than half as long as width of interocular space); supra-anal plate of female more acutely triangular than in *Agmoblatta;* male abdomen without tergal specialization; subgenital plate of female with entire, uncleft posterior margin. Male genitalia and subgenital plate are illustrated in Figs. 11-14.

Type-species: *Loboptera insularis* R. S. Albuquerque and Gurney. The name *Isoldaia* is adapted from the given name of Mrs. Isolda Rocha e Silva Albuquerque in recognition of her sustained efforts to broaden the knowledge of South American Blattaria.

A habitus figure of a female of *Agmoblatta thaxteri* is in Hebard (1932), and one of *Isoldaia insularis* is in R. S. Albuquerque and Gurney (1963). Readers are referred to page 178 of McKittrick (1964) for information about the subfamily assignment of the genera wherein the phallomeres of *Lophoblatta* Hebard, *Euthlastoblatta* Hebard, and *Supella* Shelford represent the Plectopterinae, and *Pseudomops* Serville and *Blattella* Caudell represent the Blattellinae.

The following is a key for distinguishing *Loboptera* and several similar genera:

1. Conspicuous hook-shaped sclerite of male genitalia occurs as part of left phallomere (Figs. 3-5, L3); one or both paraprocts of male armed with a hook or spines (Fig. 1); armature of ventro-anterior margin of front femur (Fig. 7) includes heavy though short spines basad of 3 terminal ones (Type A) (Old World) 2
   - Conspicuous hook-shaped sclerite of male genitalia occurs as part of right phallomere (Figs. 10, 11, R2); paraprocts of male simple, not distinctly armed (Fig. 13); armature of ventro-

anterior margin of front femur includes delicate piliform spines (Fig. 8, PS) basad of 3 terminal ones (Type B) (New World) 3
2. Tegmina present as subtriangular lateral pads; male subgenital plate simple, without styli (Fig. 2); dorsum of male abdomen unspecialized. (Canary Islands, Azores, Europe, North Africa, western Asia; other Old World records subject to change with revised definition of genus) ....*Loboptera* Brunner
- Tegmina short, subquadrate, attingent or slightly overlapping; male subgenital plate complex, with styli (Fig. 6); tergum 7 of male abdomen with 2 small pores without associated setae (Fig. 21). (Africa to Hawaii, other Pacific islands)...................... .... *Lobopterella* Princis
3. Dorsum of male abdomen specialized on tergum 7 (Figs. 15, 20); posterior margin of female subgenital plate weakly cleft (Fig. 19). (Known only from Buenos Aires, Argentina)........... .... *Agmoblatta*, new genus
- Dorsum of male abdomen unspecialized; posterior margin of female subgenital plate entire. (Known only from San Sebastian Island about 60 miles east of São Paulo, Brazil) .... *Isoldaia*, new genus

Princis (1957) stated that the male tergum is unspecialized in *Lobopterella;* perhaps the pores on segment 7 were hidden under the 6th tergum in his museum specimens.

Several genera of Old World Blattaria have been described to include species appearing by traditional generic characters to be related to *Loboptera.* Specimens of most of these genera are not available to us at present to permit us to study the characters shown by McKittrick (1964) to have special significance in higher classification. When such a study eventually becomes possible, the resulting realignment of genera may reveal which are most closely related to *Agmoblatta* and *Isoldaia* and may suggest what the lines of evolutionary development have been. Brief characterizations of *Loboptera* and 3 European species are included in Princis (1965). An illustration of the paraprocts of *Loboptera decipiens* similar to our Fig. 1, is in Bei-Bienko (1950, p. 169, fig. 67). The description of *Lobopterella* is in Princis (1957).

The present investigation tests the applicability of McKittrick's higher categories and particularly her separation by genitalia and other characters of 2 groups of genera which for many years have been regarded as a single group, the Pseudomopinae. Our studies indicate that there is a basis for a fundamental distinction between

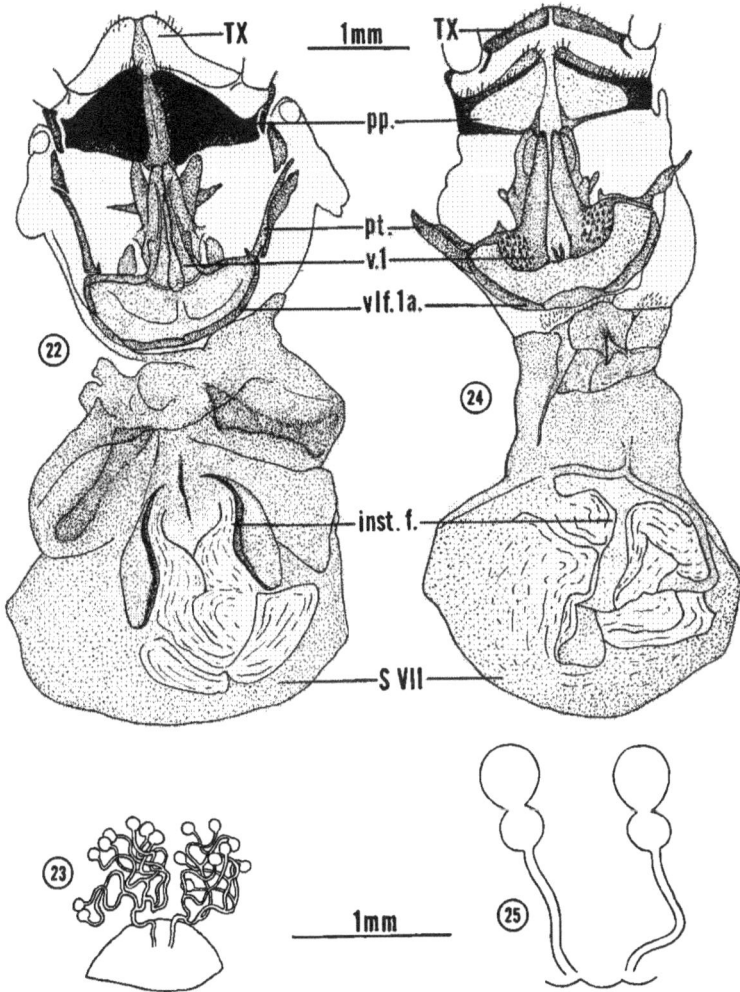

Figs. 22-23. *Loboptera decipiens* (Germar), female from Natick culture, originating in France. 22. Posterior view of genitalia. 23. Spermathecae.

Figs. 24-25. *Agmoblatta thaxteri* (Hebard), female from Natick culture, originating in Buenos Aires, Argentina. 24. Posterior view of genitalia. 25. Spermathecae.

Abbreviations: inst. f. = intersternal fold; pp. = paraprocts; pt. = paratergites; v.1 = first valve; vlf. 1a. = first valvifer arm; S VII = sternum VII; TX = tergum X.

her 2 groups, Plectopterinae and Blattellinae, though additional characters such as wing venation seem to require evaluation before all genera placed in Plectopterinae by McKittrick remain there permanently. Most genera of Pseudomopinae, in the sense used by Hebard for many years, were placed in the family Blattellidae by Princis (1960) without subfamily separation. The subfamily name Pseudomopinae dates from Burr (1910, p. 152), who also used the family name Pseudomopidae. [An earlier use of Pseudomopinae by Rehn (1903, p. 260) is invalid because the name was proposed as a substitute for Phyllodrominae, and this substitute is required by Article 39 of the International Code of Zoological Nomenclature to be based on the valid name of the original type-genus, i.e., *Blattella* Caudell.] Karny (1908) introduced Blattellidae, and that name has priority for any higher category including both *Blattella* and *Pseudomops*. [The chronology of these group names was given by Kevan and Princis (1961).]

The correlation of differences in bionomics with the higher categories was also tested in our study.

We thank Dr. K. Princis for identifying *"Loboptera" thaxteri,* Dr. Frances A. McKittrick for examining the same, Dr. R. K. Benjamin for identifying *Herpomyces lobopterae,* Mr. William Hahn for taking the photographs, and Mr. Peter Graves for camera lucida outlines of Figs. 22-24. We are also grateful to Dr. Princis for reading the manuscript and offering some very helpful suggestions.

REFERENCES

BEI-BIENKO, G. IA.
  1950. Fauna of the U.S.S.R. Insects. Blattodea. (In Russian) Zool. Inst. Akad. Nauk., S.S.S.R., Moscow, n. s. No. 40, 343 pp., 132 figs.
BURR, M.
  1910. A synopsis of the Orthoptera of Western Europe. 160 pp. London.
HEBARD, M.
  1922. Dermaptera and Orthoptera of Hawaii. Occas. Papers B. P. Bishop Mus. 7: 1-196, 2 pls.
  1932. A new species of *Loboptera* Brunner. Ent. News 43: 60-62, 2 figs.
KARNY, H.
  1908. Die zoologische Reise des naturwissenschaftlichen Vereines nach Dalmatien im April 1906. B. Spezieller Teil. etc. 6. Orthoptera und Blattaeformia. Mitt. Naturw. Ver. Univ. Wien, 6: 101-113.
KEVAN, D. K. McE., AND K. PRINCIS
  1961. *Blatta transfuga* Brunnich, 1763 (Insecta, Dictyoptera); proposed suppression under the plenary powers. Z. N. (S.) 680. Bull. Zool. Nomencl. 18 (pt. 5): 330-331.

LEFEUVRE, J. C.
   1959. Contribution à l'étude de la Biologie et de l'organogenèse des
          trachées alaires de *Blabera craniifer* Burm. 106 pp. 30 figs., 6 pls.
          D. E. S. Université de Rennes.
McKITTRICK, F. A.
   1964. Evolutionary studies of cockroaches. Cornell Univ. Agric. Expt.
          Stat. Mem. 389: 197 pp., 205 figs., 6 text-figs.
PRINCIS, K.
   1957. Zur Kenntnis der Blattarien der Kleiner Sundainseln. Verh.
          Naturf. Ges. Basel 68: 132-159, 19 figs.
   1960. Zur Systematik der Blattarien. Eos 36: 427-449, 15 figs.
   1965. Ordnung Blattariae. Bestimmungsbucher zur Bodenfauna Euro-
          pas, Lief. 3: 1-50, 56 figs.
REHN, J. A. G.
   1903. Studies in American Blattidae. Trans. Amer. Ent. Soc. 29: 259-
          290.
ROCHA, E SILVA ALBUQUERQUE, ISOLDA, and A. B. GURNEY
   1963. Records and descriptions of cockroaches from southern Brazil.
          Studia Ent. 6: 515-536, 41 figs.
ROTH, L. M. AND R. H. BARTH
   1964. The control of sexual receptivity in female cockroaches. J. Ins.
          Physiol. 10: 965-975.
ROTH, L. M. AND E. R. WILLIS
   1952. A study of cockroach behavior. Amer. Midl. Nat. 47: 66-129.
   1954. The reproduction of cockroaches. Smiths. Misc. Coll. 122: 1-49,
          94 figs.
   1958. An analysis of oviparity and viviparity in Blattaria. Trans.
          Amer. Ent. Soc. 83: 221-238, 59 figs.

NEW SPECIES OF PALPIMANIDAE (ARANEAE) FROM THE WEST INDIES*

By Arthur M. Chickering
Museum of Comparative Zoology

Members of the family Palpimanidae have been reported from many parts of the world but the number of genera and species remains small as compared to many other families of spiders. Five genera have long been recognized from the Western Hemisphere, as follows: *Anisaedus* Simon, 1893; *Compsopus* Tullgren, 1905; *Theringia* Keyserling, 1891; *Otiothops* Macleay, 1839; and *Palpimanus* Dufour, 1820. Species assigned to the genus *Otiothops* far outnumber the species belonging to the remaining four genera, taken in the Western Hemisphere, whereas species belonging to the genus *Palpimanus* have been described far more frequently than in any other genus in the Eastern Hemisphere.

Apparently, only one species of *Anisaedus* has heretofore been described from the Western Hemisphere and that was collected in Ecuador. As far as I have been able to learn, up to the present time twelve species of *Otiothops* have been described from South America, Central America and the West Indies. Both sexes are now known for *O. brevis* Simon from Venezuela, *O. macleayi* Banks from Panama, *O. walckenaeri* MacLeay from Cuba. *O. calcaratus* Mello-Leitão from Colombia is known only from the male. The eight remaining species are known only from females.

Ever since finding both sexes of *O. macleayi* Banks in Panama in 1934 and 1936 I have been interested in the family. I have taken this species in large numbers in many different localities in Panama. I have not yet found species belonging to the genus *Otiothops* in Jamaica, W. I. where I have spent considerable time on collecting trips in the last decade. The genus did not appear in my recent collection from Puerto Rico where I had hoped to find the male of *O. lutzi* Petrunkevitch. I have two immature specimens taken in the spring of 1964 on St. John, U. S. Virgin Islands which I am tentatively assigning to *O. lutzi*. In my collection made on the island of Trinidad, W. I., in the spring of 1964 I found a very interesting male and several females of a species which I am assigning to *Otiothops* even though the male palp shows features not heretofore associated with this genus. This species is described later in this brief paper. While searching through the collection of palpimanid

---

Manuscript received by the editor March 6, 1966.

spiders here in the Museum of Comparative Zoology, I found a vial
containing what appears to be a male and a female belonging to a new
species of the genus *Anisaedus* Simon, which has previously contained
only one species from the Western Hemisphere, *A. gaujoni* Simon,
1893 from Ecuador. The label in the vial gives the locality of collection as simply "West Indies." The writing appears to be that of
Miss Elizabeth Bryant, who was in charge of the collection of
arachnids in this Museum for many years. In view of the rarity of
spiders in this genus and after some discussion with colleagues, the
decision has been made to describe these specimens as representing a
new species in spite of the indefinite type locality. Types of the new
species described in this paper will be deposited in the Museum of
Comparative Zoology, Harvard University.

Genus Anisaedus Simon, 1893
Anisaedus levii sp. nov.
Figures 1-6

The species is named after Dr. Herbert W. Levi, Associate Curator of Arachnology in the Museum of Comparative Zoology at Harvard University.

Male holotype. Total length 4.81 mm. Carapace 2.21 mm. long;
1.58 mm wide opposite second coxae where it is widest; about .67 mm
tall; pedicel quite well exposed by separation of cephalothorax and
abdomen; general shape about like that of *Otiothops;* median thoracic
groove a well defined short groove in the upper and steeper third of
the posterior declivity; surface finely granulate. Eyes: eight in two
rows (Fig. 1); posterior row slightly wider than anterior row; AME
circular; all others oval or irregular to some degree; viewed from
above, anterior row gently recurved; posterior row definitely procurved; anterior medians slightly raised from general surface and
directed anterolaterally. Ratio of eyes AME : ALE : PME : PLE
= 11 : 6 : 5 : 5.5 (irregularities in shape of all eyes except AME
make it difficult to measure with desired accuracy). Viewed from in
front, anterior row gently procurved, measured by centers; posterior
row strongly procurved. AME separated from one another by about
their diameter; from ALE by slightly more than three quarters of
their diameter. Height of clypeus equal to about 2.3 times the diameter of AME; deeply grooved just above ventral margin. PME
separated from one another by a little less than four times their
diameter, from PLE by slightly less than that distance. LE separated
from one another by nearly the radius of ALE. Central ocular
quadrangle slightly wider in front than behind and slightly wider

Figs. 1-6 *Anisaedus levii* sp. nov. Fig. 1. Eyes of male holotype from above. Fig. 2. Right first leg; retrolateral view. Fig. 3. Right first metatarsus and tarsus; nearly dorsal view. Fig. 4. Lelt male palp; prolateral view. Fig. 5. Tibia and tarsus; left male palp; nearly ventral view. Fig. 6. Epigynum of female paratype; ventral view.

than long but nearly square. Chelicerae robust; flattened on anterior surface; somewhat swollen in region of fang groove; apparently with a row of 3-4 low, retromarginal teeth and a cluster of spines and hairs in region of promargin but some have been broken off and details are obscure. Lip: somewhat longer than wide at base in ratio of about 8 : 7; deeply notched at narrowed distal end; firmly united to sternum. Maxillae: moderately convergent; somewhat longer than lip but not meeting at distal ends; with lateral margins regularly rounded. Sternum: longer than wide in ratio of about 29 : 24; continued broadly between first and second coxae and narrowed between third and fourth; moderately convex; surface finely granulate; posterior end between bases of fourth coxae which are separated by their width. All coxae basally lobed but first most conspicuously so; coxae 1423 in order of length. Legs: 4123 in order of length but fourth only slightly longer than first; tibial index of first leg 16, of fourth leg 13. Figures 2-3 show essential features of first leg with its robust femur, long patella, short metatarsus and short, clubshaped tarsus; several low cusps occur on the prolateral and ventral surfaces of the patella and tibia; the metatarsus has a series of ventral teeth difficult to observe clearly because of presence of scopulae; the first tarsus and metatarsus have conspicuous prolateral scopulae with considerable iridescence; the tibia has an inconspicuous similar scopula; somewhat similar scopulae appear on other legs but they are much less conspicuous. No tarsal claws have been found on the first legs but all others have a pair; no teeth observed on them; claw tufts are present and may obscure the teeth. Palp: essentials shown in Figures 4-5; femur slender; patella very short and rounded; tibia swollen and nearly as broad as long. Abdomen: viewed from above, longer than wide in ratio of about 38 : 29; 2.47 mm long, 1.9 mm wide; broadly rounded at base and only slightly pointed posteriorly; with only two spinnerets; with a conspicuous ventral scutum anterior to genital groove and extended dorsally to cover nearly the entire basal end of the abdomen. Color in alcohol: carapace, palps, chelicerae, lip and first legs a deep, reddish brown; other legs yellowish brown with variations; sternum only slightly lighter than carapace; abdominal scutum about the same as sternum with remainder of abdomen light yellowish brown.

Female paratype. Total length 5.53 mm. Carapace 1.93 mm long; 1.43 mm wide; about .65 mm tall; considerably less robust than in male. Eyes essentially as in male with minor differences. Chelicerae: in general as in male; fang groove apparently with only two very short teeth on retromargin; promargin with a row of several long, slender spines or teeth associated with a weakly developed scopula of long, slender hairs; anterior surface finely corrugated but less flattened than in male. Lip, maxillae and sternum all essentially as in male holotype. Legs: 4123 in order of length; tibial index of first leg 15, of fourth leg 13. Only one very short claw observed on first tarsus; other tarsi apparently with two each and each claw with but one tooth. The scopulae are present but are considerably less conspicuous than in male. Anterior tarsi not clubshaped as in male but shortest of the four; first patellae much longer than others; first femora enlarged dorsoventrally much as in male. Abdomen: 3.45 mm long; 2.02 mm wide; tracheal spiracle (hidden in male) clearly shown some distance anterior to base of paired spinnerets; ventral scutum not extended dorsally to cover base of abdomen as in male. Epigynal area (Fig. 6) singularly lacking in distinctive features. Color in alcohol: essentially as in male but some differences may be noted as follows: carapace with light, irregular lines which divide the area into a series of irregular, faintly indicated stripes; sternum somewhat the same but there is a narrow median line from which radiate a series of lines toward the margin; these seem to show through from internal organs. All legs paler than in male. Abdomen also a light yellowish brown with a fine reticulation.

Type locality. As already indicated, the label accompaying the holotype and female paratype merely states that they came from the West Indies with no date of collection. It seems very likely that the specimens were sent to Miss Bryant, at that time in charge of the arachnid collections, with this very inadequate location as cited.

Otiothops carpenteri sp. nov.
Figures 7-11

The species is named after Dr. Frank M. Carpenter, Alexander Agassiz Professor of Zoology, Professor of Entomology, and Curator of Fossil Insects in the Museum of Comparative Zoology at Harvard University.

Male holotype. Total length from clypeus to posterior end of abdomen 5.27 mm; length from anterior border of slightly extended chelicerae to posterior end of abdomen 5.52 mm. Carapace 2.2 mm long; 1.54 mm wide opposite second coxae where it is widest; .77 mm tall; very convex; very gently arched along median line to beginning of posterior declivity opposite second coxae; declivity steep at first, then gradual to posterior border; with a conspicuous median pit at bottom of steepest part of declivity; surface finely granulate and corrugated throughout; with many fine hairs. Eyes: eight in two rows; viewed from above, anterior row moderately recurved and posterior row moderately procurved (Fig. 7) thus bringing lateral eyes very close together. AME circular; all others oval to some

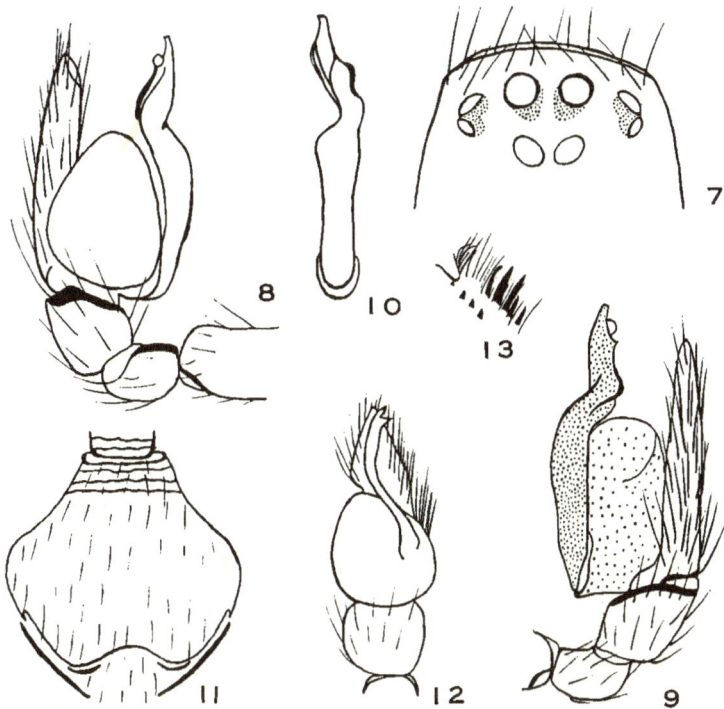

Figs. 7-11 *Otiothops carpenteri* sp. nov. Fig. 7. Eyes of male holotype
from above. Figs. 8-9. Left male palp; prolateral and retrolateral views,
respectively. Fig. 10. Embolus; nearly ventral view. Fig. 11. Epigynum of
female paratype; ventral view.
Figs. 12-13 *Otiothops walckenaeri* MacLeay. Fig. 12. Left palp; ventral
view. Fig. 13. Right fang groove of female.

degree. AME dark; all others light with PME bright silvery. Anterior row only slighly wider than posterior row. Ratio of eyes
AME : ALE : PME : PLE = 12 : 10.5 : 10 : 9 (long axes
used for measurements of oval eyes; irregularities introduce the usual
difficulties in making accurate measurements). AME separated from
one another by about two thirds of their diameter, from ALE by
about seven twelfths of their diameter. PME separated from one
another by about two fifths of their long axis, from PLE by about
1.7 times their long axis. Laterals separated from one another by
about one fifth of the long axis of PLE. Central ocular quadrangle
wider in front than behind in ratio of about 16 : 13; longer than

wide in front in ratio of about 9 : 8. Clypeus with a broad, heavily chitinized border; height equal to a little more than twice the diameter of AME. Palp: essential features shown in Figures 8-10; tarsal features quite different from others seen in the genus. Abdomen: general features as usual in the genus; ventral scutum essentially as represented for the female paratype but the area around the scutum is chitinized so that the whole basal region appears to be surrounded by this structure. Color in alcohol: carapace, chelicerae, lip and sternum a bright reddish brown; abdomen with dorsum finely dotted yellow and purplish with a clear yellowish central region and with lateral sides and venter yellowish except the scutum which is nearly like the sternum.

Female paratype. Total length 7.54 mm; base of chelicerae only slightly anterior to border of clypeus. Pedicel quite well exposed by separation of cephalothorax and abdomen. Carapace 3.05 mm long; 2.01 mm wide opposite second coxae where it is widest; 1.24 mm tall; otherwise essentially typical of the genus and as in male. Eyes essentially as in male. Chelicerae: general features as usual in the genus; with an unusual soft, membranous lobe at base of fang on ventral side; retromargin of fang groove with four small teeth and promargin with a group of several long, slender teeth or spines and long hairs. Maxillae essentially typical of females of the genus. Lip: very rugulose; a little longer than wide at base; distal end bifurcated and deeply groved. Sternum essentially as in male and typical of the genus. Legs: 4123 in order of length; tibial index of first leg 16, of fourth leg 11; first patella longest of the four and longer than first tibia; first metatarsus shortest of the four and only slightly more than one third as long as fourth. Very few trichobothria and no true spines observed. Abdomen: essentially as in male except for region of scutum and extra-scutal region; appearance of ventral scutum and epigynal region shown in Figure 11; the scutum extends dorsally a short distance above the pedicel but there is no extended chitinized region beyond the scutum as in male; a low protuberance lies just posterior to the ventral scutum. Color in alcohol: only slightly different from that of the male; light area through middle of abdominal dorsum almost absent.

Type locality. Male holotype and female paratype selected for description were taken in Caroni Swamp, Trinidad, W. I., April 14, 1964. Nine females and immature specimens were taken in Caroni Swamp and in the vicinity of the Wm. Beebe Tropical Research Station at Simla, Arima Valley, Trinidad, W. I. during April, 1964.

Otiothops walckenaeri MacLeay, 1839
Figures 12-13

Otiothops walckenaeri MacLeay, 1839, Ann. & Mag. Nat. Hist., 1839, 2: 12,
pl. 2, fig. 5. Holotype female from Cuba probably in the British Museum
(Nat. Hist.). Walckenaer, 1841; Simon, 1887, 1893; Petrunkevitch, 1911;
Bryant, 1940; Roewer, 1942; Bonnet, 1958.

This species remained known only from the female until Miss
Bryant very briefly described the male in 1940. Because this description is so brief I have thought it worth while to add some details
and a figure to aid in identification of the species. Total length 4.49
mm. Carapace 2.11 mm long; 1.43 mm wide; .91 mm tall. Essential
features of the palp shown in Figure 12; embolic spine bifurcated
distally. Eyes: viewed from above, posterior row procurved, anterior
row gently recurved; viewed from in front, anterior row slightly
procurved, measured by centers; posterior row strongly procurved.
Ratio of eyes AME : ALE : PME : PLE = 14 : 10.5 : 14 : 9.
AME circular, all others oval to some degree and with some irregularities. AME separated from one another by slightly more than
their radius; from ALE by about their radius. PME white and
shining; obliquely placed and hardly separated from one another;
separated from PLE by about 1.2 times their diameter. Lateral
eyes separated by about one sixth of the long axis of PLE. Central
ocular quadrangle wider in front than behind in ratio of about 15 :
13; longer than wide in front in ratio of about 7 : 6. Clypeus
convex; deeply grooved near ventral margin; height equal to a little
less than twice the diameter of AME. Legs: 4123 in order of length;
tibial index of first leg 14, of fourth leg 10; first femora the most
robust and slightly longer than the fourth; anterior patellae by far
the longest; fourth tibiae and metatarsi the longest of the four.
Sternum with a pair of minute cusps at lateral angle of termination between fourth coxae which are separated by 1.3 times their width. Claw
tufts throughout; claws two. Anterior tarsi club-shaped; anterior
tibiae with iridescent, prolateral scopulae or brush; anterior metatarsi
with thick scopulae along the whole prolateral surface; anterior tarsi
with similar scopulae on basal third of prolateral surface. Abdomen
with a ventral scutum extending from genital groove to pedicel and
dorsally to cover base of abdomen to dorsal anterior border. Two
spinnerets as usual; nearly surrounded by a chitinous ring incomplete
dorsally in region of anal tubercle. Tracheal spiracle apparently
indicated by a pair of minute chitinous plates a short distance anterior
to base of spinnerets.

Female. Trichobothria have been regarded as absent in this family

(Petrunkevitch, 1939) but I think I have found at least a few in the course of my study of species from Panama and the West Indies; these have been most frequently observed on the female palp. Total length 5.22 mm. Eyes: viewed from above, anterior row slightly recurved, posterior row procurved; viewed from in front, anterior row slightly procurved, measured by centers and posterior row strongly procurved. Ventral scutum much less extensive on the base of the abdomen than in male. A female from Soledad, Cuba shows cheliceral teeth as ilustrated in Figure 13.

Acknowledgements

Grant No. GB-1801 from the National Science Foundation made it possible for me to spend seven months making collections of spiders in the West Indies and Panama during the latter part of 1963 and the first five months of 1964. This grant is also making it possible for me to continue my studies in the Museum of Comparative Zoology for a considerable period. As I have frequently stated in my published papers, I am deeply appreciative of the many privileges extended to me by the staff of the Museum of Comparative Zoology, Harvard University over a period of many years. Special acknowledgements are extended to Dr. Ernest Mayr, Director; Dr. P. J. Darlington, Jr., Alexander Agassiz Professor of Zoology; Dr. Herbert W. Levi, Associate Curator of Arachnology; Miss Nelda Wright, Editor of Publications; and Dr. Frank M. Carpenter, Alexander Agassiz Professor of Zoology and Editor of Psyche for continued encouragement.

SELECTED BIBLIOGRAPHY

BANKS, NATHAN
    1929. Spiders from Panama. Bull. Mus. Comp. Zool., 69: 53-96, 4 pls.
BRYANT, ELIZABETH B.
    1940. Cuban Spiders in the Museum of Comparative Zoology. Bull.
        Mus. Comp. Zool., 86(7): 249-532, 22 pls.
CHICKERING, A. M.
    1941. The Palpimanidae of Panama. Papers of the Michigan Academy
        of Science, Arts, and Letters, 27, 1941.
PETRUNKEVITCH, ALEXANDER
    1929. The Spiders of Porto Rico. Pt. 1, Trans. Connecticut Acad. Arts
        Sci., 30: 7-158, 150 figs.
ROEWER, C. FR.
    1942. Katalog der Araneae. 1: 1-1040. Bremen.
SIMON, E.
    1892- Histoire naturelle des Araignées. Deuxième Edition.
    1903. 2 Vols. Librarie Encyclopedique de Roret, Paris.

A REVIEW OF *HALOCORYZA* ALLUAUD, WITH NOTES ON ITS RELATIONSHIP TO *SCHIZOGENIUS* PUTZEYS (COLEOPTERA: CARABIDAE).

By Donald R. Whitehead

Department of Entomology, University of Alberta

INTRODUCTION

My work on a revision of Nearctic species of the scaritine genus *Schizogenius* Putzeys has brought to light two species, one of them new, that properly belong to the otherwise African *Halocoryza* Alluaud. The major purposes of this paper are to help clarify the taxonomy of *Halocoryza*, to describe the American species, and to contrast the genus against *Schizogenius*. *Halocoryza* is poorly known and apparently very rare in collections. Despite this limitation, however, I think some interesting zoogeographic and phylogenetic points emerge. These are considered briefly, following the taxonomic treatment.

Halocoryza and *Schizogenius* belong to the "tribe" Clivinini (*sensu* Jeannel, 1946), within which they may be recognized by having a bi- or trituberculate clypeal margin (the antero-lateral angles angulate but not tuberculate), along with four to six pairs of nearly parallel longitudinal ridges between the eyes. In the closely related *Lophocoryza* Alluaud, the clypeal margin is quadrituberculate and the paired frontal carinae are reduced, the outer pairs short and oblique. At least one other genus, *Coryza* Putzeys, should probably be placed in the same group; but it is only distantly related, and lacks paired ridges on the frons.

Ball's (1960) key to North American scaritine genera, as modified by the substitution of couplet 3(1) below, can be used to distinguish *Schizogenius* and *Halocoryza* from all other Scaritini of the world.

3(1). Frons with four to six pairs of longitudinally directed carinae between eyes, AND clypeus bi- or trituberculate along anterior margin   3A.

Frons with two deep grooves, or with shallow, transverse or oblique grooves, but without a series of parallel carinae (North America); OR, if frons with four or more pairs of nearly parallel longitudinal carinae between eyes, clypeus without tubercles along anterior margin (World) .... 4.

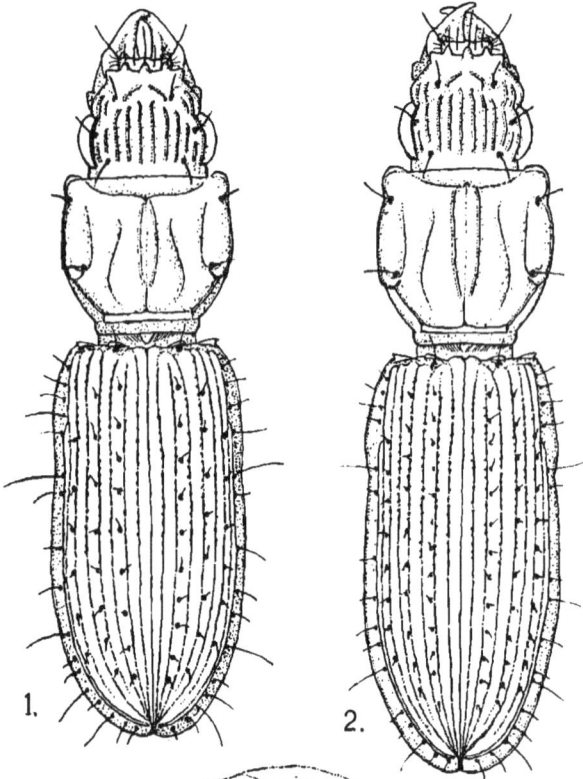

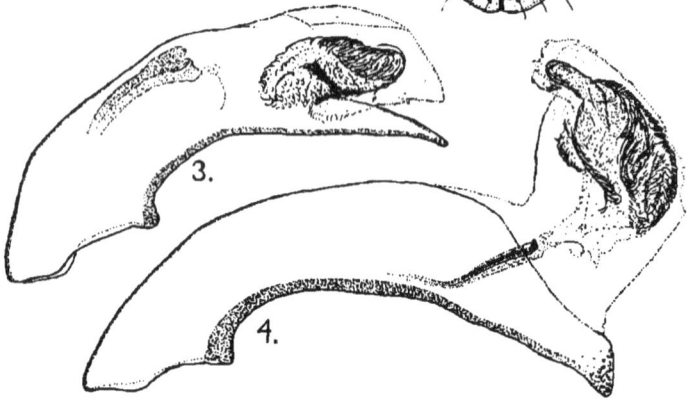

3A(3). Small beetles, length of elytra less than 1.50 mm.; second
article of antenna plurisetose; pygidium without a series of
fine paramedian longitudinal striae   *Halocoryza.*

Larger beetles, length of elytra more than 1.65 mm.; second
article of antenna at most bisetose; pygidium bearing a
series of fine paramedian longitudinal "striae" (actually
rows of small tubercles, possibly used for stridulation)
.... *Schizogenius.*

The most diagnostic characters of *Halocoryza* are the nonstriate
pygidium and the plurisetose second antennal article. But many
additional characters may be used to separate the genus from *Schizogenius,* including the following. 1. Mandibles prominent, nearly
straight laterally, abruptly bent near apices. 2. Lacinia without setae
along outer margin. 3. Frontal carinae almost perfectly regular,
parallel, equidistant, and equally raised, the frons appearing evenly
convex. 4. Neck not pitted or punctate dorsally, and not extended
along posterior margin of eyes. 5. Eyes reduced, and bordered dorsally
by a distinct carina. 6. Gula broad, at narrowest point more than
0.4 maximum width of mentum. 7. Mentum not deeply emarginate
at middle, with median tooth obsolete, and with the epilobes reduced.
8. Tarsi short, the hind leg with tarsus less than 0.6 length of tibia.
9. Paramedian carinae of second abdominal sternum short, widely
spaced and usually weakly developed. 10. Median lobe of male
genitalia neither arcuate nor abruptly deflexed in apical third.

Although *Halocoryza* and *Schizogenius* are very similar, their
separation is justifiable for several reasons. Morphologically, the
division results in two unequal but reasonably homogeneous groups.
(*Schizogenius* could be further split into perhaps four genera, but I
think subgenera would be better). The limited available biological
evidence suggests that the species of *Halocoryza* are probably all
inhabitants of the coast, whereas the species of *Schizogenius* live in
non-saline habitats. Also, their distribution patterns are best interpreted if they are treated as separate genera.

Measurements were made with an eyepiece micrometer mounted
in a Leitz stereoscopic microscope at 150 magnifications, as follows:
total length (TL), represented as the sum of the head length from

EXPLANATION OF PLATE 15

Fig. 1. Body of *H. acapulcana* (dorsal view).
Fig. 2. Same for *H. arenaria.*
Fig. 3. Median lobe of male genitalia of *H. acapulcana* (lateral view).
Fig. 4. Same for *H. arenaria* (but internal sac everted).

base of eye to antero-lateral angle of clypeus, plus pronotal length (LP) along midline, plus length of left elytron (LE, the most convenient indication of size) along suture; maximum width of head (WH) across eyes; minimum width of frons (WF) between eyes; maximum width of pronotum (WP); maximum width across both elytra (WE); length of hind tarsus (Ta), excluding claws; length of hind tibia (Ti); and length of median lobe (LA) from the dorsal margin of the basal orifice to the apex. Figures 1 and 2 were drawn with the aid of a camera lucida, figures 3 and 4 with an ocular grid.

Halocoryza Alluaud

Halocoryza Alluaud 1919:100. Type species, *Halocoryza maindroni* Alluaud 1919:101, type by monotypy. Csiki 1927:547. Jeannel 1946:228. Vinson 1956: 313.

Very small beetles (LE, 1.15-1.50 mm.); form elongate, cylindrical. Color testaceus, without metallic luster. Integument dull, with isodiametric microsculpture extensively distributed, especially conspicuous on the prothoracic pleura, abdominal sterna, and all frontal interspaces of head.

Head. Labrum slightly emarginate to biemarginate; dorsal surface with seven setae in front, the median and two outer ones longest; labrum margined laterally with four to six pairs of frayed or serrated setae, the most anterior two or three pairs curved forward and inward over mandibles. Clypeus with three subequal tuberculate teeth, the median tooth rising distinctly above plane of clypeus; paramedian carinae short and oblique, ending before reaching median tubercle; median field triangular, at base more than 1.5 greatest width of median frontal sulcus; clypeus with one pair of setae, located basally and lateral to the carinae. Clypeal suture obsolete. Frontal lobes reduced, oblique. Frons with six pairs of longitudinally directed carinae between eyes, the four median pairs very nearly straight, parallel, equidistant, equally raised, narrow and sharp throughout (the frons thus quite evenly convex in appearance); median sulcus smooth, with no trace of a median carina; carina five well developed, slightly oblique; carina six well developed, forming a distinct dorsal margin to eye, either virtually continuous (in American species) or broken on frontal lobe. Anterior supraorbital seta placed immediately in front of fifth frontal carina; posterior seta placed behind fourth carina (American species) or behind interspace between fourth and fifth carinae. Eyes reduced (WF/WH more than 0.75), coarsely faceted. Neck impunctate, not extended along posterior margin of eyes. Antennae with articles five to ten square or slightly transverse, distinctly moniliform; scape with a single subapical dorsal seta; pedicel plurisetose; articles three to eleven pubescent. Mandibles moderately elongate and prominent, nearly straight along lateral margin, abruptly bent at tips; inner ventral margin of right mandible with a small tooth near middle; scrobe oblique. Terminal article of maxillary palpus strongly swollen basally, and with a basal fan of five or six fine, appressed bristles. Lacinia with apex acute, abruptly bent, and preceded on inner margin by a series of stout setae; outer margin of lacinia lacking setae. Penultimate article of labial palpus bisetose; terminal article with a basal fan of two fine, appressed bristles. Mentum not deeply emarginate at middle, with median tooth nearly or quite obsolete, and with epilobes reduced; mentum with a paramedian and a postero-lateral seta on each side, and with a pair of large pouch-like basal sensory pits. Submentum with one paramedian and one paralateral pair of setae. Gula broad, its narrowest part more than 0.4 width of mentum.

Thorax. Pronotum usually slightly transverse, with both paramedian and paralateral longitudinal sulci (not strongly developed in American species); median sulcus closely bordered by a pair of carinae, except at base (American species only); anterior and posterior pairs of marginal setae present, posterior pair recessed from margin and situated at or near base of paralateral sulcus. Prosternum strongly compressed between coxae, broadened and convex behind where lacking setigerous punctures. Metepisternum slender, elongate.

Elytra. Lateral channel slightly narrowed at apex, shallow, lacking subapical pits; umbilicate series of punctures unbroken. Disc of elytra with at least six setae on intervals three, five, and seven; in addition, interval three has a long, whip-like seta at base. Intervals one to seven subequal, slightly convex; interval eight narrow, carinate apically, and parallel to elytral margin. Striae finely punctate in at least basal half.

Hind wings fully developed, probably functional.

Legs. Front tibiae with four well developed external teeth; apical and subapical spurs short, subequal; ventral-basal margin with three setae. Front and middle tarsi narrow and nearly glabrous in both sexes. Tarsi short (Ta/Ti less than 0.6). Paronychia subequal in length to tarsal claws.

Abdomen. One pair of paramedian ambulatory setae on sterna three to six in both sexes; two pairs of equidistant apical marginal setae on sternum six. Second sternum with a pair of straight, short, oblique, widely separated, often inconspicuous paramedian carinae. Sterna four to six each with a well developed transverse suture.

Pygidium with two paramedian setae and one large paralateral seta on each side, plus a variable number of microsetae; fine median longitudinal striae lacking; margin of pygidium entire in both sexes.

Male genitalia. Parameres subequal, slightly asymmetric, slender, with one to three setae near apex. Median lobe nearly symmetric; base non-lobate; median lobe not markedly constricted sub-basally; apical third neither compressed nor strongly bent downward, the apex strongly produced in American species. Internal sac doubly invaginated (or telescoped), with a pair of basal sclerites of variable form; apical brush lacking conspicuous spines, sclerites, or setae (American species) or with a large number of dorso-apical seta-like scales.

Immature stages. See Vinson (1956).

KEY TO THE SPECIES OF HALOCORYZA

1. Pronotum without submedian carinae; basal diameter of median lobe of male genitalia more than 0.65 ventral length, apex not produced. Old World   *maindroni, jeanneli.*

  Pronotum with submedian longitudinal carinae; basal diameter of median lobe of male genitalia less than 0.65 ventral length, apex more or less produced. New World   2.

2(1). Smaller species (LE, 1.20-1.35 mm.); pale testaceus; pronotum distinctly transverse (LP/WP less than 0.95); pronotal carinae weakly developed, separated by less than 0.1 WP; elytra sparsely setose, interval three with 10 or fewer setae; basal diameter of median lobe of male genitalia more than 0.5 ventral length, apex of median lobe acute in lateral view. Pacific coast of Mexico .... *acapulcana.*

  Larger species (LE, 1.35-1.45 mm.); dark testaceus; pronotum not distinctly transverse (LP/WP more than 0.95); pronotal carinae sharply raised and separated by more than 0.1 WP; elytra densely setose, interval three with more than 10 setae; basal diameter of median lobe of male genitalia less than 0.5 ventral length, apex of median lobe broadly truncate. West Indies .... *arenaria.*

Halocoryza acapulcana Whitehead, new species

This is the only *Halocoryza* so far known from North America. From the West Indian *H. arenaria*, it is readily distinguished by its smaller size, more transverse pronotum, less sharply elevated and more closely placed pronotal carinae, and by details of the male genitalia. See fig. 1.

Holotype male. "Acapulco, Gro., Mex. Aug. 18, 1938 Lipovsky" and "Museum of Comparative Zoology". To be deposited in the Museum of Comparative Zoology, M. C. Z. Type No. 31,168. With the characters of the genus; color pale testaceus. Sixth frontal carina of head extended unbroken onto frontal lobe. Eyes small (WF/WH, 0.80), flat, coarsely faceted, the facets all equal in size. Posterior supraorbital seta placed behind and nearly in line with the abbreviated fourth frontal carina. Lacinia appearing quadridentate, the abruptly bent apex preceded in line by three pairs of stout crossed setae. Gula at narrowest point approximately 0.48 width of mentum. Pronotum slightly transverse (LP/WP, 0.89). Paramedian and paralateral sulci shallow, inconspicuous. Median sulcus, except basally, closely bordered by a pair of weak carinae which are convergent both apically and basally; interspace at widest point less than 0.10 WP. Anterior transverse impression impunctate. Elytral interval three with nine or 10 regularly spaced setigerous punctures near midline. Intervals five and seven with six to eight setigerous punctures placed near the inner striae. Penultimate tooth of front tibia with seta submedian. Tarsi very short (Ta/Ti, 0.56). Sternum two with paramedian carinae poorly developed and inconspicuous. Median lobe of male genitalia (fig. 3) with apex strongly produced and very acute in lateral view; basal diameter of median lobe 0.55 ventral length. Internal sac with elongate basal sclerites, otherwise lacking distinct sclerites or spines; apical brush large but not heavily sclerotized, lacking enlarged seta-like plates dorso-apically.

Measurements. TL, 1.96 mm. LE, 1.20 mm. WH, 0.42 mm. WE, 0.66 mm. LA, 0.41 mm.

Allotype female. With the same label data as the holotype, to be deposited in the Museum of Comparative Zoology. This specimen differs in no significant way from the male, except for the genitalia (not examined).

Paratypes. Three males and thirteen females with the same label data as the holotype, to be distributed as follows: G. E. Ball (1 female); British Museum of Natural History (1 female); California Academy of Sciences (1 female); Institut Royal des Sciences Naturelles de Belgique (1 female); Museum of Comparative Zoology (2 males, 5 females); Jacques Nègre (1 female); United States National Museum (1 female); D. R. Whitehead (1 male, 2 females).

Variation. No important variation except size was observed: LE,

1.20-1.35 mm.; mean (17 exx.) 1.30 mm. Body proportions are quite constant: LP/WP, 0.88-0.91; WF/WH, 0.76-0.80.

Distribution. *H. acapulcana* is known only from the type series and one additional, dissected specimen from Acapulco, Guerrero, Mexico. Its name is derived from the type locality. Although no specific data are available, *acapulcana* is very probably an inhabitant of the coast, and may be intertidal.

Halocoryza arenaria (Darlington), new combination

Schizogenius arenarius Darlington 1939:84. Type locality — Rio Yaque del Sur, near Barahona, Dominican Republic; holotype in the Museum of Comparative Zoology, M. C. Z. Type No. 23,505, examined. Blackwelder 1944:27.

With the characters of the genus (see fig. 2); color dark testaceus. Larger than *H. acapulcana* — LE, 1.35-1.45 mm.; mean (5 exx.), 1.39 mm. Sixth frontal carina of head extended unbroken onto frontal lobe. Eyes small (WF/WH, 0.76-0.80), flat, coarsely faceted, the facets all equal in size. Posterior supraorbital seta placed behind and nearly in line with the abbreviated fourth frontal carina. Lacinia appearing quadridentate, the abruptly bent apex preceded in line by three pairs of stout, crossed setae. Gula at narrowest point approximately 0.48 width of mentum. Pronotum usually slightly elongate (LP/WP, 0.97-1.06). Paramedian and paralateral sulci shallow, but not as inconspicuous as in *acapulcana*. Median sulcus, except basally, closely bordered by a pair of sharply elevated carinae which are most widely separated just before apex; interspace at widest point more than 0.10 WP. Anterior transverse impression faintly punctate. Elytral interval three with twelve or thirteen regularly spaced setigerous punctures placed near the inner striae. Penultimate tooth of front tibia with seta submedian. Tarsi very short (Ta/Ti, approximately 0.55). Sternum two with paramedian carinae usually well developed. Median lobe of male genitalia (fig. 4) with apex strongly produced, broadly truncate in lateral view; basal diameter of median lobe 0.41 ventral length. Internal sac with elongate basal sclerites, otherwise lacking distinct sclerites or spines; apical brush large but not heavily sclerotized, lacking enlarged seta-like plates dorso-apically.

Distribution. I have seen six specimens of *H. arenaria*, from two localities in the West Indies: Barahona, Dominican Republic (Holotype); and Rio Piedras, Puerto Rico (one male and three females in the Museum of Comparative Zoology, and one female in my collection). In addition, one other specimen from the same

Puerto Rican locality is in the British Museum (Natural History).
Both known localities are coastal, and *arenaria* is probably an
inhabitant of the sea-shore as seems characteristic for the genus.
Darlington (1939) recorded his unique specimen as having been
taken ". . . under a deeply buried log on the sandy ocean beach . . ."
He recognized many of its essential features and (*in litt.*) suggested
to me its probable relationship to *Halocoryza*.

DISCUSSION

As noted in the generic description, Old World species of *Halocoryza* differ from New World species in at least the following
respects: pronotum lacking submedian carinae; sixth frontal carina
broken in front of eye; and apex of median lobe of male genitalia
not produced, the basal diameter more than 0.65 ventral length.
Once the genus is better known, it may be desirable to place the
American species in a separate subgenus.

Mr. Jacques Nègre (*in litt.*) has confirmed my impression that
Jeannel's (1946) description and figures of *maindroni* are very in-
accurate and misleading. The type specimen and other examples in
the Muséum National d'Historie Naturelle, Paris (including Madagascar material) resemble and may be conspecific with the Arabian
specimen of *maindroni* seen by me, and are generally in accord with
Alluaud's (1919) original description and figures. Vinson (1956)
described *H. jeanneli* from Mauritius in comparison with Jeannel's
interpretation of *maindroni;* his study seems accurate in detail, and
may portray the true *maindroni.* I suspect that these species may be
identical, since they should have a high tolerance to salinity and
desiccation and hence be able to disperse easily over sea barriers.
However, it is quite possible that the populations on both Mauritius
and Madagascar are endemics distinct from the mainland populations.

If they do disperse readily, the species of *Halocoryza* should be
widespread. However, the scanty available information indicates
that the present day distribution, though equatorial, is apparently not
pantropical. Only *acapulcana* is so far known from continental North
America, but *arenaria* may yet be found on the Atlantic coast. The
African species (*maindroni, jeanneli*) are found along the east coast
north to Arabia (Britton, 1948) and on islands in the Indian Ocean.
Although no South American or West African species are known,
at least a past occurrence in both areas must be assumed to account
for the present distribution of the genus.

Available evidence suggests dispersal from Africa, the most probable center of origin. The Atlantic was probably crossed by "rafting"

(Darlington, 1957), using the equatorial Atlantic currents. I think *Halocoryza* is unlikely to travel long distances by air, but part of the trip could have been made in this way. If so, a raft should presumably have the same catching effect as an island. Regardless of the mode of travel, however, the carabid faunas of mid-Atlantic islands are of predominantly Old World origin (e.g., Lindroth, 1960; Wollaston, 1865).

The relationships of *Halocoryza* further indicate an African origin. Its closest relative is the American *Schizogenius* (which is probably derivative or at least shared a direct common ancestor with *Halocoryza*), but no other related genera occur in the Americas. In Africa, the nearest relative is *Lophocoryza*, a relict and certainly non-derivative genus. The Indo-African genus *Coryza* is distantly related and seems to link *Halocoryza* and *Lophocoryza* with other Old World clivinine genera.

The origin of *Schizogenius* from an early invasion of the Americas by some *Lophocoryza-Halocoryza* stock, followed by a secondary invasion of *Halocoryza*, can readily be explained by the "taxon-cycle" mechanisms outlined by Wilson (1961). However, it seems unlikely that multiple trans-Atlantic migrations have taken place, even though *Halocoryza* is a relatively good candidate for such crossings. No irreversible characters of the genus conclusively demonstrate an indirect relationship with *Schizogenius*. Moreover, some characters of *Halocoryza* are found, I think primitively, in some *Schizogenius* (abbreviated paramedian clypeal carinae; paralateral pronotal sulci; paramedian ambulatory setae on sternum six in both sexes; short hind tarsi; moniliform antennae; and elytral intervals three, five, and seven with setigerous punctures).

Therefore, an alternative proposal merits mention. If but a single invasion occurred, it would follow that modern *Halocoryza* was directly ancestral to *Schizogenius*. The model for such direct ancestry is simple. *Halocoryza* at the time of invasion could have been no more different from extant Old and New World species than the latter now are from each other, and must have had the same adaptations for a seaside habitat then as now. One would not expect a rapid rate of evolution in a group of widespread species well adapted to a stable environment. That is, *Halocoryza* may be considered as an escapee from a changing environment (Maslin, 1952). But populations entering the quite different inland and freshwater habitats would have been forced to acquire new physiological adaptations at an accelerated rate. These new adaptations were doubtless accompanied by the physical modifications now found in *Schizogenius*, which can thus be considered as both a contemporary and as a descendant of *Halocoryza*.

ACKNOWLEDGEMENTS

I am indebted to Dr. Philip J. Darlington, Jr. (Museum of Comparative Zoology) for the loan of the material used in this study. I am further grateful to him for his courtesy during my visits to the Museum, and for a number of useful suggestions. Mr. Jacques Nègre (Versailles, France) has most obligingly checked material in the Muséum National d'Historie Naturelle in Paris at my request, thus providing a wealth of useful information. I wish to thank Dr. George E. Ball and Mr. John R. Barron (University of Alberta) for reading and criticising the manuscript. This study was financed in part by National Science Foundation Grant GB3312, held by Dr. Ball.

LITERATURE CITED

ALLUAUD, C.
    1919.   Contributions à l'étude des Carabiques d'Afrique et de Madagascar [Col.] XXIII. Observations sur divers Clivinides; descriptions d'une race, d'une espèce et d'un genre nouveaux. Bull. Soc. ent. Fr. 1919: 99-102.
BALL, G. E.
    1960.   Carabidae (Latreille, 1810). Fascicle 4, pp. 55-174. *In* R. H. Arnett. 1960. The beetles of the United States. Catholic University of America Press, Washington.
BLACKWELDER, R. E.
    1944.   Checklist of the coleopterous insects of Mexico, Central America, the West Indies, and South America. Part 1. Bull. U. S. nat. Mus. 185: xii + pp. 1-188.
BRITTON, E. B.
    1948.   Coleoptera: Cicindelidae and Carabidae. British Museum (Natural History) Expedition to South-West Arabia 1937-8. 1: 87-131, plates VII-IX.
CSIKI, E.
    1927.   Carabidae: Carabinae II. Pars 92, Vol. 1, pp. 315-622. *In* S. Schenkling. Coleopterorum Catalogus. W. Junk, Berlin.
DARLINGTON, P. J., JR.
    1939.   West Indian Carabidae V. New forms from the Dominican Republic and Puerto Rico. Mem. Soc. cubana Hist. nat. 13: 79-101.
    1957.   Zoogeography. John Wiley and Sons, Inc., New York. xi + 675 pp.
JEANNEL, R.
    1946.   Coléoptères carabiques de la region malgache (première partie). Faune de l'Empire française 6: 372.

LINDROTH, C. H.

    1960. The ground-beetles of the Azores (Coleoptera: Carabidae) with some reflexions on over-seas dispersal. Bol. Mus. municipal Funchal 1960 (13): 5-48.

MASLIN, T. P.

    1952. Morphological criteria of phylogenetic relationships. Systematic Zool. 1: 49-70.

VINSON, J.

    1956. A new scaritine beetle from Mauritius. Mauritius Inst. Bull. 3: 313-316.

WILSON, E. O.

    1961. The nature of the taxon cycle in the Melanesian ant fauna. Amer. Nat. 95: 169-193.

WOLLASTON, T. V.

    1865. Coleoptera atlantidum, being an enumeration of the coleopterous insects of the Madeiras, Salvages, and Canaries. John Van Voorst, London. xlvii + 526 + 140 pp.

CAMBRIDGE ENTOMOLOGICAL CLUB

A regular meeting of the Club is held on the second Tuesday of each month October through May at 7:30 p. m. in Room B-455, Biological Laboratories, Divinity Ave., Cambridge. Entomologists visiting the vicinity are cordially invited to attend.

The illustration on the front cover of this issue of Psyche is a reproduction of a drawing of a female bethylid wasp, *Pseudisobrachium terresi* Mann, from Haiti (Psyche, vol. 22, p. 165, 1915).

BACK VOLUMES OF PSYCHE

The Johnson Reprint Corporation, 111 Fifth Avenue, New York 3, N. Y., has been designated the exclusive agents for Psyche, volumes 1 through 62. Requests for information and orders for such volumes should be sent directly to the Johnson Reprint Corporation.

Copies of issues in volumes 63-72 are obtainable from the editorial offices of Psyche. Volumes 63-72 are $5.00 each.

F. M. CARPENTER
Editorial Office, Psyche,
16 Divinity Avenue,
Cambridge, Mass., 02138.

PSYCHE

A JOURNAL OF ENTOMOLOGY

Vol. 73   December, 1966   No. 4

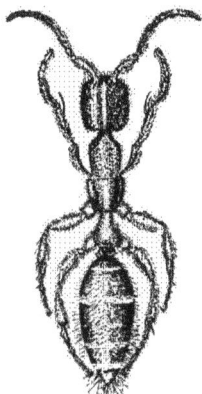

CONTENTS

PSYCHE is published quarterly by the Cambridge Entomological Club, the issues appearing in March, June, September and December. Subscription price, per year, payable in advance: $4.50 to Club members, $5.00 to all other subscribers. Single copies, $1.25.

Checks and remittances should be addressed to Treasurer, Cambridge Entomological Club, 16 Divinity Avenue, Cambridge, Mass.

Orders for back volumes, missing numbers, notices of change of address, etc., should be sent to the Editorial Office of Psyche, Biological Laboratories, Harvard University, Cambridge, Mass.

IMPORTANT NOTICE TO CONTRIBUTORS

Manuscripts intended for publication should be addressed to Professor F. M. Carpenter, Biological Laboratories, Harvard University, Cambridge, Mass.

Authors contributing articles over 4 printed pages in length may be required to bear a part of the extra expense, for additional pages. This expense will be that of typesetting only, which is about $10.00 per page. The actual cost of preparing cuts for all illustrations must be borne by contributors: the cost for full page plates from line drawings is ordinarily $12.00 each, and the full page half-tones, $18.00 each; smaller sizes in proportion.

AUTHOR'S SEPARATES

Reprints of articles may be secured by authors, if they are ordered at the time proofs are received for corrections. A statement of their cost will be furnished by the Editor on application.

The September, 1966, Psyche (Vol. 73, no. 3) was mailed January 25, 1967.

THE LEXINGTON PRESS. INC., LEXINGTON, MASSACHUSETTS

PSYCHE

Vol. 73   December, 1966   No. 4

DISCOVERY OF THE FEMALE *PLUMARIUS* (HYMENOPTERA, PLUMARIIDAE)[1]

By Howard E. Evans
Museum of Comparative Zoology

The family Plumariidae has long been a puzzle to hymenopterists. It is represented by two poorly known genera: *Plumarius*, which ranges throughout arid and semiarid regions from Ecuador to Chile and Argentina, and *Myrmecopterina*, known from semiarid situations in South Africa. The two genera are very similar; both are of generally pale coloration and possess large eyes and ocelli, not unlike other nocturnal Aculeata such as certain Mutillidae and Tiphiidae. Both genera have been known for many years from males only, and nothing whatever is known of their biology. They are commonly placed in the superfamily Scolioidea, although their strange antennae and wings, unusual development of the front of the head, long legs, lack of constriction between the first two metasomal segments, and other unusual features leave one wondering if this is, in fact, the correct taxonomic assignment for this family.

Many years ago my former professor, J. C. Bradley (1921a), remarked regarding *Plumarius* that "any one who will discover and make known the female and her habits will cover himself with well merited distinction . . . The female will undoubtedly yield important evidence of the correct systematic position for the genus." The distinction of discovery belongs to Drs. E. S. Ross and E. I. Schlinger, who collected two females in Peru and sent them to me as Bethylidae. After much study, I am convinced they can be nothing other than females of the genus *Plumarius*. The distinction of elucidating their habits remains to be claimed.

These two females were collected 22 miles north of Pativilca, in Lima Province, Peru, on January 15, 1955, at 150 meters elevation.

[1]Research and publication supported by a grant from the National Science Foundation, No. GB-1544.

Manuscript received by the editor October 22, 1966.

Dr. E. S. Ross writes that these specimens were collected in the day-time during a search for Embioptera, probably "under stones on sandy silt". "The locality was extreme desert typical of coastal Peru. It must have shown some effects of coastal fog, such as lichens on rocks, else we wouldn't have stopped for embiids" (E. S. Ross, *in litt.*). Dr. E. I. Schlinger recalls this as a "loma zone surrounded by arid to semi-arid vegetation". He collected spiders under rocks and believes the wasps may have been collected there, too. Since these females have all the features of hypogaeic Hymenoptera, their oc-curence under rocks seems logical enough.

Ross and Schlinger collected many male *Plumarius* in Peru (though none at this locality) and Dr. Marius Wasbauer has been studying these in a preliminary way. He writes that there appear to be three species in Peru and Ecuador. Since *Plumarius* is com-pletely unworked taxonomically, I shall refrain from placing a specific name on the females. The specimens have been returned to the California Academy of Sciences, where they await inclusion in a much-needed revision of this genus (hundreds of males have now accumulated in museums).

I shall present first a detailed description of these females, then a few notes on male structure, and finally a discussion of the prob-able relationships of the Plumariidae. Since both females are some-what imperfect, my description is a composite from the two specimens, parts of one of which have been mounted on a slide. The two specimens are virtually identical in size and structure.

Description of the female Plumarius. — Length about 5 mm; body somewhat depressed, wings and tegulae completely absent (Fig. 1); body light castaneous, shining, the appendages testaceous. Head strongly depressed, very thin, prognathous; eyes of moderate size, not protruding from surface of head, each containing approximately 150 facets; ocelli absent (Fig. 2). Occipital carina closely surround-ing foramen, complete but not at all visible in frontal view; under surface of head with mouth-parts far removed from occipital fora-men, the space filled by a broad genal bridge, the midline narrowly depressed but not really sulcate; hypostomal sulcus closely paralleling the margin of the broad proboscidial fossa. Labium simple, palpi with three subequal segments (Fig. 6); maxillae small, closely as-sociated with labium, bearing fairly long, 5-segmented palpi (Fig. 7); mandibles large, strongly tapered toward the apex, bear-ing three large apical teeth, each of them (but especially the large apical tooth) marked by a thick, horny plate; mandibles with many small sensilla and with numerous setae arising near the base (Fig.

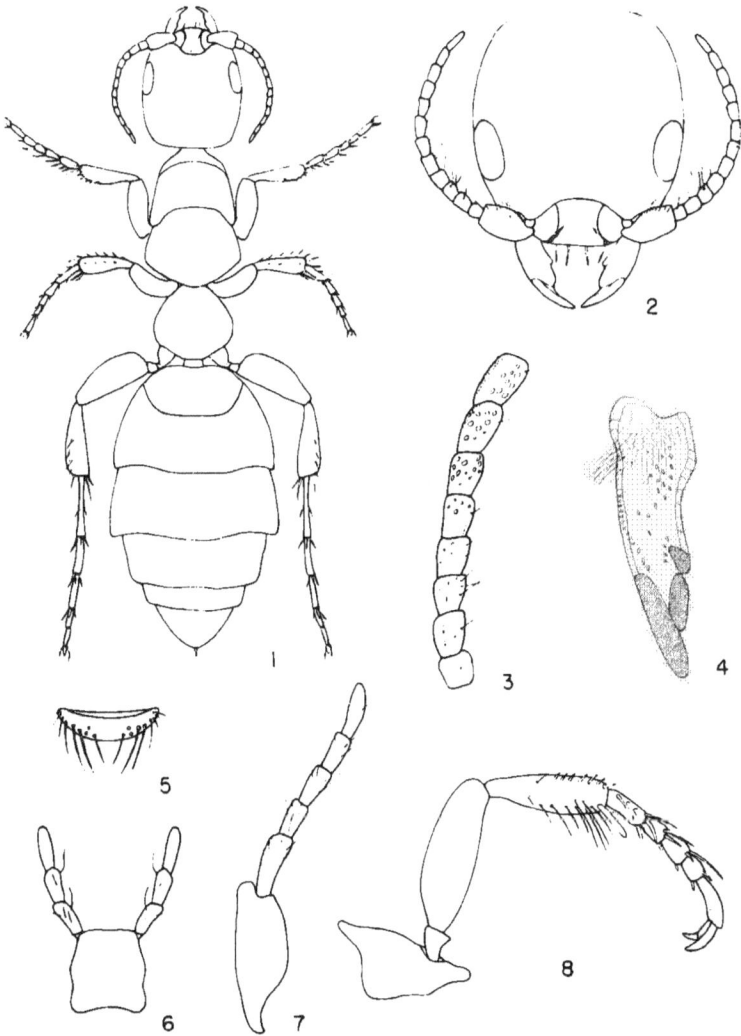

Figures 1 — 8. Structure of female *Plumarius*, from locality 22 miles
N of Pativilca, Peru. Fig. 1. Dorsal view of body. Fig. 2. Frontal view
of head. Fig. 3. Detail of antennal segments 2-9. Fig. 4. Mandible. Fig. 5.
Labrum. Fig. 6. Labium. Fig. 7. Maxilla. Fig. 8. Front leg.

4); labrum concealed by the clypeus except for some of its long apical setae, when dissected away found to be very short, semicircular (Fig. 5). Clypeus broad, weakly rounded apically, its median area rather flat, but the sides deeply hollowed out for the reception of the scape; apical margin, opposite the antennal insertions, with a pair of tufts of matted setae (Fig. 2); front weakly, evenly convex, strongly shining, without punctures or setae, distance between eyes measuring 2.6 × eye height; distance from eye tops to vertex crest much exceeding eye height, the vertex very broadly rounded, slightly concave at the midline, the crest rather sharp. Antennae with 13 well-defined segments, arising from simple orbits; middle segments weakly serrate; segments 2-9 each with one or more fairly prominent setae, segments 6-13 with a variety of prominent sensory pores and spicules (Figs. 2, 3).

Thorax and propodeum also strongly polished and virtually without surface sculpturing, with a few pale setae arising from constricted portions such as the neck region, the thoracic-propodeal junction, and the propodeal-metasomal junction; greatest width of thorax (across the mesothorax) subequal to width of head; pronotum fairly long, its posterior margin arcuate, with weakly developed, slightly rounded posterior lobes; proepisterna unusually large and convex, roughened ventrally with small, wart-like protuberances, the midventral line of the prothorax indistinctly sulcate; prosternum small, poorly differentiated; base of front coxa with a partially separated sclerite which may represent the proepimeron (Fig. 11). Mesothorax broad, smooth, with no separation whatever into scutum, scutellum, or pleura; metathorax apparently absent, the hind legs appearing to rise from the propodeum close to the articulation of the metasoma; propodeum narrowly connected to thorax, depressed, its contours very smooth. Coxae large, conical, all three pairs contiguous medially and also capable of overlapping when the legs are pressed against the body; front coxae terminating in a flattened process which extends beyond the origin of the trochanters; hind femora incrassate, front femora more weakly so; all tibiae spinose as figured; tibial spurs 1-2-2, the spur of the front tibia not forming a well defined antennal cleaner; front tarsus with a pecten of short, stout spines (Fig. 8), other tarsi very slender, rather bristly at the joints; claws simple, arolia fairly large.

Metasoma broad, attached to propodeum by a petiole which is no longer than broad; first tergite short, its posterior margin arched; first sternite short, broadened slightly behind the petiole but apparently broadly overlapped by the large second sternite. Sixth (apical) segment rather broad, simple, non-setose, giving rise to an apparently rather short sting.

Comments on characters of male Plumarius.— Evidence that the females just described represent the opposite sex of nocturnal males of the genus *Plumarius* may be summarized as follows: (1) both males and females are of generally light brown coloration; (2) Peruvian males I have seen are of about the size one would predict for males of the wasp described above; (3) both sexes have erect setae on the antennae, although these are much more abundant in the male; (4) the labium is very similar, the labial palpi 3-segmented in both sexes (much as in Fig. 6); (5) in both sexes the mandibles are tridentate, the teeth thickened and heavy, and the mandibles have numerous setae and sensilla; (6) the labrum of the male is small, bristly, and mostly or wholly concealed by the clypeus, though in general more narrow than in the female; (7) in both sexes the prosternum is very large, and there is a partially differentiated sclerite just in front of the anterior coxae which probably represents the proepimeron (Figs. 11 and 12); (8) all coxae are subconical, and the members of each pair are contiguous or nearly so; (9) the mesopleura are strongly swollen; (10) there is no constriction between the first two metasomal sternites.

In spite of these many similarities, the males are radically dissimilar to the females in many features: they have large eyes and ocelli, the wings are fully developed, and the thorax is without the many reductions associated with flightlessness; the maxillary palpi are much longer and have six segments rather than five; the face and clypeus are unusually elongate; the abdomen is sessile; and of course there are the usual differences in the form of the abdomen and in the genitalia. On the whole the sexual dimorphism is no greater than one has learned to expect in certain Tiphiidae (Brachycistidinae, Thynninae) or Bethylidae (Pristocerinae).

In the effort to determine the correct systematic position of the Plumariidae, it seemed desirable to make a preliminary study of the terminal segments of the male abdomen, since the family was omitted by Snodgrass (1941) and others who have studied the male genitalia of Hymenoptera. The apical tergite (Fig. 14) is of generalized structure and bears pygostyles much longer than any known in the Bethylidae, though not dissimilar to those of certain Mutillidae and Formicidae (Snodgrass, 1941, plates 13, 14). The apical sternite (Fig. 13) is a simple, tongue-shaped structure similar to that of certain Formicidae or Bethylidae, and quite unlike the pseudosting of most Scolioidea. The genitalia (Fig. 15) are of basically simple structure. The small basal ring and form of the aedoeagus and volsellar structures are all suggestive of the Bethylidae; however, there is no clear separation of the parameres from their basal plates, a feature more characteristic of the Scolioidea and certain Formicidae. All of this is of some academic interest, but at the same time one is left with the feeling that although the terminalia of *Plumarius* do not quite resemble those of known Bethyloidea, Scolioidea, or Formicoidea, in fact there seem to be no well defined superfamilial characters in the genitalia. One can at least say that there are no noteworthy reductions or specializations in the terminalia of *Plumarius*.

The systematic position of the Plumariidae.— It is sometimes stated that the major feature of the Bethyloidea is the lack of sexual dimorphism in antennal segmentation. If this is true, these wasps belong in the Bethyloidea. Other bethyloid features include the head shape of the female, segmentation of the labial palpi, lack of constriction between the first two metasomal segments, and the genitalic features mentioned above. However, the broad, well-veined hind wings, with distinct closed cells, tend to eliminate the group from the Bethyloidea, as do the spinose front and hind legs. The Bethyloidea must, of course, have evolved from an ancestor having a more complete venation, just as the Scolioidea undoubtedly evolved from an ancestor lacking sexual dimorphism in the antennae. I suggest that *Plumarius* is a relic of an ancient stock, one portion of which gave rise to the Bethyloidea, another to the Scolioidea and higher wasps. This ancient stock has apparently managed to survive by becoming adapted to severe desert conditions in South America and South Africa, the males being nocturnal, the females hypogaeic.

It should be noted that Sharov (1957) has described and figured the wing of a supposed wasp from the Cretaceous of Siberia, *Cretavus sibiricus* (Fig. 10), pointing out the resemblance of the wing to that of *Plumarius* (Fig. 9). Although some differences are obvious, particularly in the shape of the stigma and marginal cell, there are indeed some striking similarities, particularly in the presence of several more or less distinct veins on the outer third of the membrane which are absent in other wasps. Sharov interprets these as the termini of branches of the radial sector and of media. Bradley (1921b), however, notes the presence of "accessory spurs" in this position in many Mutillidae, and suggests that in *Plumarius* these veins arose from such spurs.

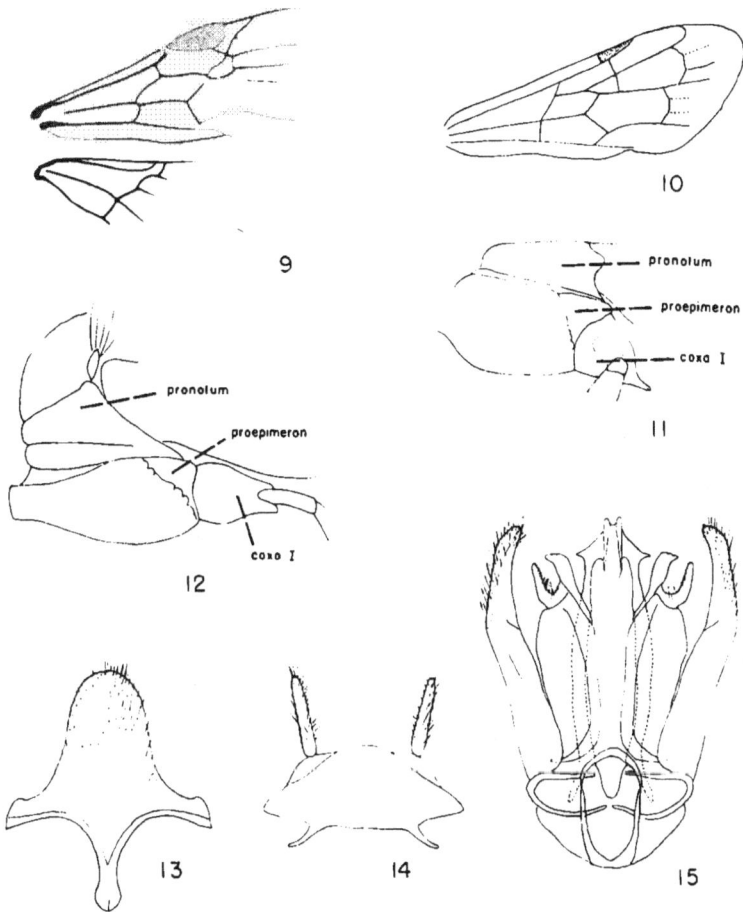

Fig. 9. Wings of male *Plumarius*. Fig. 10. Front wing of *Cretavus sibiricus* Sharov (Cretaceous) (after Sharov, 1957). Fig. 11. Lateral view of anterior part of thorax of female *Plumarius*. Fig. 12. Lateral view of anterior part of thorax of male *Plumarius*. Fig. 13. Subgenital plate (mesosomal sternite VIII) of male *Plumarius*. Fig. 14. Apical tergite (mesosomal tergite VIII) of male *Plumarius*, showing pygostyles. Fig. 15. Male genitalia.

I have described another group of wasps also having 13-segmented
antennae in the female and sharing some features with the Scolioidea
and some with the Bethyloidea. This is the family Scolebythidae
(Evans, 1963), known from one genus and species in Madagascar
and one genus and species in Brazil. Female scolebythids are winged
and apparently adapted as parasites of wood-boring insects. I described the family without knowledge of the male, after considering
and rejecting the possibility that *Plumarius* might represent the
male sex of scolebythids. This was a fortunate decision, since I have
not only discovered the female *Plumarius* but also a male of the
scolebythid *Clystopsenella longiventris* Kieffer. This male was with
a series of females of this species collected by Fritz Plaumann on
October 5, 1952, at Rondon, Paraná, Brazil. There is virtually no
sexual dimorphism in this species, except that the male metasoma
is simple, lacking the modification of sternite V of the female, and
the terminalia are of course different (though the slide mount I
made of the terminalia was lost before I studied it in detail, and
I am therefore still unable to present any notes on the terminal
structures of the male). Other minor differences from the female
are as follows: antennae considerably more slender, though otherwise
similar; vertex considerably less produced above the eye tops; front
femora less robust. The structure of the mesosoma is especially similar in the two sexes, including all details of the wings.

There is no question, then, that the Scolebythidae and Plumariidae
represent two very different families, now both known from both
sexes. In the former there is little sexual dimorphism, and one assumes that both sexes are associated with burrows in wood in which
their hosts live. In the Plumariidae there is marked sexual dimorphism, the females presumably searching for their hosts beneath the
ground in deserts, the males flying about at night. Both families
retain certain generalized features which suggest that they arose
from a very primitive aculeate near the common ancestor of the
Scolioidea and Bethyloidea: of special note are the 13-segmented
antennae in both sexes, the fairly well defined proepimeron, and the
lack of a constriction between the first two metasomal segments. The
many striking differences are in large part associated with the very
different habitats these wasps are believed to occupy. Probably the
two families have evolved independently of each other and of other
Aculeata since before the beginning of the Tertiary. A cladist would
doubtless argue that both deserve superfamilial status. A realist
might at the same time point to this as still another indication of the
difficulties of grouping the Aculeata into superfamilies. As a realist,

I would go so far as to ask if (assuming the superfamily is a useful category in other Hymenoptera) all Aculeata ought not to be placed in a single superfamily. Finally, a word should be said about *Plumarius* as a possible progenitor of the ants. Brown and Nutting (1950) point out that the venation of the male is in some ways antlike, although they remark that in general the male is "not a very promising candidate for ant ancestry". This remark seems even more applicable to the female, which has a very broad, smooth junction between the first two metasomal tergites, only five segments in the maxillary palpi, and a variety of unantlike specializations in body form. *Anthobosca,* in the Tiphiidae, remains a much better prototype for the ants.

REFERENCES

BRADLEY, J. C.
    1921a. Some features of the hymenopterous fauna of South America.
        Actes Soc. Sci. Chili, 30: 51-74.
    1921b. Plumarius, an aberrant genus of Hymenoptera. Proc. Wash.
        Acad. Sci., 11: 214.
BROWN, W. L. JR., AND W. L. NUTTING
    1950. Wing venation and the phylogeny of the Formicidae (Hymenoptera). Trans. Amer. Ent. Soc., 75: 113-132.
EVANS, H. E.
    1963. A new family of wasps. Psyche, 70: 7-16.
SHAROV, A. G.
    1957. First discovery of a Cretaceous stinging Hymenoptera (Aculeata). Doklady Academia Nauk, USSR, 112: 943-944.
SNODGRASS, R. E.
    1941. The male genitalia of Hymenoptera. Smithsonian Misc. Coll., 99 (4): 1-86, 33 pls.

RUPTOR OVI, THE NUMBER OF MOULTS IN DEVELOPMENT, AND METHOD OF EXIT FROM MASONED NESTS. BIOLOGY OF EUMENINE WASPS, VII.

By Kenneth W. Cooper,
Hanover, N. H.

Many common mason wasps of the eumenine genera *Ancistrocerus, Symmorphus*, and *Rygchium* construct nests which, for a period from a month and a half to nearly ten months, must enclose and protect the food supply and the young wasps during their helpless egg, larval and pupal stages. These nests may be made by cross-partitioning into a succession of cells ready-formed, empty, blind tunnels, such as abandoned burrows of wood-boring insects, hollow stems of plants, or even holes left by large nails. Nearly each cell, as it is made, receives an egg and sufficient paralysed prey (caterpillars or phytophagous beetle larvae, depending on the species of wasp) for development of a newly hatched larva to the adult wasp. The protective plug that closes the completed nest, and the partitions between cells, are made by the female wasp from a cohesive mortar of clay, loam or sand, worked up with water (and perhaps "saliva"). Other wasps of these genera, and of more or less related genera such as *Eumenes* and *Pseudomasaris* (a masarine), fashion their entire nests of mortar, building aggregates of masonry tubes, pots, or lumpy masses of cells affixed to plant stems, bark, or the exposed faces of rocks. Not only must the nests of mason wasps be hard and sufficiently strong to resist possible mechanical stresses and penetration by parasites but, being often subject to rain and melting snow, like man's masonry, they must withstand dissolution when built in exposed situations.

It is not surprising that the walls and plugs of such nests serve other functions than mere protection. For example, they prevent cannibalism among the brood, they serve hygienic functions, they make possible the use of lightly paralysed prey, and so on. They also serve as the channel of an essential communication system between mother and young that their very presence necessitates; these and other matters I have discussed elsewhere (Cooper 1957). But if the cement- or plaster-like masonry succeeds in keeping other insects out of the nest, as in general it does so well, by what means do the developed wasps, imprisoned within the nest, gain their exit?

Manuscript received by the editor December 5, 1966

There is an earlier point too in the life of each wasp at which, if it is to survive, it must likewise break out of an enclosure the walls of which it did not make. This first passage is of course prelude to the onset of active larval life, being penetration of the tough chorion or "egg shell". It is my aim to show how each of these escapes is accomplished. So far as I can discover, only Nielsen (1932) has disclosed the special aspect of exit from a masoned nest, and this in a species of *Symmorphus*. The means of escape from the chorion seems a wholly new observation, even though the mechanism may prove to be widespread among Hymenoptera. In addition I shall show that these wasps have a fixed number of larval moults, an aspect of the biology of hunting wasps about which there has been considerably uncertainty. The records which now follow have all been made from broods originally established by mother wasps in "trap nests".

1. Hatching of *Ancistrocerus antilope* (Panz).

When a newly completed, provisioned cell of *Ancistrocerus antilope* is opened, just as with most other eumenids, the cream colored, slightly bowed, elongate and turgid egg is normally found above or among the paralysed prey. In either case, the blunt caudal end of the egg is firmly attached to the ceiling of the cell by a short, flexible suspensory thread that is from 0.5 to 0.8 mm long and 14-16μ in diameter (fig. 1). The egg itself is about 2.7-2.8 mm long by 0.8 to 0.9 mm wide, rather small for a eumenid's egg to judge from the sample of eggs of 13 species measured by Iwata (1955). When fresh, the chorion is tough, seemingly inelastic, and leathery to manipulation by forceps, even though very thin. At 20°C, the egg hatches some 2 to 4 days after it is laid (Cooper 1953).

Shortly before hatching occurs, the brownish tips of the mandibles and the segmentation of the body of the larva can just be seen through the chorion. The first larval movements that I detected were of the forebody, and mandibles. Thereafter they may include intermittent gentle squirmings of the entire body. The larva evidently takes up most of the fluid lying between it and the envelope of the egg during its first exertions, for the still intact chorion now everywhere becomes closely appressed to the larva, and may then follow the contours of the larva's body segments as Taylor (1922) has observed. Three denticles, at the levels of the 4th, 5th and 6th postcephalic segments of the larva, thereupon burst the chorion on each side of the egg, minute amounts of fluid escaping when this happens. The caudal third of the chorion collapses and shrivels, forming two or more folds that radiate lengthwise from near the base of the suspensory filament, reducing the free space at the caudal pole of the egg (fig. 2).

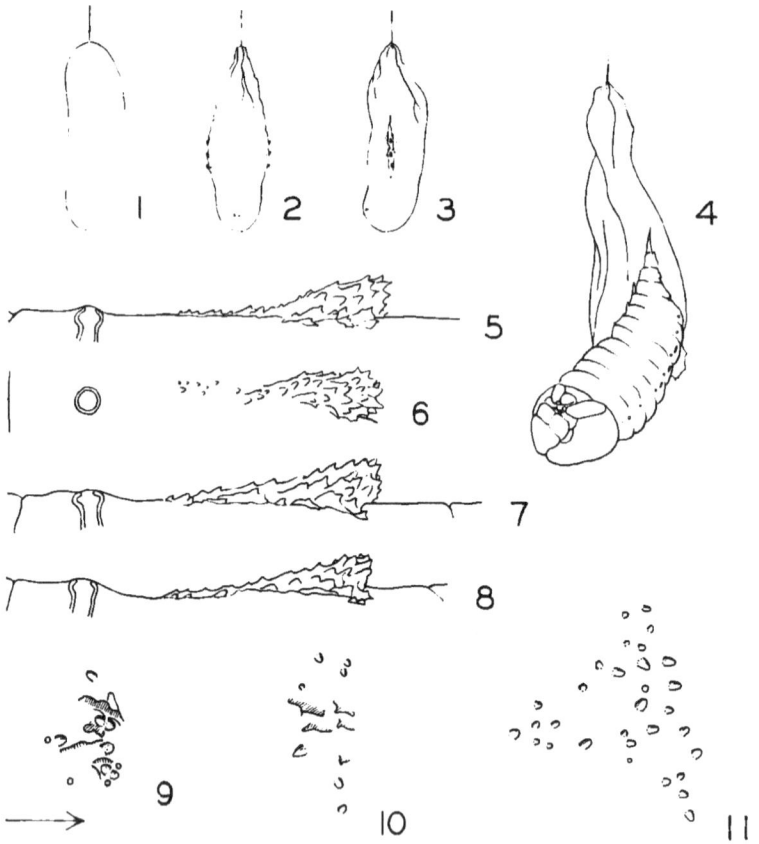

COOPER — EUMENINE WASPS

With denticles protruded through the chorion, the larva spasmodically shortens and thickens its body (for periods of three to five seconds), as though forcing itself, by creeping movements, against the lateral walls of chorion and the cephalic pole of the egg. These exertions drive the denticles, as though saw-teeth, lengthwise through the lateral chorion of the medial third of the egg, ever widening the two more or less ragged rifts both fore and aft (fig. 3). Following each period of rest, lateral pressure, renewed each time that the larval forebody thickens, tears the rent chorion more widely until, finally, the whole anterior half of the egg lies open, cut into dorsal and ventral flaps in a fashion that reminds of Wheeler's (1889) description of hatching of the beetle *Leptinotarsa decemlineata* (Say). With its anterior half free of the egg but its hinder body still enclosed and adherent within the shriveled chorion, the newly emerged larva immediately commences to feed on the nearest prey (fig. 4). Though hatched, the larva does not normally quit the chorion until it casts its first moult.

In all, I have watched 16 eggs hatch. The speediest case took 20 minutes, the longest something less than 90 minutes but more than an hour. On the average, with the temperature ranging between 20°-28°C, hatching requires 45 minutes, with a standard deviation of ± 9 minutes. The chorions of most eggs were bilaterally split as I have described, but in 3 cases the larva's denticles penetrated one side of the egg only. In each of these instances, the single rent was ultimately enlarged by the movements of the larva until the whole of its forebody emerged; these larvae seemed in no way handicapped by failure of the egg to be split on both sides.

Figures 1-3. — Hatching of the egg of *Ancistrocerus antilope* (Panz.), magnif. 9 ✕; fig. 1.-unhatched egg; fig. 2.-egg viewed from ventral surface, *ruptor ovi* of abdomen have perforated chorion on each side, chorion collapsed caudally, mandibular tips of larva visible at cephalic pole (below); fig.3-egg at mid-hatching seen from the right side, note tear in chorion, *ruptor ovi of* abdomen, and tips of manbibles at lower left.

Figure 4 — Newly hatched larva in feeding position, magnif. 15✕; the larva will normally adhere to the split chorion until instar-2.

Figures 5-8 — Abdominal *ruptor ovi*, magnif. 390✕; in each case the spiracle to the right (anterior) originates from the segmental tracheal trunk of the *preceding* body segment. Fig. 5.-ruptor of abdominal segment-1, nearly profile view. Fig. 6.-ruptor of abdominal segment-1, above. Fig. 7.-ruptor of abdominal segment-2, in "profile". Fig. 8.-ruptor of abdominal segment-3, in "profile".

Figures 9-11 — Spinous sets and laminae (hatched) of the *ruptor ovi* of thoracic segments-1, -2, and -3 respectively, magnif. 500✕, see text.

Note: — Orientation of *ruptor ovi* in figs. 5-11 is indicated by arrow below fig. 9, pointing caudally; all figures are freehand sketches, to scale.

2. The *ruptor ovi*, or egg bursters

The newly hatched larva of *Ancistrocerus antilope* has defined sets of minute, fixed spines (0.8-9μ long × 0.8-6μ in diameter) on the dorso-lateral surfaces of the three thoracic segments and the first three abdominal segments (figs. 4-11). In each case these sets of spines are located anterior and very slightly dorsal to each corresponding spiracle, at or near the mid-length of its segment; the spines are not moveable, and their bases appear to be continuous with the cuticle. Unlike the general scatter of spines in the thoracic sets, nearly every spine of each field on the first three abdominal segments is at least partially coalesced with its neighbors. The massive, caudally directed, hypertrophied, pale amber teeth thus formed on the sides of the anterior abdomen bear many smaller denticles and blade-like serrations that also point caudally (figs. 5-8). From the base of their most cephalad component spine to their caudal tip, these elongated, composite abdominal teeth are, on the average, some 60-80μ long × 20-30μ at their widest. Each rises at an average angle of 12°-15° (30° in an extreme instance) from its anterior origin on the lateral surface of the larva to a caudad peak that is some 14-18μ high.

The dentate fields of the three thoracic segments are more loosely organized, their spines and blade-like projections not coalescing into a single large structure. That on each side of thoracic segment-1 consists of 10-14 irregularly directed, stubby spines, and 4 or more blade-like ridges or denticles arrayed in a patch that is much wider (ca 30μ) than long (ca 22μ) (fig. 9). The spinous sets on each side of thoracic segment-2 are also wider (ca 30μ) than long (ca 18μ), each possessing 7-10 small spines and four or more lamina-like denticles (fig. 10). As in the case of the sets on segment-1, those on segment-2 have their spines and denticles projecting in different directions, more or less haphazardly, and several spines and blades may appear coalesced.

Each field of spines on thoracic segment-3 is much larger than those of segments-1 and-2, differing also by being roughly triangular in shape, with the apex of the triangle pointing forward (fig. 11). The wide base of this field lies caudad, roughly normal to the long axis of the larva, and approximately equal in length to the altitude (ca 60 and 55μ respectively). Individual spines are for the most part well spaced, numerous (ca 25-35), and directed caudally. In some larvae, however, 3 or more of the posterior denticles may be laminate and clustered, much as those of the first two thoracic fields.

At hatching, when the larva has taken up the fluid enclosed by the intact chorion and commences to creep, it is quite likely that the spines and laminate denticles of the thoracic fields of each side assist chiefly in the pushing and creeping movements of the larva by gaining purchase against the chorion; in doing so, they probably no more than abrade the inner face of the chorion, for they do not appear to penetrate it. It is quite otherwise, however, with the compact, high multidentate teeth of the first three abdominal segments.

Drawn forward against the appressed chorion, ratchet like, the strongly projecting teeth of the first three abdominal segments must receive litle resistance. But when moved rearwards as the larva squirms forward, their spines and blades thrust into the chorion, perforating, tearing and sawing it in the manner I have described. Once the chorion is slit open along each side of the middle third of the egg, those spines of the thoracic fields which are directed forward or laterally very likely engage the anterior end of each lateral rift as the larva alternately elongates and contracts, thereby extending the tear in the chorion still further forward.

There can be little question that all of these fields of spines are adaptations solely related to hatching, for they are present on the cuticle of the first instar larva only, and are shed with that cuticle at the first moult. Indeed the integument of the second instar has *no* vestige or reminder of either the specialized fields of spines of the thorax or of the composite teeth of the first three abdominal regments that so effectively rip the egg open at the onset of independent larval life. These structures are therefore *ruptor ovi* (or "egg bursters") in the strictest sense, and their presence marks the larval development of *A. antilope* as hypermetamorphic.

3. The number of instars

For more than a century there has been uncertainty and dispute as to whether hunting wasps normally have a fixed number of moults, hence of instars, in their development. So far as eumenine wasps are concerned, the uncertainty is very likely due to the fact that, sooner or later, most cast larval exuvia are nearly always eaten by the wasp larva as it feeds. The exuvium peels back to the tacky or viscid caudal end of the larval wasp at ecdysis, with the exoskeleton of the head capsule, split along its median suture, projecting from the ventral surface of the last abdominal segments of the larva. The exuvium is then generally held there as the larva, by arching its body and pushing with its abdomen, presses the prey against its mouth. As the last remnants of a caterpillar are eaten, so also are any moults that still cling to the larva's abdomen. For this and other reasons the only exuvium ordinarily found in the pupal cell of a wasp is that of the terminal larval moult. Accordingly there are three conditions that must be satisfied for a direct demonstration of the number of instars: (1) the first instar larva must be identified with certainty, generally by witnessing hatching, (2) exuvia must be removed when shed, or very shortly thereafter, and (3) closely and appropriately spaced observations must be continued from hatching to the emergence of the imago.

These conditions have been met for 16 individuals of *A. antilope* reared in isolation chambers on the original prey with which each was provided by its mother. In every case the full number of moults was six. The first four moults mark the limits of the first four larval stages, which are devoted solely to feeding and growth. The fifth stage larva, unlike the earlier four, does not moult to a feeding individual. It completes feeding, cleans and "varnishes" its cell, generally disposing of any exuvia that may remain, spins a cocoon (which may be incomplete in *A. antilope*), passes its meconium, and becomes a quiescent prepupa (or "mature larva"). If of the spring brood, the fifth larval moult generally occurs about 3.5 to 4.5 days after the meconium has been voided, releasing the pupa which is the sixth instar. The fifth instar larva of the summer brood diapauses after passing the meconium, and only in the following spring does the fifth moult occur. The final, or sixth moult, occurs after the pupa has become fully colored, and it is that final moult which frees the imago within its cocoon. The approximate times at which each of the first five moults occurs *after* hatching, and the average durations of each instar (at a temperature from 20°C to 28°C) are given in table 1; the fifth moult is there recorded for first (spring) brood individuals only, for that of members of the summer brood occurs in the following spring some 8 months or so after the onset of diapause. It should be noted that the egg stage is considered to have ended when the developed larva commences to cut its way out of

Table 1 (see text for explanation)

Occurrence of:	on day	duration of:	days
hatching	0	egg stage	2.5 +
ecdysis-1	3.2	instar-1	0.7
ecdysis-2	4.0	instar-2	0.8
ecdysis-3	5.0	instar-3	1.0
ecdysis-4	6.3	instar-4	1.3
ecdysis-5	17	instar-5	10.7
ecdysis-6	29-36	pupa	12-19

the egg, and the duration of instar-1 entered in the table includes the time (about 45 minutes) involved in hatching. The average duration of instar-1 *after* rupture of the chorion is 16 hours.

4. Exit from the nest

All who have reared large numbers of mason wasps in the laboratory from intact nests are familiar with the sharp, rasping scratches which foretell emergence of the imagos, as well as with the dessicated, powdery debris of the cut walls and terminal plug that remains long after the wasps have cleared the nest. But all are equally familiar with nests from which few or no wasps finally emerge, despite earlier, prolonged audible indications that emergence had been attempted. When such nests constructed in burrows are cut open, dead wasps may be found jammed in single file at the terminal plug, with the remains of dismembered and chewed sibs pushed to the rear. I suspect that such observations have led to the quite general belief that mason wasps simply cut their way out with their mandibles, as well as to the general wonder that they can do so from nests so hard, cement-like and thick as those, say, of masarid wasps (*e.g.*, see Davidson 1913, Ferton 1921, Hicks 1927, 1929). That they sometimes fail to do so seems to be taken as only natural.

It is true that the eumenid and masarid wasps (at least *Pseudomasaris* vespoides [Cress.]) do cut their way out with their mandibles, but the task is lightened in at least two ways. For one, it is easier to pass through a plug or wall from the inside than from the outside. This is because the inner faces of plugs and crosswalls are necessarily irregular and less compact in texture, as well as somewhat convex, for the masoning wasp is unable to control the irregularities and to press them down tightly with her head. For this reason portions of the inner faces of walls and plugs more readily break off when pried or rasped. For another, these wasps treat refractory regions just as their mothers did when first compounding the mortar; the eclosing adults soften the walls by moistening them to mud, as Nielsen (1932) first discovered in the case of emerging *Symmorphus sinuatus* (Fab.). Regions of walls softened in this way may then be cut with ease.

This certainly is the case for emerging *Ancistrocerus antilope* (Panz.), *A. catskill* (Sauss.), *A. tigris* (Sauss.), *Symmorphus cristatus* (Sauss.), *Parancistrocerus fulvipes* (Sauss.). *Monobia quadridens* (Linn.), *Rygchium foraminatum* (Sauss.), and *R. megaera* (Lepel.) among the eumenines, as well as for *Pseudomasaris vespoides* (Cress.), all of which I have studied. When wasps fail to cut their way out of a nest, it is often the case that one or more plugs are so thick and unworkable (a terminal plug may be as much as 20 mm thick) that the wasps run out of both fluid and energy, or that the wasps themselves are relatively dehydrated to start with, as may happen when nests have been kept in heated rooms.

A wasp ready to emerge, but still resting in its cocoon, will emit a drop of fluid from its mouth if disturbed by the observer, and the numbers of nests failing to give emergence can be greatly increased if each wasp, before it is ready to leave its cell, is "milked" of its fluid reserve. Those that do emerge after such treatment are generally from nests with relatively thin or friable walls, or presumably the wasps from them are those of which at least one regained sufficient fluid by butchering siblings. If a wall can be readily cut, even though not moistenable by water, wasps will chew through it if the thickness is not too great. Thus *A. antilope* will cut its way out of nests in which all partitions and the terminal plugs have been replaced with hard beeswax walls from 2 to 4 mm or more in thickness.

In *Ancistrocerus antilope* the source of the fluid is the proventriculus which, in a newly eclosed imago, will deliver from 5 mm³ to more than 12 mm³ of clear liquid. Very likely it is the proventriculus which supplies the fluid in all of the other cases, although that has not been determined.

Davidson (1913) suggests that the cup-like caps of the very hard, upright cells of the nest of *Pseudomasaris vespoides* collect rain which softens them, permitting each wasp to cut its way out. Hungerford (1937) of course threw doubt on this view when he showed that *P. occidentalis* (Cress.), the nest of which is also very refractory but not provided with cupped closures, emerges without a prior external softening of the region of exit. Actually *P. vespoides* itself softens the walls at the base of the cap of its cell from within, applying liquid from its mouth. It then chews away the now muddy, sandy coverings, turning from time to time, so that it nearly symmetrically enlarges a hole through the cap. It then trims the hole with its mandibles until it can wriggle its way out — which it does as though walking on the apices of its femora. In the instance observed, the male wasp at one point put its forelegs out through the hole, yet it did not try to pull itself out with them. Early during the cutting of the emergence hole, as the wasp turned in its cell, the left antenna was pushed between the mandibles. It remained there during the entire time (about 20 minutes) that the hole was being enlarged, in no way seeming to cause difficulty.

Discussion

The study of hatching and moulting, no less of many other aspects of the developmental biology of burrow-nesting eumenine wasps, is

nearly impossible without abundant material. Yet it would require
an unusual effort to collect just a few "wild" nests of *Ancistrocerus
antilope*, for example, even though the wasp abounds in the region,
and extraordinary luck were any such nests to prove recently closed
by the mother and to contain unhatched eggs. In fourteen years I
have found but one natural nest of this wasp, and that was constructed in a vacated nest of *Sceliphron* and contained but two cells.
Any who wish to check or extend my results, or to investigate other
aspects of the immature stages of *Ancistrocerus* and its burrow-nesting allies, will find the use of "trap nests" very helpful (Cooper
1953).

Although hitherto not known to occur in Hymenoptera (van
Emden 1925, 1946), it is likely that ruptor ovi will be found to be
widespread among the eumenine wasps at the very least. A second
species of eumenine nesting in my traps, which regrettably I did not
rear, also has ruptor ovi developed in the very same sites on the
thorax and on the first three abdominal segments as those of *Ancistrocerus antilope;* they have, however, a distinctly different patern
of grouping and fusion of their cuticular spines. Ruptor ovi may
thus prove serviceable in generic or specific identification of first
instar larvae of eumenine wasps. It is also probable that ruptor ovi
will be found elsewhere among the aculeates, even though the few
descriptions and figures which I have found of wasp larvae at instar-1
fail to suggest their presence; for example, the cases of *Sapyga* (Soika
1832), *Crabro* (Hachfeld 1948), *Omalus, Chrysis, Astata, Stizus,
Sceliphron, Philanthus,* and *Tachysphex* (Grandi 1961), and so on.
By analogy with the polyphagous Coleoptera, however, where a different thoraco-abdominal distribution of egg bursters is common
even though species of many genera and perhaps families are without
them (van Emden 1946), it is quite possible that closely allied aculeates do differ widely in their means of hatching, and ruptor ovi
are not universal among them.

Although five appears to be the primitive, most frequent, and upper
number of larval instars found in Hymenoptera (see Bischoff 1927,
DeBach and Schlinger 1964), it might be argued that, as in *Tineola*
and some dermestid beetles, the number of moults may in principle
be indeterminate. Certainly excessive feeding does not lead to a
sixth instar larva. When a fifth instar larva is provided continuously
with food, it may eat prodigiously (Cooper 1957), but there comes
a point at which it ceases feeding. This is not, however, followed
by a moult that gives rise to an additional larval instar. The excessively corpulent larva simply follows the normal routine that
marks the close of the fifth instar: cell cleaning, cocooning, passage

of the meconium (which is voluminous), then entrance either to the so-called pronymphal stage and succeeding sixth moult, or to diapause, remaining an eonymph. Nor have I been able to influence the numbers of moults that surviving larvae undergo by attempting to starve them from the second instar on. Five larval moults, therefore, appear to be the normal number. On enquiry, Prof. O. W. Richards informs me that it has been clearly shown that *Vespa orientalis* Linn. also has five larval instars. It is thus possible that du Buysson (1903) erred in his determination of the larval moults of *Vespa*, and that possession of five larval instars is both primitive and quite general among Vespidae just as it seems to be for many other aculeates, both bee (Berthol 1925) and wasp (DeBach and Schlinger 1964), as well as for the order Hymenoptera as a whole. Because no moult separates the fifth instar from the clearly defined prepupa, Morris's (1937) suggestion that an instar has been lost in development of the Ichneumonidae (as compared with the "lower phytophagous Hymenoptera") would seem to apply with equal force to eumenids and perhaps all other aculeates.

The prepupa, or fully-fed, quiescent fifth instar larva, or eonymph, tends regularly to enter diapause in the case of our northeastern *Symmorphus cristatus,* there being but one brood each year. Yet exceptions occur, for in one trap nest the sibs in all cells save one entered diapause as usual; the remaining individual transformed to a pupa which eclosed as a normal adult early that same fall. In principle then, *S. cristatus* is capable of being bivoltine. I have also had several prepupal *Ancistrocerus antilope* and *Rygchium megaera* remain flaccid and dormant as eonymphal prepupae through two years, even though all of their sibs broke diapause more or less together and transformed to adults in the usual time. When placed out of doors in their *third* winter, these blocked prepupae transformed to normal adults in the following spring. They were at that time not less than three years old. Meade-Waldo (1913) has had similar experience with prolonged prepupal states (of 2-3 years) in *Raphiglossa flavo-ornata* (P. Cam.) as has Williams (1919) with *Tiphia ashmeadi* Crawf. Morris (1937) comments that in Sweden nearly two thirds of the overwintering, diapaused, prepupal ichneumon fly *Exenterus abruptorius* Thb. emerged in the spring of 1935, and the remainder again over-wintered to emerge in the spring of 1936. Such instances indicate the possibility that recombinant genomes of these hymenopterans need not always be selectively tested or passed along within one generation, or even within immediately consecutive generations as may happen with regularly bivoltine species.

There have been many observers who have commented on mason

wasps' use of water in mixing mortar. Some have suggested that the masoning wasp may also use a special fluid from its mouth (e.g., Ferton 1921, Hicks 1931). This could be a secretion of its own ("saliva"), or possibly substances in solution or suspension which are derived from plants or prey and which provide an adhesive agent. Perhaps this is so, and excessively hard, masoned nests may indeed owe their refractoriness in important part to organic constituents provided by the wasp, as Ferton's (1921) comments seem to suggest. If that is the case, proventricular or other fluid used by adult mason wasps during emergence from their nests may in turn possess an added and complementary emollient, analogous to the cocoon-softener claimed for the saw-fly *Trichiosoma tibiale* which, so far as known, is unique within the Hymenoptera (*see* Hinton 1946).

Summary

The larva of *Ancistrocerus* hatches from the egg by means of thoraco-abdominal *ruptor ovi*, or egg bursters. Development is hypermetamorphic, with a total of five larval instars. Presumably one moult (and one instar) has been lost in development, namely that moult which sets the strictly prepupal instar apart in phytophagous Hymenoptera. Exit from the masoned nest by emerging eumenine and masarine wasps involves resoftening the hardened mortar with drops of fluid (from the proventriculus in the case of *A. antilope*).

References Cited

BERTHOLF, L. M.
    1925. The moults of the honeybee. Jour. Econ. Ent. 18: 380-384.
BISCHOFF, H.
    1927. Biologie der Hymenopteren. Biologische Studienbücher 5, viii + 598 pp., Springer, Berlin.
BUYSSON, R. DU
    1903. Monographie des guêpes ou *Vespa*. Ann. Soc. Ent. France. 72: 260-288.
COOPER, K. W.
    1953. Biology of eumenine wasps. I. The ecology, predation and competition of *Ancistrocerus antilope* (Panzer). Trans. Amer. Ent. Soc. 79: 13-35.
    1957. Biology of eumenine wasps. V. Digital communication in wasps. Jour. Exp. Zool. 134: 469-514.
DAVIDSON, A.
    1913. *Masaria vespoides*. Bull. So. Calif. Acad. Sci. 12: 17-18.
DEBACH, P. AND E. I. SCHLINGER (editors)
    1964. Biological control of insect pests and weeds. xxiv + 844 pp. Reinhold, New York.
EMDEN, F. VAN
    1925. Zur Kenntnis der Eizähne der Arthropoden, insbesondere der Coleopteren. Zeits. wiss. Zoöl. 126: 622-654.

1946. Egg-bursters in some more families of polyphagous beetles and some general remarks on egg-bursters. Proc. Roy. Ent. Soc. London. (A) 21: 89-97.

FERTON, C.
1921. Notes détachées sur l'instincte des Hyménoptères mellifères et ravisseurs. 9ᵉ Sér. Ann. Soc. Ent. France. 89: 329-375.

GRANDI, G.
1961. Studi di un entomologo sugli imenotteri superiori. Boll. Ist. Ent. Univ. Bologna. 25: xv + 659 + 1 pp.

HACHFELD, G.
1948. Ökologische und morphologische Beobachtungen an mitteleuropäischen Crabronen (Hym. Sphec.). I. Zool. Jahrb. (Abt. Syst., Ökol., Geogr. Tiere). 77: 49-80.

HICKS, C. H.
1927. *Pseudomasaris vespoides* (Cresson), a pollen provisioning wasp. Canad. Ent. 59: 75-79.
1929. *Pseudomasaris edwardsii* Cresson, another pollen-provisioning wasp, with further notes on *P. vespoides* (Cress.). Canad. Ent. 61: 121-125.
1931. Notes on pollen-user wasp, *Pseudomasaris edwardsii* Cresson, Bull. So. Calif. Acad. Sci. 30: 23-29.

HINTON, H. E.
1946. A new classification of insect pupae. Proc. Zool. Soc. London. 116: 282-328.

HUNGERFORD, H. B.
1937. *Pseudomasaris occidentalis* (Cresson) in Kansas (Hymenoptera-Vespidae). Jour. Kansas Ent. Soc. 10: 133-134.

IWATA, K.
1925. The comparative anatomy of the ovary in Hymenoptera. Part I. Aculeata. Mushi. 29: 17-34.

MEADE-WALDO, G.
1913. New species of Diploptera in the collection of the British Museum. Ann. Mag. Nat. Hist. (8) 11: 44-54.

MORRIS, K. R. S.
1937. The prepupal stage in Ichneumonidae, illustrated by the life-history of *Exenterus abruptorius*, Thb. Bull. Ent. Res. 28: 525-534.

NIELSEN, E. T.
1932. Sur les habitudes des Hyménoptères aculéates solitaires. II. Vespidae, Chrysididae, Sapygidae & Mutillidae. Ent. Medd. 18: 84-174.

SOIKA, A. G.
1932. Études sur les larves des Hyménoptères (1). Ann. Soc. Ent. France. 101: 127-130.

TAYLOR, L. H.
1922. Notes on the biology of certain wasps of the genus *Ancistrocerus* (Eumenidae). Psyche 29: 48-65.

WHEELER, W. M.
1889. The embryology of *Blatta germanica* and *Doryphora decemlineata*. Jour. Morph. 3: 291-386.

WILLIAMS, F. X.
1919. Philippine wasp studies. Part 2. Descriptions of new species and life history studies. Bull. Hawaiian Sugar Plant. Assoc., Ent. Series, no. 14: 19-186.

BURROWING HABITS OF
NORTH AMERICAN SOLPUGIDA (ARACHNIDA)[1][2]

BY MARTIN H. MUMA
Citrus Experiment Station
Lake Alfred, Florida

Introduction

North American solpugids, with the possible exception of a few small species of *Hemerotrecha* Banks and *Therobates* Muma, are nocturnal. During the daylight hours, the animals rest in specially constructed burrows that vary in depth from 1 to 23 cm. Burrows are also constructed for food digestion, ecdysis, hibernation, and egg deposition. An individual solpugid may, during its lifetime, dig 40 or more burrows.

Despite the extensive digging operations seemingly necessary for their survival, solpugids curiously lack special burrowing structures (Hingston, 1925). Excepting species of Hexisopodidae, this statement seems to be true for all solpugids (Lawrence, 1963). Burrowing, although conducted with extreme vigor and activity, seems to be accomplished inefficiently and laboriously.

The general facies of solpugid burrowing were presented by Hutton (1843), Turner (1916), Hingston (1925), and Fichter (1940). Although these recorded observations indicated a basic similarity in solpugid burrowing activities, differences suggested possible variations in habit between families, genera, and species.

This report presents a systematic comparison of the burrowing habits of North American solpugids.

Acknowledgments

Special acknowledgments are due the personnel of the American Museum of Natural History's Southwestern Research Station at Portal, Arizona, for the provision of living and research facilities in the collection area. Mr. Vincent A. Roth, Director, and student assistants also collected specimens.

Mrs. Thelma G. Kanavel, technician, and Michael S. Ball, student, made or assisted with many of the observations reported here.

[1]Partial report on studies supported by National Science Foundation Grant GBS-496.
[2]Florida Agricultural Experiment Stations Journal Series No. 2482.
Manuscript received by the editor September 27, 1966.

Mr. Allen G. Selhime, USDA, ARS, ENT, Orlando, Florida, assisted with photography.

Methods

Field-collected adult females or late instar nymphs were utilized primarily. Observations were made on specimens both in the field and in the laboratory. Both recently captured specimens, and specimens maintained under laboratory conditions for several weeks were observed in the laboratory. Well-fed and starved individuals of each species were observed when possible. Males of several species were also observed.

Burrowing arenas consisted of well-tamped 5 to 15 cm depths of a two to one mixture of sand and clay in 20.3 by 25.4 cm battery jars for most of the observations. Sand, clay, and a one to two mixture of sand and clay were used for a few special observations. Burrow depth and "nest" construction studies were conducted in thin-line arenas made by narrowly separating two panes of glass and filling the space with the sand-clay mixture.

Continuous observations of burrowing specimens were made between initiation of digging and disappearance of the solpugid below the soil surface in a plugged burrow. Regular interval, 10 or 20 minutes, observations were made until the solpugid appeared at the side or bottom of the arena and constructed a "nest" or until 2 hours had passed. Two hours were considered sufficient for burrow construction with an unobservable "nest." Special observations were made with an infrared viewer in the dark and sporadically with visual light on burrowing arenas maintained in the dark. Most laboratory observations were made at 26.6° C and 70% relative humidity.

Species identifications follow Muma (1951, 1962, and 1963).

General Burrowing Habits

The burrowing of subterranean North American solpugids is, in general, very similar to that reported for Asian and African species (Hutton, 1843, and Hingston, 1925). The accounts given by Turner (1916) and Fichter (1940) are too brief and generalized for comparison.

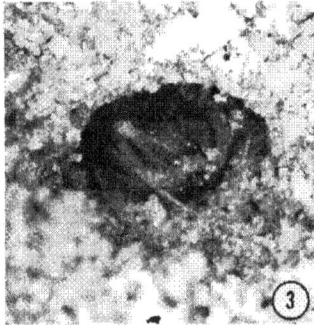

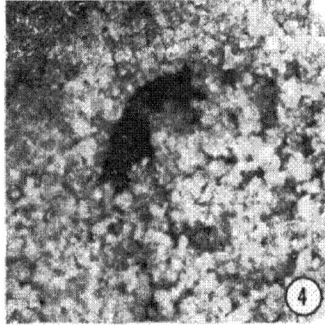

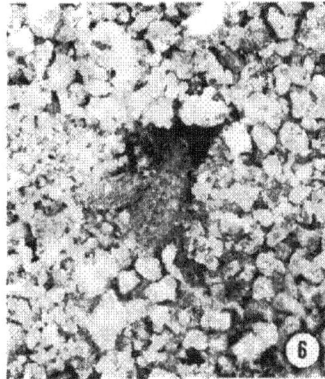

MUMA — SOLPUGIDS

Burrowing consisted of repeated irregular sequences of biting-raking, biting-raking, biting-raking-plowing or raking, raking, raking-plowing. The sequence was continued even after the burrow was plugged and the solpugid's digging was entirely subterranean. The only consistent variation occurred when obstructions such as pebbles, fragments of wood, etc., were encountered. These were bitten free and carried out of the way with the chelicerae. Some species also exhibited two palpal activities: probing, in which the palpi lightly touched unexcavated soil, and tamping, in which the palpi tapped or pushed excavated soil.

The three principal burrowing operations were analyzed. Biting involved both alternate and simultaneous use of the chelicerae. Burrows in hard, firmly packed soil were started by biting while angling, turning, and twisting the propeltidium and chelicerae, or by rotating the entire body around the area being bitten. Raking was accomplished with the laterodorsal row of spines on the tibiae of the second and third legs. The third leg was not used consistently. During raking, the legs were twisted inward and pulled backward quickly either in unison or alternately which hurled the sand and particles of clay backward under the body between the fourth pair of legs. Vigorous raking cast excavated material up to 5 cms behind the solpugid's body. When loose sand and clay accumulated under or just behind a burrowing solpugid, it turned around and plowed the pile out of the way. Plowing involved a lowering of the body to place the chelicerae at or near the base of the pile, the palpi and first legs were flexed at each side of the pile seemingly to prevent lateral scatter, and the pile was pushed as with a bulldozer, or road-grader. Plowing deposited moist excavated material in piles up to 10 cm from the burrow entrance; dry excavated material was scattered and leveled (Fig. 1).

Position reversal in the burrow, not previously reported, was accomplished as follows. The propeltidium was bent to the side or upward and backward over the meso- and metapeltidia and the palpi and legs were folded laterally along the sides of the abdomen. The solpugid then walked backward on the burrow side or ceiling which caused the peltidia and abdominal somites to undergo a backward rolling fold until the animal had completely reversed its position. The solpugid then twisted into an upright position completing position reversal. Position reversals were necessary for plowing, especially when the burrow was one or more body lengths long.

When the burrow was one or more body lengths long, the solpugid plowed only to the entrance (Fig. 3) which closed or plugged the entrance (Fig. 4). This plug, by the mechanics of digging, was extended as the burrow was deepened.

Probing usually involved only the palpi; although occasionally the first legs were used. This activity was confined to the unexcavated burrow face. Probing was interpreted as a feeling for large particles but may have assisted in the removal of loosened soil particles.

Tamping was confined to excavated and plowed soil. This activity was interpreted as a reflexive packing of loose soil which assisted in the construction of the burrow plug (Figs. 3 and 4).

When the burrow was completed, the solpugid was enclosed in a low-vaulted, oval to round space to which the term "nest" has been applied (Figs. 2 and 5). Vertical and horizontal nest location varied; this is probably governed by inherent factors, but could be an expression of soil type and condition. Nests utilized for ecdysis, egg deposition, and probably hibernation were in longer and deeper burrows than those utilized for daytime resting or digestion.

Specific Burrowing Habits

A systematic comparison of the burrowing habits of *Eremorhax magnus* (Hancock), *E. pulcher* Muma, *E. striatus* (Putnam), *Eremobates durangonus* Roewer, *E. nodularis* Muma, *E. palpisetulosus* Fichter, *Therobates bilobatus* Muma, *T. n. sp.* (*arcus* group) *Ammotrechula peninsulana* (Banks), *Ammotrechella stimpsoni* (Putnam) and *Branchia brevis* Muma, revealed variations, possibly significant at the species, genus, or family level. In the following subtitled paragraphs, these variations are presented and discussed.

Eremorhax magnus (Hancock). — Burrow depths of 1.3, 1.9, and 5.4 cm have been recorded for immatures. Immatures and females were collected from nests beneath cow dung (i.e., cow pies) and rocks. A gravid female was dug out of a burrow 22.9 cm deep. Burrows were constructed at an abrupt angle to the soil surface, 45° or more.

This species burrowed extensively in laboratory terraria, completely churning the soil in a single night. The usual biting, raking, and plowing were employed vigorously. Variation was noted in plowing. Chelicerae were slightly separated and held slightly above the base of the soil pile. Moist soil was frequently lifted and carried in the chelicerae, palpi, and first legs. The palpi were used consistently in probing.

Eremorhax pulcher Muma. — This species was not observed in burrows under field conditions.

In the laboratory, immatures utilized biting, raking, and plowing when burrowing but plowed much less frequently than *E. magnus*.

This species lifted and carried moist soils with the chelicerae and first and second legs but not extensively. This solpugid burrowed more rapidly than *E. magnus.*

Eremorax striatus (Putnam). — Females have been collected from surface nests under cow pies and rocks.

Under laboratory conditions, males and females constructed only surface nests. Burrowing involved biting, raking, and plowing, with raking predominating. The palpi and first legs swept the soil back to the second legs for raking. Plowing was accomplished with the chelicerae held together.

Eremobates durangonus Roewer. — Burrow depths of 0.6 cm to 1.9 cm have been recorded for second instar nymphs (Fig. 6). Depths of 3.8 to 12.7 cm have been recorded for females. Males (Fig. 2), females, and young (Fig. 5) were collected from surface nests beneath cow pies and stones and were also dug out of burrows 2.5 to 5.8 cm deep under field conditions. A female and eggs were collected from a 3.8 cm burrow in the field. Burrows were constructed at a slight angle to the surface, 30° or less. One immature constructed a burrow at a 45° angle. Burrows were completed in 30 to 40 minutes by both males and females.

In the laboratory, males, females, and young dug both nests and burrows. The usual biting, raking, and plowing were utilized. This species used the palpi to probe the digging surface while the first legs swept the loosened soil into the raking area. Raking was accomplished vigorously. The chelicerae were held together during plowing and the palpi and first legs used only to prevent lateral scatter of the soil. The palpi were also used regularly in tamping.

Eremobates nodularis Muma. — Burrow depths of 3.8 to 10.2 cm were recorded for this species. Males and females were collected from nests under rocks; males also from surface nests under cow pies. Burrows were constructed at a 45° to 90° angle to the soil surface. Males completed burrows in 15 to 30 minutes, females in 30 to 70 minutes.

In the laboratory, males and females dug both nests and burrows. Biting, raking, and plowing were all utilized. The palpi were used as probes during biting and raking. Palpi and first legs were both used to sweep loosened soil for raking. Vigorous raking seemed to be accomplished mainly with the second legs. Plowing was occasionally used; but most frequently, the load of loosened soil was lifted with the chelicerae, palpi, and first legs, and carried to the dumping area. During this activity, the chelicerae bit into the load but were held together or slightly open. This species frequently braced the third and fourth or fourth legs outside of the burrow while biting and raking. The palpi were also used regularly in tamping.

Eremobates palpisetulosus Fichter. — Burrow depths of 2.5 to 5.1 cm have been recorded for males, 7.6 to 10.2 cm for females. Males and females were collected from burrows and surface nests under cow pies and rocks. Burrows were constructed at an angle of 30° or less to the surface of the soil. Burrow construction time was not obtained; one male took 60 minutes to burrow out of sight.

In the laboratory, males and females constructed both nests and burrows. Chewing, raking, and plowing were all utilized. Variations were about the same as those of *E. durangonus.*

A male in a surface nest under a small cow chip burrowed to a depth of 3.8 cm in 2 hours when heat was reflected onto the surface of the substrate. Twelve hours after heat was removed, the specimen had again constructed a surface nest under cow chip.

Therobates bilobatus Muma. — Two males and one female of this species have been collected from surface nests beneath cow pies. One male was taken from a nest in a cow pie. Burrow angle and burrowing time were not observed.

In the laboratory, males and females constructed both burrows and surface nests. Laboratory-constructed burrows were angled at about 40° to the substrate surface and were laboriously constructed. Biting, raking, and plowing were all utilized but plowing was minimal. The palpi were not used by the males in plowing; the first and second legs seemed to hold the load.

Therobates n. sp. (*arcus* group). — A single male of this new species was collected at a night light. In the laboratory, he constructed a burrow 3.8 cm deep at the base of a twig pushed into the substrate. The angle of the burrow with the substrate surface was not calculated owing to its spiral nature around the twig. The burrow was closed in 95 minutes.

Biting, raking, and plowing were all utilized. The palpi and first legs swept the loosened soil back to the second legs for raking. Raking was not as vigorous as that exhibited by species of *Eremobates.* During plowing, the load was encircled by the first and second legs; the palpi were held aloft. Probing and tamping were not recorded.

Ammotrechula peninsulana (Banks).—Burrow depths of 5.1 to 7.6 cm were recorded for females. Females and immatures were collected from burrows and surface nests. Burrows were constructed at a slight angle, 20° or less, to the soil surface.

In the laboratory, males, females, and young all constructed burrows and surface nests. Biting, raking, and plowing were all utilized; but biting and raking were predominant. Soil clods and stones were removed from burrows in chelicerae, sometimes assisted with the palpi, by backing out, not using position reversal. Plowing was accomplished with the chelicerae and first legs; palpi were held to the side and aloft.

Males frequently emerged from burrows during daylight hours in the laboratory.

A female burrowed into and deposited eggs in a section of cornstalk. An immature burrowed into a section of cornstalk and moulted. Both burrows were constructed in the laboratory.

Ammotrechella stimpsoni (Putnam).—A single female and 19 immatures were collected from the Florida Keys in moist termite-infested and rotten limbs of mangrove, *Rhizophora mangle* L., and sweet bay, *Magnolia virginiana* L. During dry periods, no specimens were taken under these conditions. Two immatures were collected from nests under the bark of standing dead pine trees. In the laboratory, females, males, and young all constructed nests and burrows in soil, and nests and burrows in pith, cornstalks, and rotten wood. Subterranean burrowing involved biting, raking, and plowing with variations similar to those exhibited by *A. peninsulana*. Burrows in wood, pith, or cornstalks were constructed by biting and raking with biting predominant. Nests in such media were smaller than those constructed in soil. Young frequently utilized termite galleries or woodboring beetle tunnels rather than burrow in rotten wood.

Branchia brevis Muma.—Three females of this species were collected from surface nests beneath cow pies.

Males and females constructed subterranean burrows in the laboratory. The species did not burrow in pith or cornstalks. Biting, raking, and plowing were all utilized. No unusual variations were noted, but the species is quite small and minor variations could easily have been overlooked.

Males emerged from burrows during daylight hours in the laboratory.

Summary and Discussion

This comparative study of the burrowing habits of North American solpugids has demonstrated a broad similarity in behavior. All species used the chelicerae to bite at the substrate, pith, wood, or soil; the second and third pair of legs, particularly the second, to rake loosened particles back under the body between the fourth pair of legs; the chelicerae sometimes assisted by the palpi and first legs or first legs and second legs to plow excavated materials out of the burrow. During biting, the palpi were used as probes on the face of the excavation. The palpi were also used to tramp excavated material after it was dumped outside of or at the entrance to the burrow.

Variations in substrate, burrow angle, burrowing time, biting, raking, plowing, probing, and tamping seem to indicate the existence of specific, generic, and perhaps familial behavior.

In the family Eremobatidae, three genera and eight species were studied.

Eremorhax magnus (Hancock) and *E. pulcher* Muma, two morphologically similar short-legged species (Muma, 1951 and 1963) burrowed extensively, biting, raking, and plowing vigorously. They differed primarily in the support of soil lifted and carried in the chelicerae. On the other hand, *Eremorhax striatus* (Putnam), a long-legged species with many *Eremobates*-like characters (Muma, 1951) constructed only surface nests principally by raking.

Eremobates durangonus Roewer, *E. palpisetulosus* Fichter, and *E. nodularis* Muma constructed both nests and burrows, biting, raking, and plowing vigorously. *E. durangonus* and *E. palpisetulosus* burrowed at a slight angle, seldom lifting and carrying soil; whereas, *E. nodularis* burrowed at a 45° to 90° angle frequently lifting and carrying soil. The behavioral similarity of *E. durangonus* and *E. palpisetulosus* and the differences exhibited by *E. nodularis* become more striking when it is noted that *E. durangonus* is a species of the *pallipes*-group and *E. nodularis* one of the *palpisetulosus*-group (Muma, 1951). It should also be noted that *E. nodularis* lifted and carried soil in the same manner as *Eremorhax magnus* and *E. pulcher*.

Therobates bilobatus Muma and *T.* n. sp. (*arcus* group) burrowed slowly and laboriously, primarily biting and raking. Neither species used the palpi in plowing.

In the family Ammotrechidae, three genera and three species were studied.

Ammotrechula peninsulana (Banks) and *Ammotrechella stimpsoni* (Putnam), two generically different, similar-sized species burrowed in both soil and pith or wood. Both species primarily utilized biting and raking in the construction of subterranean burrows. *A. stimpsoni* regularly burrowed by biting in pith or wood, *A. peninsulana* only once. Furthermore, *A. peninsulana* males emerged from burrows during daylight hours; *A. stimpsoni* males did not.

Branchia brevis Muma constructed only subterranean burrows and nests by biting, raking, and plowing. The males did, however, emerge from burrows during daylight hours.

REFERENCES CITED

FICHTER, EDSON
    1940. Studies of North American Solpugida, I. The True Identity of *Eremobates pallipes* (Say), Amer. Mid. Nat., 24 (2): 351-360.
HINGSTON, R. W. G.
    1925. Nature at the Desert's Edge, Studies and Observations in the Bagdad Oasis, London, Witherby, Arachnida, pp. 192-261.
HUTTON, THOS.
    1843. On *Galeodes (vorax?)*, Ann. Mag. Nat. Hist., 75: 1-6.
LAWRENCE, R. F.
    1963. The Solifugae of South West Africa, Cimbebasia, 8: 1-28.
MUMA, MARTIN H.
    1951. The Arachnid Order Solpugida in the United States, Bull. Amer. Mus. Nat. Hist., 97, (2): 35-141.
    1962. The Arachnid Order Solpugida in the United States, Supplement I, American Museum Novitates No. 2092, pp. 1-44.
    1963. Solpugida of the Nevada Test Site, Brigham Young Univ., Sci. Bull. Biol. Ser. 3 (2): 1-15.
TURNER, C. H.
    1916. Notes on the Feeding Behavior and Oviposition of a Captive American False Spider, Jour. Animal Behavior, 6: 160-168.

THE ANT GENUS *SIMOPELTA*
(HYMENOPTERA: FORMICIDAE)*

By WILLIAM H. GOTWALD, JR. AND WILLIAM L. BROWN, JR.

Department of Entomology, Cornell University
Ithaca, New York

The taxonomic history of *Simopelta* (subfamily Ponerinae, tribe Ponerini) has been discussed in detail by W. M. Wheeler (1935) and by Borgmeier (1950). Borgmeier was the first to describe the queen of any species in the genus — that of *S. pergandei* — which he showed deserved to be called "dichthadiiform", or belonging to a particular form of queen caste characterized by extreme reduction or loss of eyes, loss of wings, hypertrophy of petiole and gaster, and other characters. He explained its "great similarity to certain females of *Eciton*" by "convergence in its hypogaeic way of life", a statement that is puzzling because, as Father Borgmeier well knows, *Eciton* is not really "hypogaeic" in its habits, at least as compared to the majority of ants that spend most of their time on or below the ground level.

At any rate, as we shall show in this paper, the convergence between the queens of at least one *Simopelta* species and certain army ants, so discerningly noted by Father Borgmeier, is only one aspect of the army-ant or legionary lifeform that two and perhaps all *Simopelta* species share with the "true" army ants of subfamily Dorylinae.

It is the purpose of this contribution to list and key the workers of the known species of *Simopelta*, to describe two new species of the genus, and to set forth on the behavior of one species some observations, however fragmentary, that will establish that it follows the army-ant way of life in important respects.

Simopelta

Belonopelta subgenus *Simopelta* Mann, 1922: 10. Type species: *Belonopelta (Simopelta) jeckylli*, by original designation.
Simopelta: W. M. Wheeler, 1935 (raised to generic rank). Borgmeier, 1950 (queen, young larva). G. C. and J. Wheeler, 1957 (young larva).

The generic diagnosis is basically that of Borgmeier modified and augmented according to the new material now available.

Manuscript received by the editor December 8, 1966

Worker: With the general characters of tribe Ponerini. Mandibles with the two apical teeth acute and forming a pair; followed basad by a short series of smaller teeth, by a single small tooth, or by a large diastema with or without one or more irregular indistinct denticles; a large acute or truncate tooth marks the basal angle. Antennae 12-segmented, second funicular segment small, no distinct club. Palpi segmented 2, 2 or 2, 3. Frontal lobes forming a raised platform, large and prominent, median part of clypeus falling sharply anteriad, sub-perpendicular to frontal region. Anteromedian clypeal margin projecting in a triangular point that in some species is produced as a slender, flattened spine or tooth. Eyes much reduced, condensed into a single, more or less convex facet, situated in front of the middle of the sides of the head, but not very close to the anterior corners. Promesonotal suture distinct and separating the segments; metanotal groove often indistinct, but more or less impressed. Petiole with steep anterior and posterior faces, apex weakly to strongly rounded. the node usually broader than long as seen from above; subpetiolar process thick and more or less triangular. Gaster with constriction behind postpetiolar segment weak to obsolescent. Sting well developed. Tibiae each with a single pectinate spur. Malpighian tubules 4 (checked only in *oculata*).

Queen (known only for 2 species: *pergandei* and *oculata*) : dichthadiiform, i.e., with broad, subquadrate head: eyes reduced, flattened, but little larger than those of worker. Ocelli absent, or only the anterior ocellus present. Antennae shorter than in worker, both scape and funicular segments. Mandibles simple, acutely falcate. Thorax reduced, permanently wingless. Mesonotum with scutum and scutellum distinct and convex, or the latter reduced and fused with propodeum (?). Petiole transverse, broader than alitrunk, divided by a median sulcus. Gaster wide, with constriction after postpetiole poorly-marked or lacking; sting present and extrusible. Legs long; femora flattened; tibiae each with a single pectinate spur. Sculpture weaker than in corresponding worker, more shining.

Male unknown.

Larva: (only small larvae of *S. pergandei* and small and medium sizes of *S. oculata* are known; see Fig. 1.) Head small, longer than broad, hemicephalic; with simple, curved acute mandibles, their apices directed ventrad, so that they apparently work much as do the mouth-hooks of higher dipterous larvae. Antennae small, situated far back on cephalic dorsum. Pronotum elongate, tapering anteriorly, partly retractile, its neck-like structure most noticeable in the smaller larvae. The very smallest larvae seen (of *oculata*) are about 0.6 mm long by 0.3 mm wide, with head capsule about 0.11 mm wide. They

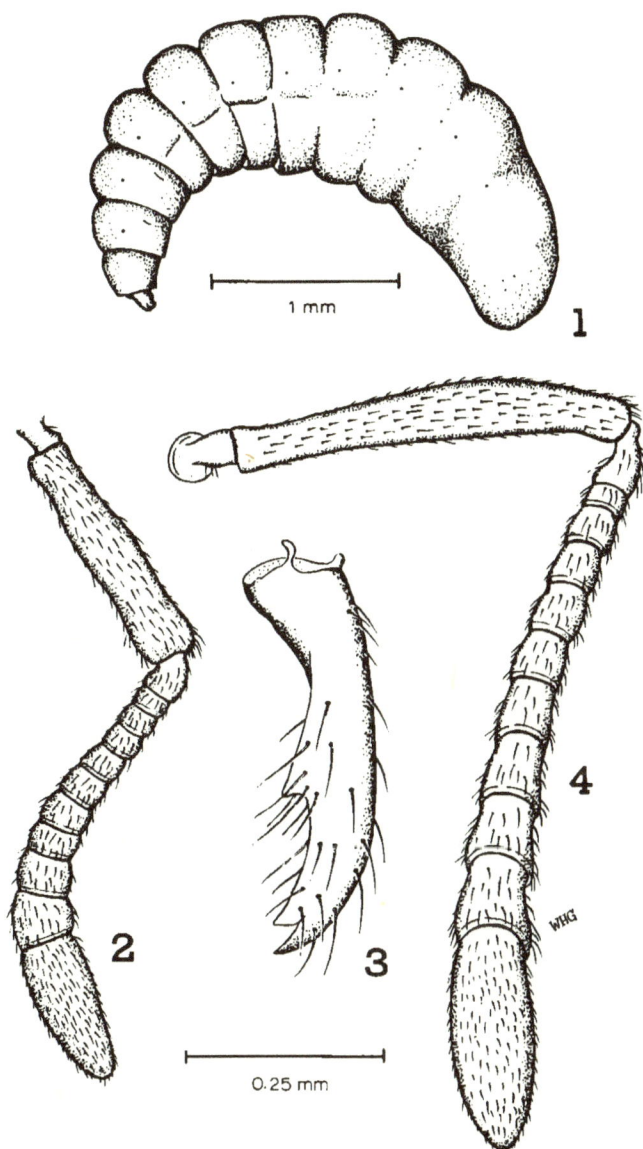

Figures 1-4, *Simopelta oculata* n.sp. Fig. 1, medium-sized (second instar?) larva, side view. Fig. 2, antenna of queen. Fig. 3, left mandible of worker, dorsal view. Fig. 4, antenna of worker. Figures 2-4 drawn to same scale.

range from this size to individuals up to 1.6 mm long and 0.9 or more mm wide, but the head capsule seems to remain at or near 0.11 mm wide throughout this series, which probably represents the first instar, or at most the first two instars. All but the smallest members of this series are very wide, due to the production of a wide, continuous longitudinal welt along each side that binds the second and all succeeding abdominal segments into one large flattened mass. Pronotum, mesonotum, metanotum and abdomen 1 are separated off by distinct constrictions in *oculata* of this instar.

Larger (second instar?) larvae of *oculata* (Fig. 1) measure about 3.2 to 3.6 mm in length straightened out, have the first 5 or 6 abdominal segments distinctly separated by constrictions, and are more nearly cylindrical in cross-section; the head capsule in this stage is still only about 0.12 mm wide.

According to the Wheelers, most abdominal segments of the small *pergandei* larva (L 1.6 mm straightened out) carry 8 minute tubercles each, 4 dorsal and 4 ventral, in transverse rows, but no tubercles of any kind could be found in the *oculata* larvae. All larvae of the genus so far found are completely hairless.

In *oculata*, the largest larvae numbered only about 10, as compared to some 690 of the smaller sizes. These largest larvae do not seem large enough to represent the final larval instar, and no *Simopelta* pupae were found. Of the smaller larvae, the vast majority were of the broad type, which possibly represents late first instar (or second instar). Whether or not we have the sequence correct, it can be seen that this particular brood had reached a peak at the older small larvae, with a few individuals having attained medium size and the succeeding instar, plus another small number of very young larvae tailing off at the other end of the size distribution. The impression of an *Eciton*-like brood cycle was further heightened by the apparently complete lack of eggs or pupae in the nest, and by the contracted state of the queen in life.

Borgmeier mentions examining 4 pupae of *S. pergandei* that were 2.8 mm long and not enclosed in a cocoon. Though cocoonless ponerines are no longer considered a great rarity, the strong possibility that *S. pergandei*, like *S. oculata*, raids ant nests for its livelihood leaves us to wonder whether the pupae may not have been those of a prey species.

Distribution. So far, *Simopelta* has been collected only in the forests of the warmer parts of the mainland Americas, from Guatemala in the north to Santa Catarina State, Brazil, in the south. *S. laticeps* was taken at about 2000 m in the Peruvian Andes, and two species have been described from Ecuador. Probably we can expect to find more species in the Transandean area as well as elsewhere. The species have been collected only rarely so far.

Habits. The observations given after the description of *S. oculata* (below), the circumstance that the queens of two species are dichthadiiform, the peculiar *Eciton*-like reduction of the worker eye, the mandibular form, and certain details of the worker form and sculpture, all go to indicate that *Simopelta* is a mass-foraging, probably nomadic genus that has evolved far toward the army ant lifeform. *S. oculata*, at least, plunders the nests of other ants (*Pheidole* in the case observed). The observations for *S. oculata* and the collection figures given by Borgmeier (loc. cit.) suggest that nest populations may reach 1,000 or more workers, but probably do not go higher than 2,000. The *pergandei* series from Costa Rica studied by Borgmeier contained one fully adult queen and one callow queen, and thus may have been on the verge of dividing (swarming). The large mass of workers and brood in this collection suggests that, like the *oculata* sample, it was taken in a hollow twig or branch from which the colony could be collected at one stroke with little loss of inmates. The *oculata* colony had only one queen.

The Species of *Simopelta*

Simopelta curvata

Belonopelta curvata Mayr, 1887, Verh. Zool.-bot. Ges. Wien, 37: 532, worker. Type locality: Santa Catarina State, Brazil.

A light reddish-brown or yellowish-brown species with a well-developed clypeal spine and anteroposteriorly compressed petiolar node. Now known to be widespread in São Paulo State as well as Santa Catarina, and also in the interior of southern Brazil.

Simopelta pergandei

Belonopelta pergandei Forel, 1909, Deutsch. Ent. Zeitschr; p. 242, worker. Type locality: Guatemala.

Simopelta pergandei: Wheeler, 1935: 11, fig. 1, worker. Borgmeier, 1950: 372, fig. 1-12, worker, queen, young larva, pupa.

Very similar to *curvata* in general form, size, color and sculpture, but mandible with only 3 well-developed teeth. Funicular segments also more slender, and there are other small differences in the form of the node and in the sculpture. Known from Guatemala and from near San José in upland Costa Rica.

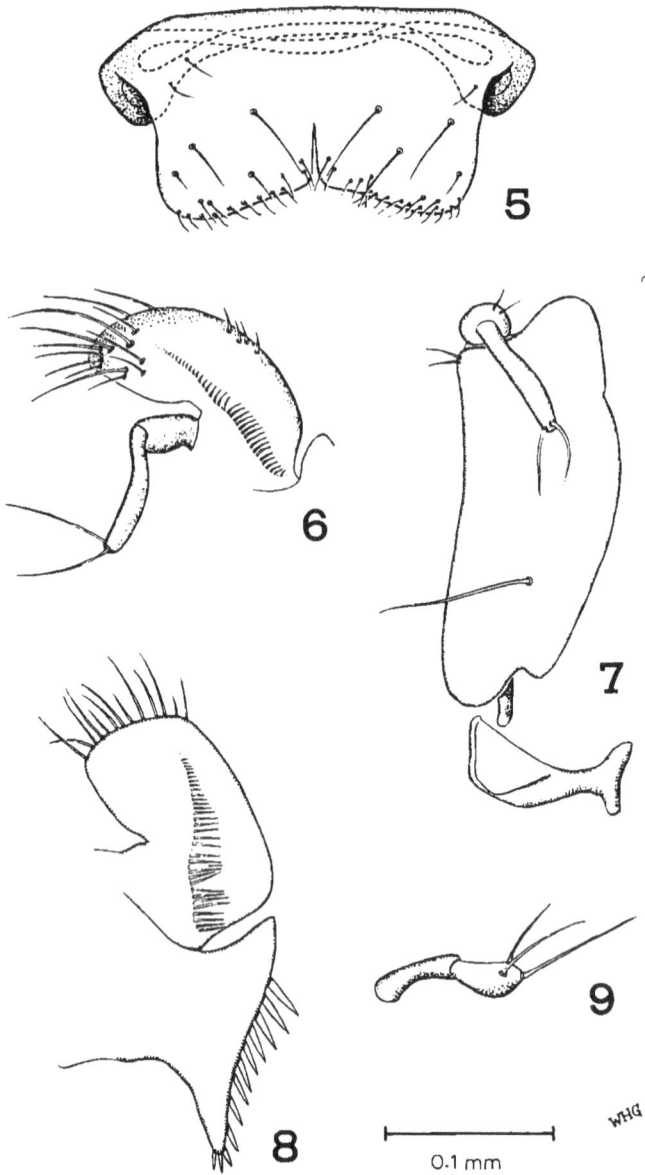

Figures 5-9, *Simopelta oculata* n.sp., mouthparts. Fig. 5, labrum, outside face. Figs. 6-8, different partial views of left maxilla. Fig. 9, labial palp. All drawn to same scale.

Simopelta jeckylli

Belonopelta jeckylli Mann, 1916, Bull. Mus. Comp. Zool. Harv., 60 415,
    pl. 2, fig. 12, 13, worker. Type locality: Camp 39, Madeira-Mamore
    R.R., Mato Grosso, Brazil.
Simopelta jeckylli: Wheeler, 1935: 14, fig. 2, worker.

S. jeckylli is a relatively large, brightly-colored form (forebody
piceous to bright ferruginous red, gaster contrasting red or yellow)
with densely punctulate head and alitrunk. Clypeal spine present;
only 3 well-developed mandibular teeth. No tooth on "mesosternum." Known only from the type collection, which consisted of
workers from under forest litter that appeared to be "traveling in
a definite direction," a description that suggests a foraging column.

Simopelta williamsi

Simopelta williamsi Wheeler, 1935: 14, fig. 3, worker. Type locality: Naran-
    japata, Ecuador, at about 600 m.

This species lacks a median clypeal spine, has very small eyes, and
has the large basal tooth of the mandible truncate, with the truncate
apex often even slightly concave. Piceous in color. Known only
from the type collection.

Simopelta oculata new species (Figures 1-14)

Holotype worker: TL 3.8, HL (without median lobe of clypeus,
i.e., measured to anterior border of frontal lobes) 0.80; HW (without eyes) 0.58; WL (diagonal length of alitrunk as seen from side)
1.34; greatest diameter of eye 0.10; scape L (chord, without basal
neck) 0.76 mm. Abbreviations as in Brown (1958: 254). Cephalic
index (CI) 73.

Similar to worker of *S. williamsi*, but differing in the following
ways:

1. Mandibles more slender, with the basal tooth simple and acute
(basal tooth broad and truncate in *williamsi*).

2. Eyes notably larger than in *williamsi* or the workers of any
other species in the genus so far known, but still composed of only a
single convex (fusion) facet.

3. Antennal scapes longer; when laid straight back in full-face
view, surpassing the occipital margin by distinctly more than their
greatest apical thickness (by less in *williamsi*).

4. Alitrunk, especially the propodeum, both absolutely and rela-

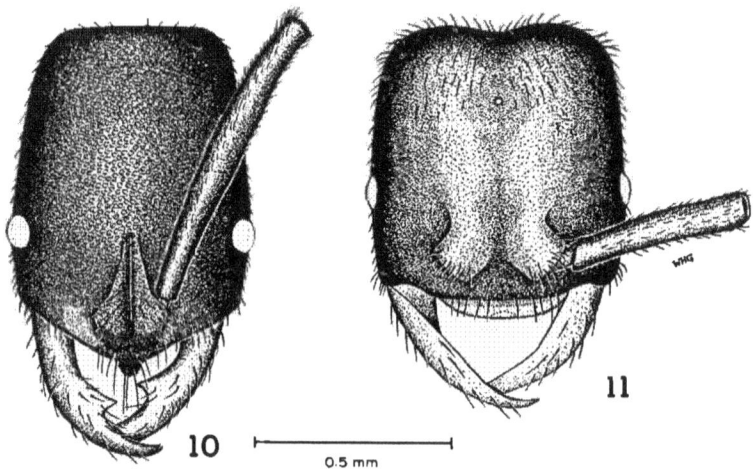

Figures 10-11, *Simopelta oculata* n.sp., heads in dorsal view. Fig. 10, worker. Fig. 11, Queen. Drawn to same scale.

tively longer than in *williamsi;* pronotum with a feeble median impression on its dorsal face; propodeum with a feeble impression about midway on its dorsal face as seen in profile from the side.

5. Petiolar node longer, scarcely higher than long; as seen from above trapezoidal, slightly wider behind than long.

6. Transversely costulate elements of sculpture looser and less extensive than in *williamsi*, especially on head, where they are only weakly indicated on the extreme occiput, and then only in certain lights. Head otherwise densely reticulate-punctulate, opaque. Anterior face of pronotum with fine indistinct striation continuing onto lateral faces; disc and lateral faces of pronotum also with numerous shallow punctures; dorsum of alitrunk indistinctly roughened, almost smooth in places, weakly shining; anterior propodeum with some loose transverse rugulae extending up from sides; posterior sides of alitrunk with loose oblique to longitudinal rugulation, also a few oblique rugules on sides of petiolar node; petiolar summit loosely rugulose, weakly shining. Gaster smooth and shining, with very fine, superficial reticulation on dorsum, as in *williamsi*.

7. Color dark brown, head brownish-black; mandibles, antennae, legs, sides of pronotum, lower petiolar node, and gaster prevailingly castaneous.

Type nest series taken a short distance (about 1/2 km) beyond (NW of) the bridge over the Rio Toro Amarillo, near Guapiles, Limon Province, Costa Rica (N. Scott and W. L. Brown, Jr. leg.). Holotype worker deposited in Museum of Comparative Zoology, Harvard University, together with queen from type nest.

Paratype series: 42 workers from type nest series taken "randomly" from a larger series in alcohol; 10 measured, including the apparent largest and smallest specimens: TL 3.6-3.9, HL 0.79-0.81, HW 0.57-0.60, ML 0.21-0.24, WL 1.31-1.40 mm. CI 72-74. Non-metric variation: Color varies from predominantly deep castaneous to piceous, with the head nearly black. Sculpture on sides of alitrunk and petiole varies somewhat in distinctness and direction.

Upon dissection, 4 live workers each proved to have 4 Malpighian tubules.

Paratypes deposited in Museum of Comparative Zoology, Harvard University; Cornell University Collection; Departamento de Zoologia, São Paulo; California Academy of Sciences, and elsewhere.

Queen (a single dichthadiiform female from type nest, gaster contracted): TL 3.6, HL (from anterior clypeal border) 0.68, HW (without eyes) 0.67, WL 1.18, greatest diameter of eye 0.11, scape L 0.46 mm. CI 99.

Shape of head and body shown in Figs. 2, 11-13. Outstanding differences from the worker may be seen in the shape of head, antennae and mandibles, thoracic sclerites, deeply bilobate petiole, and broad gaster with median sulcus on the first tergum. Eyes a bit more elongate and showing more traces of facetting, set obliquely on sides of head. Funicular antennomeres broader than long, except first and last. A single small median ocellus, in front of which is a broad, transverse shallow sulcus. Sting well developed and extrusible. Femora slightly flattened, weakly incrassate, the broad faces feebly sulcate. First gastric tergum with a broad, shallow, longitudinal median sulcus, in the middle of which is an indistinct pore. Lower edge of metapleural gland bulla cultrate, conspicuously ivory in color; meatal guard hairs 5-6 in number, long and fine.

Sculpture mainly smooth to nearly smooth, shining; head and anterior dorsum of alitrunk shallowly roughened and with indistinct punctures; finer piligerous punctures scattered over propodeum, petiole and gaster. Appendages finely, densely and shallowly punctulate, weakly shining. Entire body, including mandibles and appendages, but excluding large parts of coxae and sides of alitrunk, with abundant fine, yellowish-white, decumbent to suberect pilosity

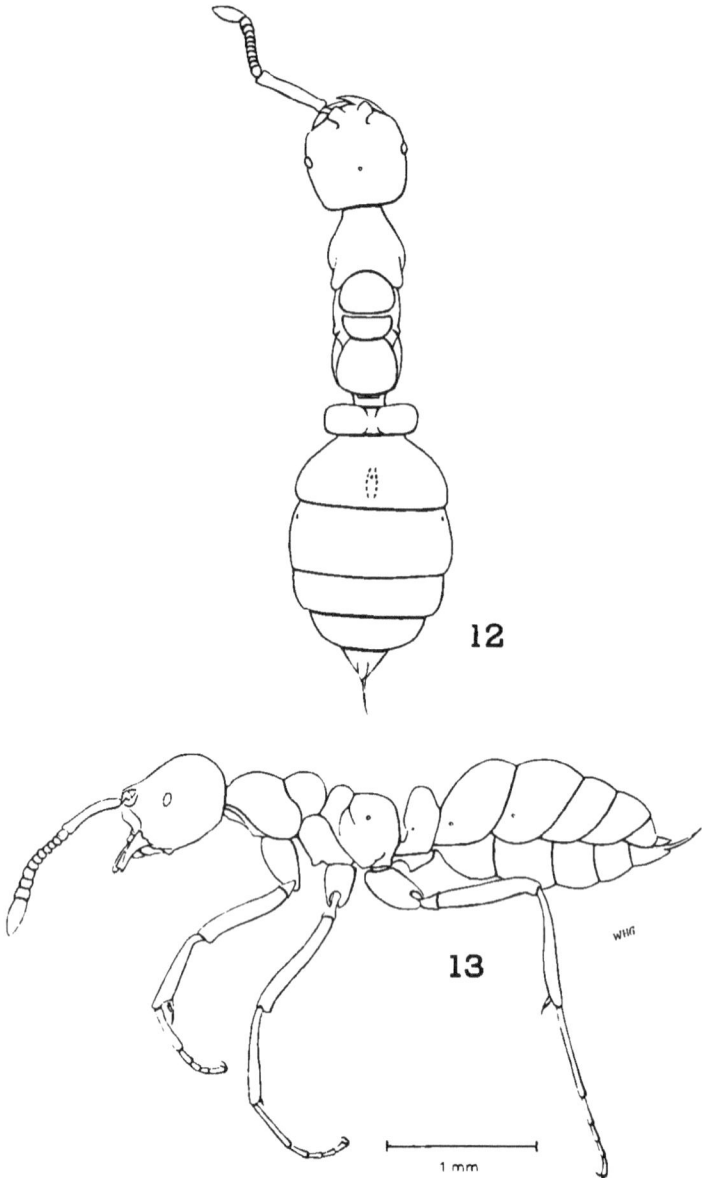

Figures 12-13, *Simopelta oculata* n.sp., queen, habitus drawings, pilosity omitted. Fig. 12, dorsal view. Fig. 13, lateral view. Drawn to same scale as Figs. 14-15.

of uneven but moderate length, most abundant and longest on gaster.
Color piceous, pronotum a little lighter and more reddish; mandibles
and appendages lighter, yellowish-brown.

The colony of *S. oculata* was found by chance at about 9 A.M.
on the morning of 2 March, 1966. Mr. Norman Scott, in charge
of the Course in Fundamentals of Tropical Biology, Organization
for Tropical Studies, and Brown were wading up a brook in second
growth rain forest. We were looking for foraging columns of an
Eciton lucanoides colony that had moved in this direction from a
log bivouac dissected by us the day before. Mr. Scott directed
Brown's attention to files of slender, dark-colored ants marching
over vines and shrub stems along the margin of the brook. On seeing
the ants, he immediately concluded that they must be some *Simopelta*
species.

The route of the ants ranged from about 30 cm to 150 cm above
ground level over vine and stem, and lay entirely in deep shade. They
moved in dense single file, almost all in one direction, which proved
to be nestward. Following the file for perhaps 6 meters stretched-out
distance, we shortly discovered the nest, which occupied a straight,
completely hollow dead twig about 1.5 cm in diameter and 33 cm
long, suspended vertically by a dead vine about 1.5 m above the
ground in dense second-growth forest.

The single incoming column was burdened with the larvae, pupae,
and pharate adult workers and soldiers of a medium-sized species of
Pheidole, clearly the dominant ant genus of this area. Partly eaten
prey specimens were later found among the nest contents. The twig
containing the nest was removed to a plastic bag and kept for later
laboratory opening. The column was not traced back toward its
origin, but we estimated that it contained at least several hundred
Simopelta ants in the files we saw. The nest twig contained 361
workers by count when it was opened, and it hardly seemed spacious
enough to contain more than 2,000 workers plus a queen, the prey,
and the brood found, about 700 in number, which consisted entirely
of small and medium larvae.

When the queen was found upon opening the nest twig, she ran
rapidly, always followed by at least one worker whose head literally
rested upon her gastric dorsum as it followed immediately in a tight
tandem. The queen with her attendant resembled some multi-legged
animal, so close and persistent was the association. Although the
exact position of the worker's head could not be seen as the pair ran

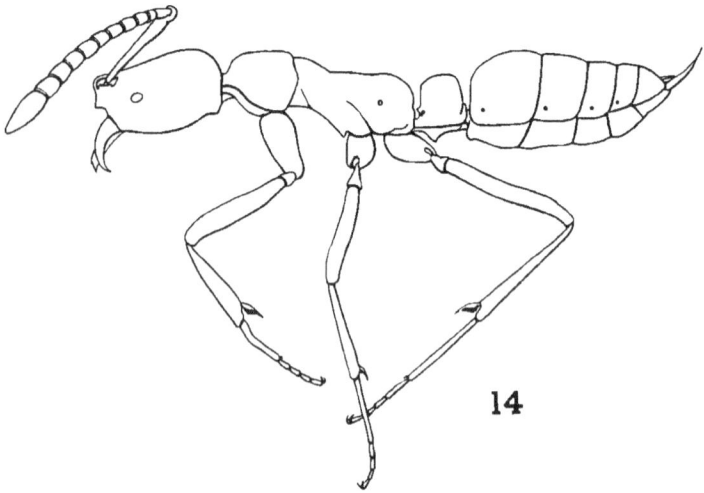

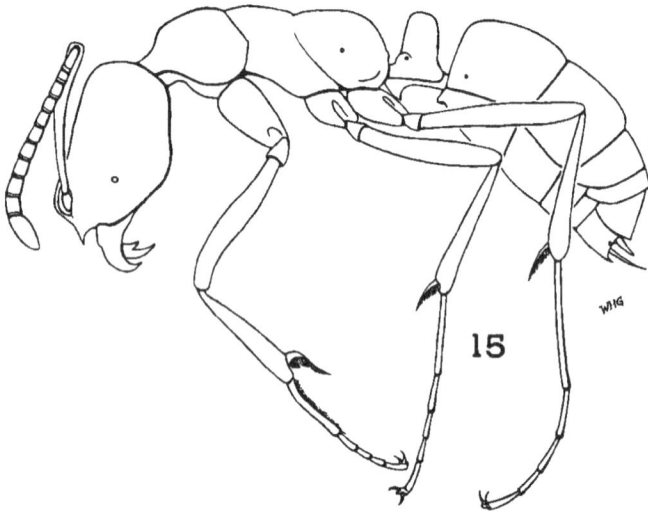

Figures 14-15, *Simopelta* n.spp., workers, habitus drawings, pilosity omitted. Fig. 14, *S. oculata*, lateral view. Fig. 15, *S. laticeps*, lateral view.

along, it seemed likely that the worker's mandibles or under-mouth-parts rested in the median sulcus of the queen's postpetiolar tergum. The workers ran rapidly, holding their antennae in much the same way as Dorylinae do, and quickly formed files along obvious odor trails newly laid on a blank paper surface. Altogther, the impression of the colony behavior received was that of an army ant. The slender bodies of the ants reminded one of mass-foraging *Leptogenys* species, such as those of the *diminuta* complex of the Indo-Australian area. *S. oculata* proved able to sting, at least through the thin skin on the back of human fingers. The sting felt about like a mosquito bite, and lasted similarly.

Simopelta manni

Simopelta manni Wheeler, 1935: 17, fig. 4, worker. Type locality: Mera, Ecuador.

This species has acutely 3-toothed mandibles and no clypeal spine. Eyes very convex, but smaller than those of *oculata*. "Mesosternal" tooth present. Pronotum and much of head smooth and shining. Petiolar node a little broader than long. Color black. Known only from type material.

Simopelta bicolor

Simopelta bicolor Borgmeier, 1950: 377, fig. 13-20, worker. Type locality: Santa Teresa, Espirito Santo, Brazil.

Mandibles with 5-6 irregular teeth basad of the apical pair. No clypeal spine or "mesosternal" tooth. Petiolar node much broader than long. Head and alitrunk densely punctulate. Bright ferruginous red; petiole and gaster yellow. Known only from type material.

Simopelta laticeps new species (Figures 15, 16)

Holotype worker: TL 4.9, HL 1.03, HW 0.93, WL 1.65, greatest diameter of eye 0.05, scape L 0.91 mm. CI 90.

Immediately separable from the other known species of the genus by means of its wide, convex-sided head with notably concave occipital margin. The median clypeal lobe bears a slender subspatulate tooth, and the mandibular armament consists of 4 strong, acute teeth.

General form of body and appendages shown well in Figs. 15 and 16. Petiolar node broader than long. Head finely and densely striato-punctulate in a longitudinal direction; dorsum of pronotum and mesonotum with similar sculpture, arched concentrically; sides of alitrunk mostly longitudinally striate; dorsum of propodeum and petiolar node shining, with spaced small punctures, mesally impunctate; declivity of propodeum and front, rear and sides of node shining, with delicate horizontal reticulo-striation. Mandibles very finely striolate, sericeous, with a few coarse elongate punctures. Legs and antennae finely and densely punctulate, the legs more shining than the antennae. Gaster smooth and shining with numerous minute, spaced punctulae.

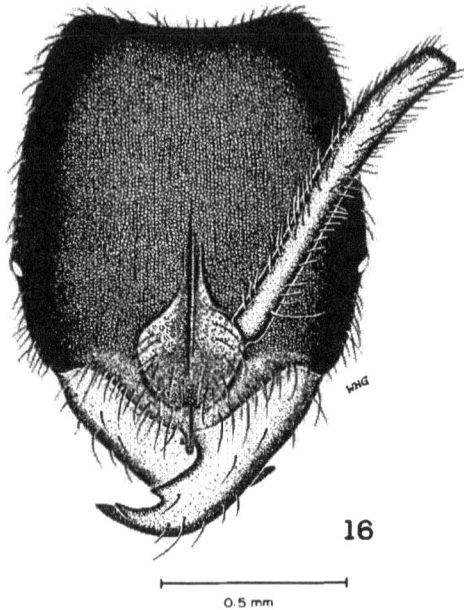

16

0.5 mm

Figure 16, *Simopelta laticeps* n.sp., head in dorsal view. Drawn to same scale as Figs. 10-11.

Body including appendages, covered with a short, fine, mostly decumbent or curved-subappressed pilosity, sparse on mandibles and sides of alitrunk, absent from anterior face of first gastric tergum. Longer fine hairs, mostly erect, are found mainly on the anterior parts of the head and near the antennal scape bases, on the underside of the head, scattered over the dorsal surface of the alitrunk, on the anterior coxae and beneath the prothorax, at the apex and on the underside of the gaster.

Color deep piceous, nearly black; mandibles and other appendages lighter, more reddish (castaneous).

Holotype and a single paratype worker on a separate pin received from Dr. E. S. Ross of the California Academy of Sciences, bearing the following label data: "PERU: 28 mi. E. Olmos, Lambayeque. 2000 m. 1-19-1955. E. I. Schlinger & E. S. Ross collectors." It seems possible that these two workers were part of a larger series, the bulk of which may still be stored in alcohol at the Academy of Sciences. My query about this collection reached Dr. Ross while he was in the midst of preparations for a long trip, when he had no time to search through the extensive collections of ants in alcohol. He did, however, furnish the additional information about the type locality in a letter: "The locality 28 mi. E. of Olmos is a curious cloud forest zone on the *west* slope of a low Andean pass. The east slope is desert!"

Paratype worker: TL 5.5, HL 1.08, HW 0.98, WL 2.00, greatest diameter of eye 0.06, scape L 0.93 mm. CI 91. Very similar to holotype in all details checked.

Holotype in California Academy of Sciences, paratype in Museum of Comparative Zoology, Harvard University.

Key to *Simopelta* workers

1. Head > 0.80 mm wide; occipital margin distinctly concave in the middle as seen in dorsal full-face view (Fig. 16); brownish black (E. Peru) .... *laticeps*
   Head < 0.80 mm. wide; occipital margin approximately straight (feebly convex to extremely feebly concave in dorsal full-face view) (Fig. 10) .... 2.
2. Pronotum smooth and strongly shining, as are a large part of the anterior dorsum of the head and various other parts of the alitrunk; black (Ecuador) .... *manni*
   Head and alitrunk, including pronotum, sculptured and more or less opaque .... 3.
3. Mandibles with a large apical tooth, followed basad by 6 or more irregular smaller teeth in series; bright ferruginous red, appendages, petiole and gaster yellow (Brazil: Espirito Santo) .... *bicolor*
   Mandibles with two large teeth at apex, followed basad by a large diastema, (containing at most 1 to 3 spaced denticles) or one moderate-sized tooth, and finally a large basal tooth .... 4.

4. Eyes large and conspicuous, greatest diameter $=$ greatest width of antennomere 4 (Figs. 10, 14); dark brown (Costa Rica) .... *oculata*
   Eyes smaller, greatest diameter distinctly $<$ greatest width of antennomere 4 .... 5.

5. Occiput, front of pronotum, mesonotum and propodeum more or less distinctly transversely striate or rugulose; median clypeal lobe without a slender tooth or process (Fig. 10); blackish brown (Ecuador) .... *williamsi*
   Head and alitrunk as seen from above uniformly and densely punctulate; median clypeal lobe with a narrow tooth or process, variable in form (Fig. 16); color lighter, brown or reddish, or bicolored .... 6.

6. Mandible 4-toothed; third tooth (counting apical tooth as first) at least half as large as basal (fourth) tooth, well-developed and acute (SE Brazil) .... *curvata*
   Mandible with only 3 well-developed teeth; broad diastema between second tooth and basal tooth unarmed or with at most a few low, irregular denticles or crenulations .... 7.

7. Larger species (head width usually $>$ 0.66 mm); punctation of head, alitrunk and node coarse, separate punctures of head not much smaller than eye; color ferruginous red to piceous, with contrasting yellow or red gaster and appendages (Brazil: NW Mato Grosso) .... *jeckylli*
   Smaller species (head width usually $<$ 0.66 mm); punctation fine and shallow, separate punctures of head not more than about 1/3 the size of the eye; color yellowish-brown to medium brown (Central America) *pergandei*

ACKOWLEDGEMENTS

We owe thanks to Father W. W. Kempf, OFM, for his sending of the sample of *S. curvata*, and to the National Science Foundation for support under grants (GB-2175, GB-5574X), W. L. Brown, Jr., principal investigator.

REFERENCES

BORGMEIER, T.
    1950. A femea dichthadiiforme e os estadios evolutivos de Simopelta pergandei (Forel), e a descrição de S. bicolor, n. sp. (Hym. Formicidae). Rev. Ent., Rio de Jan., 21: 369-380.

BROWN, W. L., JR.
 1958. Contributions toward a reclassification of the Formicidae. II.
    Tribe Ectatommini (Hymenoptera). Bull. Mus. Comp. Zool.
    Harv., 118: 171-362.
MANN, W. M.
 1922. Ants from Honduras and Guatemala. Proc. U. S. Nat. Mus.,
    61 (13): 1-54.
WHEELER, G. C. and J. WHEELER
 1957. The larva of Simopelta (Hymenoptera: Formicidae). Proc. Ent.
    Soc. Wash., 59: 191-194.
WHEELER, W. M.
 1935. Ants of the genera Belonopelta Mayr and Simopelta Mann. Rev.
    Ent., Rio de Jan., 5: 8-19.

THE ANT *CATAGLYPHIS BIRMANA* A SYNONYM —
The specimen described as *Cataglyphis birmana* by Collingwood in
1962 (Ent. Tidskr., 83: 227, figs. 8, 9; type locality Malvedaung,
Tenasserim, Burma, 300 m) is a worker minor of *Camponotus
singularis* (=*Formica singularis* F. Smith, 1868, Cat. Hym. Brit.
Mus., 6: 27; type locality "Java.") *New synonymy.* The type of
C. birmana was loaned by Dr. Eric Kjellander through the courtesy
of Mr. C. A. Collingwood, and has been returned to the Naturhis-
toriska Riksmuseum, Stockholm. — W. L. Brown, Jr., Department
of Entomology, Cornell University.

A NEW SPECIES OF MYRMECOPHILOUS COCCINELLIDAE, WITH NOTES ON OTHER HYPERASPINI (COLEOPTERA)*

By Edward A. Chapin

Museum of Comparative Zoology, Harvard University

During the past few years, Professor Daniel H. Janzen of the Department of Entomology of Kansas University has worked during the summers in Mexico and Central America on a project dealing with the relation of ants of the genus *Pseudomyrmex* to species of the thorn-bearing plants of the genus *Acacia*. In the course of the work larvae and pupae of a coccinellid were found inhabiting some of the hollowed spines abandoned by the ants. Two adult beetles were reared and sent to me for study. These proved to be the same species as two specimens collected in Mexico by Mr. N. L. H. Krauss which had been set aside as undescribed in my collection. As the species is so unlike in form from other hyperaspines known to me, the genus was not immediately recognizable. After dissection and preparation of the necessary slides, the species was found to be nearest to *Hyperaspis* and has been so assigned here. *Hyperaspis* is certainly composite as it now stands in the Korschefsky catalog and merits serious study by one who has adequate material at his disposal.

Myrmecophiles of the tribe Hyperaspini are already known from both hemispheres. J. B. Smith (1886) reported the presence of larvae of *Brachyacantha ursina* (Fabricius) in ants' nests and E. A. Schwarz (1890) reported that same species as abundant near Washington, D. C. in colonies of *Lasius claviger* Roger. F. Silvestri (1903) found *Hyperaspis reppensis* (Herbst) in the vicinity of Napoli, Italy in the nests of *Tapinoma erraticum nigerrimum* Nylander. W. M. Wheeler (1911) summed up what was known of myrmecophilous Coccinellidae and recorded the finding of *Brachyacantha quadripunctata* (Melsh.) from the nests of *Lasius umbratus* var. *aphidicola* Walsh at Great Blue Hill, Massachusetts. It is quite possible that the *B. ursina of* Smith and Schwarz is actually *B. quadripunctata*.

The genera composing the tribe Hyperaspini, as listed in the Junk-Korschefsky catalog 1931, fall into one or the other of two divisions which are based on the structure of the male and female genitalia. The first division within the tribe is composed of the genera *Brachya-*

---

*Published with the aid of a grant from the Museum of Comparative Zoology.

Manuscript received by the editor November 16, 1966.

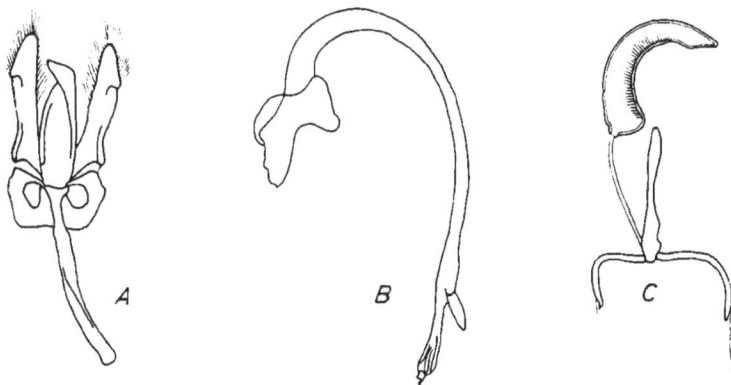

Figure 1. *Brachyacantha dentipes* (Fabricius). A. Aedeagus (without sipho); B. Sipho; C. Female genitalia, showing receptaculum seminis, sperm duct, infundibulum, and apex of bursa.

cantha Chevrolat, *Cyra* Mulsant, *Hinda* Mulsant, and probably *Cleothera* Mulsant. These genera are characterized in the males by parameres attached to the tegmen in the normal manner for Coccinellidae, that is, attached to the basal ring at the base of the median lobe and without special "roots" which pass through or almost through the ring; in the females by the presence of a complicated infundibular structure and by the possession of a normally formed, more or less sausage-shaped, receptaculum seminis. The infundibulum in these genera consists of three or four arms, two or three of which lie in the wall of the bursa copulatrix and act as supporting struts. The remaining arm stands free, and the sperm duct joins the bursa at the junction of these arms. The sperm duct is relatively short. The receptaculum lacks well-developed nodulus or ramus. These genera also agree in having eleven-segmented antennae and toothed tarsal claws.

Hyperaspis Redtenbacher, *Hyperaspidius* Crotch, *Helesius* Casey, *Thalassa* Mulsant, *Corystes* Mulsant, and *Oxynychus* Leconte and probably *Diazonema* Weise, *Tiphysa* Mulsant, and *Menoscelis* Mulsant, are included in the second division. These genera are characterized in the males by parameres which appear to be outgrowths of sclerotized but unpigmented structures or "roots," within or extending beyond the basal ring; in the females by the possession of a compound receptaculum seminis, and by the absence of an infundibulum. Among these genera one finds species with nine, ten, or eleven antennal segments and with toothed or toothless claws.

The key which follows is limited to those genera which I have
been able to study in detail and serves only to give some indication
of the relationships existing between those genera.

KEY TO CERTAIN GENERA OF HYPERASPINI

1. Parameres attached in the usual manner to the tegmen; infundibulum present; receptaculum seminis simple; antenna eleven-
   segmented 2
   Parameres attached to root-like structures within basal ring; infundibulum absent; receptaculum compound; antenna nine,
   ten, or eleven-segmented 4
2. Infundibulum with three arms; anterior tibia with a sharp tooth;
   median lobe of aedeagus asymmetrical .... *Brachyacantha*
   Infundibulum with four arms, the fourth arm a dorsal supporting strut in wall of bursa 3
3. Anterior tibia slender, not armed; median lobe asymmetrical ......
   .... *Cyra*
   Anterior tibia with expanded outer margin, which is finely and
   regularly serrulate; median lobe symmetrical, in form of a
   slender isosceles triangle; parameres modified at apices .. *Hinda*
4. Antenna eleven-segmented 5
   Antenna with less than eleven segments 7
5. Anterior tibia slender, without denticles .... *Hyperaspis* (part)
   Anterior tibia with outer edge broadly rounded 6
6. Tarsal claw with basal tooth .... *Thalassa*
   Tarsal claw simple .... *Helesius*
7. Antenna ten-segmented 8
   Antenna nine-segmented; anterior tibia broadly rounded ....
   .... *Corystes*
8. Tibia simple; tarsal claw with basal tooth .... *Hyperaspis* (type)
   Tibia simple; tarsal claw without tooth .... *Hyperaspidius*

Hyperaspis acanthicola, n. sp.

Male: Length — 13 mm. Form subcylindrical, the side margins
nearly parallel from humeri to level of apex of elytral suture
(Fig. 2A). Color piceous black, heavily marked above with whitish-
yellow; beneath, the lateral portions of the prosternum and abdominal
sternites, the mesepisterna, and legs, reddish-yellow. Head entirely
pale, pronotum with anterior half pale, posterior half dark, the dark
area strongly bilobed on disc. Each elytron has the familiar pattern
of five pale spots (2.2.1) on piceous black, so commonly found among

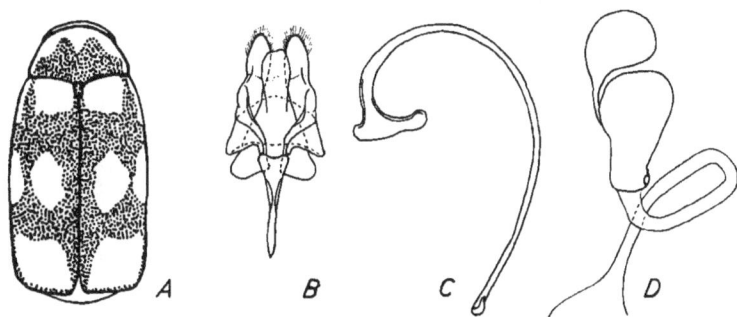

Figure 2. *Hyperaspis acanthicola* new species. A. Entire insect, dorsal view; B. Aedeagus (without sipho); C. Sipho; D. Female genitalia, showing compound receptaculum seminis, sperm duct, and apex of bursa.

the species of *Brachyacantha, Cyra,* and to a lesser extent, *Hyperaspis.* The scutellar spot is transverse, of irregular shape; it extends along the basal margin of the elytron from the scutellum to the base of the humeral callus, and is approximately one and one-half times wider than long. The humeral spot lies almost entirely on the nearly vertical flank of the elytron, is nearly rectangular and about twice as long as wide; it touches both basal and lateral margins of the elytron and extends backward slightly farther than the scutellar spot. The third and fourth spots, situated slightly postmedian, are almost connected. The outer and larger of the two extends from the lateral margin to the middle line of the elytron, is wider than long and remotely suggests a distorted hexagon. The inner spot is longer than wide, somewhat lozenge-shaped, and is well separated from the suture. The fifth and largest spot lies close to but does not touch the apical and lateral margins of the elytron and approaches the sutural margin only at its apex.

The head is finely and densely punctate on a finely alutaceous surface. Surface of the pronotum is similar to that of the head but the punctation is more sparse. Surface of the elytra is shining, slightly uneven, the punctation similar to that of the pronotum. Metasternum highly polished, virtually impunctate in median area, abdominal sternites and flanks of the metasternum noticeably more coarsely punctate than other parts of the body. The femora, especially those of legs III, somewhat inflated. Elytral epipleura narrow, ending just behind the level of legs III, without well-defined cavities for the reception of the femoral apices. Abdomen with six visible sternites, the sixth short and very broad, the corresponding tergite only half its breadth. The sternites without sexual modifications.

Genitalia (Fig. 2B, C). In general appearance most nearly resemble those of *H. reppensis* (Hbst.). The median lobe is slightly longer than wide and is almost symmetrical. The free portion of a paramere is one-sixth longer than the median lobe but only half as long as the portion enclosed within the basal ring which is twisted through an arc of 180° and which protrudes beyond the basal ring and appears to provide a surface for muscle attachment. The sipho is normal in form, slightly modified at apex.

Female: Length 3.1-3.4 mm. Form and punctation essentially as in male. Head dark beneath and with a transverse dark stripe on vertex. Pronotum largely dark, the extreme anterior margin and the anterior angles pale. Prosternum dark, propleura, mesepipleura, elytral epipleura and lateral margins of abdominal sternites pale.

Genitalia (Fig. 2D). Hemisternites broad and rounded, styli very small but with relatively long and conspicuous setae. Bursa copulatrix broad at base, rapidly tapering to meet the sperm duct of large diameter. Infundibulum absent. Receptaculum seminis is compound; the basal portion, which corresponds to the nodulus, ramus, and lower part of cornu, is pear-shaped and of moderately firm texture. There is no appendix at its apex, as in most of the species of *Hyperaspis*. Accessory gland pore located adjacent to the attachment of the sperm duct. The apical portion, which appears to correspond to the apical portion of cornu, is retort-shaped and is joined to the basal portion at about the middle of its length.

Holotype — a male, head appendages, legs, genitalia and abdominal sternites on slide, from Veracruz, Ver., México, May 1956, N. L. H. Krauss, (U. S. N. M. no. 69331). Paratypes — a male, same data as holotype, (K. U.); a female, genitalia and abdominal sternites on slide, from Temascal, Oax., México, Jan. 27, 1964, reared from larva in thorn of *Acacia cornigera* infested by *Pseudomyrmex ferruginea* F. Smith (U. S. N. M.); a female, from 2 mi. W. of Coatepeque, Quetzaltenango, Guatemala, Jan. 12, 1965, reared from larva in thorn of *Acacia hindsii* infested with *Pseudomyrmex ferruginea*, (K. U.).

This species differs from all *Hyperaspis* known to me in two, perhaps significant, characters. (1) The antennal club has the terminal (11th) segment free and considerably longer than the tenth, which in turn is as long as the ninth. In other *Hyperaspis*, both those with ten-segmented or eleven-segmented antenna, the terminal segment is very small and more or less buried in the apex of the penultimate segment, which is much shorter than the antepenultimate segment.

(2) The basal part of the receptaculum does not bear an apical appendix as in the other species of the genus known to me.

LITERATURE CITED

DOBZHANSKY, T.
    1941. Smithsonian Miscellaneous Collections, 106 (6): 1-94, 6 plates.
KORSCHEFSKY, R.
    1931. Coleop. Catalogus (Junk), pars 118: 176-209.
SCHWARZ, E. A.
    1890. Proc. Ent. Soc. Washington, 1 (4): 237-247.
SILVESTRI, F.
    1903. Ann. Mus. Zool. R. Univ. Napoli, N.S., 1 (13): 3.
SMITH, J. B.
    1886. Amer. Nat., 20: 679-687.
WHEELER, W. M.
    1911. Journ. New York Ent. Soc., 19 (3): 169-174.

THE ANT *APHAENOGASTER GATESI* TRANSFERRED TO *PHEIDOLE*.

— *Pheidole gatesi* is the necessary NEW COMBINATION for *Aphaenogaster (Attomyrma) gatesi* Wheeler, 1927, Psyche, 34: 44, worker (minor); type locality Rangoon, Burma. The types of *A. gatesi* are really minors of some species of the *Pheidole smythiesi* group (=subgenus *Ceratopheidole*). When compared directly with types of *P. smythiesi*, the *gatesi* cotypes showed differences in head shape and in details of the mesonotum and postpetiole that are strong enough to indicate distinctness at the species level, at least until we have further knowledge of intraspecific variation in this group. The type comparison was incidental to work done in European museums during 1963 under National Science Foundation Grant G-23680. — W. L. Brown, Jr., Department of Entomology, Cornell University.

CAVE CARABIDAE (COLEOPTERA) OF MAMMOTH CAVE[1]

By Thomas C. Barr, Jr.

Department of Zoology, University of Kentucky, Lexington

In an earlier paper (Barr, 1962) I listed the troglobitic beetles known to inhabit Mammoth Cave, Mammoth Cave National Park, Kentucky. The species included several trechine carabids, one catopid (*Ptomaphagus hirtus* Tellk.), and one pselaphid (*Batrisodes henroti* Park). Further investigations in this huge cavern system and in surrounding caves have shown that there are actually 6, instead of 4, species of trechines sympatric in Mammoth Cave. These include *Neaphaenops tellkampfii* Erichson, a large (7 mm) and very abundant species, and 5 species of the large genus *Pseudanophthalmus* Jeannel. The following key supersedes my earlier key (Barr, 1962: p. 279) and is applicable only to Mammoth Cave National Park and caves in the immediate vicinity of Horse Cave, Cave City, and Park City.

Key to the Eyeless Cave Carabidae (Trechini) of Mammoth Cave National Park

1 Size large (6.5-7.5 mm); one pair of supraorbital setae; elytron with only two discal punctures, the third, or posterior seta lacking; frontal grooves not extended onto sides of head; last segment of maxillary and labial palps much shorter than penultimate segment .... *Neaphaenops tellkampfi* Erichson

Size smaller (3.3-6.0 mm); two pairs of supraorbital setae; elytron with 3 discal punctures, each bearing a short, stout seta OR elytron with a single discal puncture near apex; frontal grooves extended onto sides of head; last segment of maxillary and labial palps subequal to penultimate segment *(Pseudanophthalmus)* 2

2(1) Elytron with a single discal puncture near apex; mesosternum with a prominent median tubercle; length about 4 mm; rare .... *P. audax* Horn

Elytron with 3 discal punctures; mesosternum simply declivous 3

[1] This investigation has been supported in part by grants from the National Science Foundation (GB-2011, GB-5521).

Manuscript received by the editor November 30, 1966

3(2) Size small, about 3.5 mm; humeral margins entire; anterior
discal puncture ± at level of 4th puncture in humeral margin; ♂♂ with posterior margin of last sternite notched,
aedeagus extremely elongate and slender; rare ....
.... *P. inexpectatus* Barr
Size larger, about 4.5-5.5 mm; humeral margins serrulate; an-
terior discal puncture ± at level of 2nd puncture in humeral
margin; ♂♂ with posterior margin of last sternite entire,
aedeagus not extremely elongate and slender 4

4(3) Elytral disc densely and finely pubescent, longitudinal striae
very regular and impunctate; sutural stria continued around
apical margin of elytron and connected to 3rd longitudinal
stria; aedeagus broadly truncate at apex ....
.... *P. pubescens* Horn
Elytral disc glabrous or sparsely pubescent, striae evidently
punctate; sutural stria continued only a short distance
around apical margin of elytron, not clearly connected to
apex of 3rd longitudinal stria; apex of aedeagus attenuate
.... 5

5(4) Elytral disc glabrous, longitudinal striae very shallow and
coarsely and regularly punctate; base of pronotum turned
obliquely forward behind the hind angles ....
.... *P. menetriesii* Motschulsky
Elytral disc sparsely pubescent, longitudinal striae deep and
irregular, finely and distinctly punctate; hind angles projecting backward behind base of pronotum ....
.... *P. striatus* Motschulsky

In synonymizing *P. striatus* with *P. menetriesii* (Barr, 1962: p.
280) I was in error. The male genitalia of the two species are virtually identical, and cannot be used to separate them. The characters
cited in the key are the most highly diagnostic, although *P. striatus*
is a bit more slender and less depressed, the humeri are much less
prominent, and there is usually a slight sinuosity of the elytral margin behind the humeral punctures.

The presence of several species of *Pseudanophthalmus* in Mammoth Cave raises the possibility of misinterpretation of the three
trivial names proposed by Motschulsky (1862). Professor M. S.
Ghilarov, President of the National Committee of Biologists of the
Soviet Union, kindly arranged, at my request, to have specimens of
the Mammoth Cave beetles compared with Motschulsky's types in
the Zoological Museum of Moscow. Dr. K. V. Arnoldi, of the

Moscow Branch of the All-Union Entomological Society, Academy of Sciences of the U. S. S. R., compared specimens of 5 Mammoth Cave trechines (all except *P. audax*) with the 3 examples of *Anophthalmus striatus*, 3 *A. menetriesii*, and 2 *A. ventricosus* in the Motschulsky collection. Dr. Arnoldi *(in litt.)* reports that the conventional interpretation of *striatus* and *menetriesii*, with *ventricosus* a synonym of *menetriesii* (Jeannel, 1928), is correct.

P. striatus is a riparian species in Mammoth Cave, apparently feeding on tubificid annelids in the silt banks along Lake Lethe and Echo River. In August, 1965, T. G. Marsh and I collected 30 *Pseudanophthalmus* at the margin of Lake Lethe, in dim illumination beside the electrically lighted tourist trail. Only one specimen of this series was *P. menetriesii* and the remainder were *P. striatus*. On the other hand, *menetriesii* predominates in the upper levels of the cave, where most of the older collections seem to have been made.

In a study of distribution and variation in the *menetriesii* group Barr and Marsh (in preparation) have found that the range of *menetriesii* is a narrow belt not far removed from the Dripping Spring escarpment. *P. striatus*, on the other hand, extends eastward across Barren County into the southwest corner of Metcalf County, where it is locally larger, more convex, and more difficult to separate morphologically from *menetriesii*. In Metcalf County *striatus* is sympatric with another, undescribed species of the *menetriesii* group. There is good evidence for character displacement where the range of *striatus* overlaps that of *menetriesii* or that of the undescribed species.

P. audax was known only from the type series (Barr, 1959), collected about 1880 in a cave 9 miles east of Mammoth Cave, until it was taken in White Cave, a half mile south-southwest of the Historic Entrance to Mammoth Cave, in August, 1961 (1 ♂), and August, 1965 (1 ♀). The species occurred on wet, rotting wood at the back of White Cave, near an old bridge across a shallow pit. The pit is supposedly separated from Crevice Pit in Mammoth Cave only by a narrow crevice impenetrable to man. *P. menetriesii*, *P. pubescens*, *P. inexpectatus*, *P. striatus*, and *N. tellkampfii* have all been found at this place in the cave, either on the White Cave side of the crevice, the Mammoth Cave side, or both. Although I suggested that *audax* was probably "a rather curious offshoot from the *menetriesii-robustus* branch of the genus" (Barr, 1959: p. 3), further study of the genus has shown that this species should form the type of an *audax* group (as suggested by Jeannel, 1949), to include *P.*

horni Garman (caves near Lexington, Kentucky), *P. emersoni*
Krekeler (caves near Bedford, Indiana), *P. packardi* Barr (Carter
Co., Kentucky), and various undescribed species from central Kentucky. The group is characterized by medium size (about 4 mm in
total length), prominent humeri with finely serrate margins, and a
mesosternal spine or tubercle (or at least a vertical shelf when the
mesosternum is viewed in profile).

PSYCHE

A Journal of Entomology

Volume 73

1966

Published Quarterly by the Cambridge Entomological Club

Editorial Office: Biological Laboratories

16 Divinity Ave.

Cambridge, Mass., U. S. A.

The numbers of PSYCHE issued during the past year were mailed on the following dates:

Vol. 72, no. 4, Dec., 1965: May 10, 1966

Vol. 73, no. 1, March, 1966: August 31, 1966

Vol. 73, no. 2, June, 1966: October 21, 1966

Vol. 73, no. 3, Sept., 1966: Jan. 25, 1967

PSYCHE

INDEX TO VOL. 73, 1966

INDEX TO AUTHORS

INDEX TO SUBJECTS

All new genera, new species and new names are printed in CAPITAL TYPE.

157

CAMBRIDGE ENTOMOLOGICAL CLUB

A regular meeting of the Club is held on the second Tuesday of each month October through May at 7:30 p. m. in Room B-455, Biological Laboratories, Divinity Ave., Cambridge. Entomologists visiting the vicinity are cordially invited to attend.

The illustration on the front cover of this issue of Psyche is a reproduction of a drawing of a female bethylid wasp, *Pseudiso-brachium terresi* Mann, from Haiti (Psyche, vol. 22, p. 165, 1915).

BACK VOLUMES OF PSYCHE

The Johnson Reprint Corporation, 111 Fifth Avenue, New York 3, N. Y., has been designated the exclusive agents for Psyche, volumes 1 through 62. Requests for information and orders for such volumes should be sent directly to the Johnson Reprint Corporation.

Copies of issues in volumes 63-72 are obtainable from the editorial offices of Psyche. Volumes 63-72 are $5.00 each.

F. M. CARPENTER
Editorial Office. Psyche.
16 Divinity Avenue,
Cambridge, Mass.. 02138.

FOR SALE